CW00632065

INSIDERS' GUIDE®
TO MEMPHIS

Help Us Keep This Guide Up to Date

Every effort has been made by the author and editors to make this guide as accurate and useful as possible. However, many things can change after a guide is published—establishments close, phone numbers change, hiking trails are rerouted, facilities come under new management, etc.

We would love to hear from you concerning your experiences with this guide and how you feel it could be improved and be kept up to date. While we may not be able to respond to all comments and suggestions, we'll take them to heart, and we'll also make certain to share them with the author. Please send your comments and suggestions to the following address:

The Globe Pequot Press
Reader Response/Editorial Department
P.O. Box 480
Guilford, CT 06437

Or you may e-mail us at:

editorial@globe-pequot.com

Thanks for your input, and happy travels!

Insiders' Guide®
to Memphis

Nicky Robertshaw

INSIDERS'
▶GUIDE®

Guilford, Connecticut
An imprint of The Globe Pequot Press

The prices and rates in this guidebook were confirmed at press time. We recommend, however, that you call establishments before traveling to obtain current information.

Copyright © 2002 by The Globe Pequot Press

All rights reserved. No part of this book may be reproduced or transmitted in any form by any means, electronic or mechanical, including photocopying and recording, or by any information storage and retrieval system, except as may be expressly permitted by the 1976 Copyright Act or by the publisher. Requests for permission should be made in writing to The Globe Pequot Press, P.O. Box 480, Guilford, Connecticut 06437.

Insiders' Guide is a registered trademark of The Globe Pequot Press.

Back cover photographs (left to right) courtesy of The Pink Palace, Fernando Medina / NBAE / Getty Images, the Mallory-Neely House, St. Jude Children's Research Hospital, Memphis Redbirds
Cover photograph: Wendell Metzen, Index Stock
Maps by Geografx © The Globe Pequot Press

ISBN 0-7627-2197-9

Manufactured in the United States of America
First Edition/First Printing

Publications from the Insiders' Guide® series are available at special discounts for bulk purchases for sales promotions, premiums, or fund-raisings. Special editions, including personalized covers, can be created in large quantities for special needs. For more information, please contact The Globe Pequot Press at (800) 962-0973.

Contents

Directory of Maps

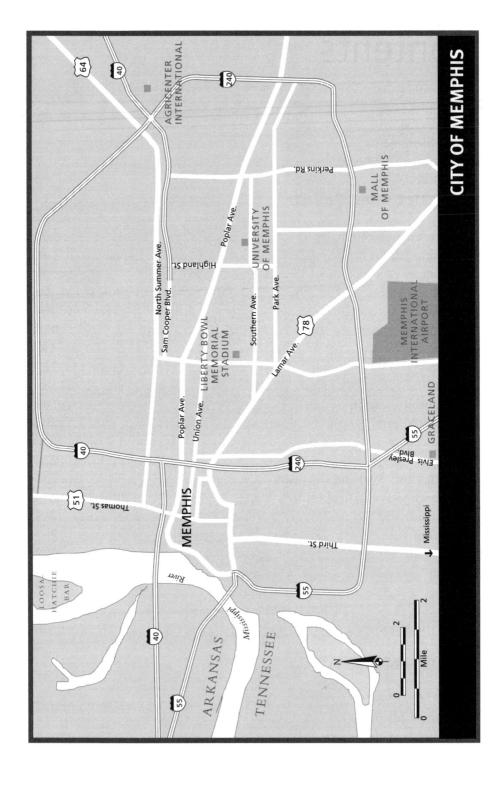

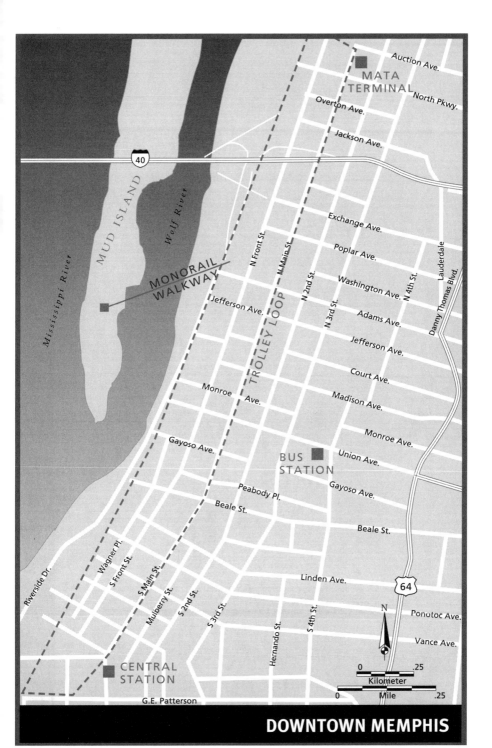

DOWNTOWN MEMPHIS

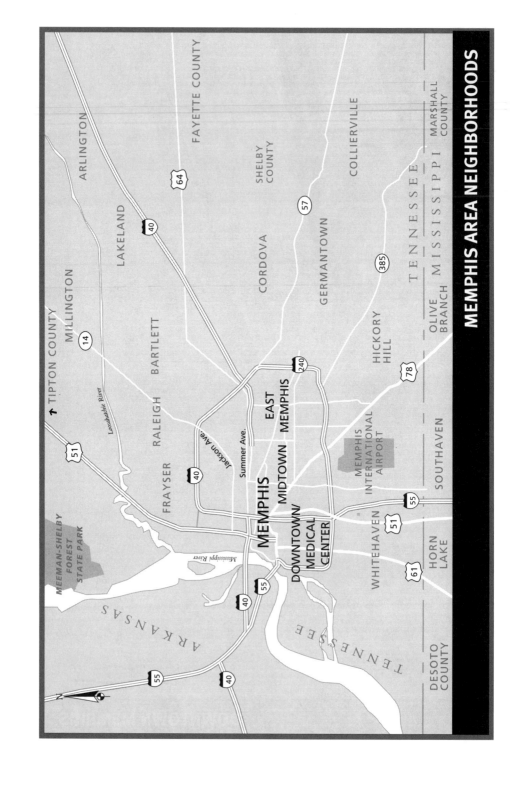

MEMPHIS AREA NEIGHBORHOODS

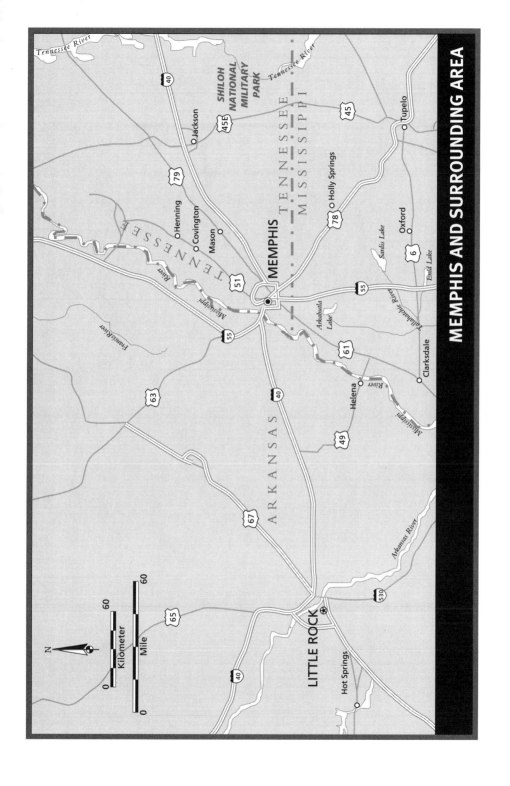

MEMPHIS AND SURROUNDING AREA

Preface

Welcome to Memphis!

Memphis is one of those mythical places in the minds of those who love rock and roll, blues, and other American music. Even if you couldn't find it on a map, you have undoubtedly heard Memphis in songs (the city's name is in the title or lyrics of some 300 songs), and you probably already know that this is Elvis Presley's hometown.

The city really is what its slogan says: Home of the Blues and the Birthplace of Rock and Roll. It's also a famous river town, which first came into being and thrived because of its location on the Mississippi River. As becomes a city in the Deep South, it's also full of friendly people with Southern drawls, for whom genuine hospitality is second nature. Of course, you'll find plenty of flatter American accents, and foreign accents as well, a sign that Memphis has attracted visitors and new residents from all over the world.

Memphis is a laid-back, easygoing place where you can relax and enjoy great music on or off the bright neon lights of Beale Street, indulge in delicacies ranging from barbecue sandwiches to outstanding eclectic American cuisine, and enjoy a wide range of sights, arts, and sports.

Insiders' Guide to Memphis was written to help you find your way around this multifaceted city, whether you are visiting the city on vacation or business, or moving to Memphis. It's also a useful tool for people who already live here, with its complete listings of restaurants, shops, and sporting events as well as ideas for entertaining the kids and the lowdown on the area's best golf courses, mountain-biking trails, and fishing spots.

We begin the book with an area overview of Memphis, a chapter on how to get around the city, and a brief history that tells how the city got to where it is today. Next are the chapters on accommodations, things to do—restaurants, attractions, nightlife, the arts, parks, and recreation—as well as chapters that spotlight an important aspect of the city, such as Memphis music. The last five chapters are for readers who are relocating in Memphis; they include information on neighborhoods and real estate, education, worship, and other topics. All these chapters include an introduction to give you a quick overview of the subject, whether it's health care, spectator sports, or day trips.

Throughout the book you'll find Close-ups, which highlight some noteworthy aspect of the city, and insiders' tips, nuggets of information you might not find anywhere else.

So have a great time in Memphis, and see for yourself why so many people never leave.

Acknowledgments

This book would not have been possible without the help of many people.

First of all, I'd like to thank my husband, Chris, for his extreme patience and understanding as this project took over our lives, as well as his incredible support during those months. I also want to thank him for his great work on the parks and recreation chapter, particularly the golf section (somebody had to test all those golf courses!). I want to thank my family and friends, particularly my sister, Sylvia, and my brother, Frank, for their support and encouragement while I was writing this book.

I want to thank Jamie Baker, as mom and innkeeper, for sharing her incredible knowledge of Memphis from a kid's perspective. Many thanks also to Jonathan Scott, a native Memphian with a great feel for the city's history, and historian Dr. Charles W. Crawford at the University of Memphis. I want to thank Scott Shepherd at the *Memphis Business Journal,* who probably knows more than anyone about Memphis health care and education. Thanks to Chris Herrington, music writer at the *Memphis Flyer,* for his help on the Memphis music and nightlife chapters, and to Alan Salomon for lending a hand on several chapters.

I also want to thank the Memphis Convention and Visitors Bureau for making available its excellent library of slides depicting Memphis attractions. I'd also like to thank the editors on this book, Lynne Arany, Laurie Kenney, and Norma Ledbetter, for their guidance and keen eye. I'd also like to thank all the editors who, over the years, have helped me develop as a writer.

Lastly, thank you, Memphis, for being such a great place to live and play. You make my job easy.

How to Use This Book

Memphis truly is, as the tourism slogan goes, the Home of the Blues and the Birthplace of Rock and Roll. But even if you aren't a music fan, you'll find plenty to enjoy in this friendly city on the bluffs overlooking the Mississippi River, whether it's world-famous pork barbecue, the bright lights of Beale Street, or Graceland Mansion.

Consider this book as your personal tool for enjoying the best of what Memphis has to offer, whether you're in town for a few days of sightseeing or moving here for an extended stay.

This book is divided into self-contained, stand-alone chapters, each about a specific aspect of Memphis such as nightlife or restaurants. We begin with an overview of the city, where you can learn about what makes Memphis such a unique place. You may be surprised to learn, for example, that Memphis is the hardwood capital of the world, home to the world's busiest airport (thanks to FedEx), and has a gigantic glass pyramid next to the Mississippi River. You can get your bearings by reading the Getting Here, Getting Around chapter.

If you're looking for a place to stay, check out the Accommodations chapter for listings of hotels, bed-and-breakfast inns, and other options. If you're looking for a great meal or just a nosh, flip to the Restaurants chapter. In addition to its general listing by area and type of cuisine, the chapter includes Close-ups on where to find both the best versions of the legendary Memphis barbecue and the best old-fashioned Southern home cooking in the form of plate lunches.

Memphis music is the reason many people visit Memphis, and you'll find out where to hear it, both on and off Beale Street, in the Nightlife chapter. Check out the Memphis Music chapter for an extensive look at how American music, including the blues, rock and roll, and soul, grew out of Memphis, and how new music still bubbles up from the city's rich musical heritage.

Downtown Memphis developed along the Mississippi River and continues to thrive.
PHOTO: MEMPHIS CONVENTION AND VISITORS BUREAU

When you're ready to see the town, turn to the Attractions chapter, where you'll get the skinny on Graceland, the National Civil Rights Museum, Sun Studio, and other sights. You'll find more choices in the Kidstuff chapter, and get the kid-friendly skinny on basic attractions including Beale Street. For other diversions check out the Parks and Recreation, Spectator Sports, Annual Events, and Day Trips and Weekend Getaways chapters. To learn more about Memphis's African American heritage, turn to the chapter bearing that name.

If you're planning to make Memphis your home, flip to the back of the book and learn more about daily life in Memphis. You'll find chapters on neighborhoods, education, media, health care, retirement, and worship.

We hope you will make good use of this book as you explore Memphis, but remember to put it away, too. Just hanging out is one of the pleasures of being here, and if you're too much the "tourist on a mission," you'll miss that aspect. Memphis is a laid-back, friendly place, so take time to relax and enjoy watching the river, listen to some blues, and make some new friends.

Bear in mind that things can change quickly even in a laid-back city like Memphis. We doubt that the Mississippi River will stop flowing or that Graceland Mansion will close its doors to visitors, but before you know it, a restaurant could move to the suburbs, an attraction change its hours, or a nightclub close its doors. It's always a good idea to call ahead before you visit the places we list here.

We've made every effort to include accurate, up-to-date information, but nobody's perfect. Let us know if we've goofed, or if you discover a great little barbecue joint or blues club that escaped our notice. This guide is periodically updated, and your input will help to improve the next edition.

Write to us at Insiders' Guide to Memphis, The Globe Pequot Press, P.O. Box 480, Guilford, CT 06437–0480. Also, check out the Insiders' Guides Web site at www.insiders. com. You'll find Insiders' Guides to more than sixty American cities and regions that range from the Florida Keys to the Oregon coast. You can order copies of the books online, or read excerpts from many of them. While you're there, send in your comments on *Insiders' Guide to Memphis*.

We hope you have a great time in Memphis. You'll see why a number of people come here for school, a work assignment, or a short visit and find they're still here five years later enjoying the mellow Memphis lifestyle.

Area Overview

The Memphis
Cityscape

A Sense of Place

Demographically
Speaking

Doing Business

Memphis at Play

There's more to Memphis than first meets the visitor's eye.

True, it's the birthplace of rock and roll, Elvis Presley's hometown, the pork barbecue capital of the world, and an important Mississippi River port. Visitors can see Graceland, take in some blues on Beale Street, enjoy outstanding barbecue ribs, and gaze out at Old Man River. The people you encounter are likely to be very friendly and only too happy to give directions or recommend a personal favorite. It's very laid-back—no need to rush around unless that's what you want to do.

Look a little deeper, however, and you'll find more in this city that got its start as a rowdy river town. Memphis has a family-friendly attitude, an employment rate that's consistently better than the national average, and a diversified economy that makes the city resilient to downturns. Memphis over the years has spawned innovations that change the way we live. These include the modern supermarket (Piggly Wiggly, 1916), the modern hotel chain (Holiday Inn, 1952), and overnight package delivery (FedEx, 1972).

The city has its share of paradoxes. Despite a basically conservative atmosphere, the city has produced musical revolutions that shaped the complexion of American music. Remember how shocking Elvis's gyrations were considered in the 1950s, yet his act originated in the conservative Southern city of Memphis. And despite the extreme poverty within much of the black community and the fact that Dr. Martin Luther King, Jr., was assassinated here in 1968, Memphis in 2001 rated as one of the best places in the United States for African Americans to live, according to *Black Enterprise* magazine.

The city also has a low cost of living, affordably priced homes, and ranks among the best cities in the country for starting a small business. In Memphis, as becomes a city in the midst of the Bible Belt, many are church-going citizens, often building their personal lives around the church or synagogue of their choice.

Memphis is also one of the country's most important distribution centers, a growing center for medical research (St. Jude Children's Research Hospital scientist Peter Doherty won the 1996 Nobel Prize in medicine), and the southern hub for Northwest Airlines. In addition, Memphis remains a strong river port and a center for marketing of U.S. cotton crops, the businesses that first put Memphis on the map in the 1800s.

The city's jobless rate is usually lower than the national average, and if anything, the city's biggest labor problem is finding enough people to fill the high-tech jobs. When the labor market is really tight, employers have trouble filling jobs at the low-skill end of the scale, such as busboy, dishwashing, and domestics jobs.

But there's something intangible about Memphis that grows on you. Just ask around, and you'll likely encounter more than a few people who came to Memphis intending only a short stay. Yet here they are five or ten years later, feeling very much at home but not really sure how it happened. You might also be surprised at how many native Memphians choose to stay here. While many are proud of their city and delight in its successes, there's an unfortunate propensity among some native Memphians to complain that the city isn't Manhattan or Atlanta. Yet even these malcontents find a place for themselves in Memphis; after all, flights leave daily for New York and Atlanta, and they're still here.

It's an exciting time to be in Memphis, as long-held dreams, including the revival of downtown Memphis and professional sports, have become a reality. Now attention is being focused on redeveloping the city riverfront in such a way as to make it more accessible to visitors and residents alike. Economic-development activity continues, as new businesses come to town and existing ones expand their operations.

The Memphis Cityscape

Graceland Mansion may be the city's most recognizable building, but in fact most of the city looks very different from the Presley home.

Built on flat, sometimes rolling, terrain and dotted with parks and stately oaks, magnolias, and other trees, the Memphis cityscape includes a variety of architectural styles, ranging from antebellum homes and 1800s commercial buildings to skyscrapers and modern shopping centers. It's eclectic, to say the least, so you can't really point to a Memphis style that's as distinctive and characteristic as what you'd find in other Southern towns such as New Orleans or Savannah.

Memphis does boast a large number of historic buildings, particularly in the downtown area, more than you'd find in Charlotte, Atlanta, and other Southern cities where many more older buildings were cleared to make way for progress.

Downtown is also where the variety is most pronounced; within 10–20 blocks you find austere government buildings from the 1960s, restored Victorian homes, a few antebellum structures, and several skyscrapers. There are many lofty commercial buildings dating from the early 1900s, some of which have been put to new uses and others that remain vacant. Among them is a former Kress Variety Store with a colorful, beautifully preserved glazed terracotta facade. Just across the Auction Bridge on Mud Island is Harbortown, a residential neighborhood built in the 1980s and 1990s with award-winning new homes that incorporate many elements of traditional Southern architecture.

As you leave the downtown area on the main thoroughfares such as Union or Poplar and move into midtown, you'll see some of the stately homes that formerly lined these streets, now interspersed with commercial and medical buildings, gas stations and fast-food joints, apartment buildings, churches, and strip shopping centers. Central and Peabody Avenues in midtown have remained residential, and here you can still see many of the city's beautiful old homes, particularly in the Central Gardens area.

If there's any such thing as a typical Memphis building, it has to be the bungalow,

The lights of downtown Memphis brighten up the surface of the Mississippi River at night.
PHOTO: MEMPHIS CONVENTION AND VISITORS BUREAU

a style of middle-class home with a front porch and extended eaves popular in the 1910s and 1920s. You'll see many bungalows in midtown neighborhoods, as well as "foursquares," so called because each floor has four big rooms. Once you reach East Memphis, residences are mostly tract housing from the 1950s through the 1980s, whereas commercial buildings include shopping centers, low retail and office buildings of up to four floors, and a few high-rise buildings. The far suburbs such as Germantown and Collierville have some historic buildings, including the Collierville town square, but otherwise homes, apartment complexes, office buildings, and shopping centers are typical modern suburban in their design. Standouts include FedEx World Headquarters campus in Collierville.

A Sense of Place

To understand what makes Memphis the city it is today, you must start with its location. Perched above the Mississippi River on what is known as the Fourth Chickasaw Bluff, it's safe from flooding yet benefits from the remarkably rich soil created by annual flooding in surrounding areas. Memphis started as a shipping and marketing center for locally grown cotton and other crops in the early 1800s and continues to be active in bringing cotton to market. Memphis also is still an active river port, and although port operations have been moved south of downtown, you can see barges and towboats plying the Mississippi.

Memphis rests in the southwest corner of Tennessee, several hundred miles away culturally and geographically from the Great Smoky Mountains of east Tennessee. Memphis is the capital of the Mid-South, a region that includes west Tennessee, northern Mississippi, eastern Arkansas, and the Missouri boot heel. As in years past, Memphis continues to be big lights, big city for that part of the country.

Because it sits on the top of the state of Mississippi and draws many residents from that state, Memphis has traditionally been viewed as the capital of Mississippi. Southern writer David Cohn famously underscored that point in the

Insiders' Tip

For more information check out these Web sites: www.cityofmemphis.org (City of Memphis), www.memphischamber.com (Memphis Regional Chamber), www.memphis travel.com (Memphis Convention and Visitors Bureau), and www.gomemphis.com (*The Commercial Appeal*, the city's daily newspaper).

1930s when he wrote, "The Mississippi Delta begins in the lobby of The Peabody Hotel in Memphis."

Delta people have traditionally come to Memphis not only to socialize at the Peabody (still a favorite pastime) but also to shop, do business, and to amuse themselves, whether it's fine dining, the clubs on Beale Street, a Redbirds game, or a touring Broadway show.

Mid-Southerners also flock here to live, whether to attend college, find work, or get away from their small towns and farms.

At present, in terms of the city's economy, location is just as important as it was in the 1800s, but in a different way. Because Memphis is centrally located in the North American continents and within a 24-hour drive of about two thirds of the U.S. population, it has become a major distribution and transportation hub, with cargo traveling via rail, truck, and air as well as by river barge. Memphis is far enough south that it's rarely snowed in, an important reason that Memphian Fred Smith decided to base his Federal Express operations here. FedEx is the city's largest employer, with some 32,000 employees, and has helped Memphis International Airport hold its position as the world's busiest air-cargo airport since 1992, handling 2.7 million tons of cargo in fiscal 2000. The presence of FedEx

A ride on a Memphis Queen riverboat is a great way to experience the Mississippi River up close and enjoy the sunset. PHOTO: MEMPHIS CONVENTION AND VISITORS BUREAU

continues to attract companies to set up their own distribution centers here for the quickest possible delivery to their customers.

The annual average temperature here is 62 degrees, with the temperature averaging 41 degrees in January and 81 degrees in July. Humidity averages 69 percent. Summers can be scorchers with highs often in the upper 90s, especially in late July and August (luckily, air conditioning is ubiquitous). May and October generally have the best weather. In winter Memphis sometimes gets ice storms, and temperatures are sometimes in the 20s or even the teens. But it's also prone to winter warm spells, so you're just as likely to find Memphians wearing shorts as down jackets in February.

Rainfall averages 49 inches, and snowfall averages 5.3 inches a year, although many years there are only flurries. Memphis often is a standout on national weather maps because it's situated where the plains to the west end and the mountains to the east begin. Thunderstorms here are dramatic, a far cry from the misty rains of Seattle. Tornadoes also threaten and sometimes strike Memphis and the surrounding area.

Another geographical quirk is that the city sits on the Memphis Sand Aquifer, an enormous underground reservoir of naturally purified water that's retrieved through drilled wells for the city water supply. Memphis is the largest city in the world to rely exclusively on artesian wells for its water supply.

Demographically Speaking

Memphis is Tennessee's largest city, situated in the extreme southwest corner of Tennessee in Shelby County, the state's most populous county. It's the 18th-largest city in the country, with 650,100 people, according to the 2000 census. The Memphis MSA (metropolitan statistical area) is the 44th largest and consists of five counties in three states: Shelby, Tipton, and Fayette Counties in Tennessee, DeSoto County in Mississippi, and Crittenden County in Arkansas. The MSA population is 1,135,614, an almost 13 percent increase over 1990, according to 2000 census figures. In contrast the population of Nashville is 569,891,

according to the 2000 census. During the 1990s the Nashville MSA grew by 25 percent compared with Memphis's 13 percent growth; as a result Nashville overtook Memphis as the most populous MSA, with 1,251,509, according to the 2000 census.

Most of the current growth in population is in the suburbs, although downtown Memphis saw a huge increase in population during the 1990s as new homes and apartments were built and some historic buildings were renovated into apartments. The strongest suburban growth during the 1990s took place in DeSoto County, Mississippi, with a 58 percent increase in population; Tipton, with 36 percent growth; and Fayette County, with 13 percent growth. In Shelby County the hot 1990s growth spots were Collierville, which grew by 120 percent, and Lakeland, which grew by more than 400 percent.

The city continues to build out to far eastern Shelby County towns including Oakland, Arlington, and Eads, and north to Tipton County towns such as Atoka and Covington. In DeSoto County, Mississippi, further development is expected in

Insiders' Tip
Did you know that Memphis was the home of the first Welcome Wagon in 1928? The home of the first Greyhound and Continental Trailways bus lines? It's also home to the world's largest producer of Christmas wrapping paper and was named the cleanest city in the nation, according to National City Beautiful Commission, and the only city that's a five-time winner of that award.

Olive Branch and Hernando. See Neighborhoods and Real Estate chapter for more details.

It shouldn't surprise anyone that the demographics of Memphis differ dramatically from those of Tennessee as a whole. After all, Tennessee stretches some 500 miles over the top of the states of Mississippi, Alabama, and Georgia, and because of its extreme width, west Tennessee (where Memphis is), middle Tennessee (where Nashville is), and east Tennessee (home to Knoxville and Chattanooga) are so distinct they could easily be three separate states.

For example, Memphis has higher concentrations of minority populations than the state as a whole. The Memphis MSA population is 51.2 percent white, 43.2 percent black, 2.4 percent Hispanic, and 1.4 percent Asian, according to the 2000 census. In contrast Tennessee's population is 80.2 percent white, 16.4 percent black, 2.2 percent Hispanic, and 1 percent Asian. Although figures for the Memphis MSA and Shelby County show that whites slightly outnumber blacks, in the city of Memphis the black population exceeds the white population.

Per-capita personal income for the Memphis MSA was $28,828 for 1999, a figure that's just above the national per-capita figure of $28,546, according to government statistics. The city's cost of living is lower than the national average, according to the American Chamber of Commerce Researchers Association, which calculated that as of September 30, 2001, Memphis's cost of living was 88.9 percent of the national average.

In terms of the job market, unemployment levels for the Memphis MSA are lower than the national average, as they have been through most of the 1990s. As of November 2001 local unemployment was 4.6 percent, compared with 5.7 percent for the country as a whole.

Doing Business: From Cotton to E-commerce

Memphis is an economically diverse city, a characteristic that helps the city to weather the ups and downs in the economy. For example, except for a slight increase in unemployment, Memphis barely felt the early 1990s recession that was devastating to other parts of the country. One reason is that manufacturing accounts for less than 10 percent of local employment, a key factor because manufacturing is hit hardest by tough times. Instead, most jobs are in the service sector, where large employers include FedEx, the health-care industry, retail, and other transportation/distribution companies.

FedEx is the city's largest employer, with about 32,000 Memphis employees, so it's an important engine to the local economy. The company's headquarters are here, and about half of the company's worldwide package volume comes through Memphis. FedEx is a big reason that Memphis International Airport is the world's busiest air-cargo airport.

It's also a big reason companies continue to flock to Memphis to open their own distribution centers. Among these are e-commerce companies including barnes andnoble.com and toysrus.com, catalog retailers such as Williams-Sonoma, and computer hardware and software companies such as Ingram Micro.

Other modes of transportation are strong here, including railroad, river, and trucking. Memphis is the country's third-largest rail center, its fourth-largest inland port, and home to more than 200 trucking companies. Because of the city's central location, products moved by truck and rail can reach 66 percent of the U.S. population within 24 hours.

Memphis has exported cotton and other products to overseas markets since the early 1800s, but in 1999 the Memphis area sold more than $3.1-billion worth of goods for export worldwide.

Although not the reigning economic king it once was, cotton continues to be an important part of the local economy. The Mid-South cotton industry (from farming to textiles) generates some $7.5 billion in revenues, and Memphis-based merchants market about 30 percent of the total U.S. cotton crop. Memphis is home to the largest spot cotton-trading market in the world and cotton-trading giant Dunavant

Enterprises as well as the National Cotton Council and other cotton organizations. Memphis is also home to the National Hardwood Lumber Association and was at one time the hardwood capital of the world.

Memphis is also strong in health care, given the two large hospital systems as well as St. Jude Children's Research Hospital and the University of Tennessee Health Science Center. The retail industry is also a big player in the local economy because Memphis is where the Mid-South comes to shop. The federal and local governments also are large employers, as are the city and county school systems.

Memphis economic development has been on the rise. Each year from 1997 to 2000 saw more than $1 billion in capital investment through major projects, while during that time Memphis economic development accounted for 25 percent of total economic development within the entire state, according to the Memphis Regional Chamber. In 2000 some 41 companies announced relocations to Memphis, while 230 Memphis companies announced major expansions. While the Memphis economy suffered from the fallout of September 11, the effects seem to have been short-lived. Such resiliency is in keeping with the city's history of being better able than many other cities to weather downturns in the economy. One reason is that the Memphis business community is pretty conservative, so expansion doesn't get out of hand during good times. That means there's not as far to fall when business slows down. Its relatively low level of manufacturing also protects the city economy during bad times, even though that also means that economic booms here are not as great as in cities with a larger portion of manufacturing.

The job market looks pretty good as unemployment here is generally below the national average. Low unemployment rather than high unemployment has been the problem, as employers struggle to find enough people to man lower-paying jobs and the skilled people necessary for high-tech and other jobs. Cognizant of this challenge, city leaders have focused their attention on improving the local education system as a way to produce more skilled workers.

Cotton, the white gold that launched the Memphis economy in the 1800s, is still an important crop in the surrounding Mid-South area.
PHOTO: MEMPHIS CONVENTION AND VISITORS BUREAU

Despite the city's economic resilience, its attractions, conventions, and aviation industries were initially devastated by the slowdown in travel that followed the events of September 11, 2001, although within a few months these businesses were recovering. The city usually brings in some eight million visitors each year. The Memphis Cook Convention Center is being expanded and rebuilt to the tune of close to $100 million, and the city is anticipating stronger convention business once the work is done in late 2002.

The city is making great progress toward its goal of creating a strong downtown. In

Memphis Vital Statistics

Founded:

In 1819 on the fourth Chickasaw bluff overlooking the Mississippi by Andrew Jackson, James Winchester, and John Overton

Nickname: Bluff City

Mayors/Governor:

Memphis: Mayor W. W. Herenton
Shelby County: Mayor Jim Rout (until September 2002)
Tennessee: Governor Don Sunquist (until January 2003)

Population:

Memphis: 650,100
Shelby County: 897,472
Memphis metropolitan statistical area: 1,135,614
Tennessee: 5,689,283

Area:

Memphis: 296 square miles
Shelby County: 772 square miles
Memphis MSA: 3,012 square miles

Counties in the Memphis MSA:

Shelby, Tipton, and Fayette Counties in Tennessee, Crittenden County in Arkansas, and DeSoto County in Mississippi

Average temperatures:

January: 41° F
July: 81° F
Annual: 62° F

Average annual rainfall: 48.6 inches

Average snowfall: 5.3 inches

Major airport:

Memphis International Airport, the world's busiest cargo airport since 1992 thanks to FedEx, and the southern hub for Northwest Airlines

Major interstates: I–40 (east-west) and I–55 (north-south)

Maritime and railroad activity:

Memphis is the fourth largest inland port in the United States (second largest on the Mississippi) and the third largest rail hub in the United States.

Major colleges and universities:

University of Memphis, University of Tennessee Health Science Center, Christian Brothers University, Rhodes College, and LeMoyne-Owen College

Important dates in Memphis history:

1541: Hernando DeSoto and his party are the first white men to view the lower Mississippi and may have been the first white men to visit the fourth Chickasaw bluff.

1739: The French build a fort on the fourth Chickasaw bluff.

1795: The Spanish build Fort San Fernando on the fourth Chickasaw bluff, which lasts only two years until the Americans build Fort Adams on its ruins.

1819: Memphis is founded.

1826: Memphis is incorporated as a town.

1857: The Memphis-Charleston Railroad is completed, launching the city's position as an important rail hub.

1862: Memphis falls to Union forces but continues to operate as a major center of commerce for both sides.

1879: Memphis declares bankruptcy and loses its charter after a series of yellow-fever epidemics kill or drive off most of its population.

1880s: Memphis becomes the largest hardwood market in the world.

1893: Memphis regains its charter.

1899: Church Park and Auditorium are built for the city's African Americans by black millionaire Robert Church, cementing Beale Street as the center of African American culture and commerce.

1909: Beale Street bandleader W. C. Handy publishes the first blues music, becoming "father of the blues" for his role in bringing this style of music to the American mainstream.

1916: The first self-service grocery store in the country opens in Memphis under the name Piggly Wiggly, which evolves into the modern supermarket.

1948: WDIA becomes the first radio station to adopt an all African American format, launching the careers of B.B. King, Rufus Thomas, and others.

1952: "Rocket 88" is recorded at Sun Studio by Jackie Brenston and the Delta Cats, considered the first rock-and-roll recording.

Memphis entrepreneur Kemmons Wilson opens his first Holiday Inn, pioneering the modern hotel/motel chain.

1955: Elvis Presley records his first hit, "That's All Right (Mama)," at Sun Studio, quickly becoming an international superstar.

1960: Stax Records has its first major hit, "Cause I Love You" by Rufus Thomas and his daughter Carla Thomas, to be followed by many more hits by Otis Redding, the Staple Singers, Isaac Hayes, and others.

1968: Dr. Martin Luther King, Jr., in town to support striking African American garbage workers, is assassinated at the Lorraine Motel.

1972: Frederick W. Smith starts Federal Express Corp. in Little Rock, soon moving the operation to Memphis.

1977: Elvis Presley dies at his south Memphis home Graceland at age 42.

1980s: Memphis tourism heats up as The Peabody hotel is reopened, Beale Street is revived, and Graceland and Sun Studio are opened to visitors.

1992: The city elects its first African American mayor, City Schools Superintendent W. W. Herenton.

1994: Memphis International Airport, already a major Northwest Airlines hub, begins direct international service when KLM Royal Dutch Airlines launches its Memphis-to-Amsterdam flight.

2000: The AAA Redbirds baseball team opens its first season at a new downtown ballpark.

2001: Memphis lands an NBA team, the Grizzlies, from Vancouver, which begins its first season here.

Major area employers:

FedEx, U.S. Government, Memphis City Schools, Methodist Healthcare Corp., Baptist Memorial Health Care Corp., City of Memphis, Shelby County Government, Wal-Mart Stores, University of Tennessee Health Science Center, AutoZone

Memphis companies with more than $1 billion in annual revenues (2000):

FedEx Corp. (express delivery), AutoZone (auto parts retailer), First Tennessee National Corp. (financial services), M.S. Carriers (trucking), Thomas & Betts (electrical components), Union Planters Corp. (financial services), Dunavant Enterprises (cotton merchandising, etc.), Hohenberg Bros. Co. (cotton merchandising, etc.)

Famous sons and daughters:

Actors Cybill Shepherd, Kathy Bates, and Morgan Freeman; DJ Rick Dees, basketball player Penny Hardaway, game-show host Wink Martindale, musician Isaac Hayes, Elvis Presley, Machine Gun Kelly, early 1900s adventurer Richard Halliburton, Confederate General Nathan Bedford Forrest, sportscaster Tim McCarver, 'N Sync's Justin Timberlake, television's Judge Joe Brown

Famous Memphis residents:

Historian Shelby Foote, soprano Kallen Esperian, Debbi Fields Rose (Mrs. Fields' Cookies), civil rights leader Benjamin Hooks, preacher/musician Al Green, Nobel Prize-winning researcher Peter Doherty, entertainer Jerry Lee Lewis

Major American music innovations from Memphis:

1910s: the blues, first published by W. C. Handy
1950s: rock and roll, first recorded at Sun Studio
1960s–early '70s: Southern soul, recorded at Stax Records

Public transportation:

Memphis Area Transit Authority operates bus lines, the downtown trolley, and an airport shuttle service for downtown hotels.

Military bases:

Naval Support Activity Memphis in Millington, Tennessee, home of the Bureau of Naval Personnel

Driving laws:

Speed limits are usually 35 mph or 40 mph on the city's main streets.
Turning right at a red light is allowed unless signs say otherwise.
Where you see an HOV lane, travel in that lane is limited to cars with at least two passengers during the rush hours posted on the signs.

Alcohol laws:

You must be over 21 to drink alcohol.

Liquor may be served until 3:00 A.M. except on Beale Street between Second and Fourth Streets, where establishments have permission to serve until 5:00 A.M. Only in this section of Beale Street is it legal to carry an open container of alcohol.

In 2002 under Tennessee law, drivers are considered to be illegally impaired if their blood alcohol level reaches .10. This is likely to be lowered to .8 within a few years.

Daily newspaper: *The Commercial Appeal*

Taxes: Sales tax: 8.25 percent (6 percent Tennessee tax, 2.25 percent Shelby County tax)
Hotel-room tax: 14.95 percent (includes sales tax; may vary outside Shelby County)

2001 there was some $2 billion in renovations and new construction underway, including the extension of the Main Street trolley and the expansion of the convention center.

Memphis at Play

On the leisure side Memphis is also seeing the results of many years of planning downtown. AutoZone Park, a beautiful baseball park designed along the lines of Baltimore's Oriole Park at Camden Yards, is home to the Triple A Redbirds, a Cardinals farm team that draws more fans than most other teams in the Pacific Coast League.

The city also experienced its first season in 2001–2002 as a professional basketball city, when the NBA Vancouver Grizzlies became the Memphis Grizzlies. Plans for a new arena for the Grizzlies are in the works for the south end of downtown, but for now the team plays at the Pyramid Arena.

Peabody Place opened in 2001, with a large movie theater, restaurants, Tower Records, and other stores. A few blocks away, South Main Street has become the gallery district for the city, with galleries as well as chic shops.

There are plenty of restaurants and bars of all kinds downtown, so visitors can easily have a meal or drinks before or after the game, the movies, and other entertainments.

Beale Street is a huge destination for visitors, locals, and residents of nearby towns and farms, drawing more visitors than any other attraction in the state. Good local blues and other live music can be found on the street every night, and sometimes national acts that have included B.B. King, Alvin Youngblood Hart, and Buckwheat Zydeco. Outside of Beale Street you'll find all kinds of live music, ranging from big concerts by stars such as the Rolling Stones and Pearl Jam at the Pyramid Arena to club performances ranging from heavy metal to jazz, blues to bluegrass.

Beyond downtown Memphis you'll find good shopping, numerous parks that include 5,000-acre Shelby Farms, and many places to enjoy your favorite activity, whether it's skateboarding, bowling, hanging out in bookstores, or catching the game at a local bar. Check out the Nightlife, Parks and Recreation, and Shopping chapters for a full rundown, not to mention our listing of Annual Events.

The Pyramid Arena, built on the banks of the Mississippi River, recalls Memphis's namesake, the ancient Egyptian city on the Nile. PHOTO: MEMPHIS CONVENTION AND VISITORS BUREAU

Getting Here, Getting Around

Memphis is near the geographical center of the country and is well connected by highway, air, railroad, and even the Mississippi River for passengers on the *Delta Queen* or *Mississippi Queen* riverboats. KLM Royal Dutch Airlines makes the city easily accessible from Europe and beyond, flying daily to and from Amsterdam. Once here, unless you are staying downtown (where there's the Main Street trolley and cab stands) and plan to spend most of your time there, you'll want to have a car. True, Memphis has a well-run bus system, but relying on the bus can prove time-consuming and not always very convenient. For a taxi you must call a cab company to arrange your rides, as it's generally not possible to hail a cab on the street.

To get your bearings from downtown, face the Mississippi River, which is west, looking into Arkansas. To the left is south Memphis, where you find Graceland and the airport, and just beyond, the state of Mississippi. Much of the city's residential and commercial growth over the years has been to the east, so that's where you'll find many of the city's homes, restaurants, hotels, and shopping centers.

For driving Memphis could be called a 20-minute city, since by taking the I–240 loop around the city, you can get just about anywhere except the far suburbs within 20 to 25 minutes. Avenues run east and west, including Poplar and Union, and streets run north and south, with the dividing line between north and south at Madison Avenue. Of course, traffic is always a wild card, and if it's bad, it can add considerably to the length of your trip.

Remember, if you get lost or need assistance in finding your way, don't hesitate to ask someone for help. You'll find that Memphians are very friendly and glad to give you directions.

The city isn't very well set up for biking. Memphis thoroughfares rarely have bike lanes, and local drivers aren't used to accommodating bicycles. Stick to the smaller streets, park bike paths, and less-busy thoroughfares (such as Jefferson and North Parkway) if you must rely on your bike to get around.

Getting Here

By Roadway

Two major interstate arteries cross at Memphis: I–40, which runs east and west, and I–55, which runs north and south. From the west and north, they converge in West Memphis, Arkansas, a town just across the river that seems like a huge truck plaza, given all the commercial traffic. Two highway bridges bring cars across the Mississippi into Memphis: the I–40 bridge, which crosses the Mississippi near the Pyramid Arena at the northern end of downtown, and the I–55 bridge, from which you take Riverside Parkway to get downtown. I–40 East comes in past Wolfchase Galleria, the city's newest regional shopping mall, and feeds into the I–240 loop around Memphis. To go directly into the heart of the city from I–40 East, take Sam Cooper Boulevard. If you're coming in from Mississippi on I–55, you'll be well inside the city before you link up with Riverside for direct access into downtown (and a great view of the river). Alternatively, from I–55 you can take the I–240 loop near Graceland to reach other parts of the city.

By Air

Memphis is well served by commercial airlines, with more than 600 departures and arrivals each day, and an excellent on-time arrivals record; if anything, flights sometimes arrive early. Because Memphis is a Northwest Airlines hub, Memphis has direct flights to and from just about any U.S. city. At least nine other airlines serve the Memphis airport as well, and KLM Royal Dutch Airlines connects Memphis to Europe and beyond, flying daily to and from Amsterdam. It's likely that flights to other European cities and to Japan will be added in the near future. On the cargo side Memphis International Airport has been the world's busiest cargo airport for the past decade by virtue of Federal Express, moving some 2.7 million tons of cargo in fiscal 2000. This hometown company has its SuperHub package-sorting facility at the airport, and many companies have opened distribution centers near FedEx to expedite shipments. Memphis International Airport is one of the 10 fastest-growing airports in the United States, and to meet future needs, the airport has been spending some $400 million on capital improvements to runways, terminals, and parking areas.

The airport has three terminals, designed with a triangular pattern on the exterior so that from afar they resemble trays of martinis. Each has baggage claim on the ground floor and ticket counters, gates, shops, and restaurants on the second level.

When your flight arrives at the airport, follow signs to the baggage-claim area on the ground floor. Skycap porters are available to handle your luggage for a minimum of 50 cents per bag; baggage carts are available from a vending machine ($2.00 in cash or paid with a major credit card, with a 25-cent reward for returning the cart to the machine) in each terminal's baggage-claim area.

Terminal B is where you'll find most shops, including a PGA Golf Shop and Sunglass Hut. You'll also find Elvis Presley's Graceland Gift & Tour Shop, where you can buy Elvis gifts and music, or, if time allows, get a tour of Graceland Mansion (just a few miles from the airport). There are a number of mostly fast-food

Memphis International Airport has a distinctive design that enhances its passenger terminals.
PHOTO: MEMPHIS CONVENTION AND VISITORS BUREAU

Insiders' Tip

If you're getting a cold, have a minor injury or other health concern, visit the Dorothy L. Bobbit Health Station near the Terminal B security checkpoint at Memphis International Airport. A registered nurse is there Monday through Friday, 8:00 A.M. to 4:30 P.M. to cater to airport employees and the traveling public.

Car Rental

Car-rental agencies, which are located just off the airport property, have free shuttles that stop in the far lane outside the baggage area.

Alamo, (901) 332–8412
Avis, (901) 345–3514
Budget, (901) 398–8888
Dollar, (901) 396–2495
Enterprise, (901) 345–8588
Hertz, (901) 345–5680
National, (901) 345–0070
Thrifty, (901) 345–0170

Taxis and Hotel Shuttles

Taxis cost $1.50 for the first $\frac{1}{7}$ mile, then 20 cents for each additional $\frac{1}{7}$ mile, plus a 75-cent airport surcharge and fees for extra passengers and luggage. A cab ride downtown costs about $21 plus tip. Try Yellow Cab (901–577–7700).

If you're staying downtown, a special airport shuttle (DASH) provides service to the downtown hotels for a cost of $17 round-trip or $10 one way. Many hotels operate free shuttles for their guests. Ask when you make your reservations or try the courtesy telephones in the airport baggage-claim area.

As for transportation back to the airport, ask your hotel's front desk for their recommendation. Often they have a shuttle or other arrangements for getting guests to the airport. You can call a taxi, but taxis don't always arrive on time, which can be pretty nerve-racking if you have a plane to catch. If you are dropping off a rental car, you'll probably want to allow an extra 15 minutes for the shuttle ride from the agency to the airport terminal.

By Train

Amtrak's *City of New Orleans* train stops in Memphis's Central Station on South Main Street, with service to New Orleans or Chicago. If you don't already have your tickets, it's best to arrive an hour early to buy them (the entrance is on Main Street). The northbound train leaves at 10:30 P.M. and arrives at 9:00 A.M., so you may want to invest in a sleeper car for a more comfortable trip. The southbound train leaves at 6:30 A.M. and

restaurants and bars. You'll find Starbucks near gate B8, and if you didn't get your barbecue fix already, check out DaBlues Memphis near gate B34, which has live blues and Corky's BBQ (also available for takeout). Another Memphis favorite, Interstate BBQ, operates a restaurant and takeout window near gate B14. A whole slew of services, including a hair salon, a travel agency, and a business center, are also available at the airport. Northwest Airlines has its World Club near the security checkpoint at Terminal B (both are for members only). For a complete listing of airport amenities, check out www.mscaa.com.

Smoking is not allowed in the airport terminals, except in The Bud Bar & Restaurant in Terminal B. Otherwise, smokers must go outside the terminal and at least 20 feet away from the public entrances to smoke.

Getting from the Airport to the City

A taxi stand, courtesy shuttles, and other transportation are located outside the lower-level exits. If you are renting a car or intend to use your hotel's shuttle service, look for free indoor courtesy phones, just inside the door of each terminal's baggage-claim area. Call your hotel to let them know you arrived or to make reservations.

arrives in New Orleans at 3:40 P.M. Call (800) 872-7245 or check out www.amtrak.com for more information. It's a good idea to call the station (901-526-0052) beforehand to make sure the train is on schedule.

By Bus

Greyhound Bus Lines offers service between Memphis and destinations across the country. The phone number for the downtown bus station is (901) 523-9253; or for reservations call (800) 231-2222. *Note:* The Greyhound bus station, which has operated at 203 Union Avenue for many years, is likely to move to a new location in south Memphis near the airport. So call before you head for the station.

By Boat

The Delta Queen Steamboat Company operates paddlewheel steamboat cruises on the Mississippi, which stop in Memphis. For information call (800) 543-1949 or check out www.deltaqueen.com.

General Aviation

Memphis International Airport has two fixed-based operators, Wilson Air Center (901-345-2992) and Signature Flight Support (901-345-4700). Both provide services to private and corporate aircraft, including fuel, repairs, hangar, and tie-down.

In addition, the airport authority operates two secondary general-aviation airports. General DeWitt Spain Airport (901-922-8004), just north of downtown Memphis, has services available through Downtown Aviation (901-353-9151). Charles W. Baker Airport (901-922-8004) is 22 miles north of Memphis International in Millington, with services available through Shelby Aviation (901-873-3838).

Getting Around

By Car

Memphis likes to name its highways, but for some reason people never use the

The Tennessee Welcome Center in downtown Memphis, with its knowledgeable staff, is a good first stop as you familiarize yourself with the city. PHOTO: MEMPHIS CONVENTION AND VISITORS BUREAU

Insiders' Tip

While driving in Memphis, be on your guard for bad drivers. The biggest problems are drivers going too fast, going too slow, and changing lanes or turning without first signaling and/or looking carefully.

names. Although segments of the loop around the city have names including Avron B. Fogelman Expressway and Martin Luther King Expressway, locals always refer to it as I–240, 240, or the Expressway. Tourism officials have named I–40 between Memphis and Nashville Music Highway, but everybody else calls it I–40, or the Interstate. Highway 385, the freeway from East Memphis to Collierville, was renamed Bill Morris Parkway, but everybody still calls it by its original name, Nonconnah Parkway, just plain Nonconnah, or sometimes 385.

If someone recommends that you take Sam Cooper Boulevard, they're referring to the newly widened freeway that connects midtown Memphis to I–40 East. This is a popular shortcut favored by midtowners to get out east. Another eccentricity in midtown and downtown is streets that stop and start. If you're in the 200 block of Jefferson Avenue in downtown Memphis, you can't drive straight east on Jefferson to reach an address in the 2000 block.

The main east/west arteries out of downtown are Union, Madison, and Poplar (locals always call them by their "first names," never adding Avenue). Union (not to be confused with Union Extended, a different street) turns into Walnut Grove Road, continuing east across I–240 to Shelby Farms Park, the International Agricenter, and Germantown. Madison dead-ends into East Parkway, just

east of Overton Square, but a quick left, then right at the first light puts you onto Poplar. Poplar continues past I–240 through Germantown to Collierville, where it's renamed West Poplar and then turns into Highway 72. (Any address with West Poplar is in Collierville.) Arteries that run north/south include Danny Thomas Boulevard just past downtown, Eastern Parkway in midtown, Highland just past midtown; Perkins, Mendenhall, White Station, and Ridgeway in East Memphis; and Germantown Parkway in Germantown.

Bear in mind that the law requires the use of seatbelts for passengers and child-safety seats for children under age 4. It's legal to turn right on red at an intersection, as long as you come to a complete stop first. Look for signs, for turning right on red is prohibited at specified intersections. The speed limits vary, usually between 35 mph and 55 mph. Remember that if the stoplights aren't working at an intersection, it should be treated like a four-way stop.

Also, during the 2002–2004 time frame, parts of the interstate system in and around Memphis will be under construction. Not all these projects will take place simultaneously, however. Plans call for new interchanges between I–40 and I–240 to be built, first at Summer Avenue, then at the midtown exchange north of the medical center, and then at Perkins in east Memphis. Portions of I–240 also will be under construction. East of the city there will be construction around Highway 64, as crews build what will basically be an outer semiloop around the city by linking Nonconnah (Highway 385) to I–40.

As you drive into town, look for detailed signs on how to avoid trouble spots. We recommend that before you come to Memphis, check out www.co.shelby.tn.us or www.tdot.state.tn.us for an update on construction and recommendations on how to avoid congested areas.

Also be aware that I–40 has HOV lanes for 4 miles east of the city during rush hour to help manage traffic. During the posted hours the lanes are limited to vehicles with at least two passengers. HOV lanes are expected to take effect on I–55 in mid-2002 and are in the works for parts of I–240.

Parking

Parking is free in most of the city, with the exception of downtown. While there's some parking on the streets (with meters), it's snatched up quickly, so parking lots in the area are usually your best bet. Downtown lots cost $2.00 to $7.00, except during big events, when the capitalist spirit pushes prices to $10 or whatever the market will bear. Parking meters are in use only during weekdays until 6:00 P.M., so don't worry about feeding the meters at other times. Pay attention if you park on the street during Redbird games, when there are additional parking restrictions.

By Public Transportation

MATA Buses

The Memphis Area Transit Authority operates air-conditioned buses all over the city and the immediate suburbs. The base fare is $1.25 one way (exact change required; 10 cents extra if you transfer to another route). To find out how to get to a destination, call the MATA Hotline (901-274-6282) Mon-

day through Saturday and press "0" to reach someone who will tell you exactly which bus or buses will take you there. You can also visit the MATA North End Terminal, 444 North Main Street (at the corner of Auction Street), for a map or directions. Disabled passengers can arrange transportation by calling MATAplus at (901) 722-7171.

Main Street Trolley

The downtown trolley operates along Main Street and loops along the riverfront. A two-mile extension, expected to be completed in 2004, is under construction east along Madison Avenue past the medical center. The Riverfront Loop allows for an excellent panorama of the Mississippi River and also stops at the Tennessee Welcome Center and the Pyramid Arena. (For more details on the Main Street Trolley, see the Kidstuff chapter.)

Tickets are 60 cents per ride for all ages, except seniors and disabled persons, who pay 30 cents. You can also get a $2.50 day-long pass or a $6.00 three-day pass. Exact change is required. Call (901) 274-6282 for more information.

The Main Street Trolley is a fun and practical way to get around downtown Memphis and to get a great view of the Mississippi River. PHOTO: MEMPHIS CONVENTION AND VISITORS BUREAU

Airlines

AirTran Airways, (800) AIRTRAN
American Airlines, (800) 433–7300
ComAir, (800) 354–9822
Continental Express, (800) 525–0280
Delta Air Lines, (800) 221–1212
KLM Royal Dutch Airlines, (800) 374–7747
Midway Airlines, (800) 446–4392
Northwest Airlines, (800) 225–2525
United Airlines, (800) 241–6522
U.S. Airways, (800) 428–4322

Insiders' Tip

One of the bonuses of living in a Northwest Airlines hub city is Cyberfares, a program that allows you to book last-minute travel to certain destinations at low fares. Check www.nwa.com after midnight Tuesdays for the cities and fares available for the following weekend. Sample fares are round-trip to Philadelphia for $149 or to Dallas for $119.

History

Location and transportation: These are the two main elements responsible for the founding of Memphis and its development and which continue to influence this Mississippi River city today.

This was true more than 1,000 years ago when Native Americans used crude stone tools to build a village on one of the high bluffs of the river and brought their canoes to navigate the waterway. It remains true now as this diverse multicultural community uses the latest high-tech equipment to move information, people, and services around the globe.

Between then and now, the city has repeatedly bounced back and forth between prosperity and ruin and has served as the capital of an area known as the Mid-South. This region can be defined as the area stretching 200 miles on all sides of the city. Throughout Memphis's history fascinating and legendary people have made their mark in the worlds of civil rights and politics (Ida Wells and Benjamin Hooks), literature (William Faulkner), entertainment (Elvis Presley), and business (Fred Smith with FedEx and Kemmons Wilson with Holiday Inns).

As frequently happens, this development occurred by chance because of the natural amenities provided by a small patch of land situated along a mighty river. People could either traverse the waterway or, due to the safety afforded by the bluffs from the catastrophic floods, settle here. This patch of land was known as the Fourth Chickasaw Bluff.

Birth of the Bluff City

Hundreds of years before European explorers claimed the land upon which Memphis would eventually rise, Native Americans had a thriving culture. Evidence of this culture can be found at Chucalissa, an Indian village located just 6 miles south of where downtown Memphis bustles today. Although abandoned in the 1500s, Chucalissa was reconstructed in the late 1950s and now remains open as the Chucalissa Archaeological Museum and Reconstructed Indian Village. Guided tours provide a glimpse into what life was like for the area's first permanent settlers. (See Attractions chapter for details.)

Like the people of European descent who would follow in their footsteps, the Native Americans built permanent settlements in the area because the high bluffs protected their shelters from floods. From the many remnants of graves, tools, weapons, and pottery found at Chucalissa, it is obvious that the Mid-South flour- ished as a center for trading, hunting, and farming for Indians for hundreds of years, but that began to change in the 1500s.

In 1541 Hernando DeSoto led his army to the Mississippi River, although exactly where along the river is still debated to this day. Most historians, however, agree that DeSoto's party was the first group of Europeans to view the lower half of the river and that they made camp somewhere near Memphis. Although DeSoto claimed this area for Spain, for the next 200 years the ownership of the Memphis area changed hands and was held by the English and the French as well. Eventually it was made the westernmost border of North Carolina, and in 1796 this area was included as part of Tennessee, the 16th state admitted to the Union.

An interesting footnote is that when the Fourth Chickasaw Bluff was home to an American frontier outpost known as Fort Adams, its commandant, Captain Meriwether Lewis, was visited by a friend named William Clark. Little did they know that five years later the two men, at the request of President Jefferson, would come to the banks of the Mississippi River again—although farther north—to begin their famous expedition.

Even though various outposts were built on the Fourth Chickasaw Bluff, the city of Memphis didn't come into existence until the 1800s. In 1818 the Chickasaw Indians sold the land encompassing Memphis to the United States, resolving once and for all the question of ownership. That same year, three entrepreneurs decided to become absentee landlords of their own city, which they decided to name Memphis.

Future president Andrew Jackson joined with two other middle Tennesseans, John Overton and James Winchester, and together this trio of entrepreneurs not only recognized the two natural geographical advantages—high bluffs and harbor access created by the convergence of the Wolf and Mississippi Rivers—but also were foresighted enough to see the financial possibilities of erecting a city there. In May 1819 the three founders ordered a survey of a 5,000-acre tract on the banks of the river, which would form the heart of downtown Memphis. A mere five months after this survey, a new county named Shelby was carved into the southwest corner of Tennessee. (Within a few years Andrew Jackson sold his share to a fourth entrepreneur, John G. McLemore, who later became president of the first railroad built in Memphis.)

The state may have had a new county, but this county still needed a name for its laid-out-on-paper city. Like many of the nation's early settlers and founders, the fathers of this new city turned to their history books to find a name suitable for this new river town. In these books they settled on the name "Memphis," which seemed especially appropriate as it was originally the name of a once-thriving metropolis on the banks of the Nile River in ancient Egypt. The Egyptian word translates roughly into the expression "place of good abode."

By naming the new city Memphis, the founders conjured images of a great cosmopolitan town for this fledging community. Of course, during its first decades, Memphis was anything but a thriving, pro-gressive city. The city was officially incorporated in 1826, and shortly before that, when the first census was conducted in 1820, Memphis was a small village of only 663 residents. At the time Memphis wasn't much more than a rowdy settlement for transients. Many viewed the city as little more than an outpost as they passed through Memphis on their way to explore the Wild West, which started just across the river in Arkansas. Memphis was also frequented by river men, who stopped for a night or two as they dropped off or picked up goods for their steamboats or flatboats.

Memphis may have been a backwater hamlet, but it was on the verge of a boom: The city's population nearly tripled by the time the 1840 census came around.

The primary economic force responsible for this population explosion was the so-called "white gold." Cotton was quickly becoming king of the Mid-South's agrarian economy. Built on the backs of enslaved labor, the cotton trade was quite profitable and quickly planted thousands of acres. In 1825, 300 bales of cotton were recorded in Memphis. Just 15 years later cotton merchants reported 35,000 bales shipped from Memphis. By 1850 Memphis was acknowledged as the largest inland cotton market in the world. In 1859, the eve of the Civil War, more than 400,000 bales of cotton were transported out of Memphis. In the time since its birth on the banks of the Mississippi River just four decades earlier, Memphis had become one of the nation's busiest river ports, rivaling New Orleans to the south and St. Louis to the north. The Bluff City's population had grown from nothing more than a crowd to a lively metropolis of more than 22,000. Most of the growth was due to the valuable commodity known as cotton. But Memphis's economic success came at a high price. It had been built on an inhuman foundation of slavery, and this foundation was about to crumble. In the process the young nation was ripped apart.

The Civil War Years

With its strategic location on the Mississippi River, its strong economy, and its designation by the 1860 federal census as the 38th-largest city in the nation, Memphis would prove to be a valuable asset to whichever side—the Union or the Confederacy—had possession of it.

Of course, given its location in the Deep South, once the Civil War began in earnest, Memphians were firmly on the side of the Confederacy. When shortly after the war began there was a vote on the matter, the voters of Memphis spoke unanimously: A mere five voters in Memphis cast ballots against secession.

In 1861 a Confederate Army headquarters and supply depot was established in Memphis. Many of the city's 22,600 people signed up to join the Army of the Confederacy. Some 72 Confederate companies were formed by the Memphis recruits. Initially, Memphians were confident the war would end quickly and favorably for the Confederacy. That point of view, however, proved short-lived.

In 1862 Union naval forces gathered on the river not far from Memphis, and the Confederate gunboats prepared to defend the city. As daylight broke across the river on June 6, hundreds of Memphians lined the bluffs to witness what they were sure would be the swift defeat of the Union forces. Yet just two hours after the first shots were fired, the Union vessels had soundly defeated the Confederates. That afternoon, the Confederate flag was lowered, and the United States flag once again flew over the city. Memphis had returned to the Union only 363 days after its residents had voted to secede.

The Confederate Army headquarters and supply depot quickly became a Union headquarters and supply depot. Memphis also became a prisoner-of-war center. The victorious Union leaders soon learned that a military occupation of Memphis was not the same as a city voluntarily rejoining the United States. First General Ulysses S. Grant and then General William T. Sherman found out for themselves how hard it was to actually retain control over the citizenry. Memphis merchants quickly adapted to the occupation and discovered that Union money was as good as, if not better than, Confederate money since many Yankees paid in gold

Cotton, also known as white gold, was a key for the settlement and economic growth of Memphis.
PHOTO: MEMPHIS CONVENTION AND VISITORS BUREAU

and silver. Although they may have been under Union occupation, many members of the local business community remained loyal to the Confederacy. Thus, much of the money businesses earned by Memphians trading with the Union ended up back in the hands of the Confederates, which the Southern Army then used to buy the supplies that allowed them to continue its war with the Union. Although Grant and Sherman tried one initiative after the other to stop the flow of money and/or contraband from Memphis to the Confederacy, neither one had much success.

One of the most stubborn supporters of the Confederacy was a local newspaper,

An Early Experiment: The Nashoba Plantation Colony

Although not generally regarded as a hotbed of progressive politics or a haven for freethinkers, Memphis was the site of one of the nation's earliest interracial communes. And, of all things, the founder of this utopian colony was a woman.

Frances Wright, a native of Scotland, was a freethinker and someone who was years ahead of her time. She left Scotland and traveled around much of the United States in the 1820s, observing the people and absorbing the culture of this new nation. She made a favorable impression on many of the leading intellectuals of the day, including Ralph Waldo Emerson.

One aspect of this new nation that truly appalled her was the institution of slavery. Wright eventually made her way to an area located near what would soon become Memphis, Tennessee, (and presently is in Germantown, Tennessee), and there in 1825 she founded the Nashoba Plantation Colony.

Wright's plan was to establish a community where slaves could earn their freedom by living and working on this plantation. Her long-range goal was to have others replicate this colony in other parts of the country so that over time, slavery would eventually disappear.

Before this radical Nashoba Plantation concept could move much beyond the planning stages, however, Wright was forced to return to Scotland due to illness. Although others had promised to fulfill Wright's dream, the colony foundered without the strong leadership and vision provided by Wright herself.

The Nashoba experiment was abandoned, but the name "Nashoba" is still used by developers and businesspeople in Germantown.

The Appeal (forerunner of today's *Commercial Appeal*). Following the fall of Memphis in 1862, the newspaper operators gathered up their presses and fled to Mississippi. In order to continue to provide the news from a Confederate point of view and avoid capture, the newspaper staff was forced to relocate from one city in one state to another city in another state throughout the Civil War.

It wasn't until the final weeks of the war that the support for the Confederate army waned in the Memphis community. By this time it was clear that the South was going to lose the war, and the Memphis economy was gradually grinding to a halt.

When the war ended in 1865, Memphis had managed to avoid the serious damage experienced by many of its sister cities in the South. For instance, it wasn't torched like Atlanta, and, because the battle for Memphis was over so quickly and

took place only on the river, the city wasn't terrorized by artillery fire like Richmond, Virginia, or Vicksburg, Mississippi. Although a horrific four-year-long civil war left little mark on Memphis, a tiny mosquito was about to harm the city in ways that a war couldn't.

Yellow Fever

Memphis's location along the Mississippi River may be responsible for the city's founding and success, but it also harbored the cause of a disease that would almost destroy the city. Along with its desirable bluffs, Memphis had swampy areas and lowlands that flooded. Both types of terrain formed ideal breeding grounds for mosquitoes. The unsanitary conditions of the formative decades of Memphis had made the city prone to diseases such as cholera, dengue, dysentery, and smallpox. Worst of all, however, was the mosquito population that spread yellow fever, or as it was commonly called, yellow jack.

The first reported yellow-fever epidemic to strike Memphis occurred shortly after the city was incorporated in 1826, and it returned every few years. While these earlier epidemics were responsible for the deaths of hundreds of Memphians, it wasn't until after the Civil War that the city found out just how devastating yellow fever could be.

During the 1873 epidemic 5,000 cases were reported, and 2,000 deaths were attributed to yellow fever. But yellow jack would prove even more deadly five years later. In 1878 it seemed as if the mosquitoes would not be content until they had wiped out the human population of the city. Records of that year indicate that 17,600 cases of yellow fever were treated in Memphis. Of these, however, 5,150 perished. The next year, the city experienced yet another bout of yellow-fever cases, although on a lesser scale. A mere 2,000 cases were treated, and only 600 yellow fever deaths were reported. By the time of the climactic 1878 yellow-fever epidemic, so panicked were the citizens of the city that one month after the first yellow-fever death was reported, fewer than 20,000 residents remained in the city. Most of those who were able fled the city.

Memphis had been hit so hard by the sickness and death that the city's economy was a catastrophe. The city was forced to declare bankruptcy and surrender its charter, thereby being reduced to a state taxing district in 1879.

By this time the population no longer had a city, but the leaders of the community did realize what was needed to return Memphis to the thriving metropolis it once had been: a massive upgrading and sanitizing of the city's water and sewer system. Memphis may have been at its lowest point in its 60-year history, but what remained was positioning itself to be revitalized and ready for the modern 20th century that was just around the corner.

Memphis Reborn

As the 19th century came to a close, so did Memphis's economic hard times and its reputation as an unsanitary and disease-ridden community. The Bluff City still contained some untamed, crime-infested pockets, and the white, male leaders certainly retained plenty of the conservative, often racist views shared by their counterparts in many other Southern cities (especially their views of African Americans). Nevertheless, compared with the squalid conditions and backward, corrupt political systems in Memphis just a few short years before, the city in 1900 was entering one of its most progressive periods.

Following the devastating yellow fever epidemics of the 1870s, Memphis officials could no longer ignore the importance of providing clean water and a sanitary sewer system, so in the 1880s, the city began a major push to make the community more sanitary. It built a sewer system and began testing the water supply located deep beneath the city. Memphis began supplying its residents and businesses with clean, safe drinking water through artesian wells. The city's ample supply of pure artesian-springs well water continues to serve as a key economic development tool to city officials in the 21st century.

A number of other infrastructure-improvement projects began in the 1890s that helped boost the city's reputation in the nation and made it more attractive to businesses and families. The first electric streetcar was inaugurated. The Frisco Bridge was completed in 1892, thereby becoming the first bridge to span the Mississippi River south of St. Louis. A public library was opened, a new general hospital was built, and competing street rail lines entered the Memphis market. In 1895 the city's first steel skyscraper, the Porter Building, was such a wonder to the local community that many residents eagerly paid 10 cents to ride on the "high-speed" elevator. The 11-story structure remains downtown on Main Street.

Another important public-improvement program involved the community's investment in its public-education facilities. Between 1890 and 1910, 23 new schools were constructed, including four for black students. Providing public schools for blacks is notable for a number of reasons. Since 1864, the city had provided a public education for African Americans and was finally making a financial commitment to this education. Also, these new schools reflected the steadily growing number of blacks moving into Memphis. This agrarian-based community had relied on slave labor in its formative years, but with the Civil War and its subsequent reconstruction era, Memphis became popular with freed blacks. The city's minority population swelled even more toward the end of the 19th century, when mechanization forced thousands of black farmers and farmhands to move to the city to find jobs. During the time of the two world wars of the past century, African Americans continued to find Memphis a fairly agreeable city in which to enjoy a modest, if second-class, quality of life.

Of course, although there were rare exceptions, by and large, blacks were denied leadership roles in the community. Robert Church became a millionaire and city leader, but for every successful black businessperson such as Church, thousands of other minority store owners and operators were ignored by white business leaders. And for every social reformer such as Ida B. Wells, hundreds of other civil rights advocates in the black community were never given an opportunity to raise their voices. Still, the cultural and economic impact of this burgeoning segment of the population cannot be underestimated. During this time blues and jazz were born, and the sounds of these new musical genres could be heard on Beale Street and other parts of Memphis where blacks congregated for social interaction. (See the African American Heritage and Memphis Music chapters for more details on these subjects.)

By 1900 the city's population hit 102,320, topping the 100,000 mark for the first time and making it a top-tier Southern metropolis. The city also had managed to have its charter, which was lost in 1879, restored in 1893. In this atmosphere of change, a young man named Edward Hull Crump from North Mississippi walked onto the political stage of Memphis. He wouldn't budge from this stage for nearly 50 years, and faint traces of his fingerprints can still be found on the city.

The Crump Years (1909–1954)

E. H. Crump, or "Boss Crump" as he is most often referred to, established a political machine that managed to implement some much-needed public improvements, yet he often relied on questionable political tactics to achieve these accomplishments.

Crump was elected mayor of Memphis in 1909 and was ousted from the mayor's office just six years later. Yet, for more than three decades after he left his position as mayor, Crump still pulled the political strings in Memphis and Shelby County. Until his death in 1954, Crump was a powerful political force in local, state, and even national politics.

When he was elected mayor of Memphis, Crump touted himself as a reformer. At that time Memphis was infamously known as the "murder capital" of the nation after a 1912 study found that the city had 47.1 homicides per 100,000 population compared with the national average of 7.2 homicides per 100,000. (Later, Prudential Insurance Co. of America found that in 1916 Memphis had a jaw-dropping 89.9 homicides per 100,000, more than twice as many as its nearest competitor.)

Crump pledged to clean up the city by clamping down on saloons, gambling halls, and houses of ill repute. He managed to get elected mayor, but only by a margin of 78 votes. Sure enough, shortly after taking office, Crump did crack down on the dives, crap games, and prostitutes. It is worth noting, however, that during his time as mayor, the murder rate of Memphis continued to climb, and it was not by accident that whenever election time approached, Crump would loosen his grip on the enforcement of these laws, and once again the booze would flow, the dice would roll, and the streetwalkers would stroll. Ironically, while Crump was elected as someone who would rid the city of vice, he ended up being ousted

The city honored Memphians who served in World War I with this statue at Overton Park.

PHOTO: CITY OF MEMPHIS DIVISION OF PARK SERVICES

from the mayor's office by an act of the state legislature on a charge that he willingly failed to enforce the state liquor laws.

Even though he was forced out of the mayor's office in 1916, by some shrewd political maneuvering he resigned his post and had the city commissioners appoint his hand-picked successor to the office. Just six months after resigning as mayor, Crump was elected County Trustee, and, some years later, he was elected to two terms to Congress. Whether in an elected office or out, Crump ran a highly organized political machine. Crump not only influenced who got elected in Memphis and Shelby County, but his ability to "deliver" the voters of the city and county in state and federal races allowed him to have an effect on races for governor and Congress.

During the Crump era Memphis did enjoy much prosperity and growth. One of Crump's most hard-fought initiatives and proudest accomplishments was wrestling control of the utility services from the private sector into the hands of local government. The repercussions of this Crump achievement are enjoyed by every resident and business in Memphis today in the form of high levels of service and some of the lowest costs in the United States, because the city continues to own and operate Memphis Light, Gas & Water, the largest three-service municipal utility in the nation.

The Crump era began shortly before World War I and ended shortly after World War II. Like other American cities during these wars, Memphians rallied to the defense of the nation as patriotic pledges were renewed.

Anti-German sentiments grew so strong during World War I that the City of Germantown, essentially a suburb of Memphis, temporarily changed its name to Nashoba. In Millington, a city just north of Memphis, Park Field was used as a training field for World War I pilots. When World War II came along, Park Field officially became the Millington Naval Air Base.

Between the world wars many Memphians participated in the prosperous years of the 1920s; however, even more Memphians participated in the economic downturn period known as the Great Depression. When the stock market crashed in 1929, the price of cotton fell as well. Since much of the city's economy was still tied to the cotton industry, businesses throughout Memphis were hurt. With the financial means of the private sector severely limited, the federal government stepped in to pump money into the local economy. During the 1930s some $20 million in work-relief construction projects were started in the city.

The Memphis economy was regaining its strength as the cotton market improved when World War II erupted. Once again the city mobilized in support of the war effort. Its young men signed up for the various branches of the armed services, and the civilians at home did their part by supporting war-bond drives. Several defense-related industries had started locating in Memphis even before the war started, but once the United States entered the war, these businesses flourished. The city's economy also got a boost as a result of the thousands of naval personnel who were stationed at the Millington base. World War II also provided Memphis with one of its most enduring symbols—the *Memphis Belle*. The *Memphis Belle* was the first B-17 to complete 25 missions. The bomber and its crew logged more than 20,000 combat miles and dropped more than 60 tons of bombs during World War II. All missions were completed without a single casualty. This famed bomber, named for Memphian Margaret Polk, is considered the most celebrated bomber of the war. It remains on view to the public today in Memphis.

Although World War II ended, the boom in the Memphis economy didn't. Crump continued to push for economic development and was not satisfied to wait for industry to come to the city; instead, he took a proactive approach to business recruitment. One of the last Crump initiatives was the development of Presidents Island, a peninsula of land jutting out into the Mississippi River just south of the downtown section of the city. This area remains the most industrialized corner of Memphis.

It's interesting to note that in the 1950s, Memphis had a slightly larger population than Atlanta (Memphis had 396,000 inhabitants compared with 331,314 for Atlanta, according to the 1950 census). The subsequent development of Atlanta into the Capital of the New South, with a metro population of more than 4 million people compared with little more than 1 million in the present-day Memphis metro area, has been thought-provoking for city leaders, and has led some to question whether Memphis might not have pushed harder during that time to attract more new industry.

Although the Crump political era did eventually fade, the Memphis business community has steadily moved forward at its own pace.

A Brief History of Memphis Business

As the local adage affirms, cotton was certainly king in Memphis and was instrumental in the city's development. This commodity continues to provide hundreds of jobs and millions of dollars to the community, but other products and services have played an important role in the city's economy as well.

Cotton wasn't the only crop of note in the region. After the Civil War Memphis became home to one of the nation's largest hardwood lumber industries in the nation. By the start of the 20th century, Memphis officials adopted the slogan that the city was the "First Hardwood Market" in the nation. At that time more than 500 lumber mills operated within a 100-mile radius of Memphis, producing more than

1 billion feet of lumber a year. Naturally, with all the lumber in the region, spin-off industries blossomed, including furniture manufacturers. The Mid-South continues to be a center for furniture production in the United States in the 21st century.

Manufacturing thrived in Memphis for about 100 years after the Civil War. The city became an attractive place in which to relocate a plant from the North for two reasons: a cheap labor market and a centrally located distribution network.

Because it was surrounded by hundreds of miles of rural farmlands, Memphis attracted workers, black and white, from throughout the Mid-South who were losing their jobs due to the mechanization of farming. These unskilled laborers were willing to work for wages much lower than their counterparts in many other parts of the United States. Memphis economic-development officials never hesitated to tout the cost savings a company could realize by moving their production lines to the Bluff City.

With the river at its doorstep, Memphis has always been attractive to businesses that needed to move their goods by water. From the riverboats of yesteryear to the barges of today, Memphis has consistently been one of the busiest inland ports in the nation. It has the fourth-largest inland port in the nation, and the Memphis harbor contains 44 private terminals and eight public terminals.

With the advent of the locomotive, rail lines tended to traverse Memphis, once again enhancing the city's transportation amenities. Presently, five Class 1 rail systems serve Memphis at six rail yards. The city still does a fair amount of passenger service by rail with Amtrak's *City of New Orleans* running daily between New Orleans and Chicago.

Once automobiles became the rage and a highway system was developed, Memphis found itself a key crossroads for the nation. The nation's major north/south interstate route for the central United States, Interstate 55, runs through Memphis, as does Interstate 40, the nation's major east/west route across the country. Another seven U.S. highways converge in Memphis, and one of the nation's most

Clarence Saunders, the Founder of the Modern Supermarket

Few people realize it, but Memphis is the birthplace of the modern supermarket.

In 1916 entrepreneur Clarence Saunders opened the first Piggly Wiggly grocery store on Jefferson Avenue, between Front and Main Streets, in downtown Memphis. The store contained a feature that few shoppers had ever seen before: self-service. Previously, shoppers would typically enter a store with a list, tell clerks what they wanted, and clerks would pick the merchandise for them from the store shelves and bins. At Piggly Wiggly they picked the items themselves. Saunders took his modern approach a step further. He figured out how best to accommodate shoppers and patented his own "traffic-flow pattern."

Whatever he did worked. By 1923, just seven years later, 2,600 Piggly Wiggly grocery stores dotted the nation.

Saunders became a millionaire, and in the early 1920s he started building a 22-room mansion to be constructed with pink marble. He spent about $1 million on his grand home, which would feature such lavish elements as an indoor swimming pool and a bowling alley.

Saunders's prosperity did not last. In 1923 he lost the company and found himself penniless. As a result, he also lost the mansion, dubbed the Pink Palace because of the pink-marble construction. Saunders tried other ventures over the years, notably, a grocery store with an electronic picking system called Keedoozle, but none met with the success of Piggly Wiggly.

The City of Memphis now owns his home, still known as the Pink Palace, where an IMAX theater, a planetarium, and a popular museum make their home. Appropriately, the museum contains a permanent exhibit that features a replica of Saunders's pioneering self-service Piggly Wiggly grocery store.

ambitious new road projects, Interstate 69, will pass through Memphis as it connects Toronto, Canada, with Monterrey, Mexico.

Naturally, this combination of a central location and confluence of major highways and interstates has proved to be a fertile breeding ground for truck companies. At last count more than 300 motor-freight companies are operating in Memphis.

Finally, with the dramatic growth in air transportation, especially air cargo, in the past 50 years, Memphis has found itself ideally suited to take advantage of its location in the central part of the United States. While 15 cargo airlines operate in Memphis, the internationally renowned FedEx was founded here in 1972 by Fred Smith. At present, FedEx is the city's largest employer with more than 32,000 employees.

Combining FedEx's enormous volume of packages with those of the other air cargo companies, Memphis International Airport is acknowledged as the world's busiest cargo airport.

The Civil Rights Era

The city's unique location and transportation advantages have certainly served as the backbone of the Memphis economy for decades, but these two natural elements have also served as a key backdrop to what is perhaps this area's unifying feature when it comes to its people: the struggle for racial equality and harmony.

The city's population has almost always had a large percentage of black residents, and after the Civil War, this segment of the community gradually increased. During the Jim Crow era of the 1880s to the 1950s, within the city limits of Memphis were, essentially, two cities: one for whites and one for blacks. Whites may have held all the elected positions and other leadership positions generally recognized by the white media, but within the black community, neighborhood, education, business, and religious leaders have played important roles. Yet few of these black leaders were recognized by the white establishment, and blacks were forced to remain second-class citizens, a situation that began to change after World War II.

From the pulpits of black churches, and, eventually, to the ballot boxes, community centers, and union halls, a call for equality started to be heard. While the civil rights movement was gaining momentum in other large urban centers in the South in the late 1950s and early 1960s, Memphis seemed to avoid stepping onto that emotional and all-too-often dangerous stage. By the mid-1960s black leaders in Memphis had managed to quietly and nonviolently integrate many of the city's public facilities. Then the city's sanitation workers went on strike, and Rev. Martin Luther King, Jr., came to Memphis in 1968 to support their cause. The city's black sanitation workers had walked off their jobs in protest of what they claimed were discriminatory work conditions and wages.

The assassination of King on April 4, 1968, in Memphis shocked the nation, set off riots, and shook the morale of the city, particularly in the black community. Memphis was forced to confront the complicated issues associated with racial intolerance and inequality unlike it had at any other time in its history. (See the chapter African American Heritage for more details.)

Yet, during the 1960s in Memphis, anyone who stepped outside of City Hall and simply turned on the radio would have heard less political rhetoric about integration and instead discovered the sound of integration in practice. The black and white musicians in places like Stax showed Memphis and people all around the world what a beautiful noise could be made when they worked it out together. (See the chapter Memphis Music for more information about the golden era of music making in Memphis.)

As the inspired and talented people at Stax and Hi Records were amassing an enormous music catalog during the late 1960s and early 1970s, Memphis itself was expanding its catalog of new neighborhoods. Every few years city officials were gobbling up more neighborhoods as the community grew eastward. With the river on the west and the Mississippi state line to the south, about the only direction the city could move was east. People moved farther east at a rapid pace, and as they did, the jobs followed.

As a result, the once-vibrant downtown section of Memphis, like many other urban centers around the nation, was all but abandoned.

Modern Memphis Takes Shape

During the late 1960s and early 1970s, the political landscape and the community began to change. The public schools were integrated during this time, and while there were heated arguments and hints of violence when they were forced to integrate, the so-called "busing" program was implemented with far more ease than integration efforts in many other urban cities such as Boston and Little Rock.

At the same time the city's African American political leaders began to rise to the top. Blacks started being elected, first to local political bodies such as the school board and city council, and then to national offices. Beginning in the 1970s the machine politics formerly so common in the white community became popular in the black community with the emergence of the Ford family. Harold Ford, Sr., and his brothers began getting elected to local, state, and national offices in the early 1970s. During this time a political dynasty was formed that continues to this day.

On the surface little seemed to happen in Memphis during the 1970s. Instead of progress, many of the best attributes of the city seemed to be dying. The hugely popular and influential Memphis sound grew

For more information on the history of Memphis, you may want to check out these books, which provide some of the information for this chapter:

- *Memphis during the Progressive Era 1900–1917* by William D. Miller; the Memphis State University Press, Memphis, Tennessee; the American History Research Center, 1957.
- *Metropolis of the American Nile* by John E. Harkins; the Guild Bindery Press, 1982.
- *Mr. Crump of Memphis* by William D. Miller; Louisiana State University Press, 1964.
- *Yesterday's Memphis* by Charles W. Crawford; E.A. Seeman Publishing, Inc., 1976.

Other books about Memphis history:

- *At the River I Stand: Memphis, the 1968 Strike and Dr. Martin Luther King, Jr.,* by Joan Turner Beifuss; Carlson Publishing, 1989.
- *Memphis Memoirs* by Paul R. Coppock; Memphis State University Press, 1980.
- *Race, Power, and Political Emergence in Memphis* by Sharon D. Wright; Garland Publishing, Inc., 2000.

---

faint with the closing of Stax Records. Beale Street's lascivious luster had long since faded. Downtown was on life support, and the city even lost its most famous son when Elvis Presley died in 1977 at age 42.

But just as Elvis's career was to rise after his death, Memphis was about to launch its own comeback. During the 1970s a new vision for the city came into view. Community leaders agreed on the need to revitalize downtown and bring back Beale Street. The once-glamorous Peabody hotel had been shuttered, but it was about to get new owners and a new life. And a little overnight delivery company named Federal Express was founded, which was destined to remake the city's economy and bring Memphis closer to the rest of the world.

As Memphis moved into the 1980s, city leaders began to finally realize the enormous appeal of Memphis's one-of-a-kind music history and began to build the tourism business around this unique advantage. Graceland and Sun Studio were opened to the public as tourist attractions. Money was pumped into Beale Street redevelopment. Capitalizing on its odd Egyptian namesake,

city leaders decided to fund the construction of a new pyramid-shaped arena that would rise from the banks of the river.

The city managed well during the economic recession of the late 1970s and early 1980s (and those that followed in later years), mainly because it has such a diverse base of businesses. Because Memphis has this mix of medical, government, agriculture, distribution, manufacturing, retail, and tourism industries, it never suffers too seriously during an economic downturn. On the other hand, during the periodic boom periods experienced by many other parts of the country, the Memphis economy never seems to explode either.

While the city's business economy remained relatively stable in the 1980s and 1990s, Memphis's political landscape changed drastically.

In 1992 the city's former school superintendent, Willie Herenton, surprised virtually all the local election prognosticators by unseating Dick Hackett, Memphis's popular white mayor, and becoming the first elected black mayor in the city's history. Herenton's first dramatic mayoral victory was achieved with fewer than 200 votes. In the two subsequent city elections, however, Herenton has been reelected by wide margins, proving how popular he has become with both white and black voters.

In 1996 U.S. Representative Harold Ford, Sr., retired from Congress, but his son, Harold Ford, Jr., was elected in his place. Representative Ford, Jr., now in his early 30s, is viewed as one of the most astute young political leaders in the nation today and appears poised for much success in the future.

A 21st-Century City

Memphis has momentum as it enters the 21st century. The 2000 U.S. Census reveals a city of more than 650,000 that not only has about the same percentage of white and black residents, but a population that is becoming much more culturally diverse. The city's Hispanic and Asian American residents are rapidly expanding, and business and community leaders from both these segments are emerging.

The city's efforts in reviving downtown Memphis after decades of neglect and economic stagnation is paying off. The city's downtown is now thriving. Not only are businesses returning to the oldest section of Memphis, but new residential development also is attracting hundreds of new homeowners and apartment dwellers to downtown. Redbird's stadium continues to bring families and other baseball fans downtown during the season. And, with the recent relocation of the NBA's Grizzlies from Vancouver, Canada, to Memphis, a new state-of-the-art professional basketball arena is being constructed and is expected to be complete for the 2004 season. The next downtown focal point is the riverfront. Elected officials are devoting new energy and discussing the investment of some $300 million in a revitalization of the city's historic riverfront area.

Given its diverse economic base, reenergized downtown, prospering suburban communities, and improved racial and cultural environment, Memphis appears headed toward a healthy future.

African American Heritage

No book about Memphis would be complete without a description of the city's rich African American history and culture. Many of the things Memphis prides itself on most—including the blues, rock and roll, and the Memphis sound—have their roots in the city's African American community.

Memphis has the ninth largest concentration of African Americans in the country, and has produced such luminaries as former NAACP chairman Benjamin Hooks and Congressman Harold Ford, Jr., a rising star on Capitol Hill in Washington, D.C. The city's first black mayor, Dr. W. W. Herenton, was elected in 1992. Basketball greats Penny Hardaway and Eliot Perry hail from Memphis, as do colossal music legends Isaac Hayes, Al Green, and Aretha Franklin (she was born here). More recent Memphis musical sensations include O'Landa Draper's Associates and Three-6 Mafia.

The city also boasts its share of black visual artists, including painter Brenda Joy Smith and photographer Ernest Withers. He captured some of the country's most moving images during the 1968 garbage workers strike as well as during the riots and other events that followed the assassination in Memphis of Dr. Martin Luther King, Jr. Memphis is also home to one of the South's oldest historically black colleges, LeMoyne-Owen College, which dates back to 1862. Local entrepreneurs include Fred Jones, who started the Southern Heritage Classic football event that draws many thousands to Memphis each year. In athletics, the city has produced some great talent, including basketball players Eliot Perry and Penny Hardaway, and continues to do so.

Memphis also is the seat of two large African American churches, the Church of God in Christ, and the Christian Methodist Episcopal Church. Some of America's greatest gospel music came from here, with hundreds of gospel songs flowing from the pen of the late Herbert Brewster. It's also home to the Full Gospel Tabernacle, the church headed by the Rev. Al Green, the recording-artist-turned-pastor, and Mason Temple, where Martin Luther King, Jr., made his famous "I've Been to the Mountaintop" speech.

Those interested in learning about the city's heritage can visit a number of African American attractions, including Beale Street, which was the birthplace of the blues and the center of African American culture and commerce during segregation. There's also the

This modest farmhouse, owned by Jacob Burkle, sheltered runaway slaves as a stop on the Underground Railroad, according to local legend. PHOTO: KENT PHILLIPS/MEMPHIS CONVENTION AND VISITORS BUREAU

33

National Civil Rights Museum, and Slavehaven, a house that as a reputed stop on the Underground Railroad is said to have sheltered runaway slaves on their way north. The Stax Museum of American Soul Music provides a thorough education on how musical history was made here in Soulsville USA and in other cities.

You can also tour the National Civil Rights Museum, and follow Martin Luther King's footsteps during his fateful trip to Memphis in 1968. You may want to take a self-guided civil rights walking tour, using the "I Am a Man" map published by Memphis Heritage, Inc. (See Close-up on Martin Luther King in this chapter for more information.)

History

African Americans first came to this area in the early to mid-1800s as slaves, brought by white plantation owners to work the fertile Delta land surrounding Memphis. The owners relied on slave labor to produce cotton, the "white gold" that fueled the Southern economy. Slave labor built the city's first roads and buildings.

During slavery days, one of the main escape routes for slaves fleeing the South was through Memphis, and the home of Jacob Burkle (open to the public as Slavehaven; see Attractions for more information) is believed to have been a stop on what history calls the Underground Railroad.

Slaves were freed in 1863, and many of them migrated from the plantations to Memphis and other urban areas. In 1874 blacks were admitted to the Memphis public school system for the first time.

In 1878, the final and worst of three yellow fever epidemics struck Memphis, driving half of the city's 40,000 inhabitants out of the city and killing some 5,000 people. During the epidemics, blacks took on much of the burden of nursing the sick. Their survival rates were much higher than those of the whites, because of an immunity to the disease passed down from African ancestors.

As whites fled the city, many sold their property to a young African American

This house was the home of W.C. Handy, the father of the blues, and his family when they lived in Memphis.
PHOTO: KENT PHILLIPS/MEMPHIS CONVENTION AND VISITORS BUREAU

If Beale Street Could Talk

Beale Street was the center for African American culture and commerce in Memphis from the beginning of the 20th century until the end of segregation in the 1960s. While many Southern cities had areas where African Americans gathered, conducted business and amused themselves, Beale Street was renowned for its music and even had a song, W.C. Handy's "Beale Street Blues," named after it.

Today, the street is an entertainment district and tourist attraction for all people, with music clubs that include B.B. King's Blues Club.

Beale Street was home to wealthy whites until the 1878 yellow fever epidemic, when Robert Church, Sr., bought up the land and built Church Park and Auditorium on Beale Street, exclusively for blacks. He built Beale into the city's center of African American life. It continued to be segregated for the most part, and only starting in the 1940s were whites allowed to visit the street's club during designated hours. Today, in addition to the commercial businesses, you'll find several historic buildings on Beale, including the Old Daisy Theatre at 329 Beale, a theater originally built for African Americans.

Beale Street Baptist Church at 379 Beale was the first brick-constructed, multi-story church in the U.S. built for African Americans (today it's the First Baptist Church Beale). Church Park at Beale and Fourth Street honors Robert Church, who first developed it many years ago.

On the street you'll also find historic markers describing luminaries including journalist/activist Ida B. Wells and WDIA radio announcer Nat D. Williams. Brass musical notes embedded in the sidewalks honor musicians including many R&B greats.

Today, the street is a tourist attraction by day and an entertainment district at night featuring live music. See the Memphis Music, Nightlife, and Kidstuff chapters for more information about Beale Street.

named Robert Church. Eventually, Church owned much of Beale Street, started the city's first bank for blacks, and became the South's first African American million-aire. As a result of the fever epidemic, the city defaulted on its obligations, and in 1879 the state revoked the city charter. But when it was time to get the charter restored, Church bought the first $1,000 bond issued by the city.

The city's charter was restored in 1893, and by 1900, blacks accounted for about 50,000 of Memphis's 102,000 citizens.

A prominent black Memphis citizen during the latter part of the century was Ida B. Wells, a schoolteacher who wrote editorials denouncing the practice of lynching and the condition of schools for African American children. She was forced to leave Memphis, and later moved to Chicago, where she became a founding member of the NAACP.

Beale Street and the Birth of the Blues

Around the turn of the century Robert Church was actively developing Beale Street into a haven for the city's African

Insiders' Tip

As you walk around Beale Street and nearby areas, look for historic markers that provide information about individuals, including W.C. Handy, Ida Wells, and Nat D. Williams, as well as businesses, including Universal Life Insurance, PeeWee's Saloon, and WDIA radio. On Beale Street itself, you'll also find brass musical notes in the sidewalk honoring some of Memphis's greatest musicians.

American population. He set about building a park, theater, and other amenities for blacks, who were denied these pleasures elsewhere in the city, and started The Solvent Bank in 1906, which by 1921 claimed to be the largest black-owned bank in the world. By night, though, Beale was a wild place, with rowdy saloons, gambling halls, and brothels.

W.C. Handy, an accomplished African American musician who had lived all over the country, moved to Memphis in 1909, and after publishing the blues he heard on Beale, became known as the "Father of the Blues." A few decades later, the city honored Handy with a parade in appreciation for putting Memphis on the musical map, and established Handy Square (today Handy Park).

In the 1920s many early Memphis blues musicians were active on Beale, including Furry Lewis, Sleepy John Estes, and Memphis Minnie. In fact, some of the music was recorded, until the onset of the

Depression discouraged record labels from returning to Memphis.

Since the Depression, Memphis African American blues musicians, including Robert Johnson, Howlin' Wolf, and B.B. King, have continued to make music history. See the Memphis Music chapter for more information on the city's African American musicians and the musical history they created, from the earliest blues to current hitmakers.

Also during the 1920s the Memphis Red Sox baseball team, part of the Negro Baseball League, threw out its first pitch, and Dr. J. E. Walker founded Universal Life Insurance, which became one of the largest African American–owned insurance companies in the country. In 1925 another Memphis African American emerged as a hero. In an amazing feat, Tom Lee rescued 32 people from a sinking steamship, despite the fact he couldn't swim. Today, Tom Lee Park in downtown Memphis is named in his honor.

In the 1940s WDIA became the first radio station in the U.S. to have an all-black format and black disc jockeys, including Nat D. Williams, B.B. King, and Rufus Thomas. In the 1950s, King, Thomas, and many other African American musicians began recording at Sun Records, an unassuming small recording studio just east of downtown Memphis. In 1960 Stax Records was started, launching the careers of Carla Thomas, Otis Redding, and Isaac Hayes before closing its doors in the late 1970s. The newly-built Stax Museum of American Music tells that story.

Civil Rights and Martin Luther King, Jr.

As the civil rights movement hit its stride in the 1950s and 1960s, the Memphis African American community was a leading participant. In 1968, the city's black sanitation workers went on strike, wearing signs that read, "I Am a Man." Dr. Martin Luther King, Jr., came to the city to support the strikers, and on April 3, gave his famous "I've Been to the Mountaintop" speech at Mason Temple. The next day Dr. King was killed by an assassin's bullet on the balcony

Martin Luther King, Jr., and the Memphis Black Sanitation Workers

In 1968 the city's black sanitation workers were fed up with being treated unfairly by their employer. For example, in January of that year, black sanitation workers were sent home from their jobs because of the weather, and given two hours' show-up pay, while their white counterparts remained and earned a full day's wage. In February two black workers were killed in an on-the-job accident. The black workers went on strike February 12, with immediate results: Only 34 of the city's 180 garbage trucks were able to operate the first day of the strike.

The strike also was about dignity, and to underscore that point, the strikers carried and wore placards bearing the message, "I Am a Man." The mayor refused to negotiate with the workers, saying their strike was illegal. The standoff continued, mediation was tried and failed. Marches, sit-ins, and boycotts became commonplace.

In support of the strikers, Dr. King came to Memphis on several occasions, the last of which was April 3. A few days before that, King had decided to cancel a trip to Africa in order to lead a peaceful march in Memphis.

On the evening of March 3, King addressed a crowd at Mason Temple, and in his famous final speech told listeners that he knew his people would one day reach the promised land.

The next day Southern Christian Leadership Conference lawyers were successful in getting an injunction against the planned march overturned. However, before the march could take place, King was killed by an assassin's bullet on the balcony of the Lorraine Motel. Riots ensued, in Memphis and across the country, while the FBI initiated an international manhunt for the killer. A few days later, Coretta Scott King and other civil rights figures led a peaceful memorial march through downtown Memphis in memory of King and to support the strike. On April 16 the workers voted to accept an agreement that had been worked out.

This series of events had a profound impact on Memphis, creating wounds that would take years to heal. Beale Street and other areas of the city began to deteriorate as many whites moved to the suburbs and a number of businesses followed. For black Memphians, the fact that King was murdered in their city depressed morale considerably despite the positive outcome of the strike.

Today, using "I Am a Man: A Civil Rights Walking Tour," a brochure published by Memphis Heritage Inc., you can retrace the steps of the 1968 striking black sanitation workers as they attempted to march from Clayborn Temple AME Church to city hall, and see other places of importance to the civil rights movement. Look for the "I Am a Man" map on the visitors information racks found in hotel lobbies and attractions, or call Memphis Heritage (901–529–9828).

Also, visit the National Civil Rights Museum for more information about King's legacy as well as the controversy over who actually killed the civil right leader.

—Much of this information is excerpted from "I Am a Man: A Civil Rights Walking Tour," with permission from Memphis Heritage Inc.

Historic Sites

If you're interested in Memphis's African American heritage, you won't want to miss these attractions. See the Attractions chapter for more details.

Beale Street
Downtown Memphis
www.bealestreet.com
The center of African American cultural and commercial life for many years, and today home to thriving clubs, bars, and shops. See Close-up, If Beale Street Could Talk, for details.

Burkle House/Slavehaven
826 N. Second St.
(901) 527-3427
This home is thought to be a stop on the Underground Railroad, where runaway slaves could find refuge.

Center for Southern Folklore & Cafe
119 S. Main St.
(901) 525-3655
www.southernfolklore.com
Music, art, and performances here demonstrate the African American roots of much of the South's folklore and culture.

W. C. Handy House
352 Beale St.
(901) 522-1556
Bandleader W.C. Handy lived in this Memphis house at the time he "discovered" the blues.

Historic Elmwood Cemetery
824 S. Dudley St.
(901) 774-3212
www.elmwoodcemetery.org
This cemetery tells the story of African American Memphians ranging from slaves in unmarked graves to millionaire and political leader Robert Church, Sr.

Mason Temple
930 Mason St.
(901) 578-3800
This is where Martin Luther King, Jr., gave his famous "I've Been to the Mountaintop" speech the eve of his assassination.

National Civil Rights Museum
450 Mulberry
(901) 521-9699
www.civilrightsmuseum.org
Housed in the Lorraine Motel, where Martin Luther King, Jr., was assassinated, this museum tells the story of the civil rights movement.

Stax Museum of American Soul Music
926 E. McLemore St.
(901) 946-253
www.soulsvilleusa.com
This museum, built on the site of the former Stax Records studio, tells the story of Otis Redding, Isaac Hayes, and other Southern soul stars and their contributions to American music.

of the Lorraine Motel. Riots ensued, and by the end of the month the workers had succeeded in having their demands met.

The assassination and subsequent riots had a profound impact on Memphis, creating wounds that would take years to heal. Beale Street and other areas of the city began to deteriorate as many whites moved to the suburbs and a number of businesses followed.

But by the 1970s things were picking up on another front, as the city's black politicians began to make some inroads. Lois DeBerry was elected as the first female

African American state representative from Memphis, and Harold Ford became the first black elected as the U.S. congressman from the ninth district, which includes Memphis. He served for 26 years, helping to pave the way for his son's success. Today, the city has an African American mayor (W. W. Herenton) and Congressional representative (Harold Ford, Jr.), as well as numerous other black officeholders and leaders.

Memphis Today

Visitors to Memphis these days will find that the city's rich African American heritage is being preserved and celebrated. Beale Street—once deserted—has been converted into a thriving entertainment district, and the Stax museum is not only educating people about Memphis music, but is also helping to revive the Soulsville USA neighborhood that surrounds the spot where the legendary recording studio once operated.

What's more, Memphis is being talked about as a great place for African Ameri-

> ## Insiders' Tip
> You can book a guided tour of the sights of importance to the city's African American heritage. One of the best ones is operated by Heritage Tours at (901) 527-3427. It's best to call ahead for reservations.

cans to make their homes. *Black Enterprise* magazine in 2001 named Memphis as one of the top 10 places for African Americans to live, work, and play. The magazine cited the city's affordable new home prices and low cost of living, and gave Memphis high marks in the categories of satisfaction with African American power and influence, and church outreach.

Accommodations

Hotels and Motels

Bed-and-Breakfasts
and Country Inns

RV Parks

Youth Hostel

Memphis has some 20,000 hotel rooms at all price levels. At the top is The Peabody, one of the South's premier grand hotels. You'll find plenty of comfortable accommodations here, including a handful of bed-and-breakfast inns, but for the most part, it isn't a travel destination you would choose for its quaint inns (like St. Augustine, Florida) or fabulous hotels (like San Francisco).

Memphis is the birthplace of the modern hotel. The whole concept of standardized lodging originated here in 1952, when local entrepreneur Kemmons Wilson opened the first Holiday Inn. Even though the idea of a brand-name hotel chain, with hotels that are the same from city to city, is commonplace today, at that time it was radical. As befits the birthplace of the chain hotel, the city has many familiar lodging names representing every major hotel company. You'll notice more Hampton Inn properties here than in most cities this size, because its parent company, Promus Cos., was headquartered here until it merged with Hilton Hotels Corp. in 2000 and moved away.

In this chapter we list hotels in five areas of the city: downtown, medical center/midtown, east Memphis, southeast Memphis, and the Graceland/airport area (south Memphis). Downtown is home to most tourist attractions including Beale Street, but if you choose to stay outside this area, you still won't be too far away. By taking the I-240 loop around the city, no destination is more than 20 or 25 minutes away, as long as you're not going to or from the far suburbs such as Collierville or Southaven, Mississippi. A car trip can sometimes take longer, as Memphis has its share of rush-hour snarls and other traffic problems, which invariably seem to happen when you're in a hurry.

We don't list hotels in the far suburbs, although you'll find many chains represented at the exits along I-40 and I-55 as you come into town. If you come in from Arkansas via I-40 West and I-55 North, most of the hotels you'll see cater to truckers rather than leisure travelers. Along I-40 East familiar chain hotels are clustered around the exits, particularly Sycamore View (exit 12), Germantown Parkway (exit 16), and Highway 64/Bartlett (exit 18). Exits 16 and 18 are convenient to Wolfchase Galleria, the city's best regional shopping mall, and other shopping, as well as the Agricenter International, where events such as the Ducks Unlimited Outdoor Festival take place. You'll find Wingate Inn (800–228–1000), Comfort Inn (800–228–5150), and LaQuinta Inn (800–531–5900), among others, at Germantown Parkway and at Highway 64, Holiday Inn Express (800–HOLIDAY), Country Inn & Suites by Carlson (800–456–4000), and others. The Sycamore View exit has Baymont Inn and Suites (877–229–6668), Holiday Inn (800–HOLIDAY), and other options. If you don't see your favorite hotel chain listed, check out its Web site or call its reservations number.

Near the airport the Millbranch Road exit of I-240 has a number of hotels. Baymont (877–BAYMONT), Best Western (800–WESTERN), and Hampton Inn (800–HAMPTON) are along Millbranch proper but in a gritty industrial area. In the neighboring office-park area of Nonconnah Boulevard, you'll find Courtyard by Marriott (800–321–2211) and Homestead Studio Suites (800–STAYHSD), both well-maintained hotels that offer good values on weekends if you don't mind an office-park setting.

Although bed-and-breakfast inns are rare within the city limits, they can be found, along with at least one country inn, farther out. We list a few, but you can also check our Day Trips chapter or your favorite B&B Web site or directory for other options close to Memphis.

Downtown Memphis is the most convenient place to stay if you're taking in the sights, partying on Beale Street, or attending an event on the riverfront or at the Memphis Cook Convention Center. You can walk or take the Main Street trolley to Beale Street, the convention center, and top attractions including the Rock 'n' Soul Museum,

National Civil Rights Museum, and The Peabody with its famous ducks—a plus that easily outweighs the fact that some downtown guest rooms are a bit smaller and more expensive than their suburban counterparts. More than 3,000 of the city's hotel rooms are downtown, mostly clustered between Beale Street and Madison or a few blocks to the north around the convention center. It's by far the most pedestrian-friendly place to stay, and probably the only area where you won't miss having a car. It's also the most popular.

The next neighborhood to the east as you leave downtown is the medical-center area, which has a handful of hotels catering mainly to families of hospital patients and medical personnel, then midtown. The Hampton Inn is the best of the bunch at the medical center, but if you need that location, Red Roof Inn (800–RED ROOF) and LaQuinta Inn (800–687–667) are cheap alternatives.

Midtown is home to just a few accommodations, so basically, except for those few choices, there's a gap of about 10 miles as you go east on Poplar between the downtown cluster of hotels and the next concentration of rooms.

East Memphis has many lodging choices, including modern suites in hotels with a kitchen, separate living area, and other at-home amenities. This area is probably the best alternative to downtown. Many of these hotels are clustered around the intersection of Poplar Avenue and I-240, accessible by car, taxi, or the free airport shuttles operated by many of the hotels. They're convenient to events such as the FedEx St. Jude Golf Classic and the Germantown Charity Horse Show.

The area also has many of the best restaurants and shopping centers in town, including locally owned and chain eateries and Oak Court Mall, a regional shopping mall. It's family-oriented and home to many schools, so on the weekends the hotels draw a number of student sports teams and their families in town for games and tournaments.

Southeast Memphis is home to shopping centers and several regional shopping malls, including Mall of Memphis, and puts you within a few miles of the airport and Graceland. You'll find lodging options clustered on either side of Mall of Memphis, including a spiffy full-service Marriott and some family-oriented hotels.

Although the Marriott and hotels next to it are well-patrolled, you should still exercise caution in this neighborhood once you leave the hotel properties, especially at night and on weekends. The area around the mall has had problems with crime in recent years.

The Graceland/Memphis International Airport area is a good bet for visitors with limited time in Memphis who mainly want to see Graceland. A number of South Memphis hotels operate within a few blocks or a few miles of both the popular tourist attraction and the airport, including a handsomely renovated Holiday Inn Select. Sadly, the neighborhood of Whitehaven, which was one of the best areas of town when Elvis bought Graceland, has become extremely run-down. We recommend two hotels and an RV park there but have chosen to skip the other properties in the area. We would caution you that if you see hotel deals in this area that sound too good to be true, pay attention, as they may put you too close for comfort to the seedy side of the city. That's equally true of Brooks Road and the rest of the area near the airport, an industrial part of town with a scattering of strip joints.

The prices we quote are the basic off-the-street rates known in the industry as rack rates; they do not include a 14.95 percent tax (8.25 percent state sales tax plus 6.7 percent local room tax), tips, and extra charges. It's always worth asking if you qualify for a better rate, and sometimes just the fact you're staying on the weekend will lower the price. Don't forget to inquire about weekend packages that sometimes include extras such as a bottle of champagne or passes to local attractions. Unless we note otherwise, all the listed hotels accept major credit cards. Bear in mind that some hotels will up their rates for the busiest weekends.

In general Memphis hotels all have nonsmoking rooms and wheelchair-accessible rooms. Most do not accept pets, and the ones that do often require a nonrefundable deposit. Hotels usually allow children under 18 to stay free with their parent or parents but charge an additional $5 to $10 for an extra adult in the room. Virtually all properties have coffeemakers, hair dryers, ironing boards and irons, dataports, air-conditioning, cable television with a free movie channel in the guest rooms, and at least one free newspaper. We note the exceptions in the individual hotel write-ups. These amenities are not ubiquitous among country inns and bed-and-breakfast inns, however.

Free parking is a standard hotel amenity in all parts of the city except downtown. We'll note which hotels charge extra for parking. DASH, an airport shuttle service operated by Memphis Area Transit Authority, serves the downtown hotels (see Getting Here, Getting Around for details), and many hotels in other parts of the city operate free airport shuttles for their guests.

Remember that hotels, especially those downtown, fill up fast during the May weekends when annual Memphis in May events such as the Beale Street Music Festival take place, the busy summer tourist season, Elvis commemorations, popular sporting events, and large conventions. (See the Annual Events chapter.) Rooms are particularly hard to find during the huge Church of God in Christ convention that takes place the second week of November. If you have to be in Memphis during one of these times and you have trouble finding a room, try the far suburbs.

Price Code

The following price code is the average cost of a double-occupancy room (two adults) during peak season. For hotels with a substantial number of suites, the price is a range that includes the cost for a room and for a suite. Prices do not include a 14.95 percent tax (8.25 percent for sales tax, 6.7 percent for room tax) charged for hotel rooms in Memphis. The tax varies slightly in areas outside the city limits.

$	Less than $90
$$	$90 to $119
$$$	$120 to $149
$$$$	$150 and more

Hotels and Motels

Downtown

Hampton Inn & Suites at Peabody Place
$$$
175 Peabody Place
(901) 260–4000, (800) HAMPTON
www.hampton-inn.com

This 144-unit accommodation is as close as you can stay to Beale Street unless you decide to sleep in W.C. Handy Park. It is one of the most luxurious Hampton Inns in that chain, opened by the owners of The Peabody in 2000 as an alternative for visitors when the grand hotel is full. The Hampton lobby may not have ducks, but it does have bronze-toned stone floors, several conversation areas with plush sofas and chairs, a big TV, a working fireplace, and a small business center. Its large, cheerful breakfast bar is appointed with brick-red tile, kitchen-style cabinets, and tables and chairs for serving its free continental breakfast for guests. A small indoor swimming pool and modern fitness center are around the corner. The Hampton has 108 modest-sized guest rooms and 36 suites. The king suite features a kitchen outfitted with basic cooking and serving items, microwave, full-size refrigerator, dishwasher, and breakfast bar. It also has four phones, a large work area and three recliners, and plenty of room. All rooms include the usual amenities, plus pay-per-view movies and Nintendo. The property has its own parking garage, available for $8.00 a day. Some of the biggest amenities are just outside the hotel: Beale Street a block to the south, Peabody Place Entertainment Center across the street to the north. Most guests like being close to the action, but as the street often goes all night on the weekends, it can be a bit noisy. If you're susceptible, ask for a room facing the courtyard, and remember that earplugs are available at the front desk.

Holiday Inn Select Downtown $$$
160 Union Avenue
(901) 525–5491, (888) 300–5491

Its central location across the street from the Peabody is a good reason to select this full-service hotel, which was converted into a Holiday Inn and completely renovated in 1996. The spacious, carpeted lobby features a marble fireplace and marble cornices around the elevators plus a tiny business center with fax machine and computer. The 15-story hotel has 192 rooms, each with big windows and mahogany-finish furniture. Each room includes the usual amenities, and for an extra charge there are in-room Nintendo and movies available. The hotel also has what it calls Executive Edition rooms, which cost $30 extra per night. These slightly larger corner rooms come with a sleeper sofa (in addition to the bed) as well as such extras as a minirefrigerator, a microwave, and terry bathrobes. The hotel's fourth-floor outdoor pool feels private and relaxed. (*Hint* for swimmers: Ask for a fourth-floor room with direct access to the pool.) Holiday Inn Select Downtown has two restaurants. The Union Café serves a buffet breakfast (not included in room rates) every morning and offers basic American fare for other meals plus a full bar. There's also Sekisui, a popular Japanese eatery featuring a sushi bar. Food from both restaurants is available for room service. The Union Café bar and Sekisui both have big windows at street level, allowing for good people-watching. Meeting rooms are available on the top floor.

Madison Hotel $$$$
79 Madison Avenue
(901) 333–1200, (866) 44–MEMPHIS
www.madisonhotelmemphis.com

The Madison Hotel has just one goal: to be the finest hotel in Memphis. Opened in 2002 and operated by a former Peabody general manager, this luxury boutique hotel has spared no expense in furnishing the rooms with silks and unique artwork. The 16-story former bank building, built in 1905, was gutted in 2001, then renovated into a European style, small luxury hotel (affiliated with the Small Luxury Hotels of the World group). The elegant lobby features plush sofas and chairs, a musical motif, and cocktail service. There's also a 65-seat restaurant featuring Mediterranean cuisine. A free continental breakfast and afternoon happy hour take place on the mezzanine, with heartier fare available in the restaurant/bar. The 110 rooms and suites feature granite-topped wet bars with refrigerators, microwaves, coffeemakers, and an honor bar. All feature high-speed Internet. The top rooms have great views of the river, and 28 rooms have Jacuzzis. The hotel also has two presidential suites available for $900 a night. Valet parking is available for an extra charge.

Memphis Marriott Downtown $$$$
250 North Main Street
(901) 527–7300, (800) 557–8740
www.marriott.com/memdt

The Memphis Marriott Downtown becomes the city's largest hotel, with 600 rooms and suites, as it completes work on an addition consisting of a 13-story tower in 2002. Across Main Street from Memphis Cook Convention Center, this hotel is very popular with visitors attending events and conventions at the center as well as other business travelers. Marriott has spent some $50 million on the property, buying the former Crowne Plaza in 1995, renovating guest rooms, meeting facilities, and common areas plus adding the new tower. The investment is being driven by a $100-million expansion of the convention center, which should be wrapping up in late 2002. The hotel has all the amenities you would expect from a full-service Marriott hotel, including room service, a spacious, well-equipped fitness center, an indoor pool, a whirlpool, and a sauna. The lobby is a lofty atrium with white marble floors, tall large windows looking out onto Main Street, and a number of sitting areas. An escalator goes up to the meeting rooms as well as the covered crosswalk over to the convention center. The rooms, which seem bigger and fresher than most downtown rooms, are outfitted in cheerful furnishings. Three concierge floors feature slightly more expensive rooms with added amenities such as terry robes and bottled water as well as access to a lounge that serves a free continental breakfast in the mornings and honor bar and hors d'oeuvres in the early evenings. The hotel lobby restaurant, Magnolia Grille, serves a Southern menu and daily breakfast buffet, whereas Trolley Stop Bar features appetizers and snacks plus a full bar. Valet parking is available for $10.00 (unlimited in and out); self-parking is $5.00 for each entry.

The Peabody $$$$
149 Union Avenue
(901) 529–4000, (800) 732–2639
www.peabodymemphis.com

This gracefully restored historic downtown hotel promotes itself as the South's Grand New Hotel, and with good reason. It preserves traditional charms such as the Italianate fountain with its famous ducks while offering attentive service and modern amenities such as award-winning meeting and convention facilities, a fitness center, and all the conveniences today's executive travelers expect. The Peabody, first established in 1869, was closed in the 1970s amid the urban decline of the downtown area. Its restoration—to the tune of $25 million—and reopening in 1981 were the opening salvo of the battle to return downtown Memphis to prominence. Over the years writer William Faulkner, U. S. presidents from Andrew Jackson to Bill Clinton, the Rolling Stones, Barbara Streisand, and Cary Grant have all stayed here. The Peabody has always been the social and commercial hub of the city and the surrounding Delta region. Mississippi writer David Cohn in 1935 wrote that "the Delta begins in the lobby of The Peabody Hotel and ends on Catfish Row in Vicksburg. The Peabody is the Paris Ritz, the Cairo Shepheard's, the London Savoy of this section." Other hotels offer luxurious accommodations and nice lobby areas, but The Peabody Lobby, where visitors and locals alike meet for drinks or afternoon tea, is peerless. People also gather here for elegant weddings and other festive occasions and to enjoy the haute cuisine and dazzling elegance of Chez Philippe.

Railroad builder Col. Robert C. Brinkley opened The Peabody shortly after the Civil War, naming it after philanthropist George Peabody. At that time the hotel charged $3.00–$4.00 a night (including meals but charging extra for fire and gaslight) for the 75 rooms, each with a private bath. Its saloon was the site of high-stakes poker games, at which plantations were won and lost, according to local lore. In 1925 The Peabody moved to its present location. Built in the colonnaded Italian Renaissance style, it features a two-story lobby with a fountain carved from a single piece of marble. Subsequent renovations have carefully preserved this design.

The Peabody's restaurants have recently been revamped. Capriccio features northern Italian cuisine, whereas Café Expresso sells coffee and luscious homemade pastries to go. The Peabody's culinary jewel is Chez Philippe, one of the city's finest haute-cuisine restaurants. (For more information see Restaurants chapter.) Room service is available around the clock. The hotel has a day spa (services range from haircuts and facials to massages) and a decent-sized fitness center on the lower level as well as a small but elegant indoor swimming pool, sauna, and whirlpool spa. Shops line the Union Avenue side of the ground floor, selling souvenirs, T-shirts and finer apparel, jewelry, and artwork. Next door is Peabody Place Entertainment Center, which includes Jillian's, a multi-screen movie theater, and other shops and hangouts. The roof of The Peabody features an Art Deco style Skyway and a well-groomed terrace where "Sunset Serenade" parties offer live music on Thursday evenings during summer. Sometimes the roof is closed or in use for a private party, but it's always worth asking if you can go up there to enjoy the great views of the Mississippi and surrounding city and perhaps visit the famous Peabody Ducks in their off-hours digs, the Duck Palace.

The Peabody's 468 guest rooms range from lavish $1,000-plus-a-night luxury suites to modest-sized standard rooms around $200. Because of the building's quirks, no two rooms are alike. They're decorated in muted pastel tones, with floral patterns on bedspreads and curtains, cherry furniture, and moss-green carpeting. The bathrooms are standard-sized (larger with whirlpool baths for the more luxurious units). All rooms have pay-per-view movies and toiletries that include duck-shaped

Suites at The Peabody Memphis's historic grand hotel are much in demand by discriminating visitors.
PHOTO: THE PEABODY MEMPHIS

soaps. Parking and breakfast are extra, and it's $30–35 for an extra adult staying in the room. The concierge floor, which requires a special key for entry, has its own concierge desk, a comfortable lounge, and a separate room for smokers. Guests on this floor get free continental breakfast, happy-hour hors d'oeuvres, and sweets in the evenings as well as such extras as terry-cloth robes.

With its 80,000 square feet of meeting and function space, the hotel is a popular site for conferences and social functions. Its largest ballroom can seat as many as 1,200 for dinner and up to 1,600 for a reception or other function.

One practical note: Though its main pedestrian entrance still faces Union Avenue, The Peabody has moved its motor entrance and parking facilities farther down Second Street. To check in or park your car, go south on Second past the hotel and look for the entrance to the left. Valet parking is $13.00 per day, and self-parking is $8.00 per day. Ask about special weekend packages that may include such extras as a limousine ride to and from the airport, dinner at Chez Philippe, and a bottle of champagne.

Radisson Hotel Memphis $$$$
185 Union Avenue
(901) 528–1800, (800) 333–3333
www.radisson.com

Located just across Union Avenue from AutoZone Park and close to Beale Street and Peabody Place Entertainment Center, the Radisson Hotel Memphis has TGI Fridays restaurant downstairs and 272 rooms upstairs. It opened in 1996, after its owners invested $24 million to convert the old Tennessee Hotel (built in 1929) and other buildings into a modern hotel. The brick arched wall that separates Fridays from the main lobby is the facade from one of those buildings. The dimly lit lobby, a six-story atrium, has dark-green granite floors and a large central structure made of dark wood—a bookshelf facing the entrance with a bar (open 4:00 P.M. to midnight)—on the other side. The lobby is outfitted with comfortable chairs and sofas as well as tables and a fountain. All three meals, including breakfast, are available at Fridays, part of the chain famous for its festive atmosphere and frozen drinks.

The Peabody Ducks

Celebrities may stay there from time to time, but the most famous inhabitants of The Peabody hotel aren't people at all. They're the mallard ducks you see swimming in the elegant fountain in the hotel's grand lobby.

Every day at 11:00 A.M., a red carpet is unrolled in the lobby, and the ducks, after taking the elevator down from their penthouse suite, march down the red carpet to John Philip Sousa music. They go up a small ramp and plop into the fountain for the day. At 5:00 P.M. they leave the fountain for their rooftop home, with similar pomp and circumstance.

The tradition began in the 1930s, when it was legal for duck hunters to use live ducks as decoys instead of the plastic ones now used. Hotel general manager Frank Schutt and a friend returned to the hotel after a weekend hunting trip, and, as a joke, they put some of their decoys in the elegant fountain to swim around. The guests loved it, so the practice continued. Edward Pembroke, a bellman who had worked as a circus animal trainer, took charge, and created the ritual of the daily musical march to and from the fountain. (He was Duckmaster until 1991.)

At present the five ducks that grace the fountain are raised by a local farmer. They live at The Peabody until fully grown; then they are returned to the wild upon their retirement.

It seems, though, that the spectators are a very important part of the march. When the Peabody ducks first went on tour to other cities, their march down the red carpet was a disaster— the spectators kept at a distance, and the birds scattered. It was found that they rely on the rows of toes on either side of the carpet created as everyone crowds in for a closer look.

The famous ducks in The Peabody hotel lobby make their way home after a day's swim in the lobby fountain. PHOTO: THE PEABODY MEMPHIS

Hotel rooms are larger than in most downtown hotels, and many include good-sized bathrooms, which often have a separate shower stall and tub, as well as the usual amenities. An outdoor swimming pool and a small fitness center are on the third floor. Capitalizing on its proximity to the baseball park, the Radisson offers special Redbirds package and other deals. Because parking is so tight in the area, valet parking is advisable ($5.00 a day). You'll probably want to steer clear of the Greyhound Bus station next to the Radisson. There are discussions, however, about moving it to south Memphis, so that may be a moot point when you visit the city.

Sleep Inn at Court Square $$$
40 North Front Street
(901) 522–9700, (800) SLEEPINN

A central downtown location and simple, well-maintained rooms have made this 124-room hotel a popular option for leisure and business travelers since it first opened in 1996. The hotel's motor entrance is on Front Street, with its other side facing the pedestrian Main Street, allowing guests to walk right out the door and a few blocks to restaurants, bars, and attractions. A trolley stop is just in front as well. Although this moderately priced, limited-service hotel faced opposition when first proposed, the hotel blends nicely with the old and the new, and its developers had little trouble getting permission to build a second hotel just south of Sleep Inn (SpringHill Suites by Marriott; see below). The small but cheerful lobby of teal and burgundy offers a dining room where guests enjoy a complimentary continental breakfast, as well as a modest fitness center. Parking is free for guests. Each room has pay-per-view movies.

SpringHill Suites by Marriott $$
21 North Main Street
(901) 522–2100, (888) 287–9400
www.springhillsuites.com

This newly built suites hotel has the best of both worlds: a convenient downtown location right on the trolley line and bigger rooms more in keeping with what you find in the suburbs. The seven-story hotel has 102 suites, each with separate areas for work, relaxing, sleeping, and eating as well as a pull-out sofa, a small refrigerator, a microwave, and the usual line-up of amenities. You'll find an outdoor swimming pool and spa, as well as an exercise room, a business center, and guest laundry facilities. The room rates include a free continental breakfast, and although there's no restaurant, many dining options are available within walking distance of the hotel. SpringHill Suites, which operates next to the Sleep Inn at Court Square, is owned and managed by the same group. Parking is available for a nominal charge.

Talbot Heirs Guesthouse $$$$
99 South Second Street
(901) 527–9772, (800) 955–3956
www.talbothouse.com

Just across Second Street from The Peabody stands Talbot Heirs, a discreet, quiet, homey hotel that feels miles away from the social hubbub of The Peabody's grand lobby. That's by design: Owners Jamie and Phil Baker, former road warriors who grew weary of hotels, converted this Gayoso Historic District apartment building into a guest house in 1995 specifically for people who hate hotels. It has attracted such luminaries as filmmaker Francis Ford Coppola and model Claudia Schiffer. Jamie decorated the nine units herself with an eye to making it feel as though you're staying in a friend's apartment, including original artwork in many rooms. Each has an apartment-sized kitchen equipped with basic cooking and eating utensils, and the full-sized refrigerator is stocked with milk, yogurt, cereal, juice, soft drinks, and snacks. Each unit is different, ranging from a funky yellow studio with black-and-white linoleum floors to a spacious apartment with deep-peach walls, a four-poster bed, and a private deck. The staff prides itself on taking care of its guests, whether it's recommending restaurants, engaging a personal chef to cook a meal, or arranging transportation. Some guests fax a grocery list ahead of their arrival so that their cupboard is prestocked to their liking. Other amenities include free high-speed Internet access and, upon request, a VCR, a treadmill, or a fax machine at no extra charge.

Wyndham Garden Hotel   **$$$**
300 North Second Street
(901) 525–1800, (800) WYNDHAM
www.wyndham.com

This 230-room hotel, 9 blocks from The Peabody, is a bit off the beaten path for tourists but convenient to the Memphis Cook Convention Center and the Pyramid Arena. (If you cross Second and go through the Memphis Marriott Downtown, you'll find the convention center and a trolley stop.) This hotel was gutted and renovated in 1999, when Wyndham purchased the property. The airy lobby features marble floors and a round table at the center, where you'll find complimentary newspapers. Relax in the small library just off the lobby, where you can order drinks from the adjacent restaurant/bar. The restaurant features basic American fare including sandwiches, salads, and pastas and is available for room service at dinner only. A breakfast buffet is served in the restaurant. There's also a small fitness center, and there's a pool across the driveway from the entrance. The rooms feature handsome striped curtains, cocoa carpeting, furniture with a walnut finish, and a standard-sized bathroom. In-room video games and movies are available for an extra charge.

Medical Center/Midtown

French Quarter Suites Hotel   **$$**
2144 Madison Avenue
(901) 728–4000, (800) 843–0353
www.memphisfrenchquarter.com

Spacious rooms and suites with large whirlpool bathtubs make this midtown hotel a favorite for romantic weekends, and it's just down the street from the restaurants, shops, and bars of Overton Square. Both the exterior and the atrium interior are decorated with New Orleans–style wrought iron, and some of the rooms have large (although shared) balconies. Its location, about 4 miles from downtown, and room size are reason enough to stay here, even if the hotel and its lobby are not as happening as in the late 1970s and early 1980s, when the surrounding Overton Square entertainment district was the place to party in Memphis. The large, somewhat scruffy atrium

lobby has a restaurant, which serves Southern specialties and Sunday brunch, as well as a gazebo bar and live music, but you'll do better walking a few blocks to the Square, where options include a wine bar (Le Chardonnay), a brewpub (Bosco's) and the romantic French favorite Paulette's. The 105 suites and rooms, with either a king bed or two queen beds and a living-room area, are traditionally decorated and include wet bars with minifridges. The suites have a separate bedroom. Other amenities include free shuttle to and from the airport and destinations within 5 miles, free parking, and an outdoor swimming pool. When making reservations, make sure to ask about romantic weekend-getaway packages, a French Quarter specialty.

Hampton Inn — Medical Center Midtown   **$**
1180 Union Avenue
(901) 276–1175, (800) HAMPTON
www.hampton-inn.com

This modest hotel, just a mile from downtown next to the I-240 exit, is favored by families of patients being treated at nearby hospitals and clinics. It has a swimming pool and offers free continental breakfast. The small lobby has a sunken sitting area with a TV and breakfast tables. The rooms, decorated in dark colors with oak furniture and chintz bedspreads, have either a king or two double beds. The hotel offers special rates if you or a relative are being treated at an area hospital.

East Memphis

Adam's Mark Hotel   **$$$$**
939 Ridge Lake Boulevard
(901) 684–6664, (800) 444–2326
www.adamsmark.com

This splendid, 27-story, cylindrical glass hotel, an East Memphis landmark, offers upscale accommodations with wonderful views in all directions from its location off Poplar near I-240. Built in what its executives call a SlickTech/HighTech, or late modernist, style, it opened in 1975 and became the Adam's Mark in 1992. The urbane, two-story lobby has floor-to-ceiling windows, soothing green carpeting, and plenty of plants. In the center you'll find Satchmo's, a popular cocktail lounge and casual restaurant that features live music on weekends and a statue of Satchmo himself. An escalator leads to another dining option, the lively Bravo! Ristorante that overlooks the lake. Musicians perform opera and Broadway tunes at dinner. The well-stocked gift shop and plentiful meeting rooms betray the Adam's Mark's status as one of the area's most popular sites for conferences and special events. Here local politicians gather on Election Night with their supporters. Amenities include room service, a business center with Internet access, free transportation to and from the airport, a large outdoor swimming pool and nearby whirlpool (open year-round), and a spacious, modern fitness center. The hotel often has special rates and weekend packages including romantic getaways, so ask when you call for reservations. Adam's Mark has 408 rooms as well as a few suites (where Lisa Marie Presley stays when she's in town.) The rooms are plushly furnished with colorful geometric-patterned bedspreads and curtains and oversized sofa and chairs. In addition, each room has Internet, Play Station video games, and movies available on TV for a fee, a standard bathroom with dressing area, and, of course, a fabulous view.

The 27-story Adam's Mark Hotel is an East Memphis landmark. PHOTO: ADAM'S MARK HOTEL

AmeriSuites $$
1220 Primacy Parkway
(901) 680–9700, (800) 833–1515
www.amerisuites.com

One of a trio of hotels across the street from St. Francis Hospital, this all-suites property is a good value, especially on weekends, when the rates drop down. The 128-unit hotel, built in 1997, has a small tiled lobby that opens onto a breakfast room, with plenty of tables and chairs, where guests get a free deluxe continental breakfast. Nestled in next to the front desk is a small, modern business center. Other amenities include a small but cheerful fitness center, a good-sized outdoor pool, and guest laundry facilities. All rooms have tiny kitchens, complete with minifridge stocked with snacks, microwave, and dishes; a 25-inch TV with VCR; sleeper sofa; and the usual amenities. The hotel allows pets weighing under 10

pounds. Park Place Centre shopping center is just to the east, and Poplar is just a block or so north.

Comfort Inn East $
5877 Poplar Avenue
(901) 767–4300, (800) 228–5150

Sandwiched between The Ridgeway Inn and Holiday Inn Select East Memphis, this modest hotel offers rates that are well below those of its more upscale neighbors. With a cozy lobby, a small fitness center, and a small swimming pool (which unfortunately looks out onto the parking lot), this 126-room hotel also offers free continental breakfast and a free shuttle to the airport or (depending on availability) to destinations within 5 miles. Pets are allowed for a $15 fee. There's a Chinese buffet restaurant downstairs, with a separate area for the continental-breakfast buffet.

Courtyard by Marriott $$–$$$
6015 Park Avenue
(901) 761–0330, (800) 321–2211
www.courtyard.com

This 146-room hotel caters to a corporate clientele during the week and to soccer teams, groups, and families on the weekends, when rates drop by as much as $30. Attractive even before being redone in 2002, the lobby has plenty of private sitting areas, a small bar, and the Courtyard Café, where a breakfast buffet is served. Just beyond and accessible from the lobby is the chain's signature courtyard, with a small swimming pool and a gazebo. There's also a whirlpool spa, guest laundry facilities, and a small fitness center. The spacious guest rooms face either the courtyard or outside. You'll find the hotel on the corner of Park, just across Primacy from St. Francis Hospital, and just a block from Park Place Centre shopping center and its restaurants and shops.

Embassy Suites $$$
1022 South Shady Grove Road
(901) 684–8185, (800) EMBASSY
www.embassy-suites.com

This exceptional all-suites hotel has a beautiful atrium with hundreds of plants and one of the city's best Italian restaurants. They do not scrimp on the amenities for families and business travelers alike. All 220 suites open onto the five-story, skylighted lobby. You'll find plenty of comfortable sitting areas, among a series of ponds and waterfalls that run through the middle of the lobby, complete with fish and even some small ducks. In the back of the lobby is an enormous dining room and two buffets, where cooked-to-order breakfast is served every morning and a social hour with drinks and hors d'oeuvres every evening. Both are included in the cost of your room. In addition, Frank Grisanti's restaurant, a popular East Memphis Italian restaurant near the front of the lobby, serves lunch and dinner and provides room service. There's also a business center, a gift shop, a well-furnished fitness center, an indoor pool, a whirlpool bath, and a sauna—all grouped together just off the lobby. Families will appreciate the

video arcade, with all kinds of games, and guest laundry facilities.

The suites are spacious and plush, with a sleeper sofa and a granite-topped wet bar with minifridge and microwave in the living room. The bathrooms have standard tubs and good counter space, and with an extra sink and vanity in the bedroom, two people can get ready at the same time. Other amenities include video games, movies, and Internet access, all available on the room TV for an extra charge. Be sure to ask about family weekend packages, a hotel specialty. Meeting rooms are available, too, with full catering. This hotel is right next to Regalia, an upscale shopping center with several restaurants including Owen Brennan's.

Hampton Inn—Poplar $
5320 Poplar Avenue
(901) 683–8500, (800) HAMPTON
www.hampton-inn.com

Located in East Memphis across the street from Corky's, one of the city's most famous barbecue restaurants, and 1.5 miles from Oak Court Mall and other shopping, this 125-room hotel offers free continental breakfast and an outdoor swimming pool. The small lobby opens onto a sitting area/dining room with upholstered furniture, TV, and tables for breakfast. Much of the clientele is short-term—families in town for a soccer game or event or business travelers in town for just a night or two. The hotel doesn't have a fitness center, but it provides guests with free passes to a health club. The entrance is just east of the hotel on Estate Place.

Hampton Inn & Suites Shady Grove $$
962 South Shady Grove Road
(901) 762–0056, (800) HAMPTON
www.hampton-inn.com

This 133-unit property offers suites as well as rooms. With a lofty two-story ceiling and attractive fireplace, the large, handsomely decorated lobby includes an extensive kitchen-style buffet area, where a free continental breakfast is served to guests. Outside is a patio with barbecue grills and a swimming pool. Other hotel amenities include a small fitness center, a guest laundry facility, a tiny convenience store, and free shuttle both to the airport and (depending on availability) to destinations within a 5-mile radius. Dining and room service are available from Frank Grisanti's, the Italian restaurant at the Embassy Suites Hotel next door. The suites feature a small kitchen with microwave, full-sized refrigerator, dishwasher, toaster, and utensils for cooking and serving a simple meal. The living area has a TV with movies and video games available for a fee, as well as a VCR and a sleeper sofa; the bedrooms have an extra vanity and sink. You can walk across a parking lot to visit the shops and restaurants of The Regalia shopping center.

Hawthorn Suites $$$
1090 Ridge Lake Boulevard
(901) 682–1722, (800) 527–1133
www.hawthorn.com

This 113-unit hotel, in a quiet area just a few blocks off busy Poplar Avenue, offers many of the comforts of home. The suites, cheerfully decorated in peach and teal, have small bedrooms, each with either a king or two double beds, a living room with tables and four chairs, and a full kitchen complete with full-sized refrigerator, microwave, dishwasher, and the basics for preparing and serving a simple meal. There's a VCR, too. Cinema buffs will find a movie theater (Ridgeway Malco) just across the street, and nearby restaurant choices include Benihana and Ruth's Chris Steakhouse. The Hawthorn also has other entertainments, including a swimming pool, a basketball court, and a fitness center. It serves a full hot breakfast in the mornings, and from 5:00 to 7:00 P.M. during the week there's a happy hour featuring a keg of beer and appetizers. Other amenities include a restaurant with dinner buffet, coin-operated laundry facilities, and whirlpool spa.

Hilton East Memphis $$$
5069 Sanderlin Avenue
(901) 767–6666, (800) HILTONS
www.hilton.com

This 264-room hotel (sometimes listed as the East Memphis Hilton) underwent a $2.8-million renovation in 2001, freshen-ing up the lobby area and adding an Art Deco feel to its guest rooms, meeting rooms, and new restaurant/bar. The hotel is 1 block north of Poplar, next to an upscale shopping center. Of all the East Memphis hotels, it's the closest to down-town (about 10 miles). The sunny, sleek lobby features cream-and-black tiled floors and terrarium-style windows that rise five stories. Just off the lobby is Cal's Champion Steakhouse, named for basket-ball coach John Calipari, whom University of Memphis hired to revive its team. Cal's serves steaks and casual American cuisine for lunch and dinner and a breakfast buffet in the mornings. The property also has Hilton's signature indoor-outdoor pool (you swim under a dividing wall to get outside), and a medium-sized fitness room. Other amenities include passes to the nearby Memphis Racquet Club (great for tennis and racquetball buffs) or local health club, free newspapers, and a shuttle service to and from the airport or (depending on availability) to destinations within 3 miles.

The hotel's executive floor offers larger rooms with extra amenities such as desks with slide-out extensions. A communal lounge serves a free continental breakfast and happy hour with hors d'oeuvres. Also available are a business center and concierge staff. Ask about weekend rates, and remember that if you're in town for the star-studded Kroger St. Jude International Indoor Tennis Championship, you can walk to the matches from the East Memphis Hilton.

Holiday Inn Select East Memphis $$$
5795 Poplar Avenue
(901) 682–7881, (800) 300–5491

This 10-story Holiday Inn, built in 1986, was recently upgraded to Holiday Inn Select after a $5-million renovation of its guest rooms, meeting facilities, and common areas. Its lobby area, with a sunken living room that offers views of a pretty blue-tiled fountain through terrarium-style windows, connects to Monterrey Grill, a new restaurant serving American food for all three meals, complete with a spiffy new lounge. You'll find the large indoor pool, with a nice-sized whirlpool spa nearby, on the other side of the restaurant. The hotel's refurbished second-floor meeting and special-event facilities, a popular spot for wedding receptions and corporate powwows, has been enhanced with a new ballroom on the first floor. Holiday Inn Select has 243 rooms, including a concierge floor with rooms and luxury suites on the 10th floor. The traditional-styled suites (which cost extra) are spacious, with the largest, nicest bathrooms of just about any hotel in the city. Guests staying in the suites or other 10th floor rooms have access to a small but elegant concierge lounge, where there's free continental breakfast and happy hour in the evenings. The standard rooms are generous in size, with either two queen beds or a king bed plus sleeper sofa (no charge for extra guests). These rooms also have fresh new bathrooms. Other amenities include room service, passes to a nearby health club, and a free airport shuttle, which, depending on availability, can also take guests to destinations within 3 miles. The hotel does accept pets but requires a $25 fee.

Homestead Studio Suites $
6500 Poplar Avenue
(901) 767– 5522, (888) STAY HSD
www.homesteadhotels.com
Opened in 1999 just west of Germantown, this sparkling-clean, few-frills hotel may cater mostly to business travelers, but at $59 to $74 a night, it's a great value for vacationers, too. The small lobby has a tiny front desk, a convenience store, and a small sitting area with a TV and a few tables and chairs; on the second floor there's a modern coin-laundry facility equipped with six washers and six dryers. The 134 guest rooms are bedroom–living room–kitchen combos with a king or queen bed, a work desk, and a breakfast bar with two barstools that separates the tiny kitchen area from the rest of the room. The kitchen has a full-sized refrigerator, a stovetop with two burners, a small microwave, and enough cooking and dining utensils for a simple meal. Given the small-but-not-claustrophobic size of the rooms, three or four could definitely be a crowd. Pets are allowed for a $75 fee. The price drops if you stay at least seven nights.

Homewood Suites by Hilton $$$
5811 Poplar Avenue
(901) 763–0500, (800) CALL HOME
www.homewood-suites.com
Staying at Homewood Suites is more like living in an apartment complex with generous amenities than staying at a hotel. When you arrive to check in, you enter a spacious "lodge" decorated with pine paneling and furniture, brick flooring, and homey fabrics. There's plenty of room for watching TV, reading in front of the fireplace, and holding impromptu meetings. The large kitchen-style buffet is where the staff serves a lavish free continental breakfast daily and for the early evening social, beer, soft drinks, and a light supper (burgers, nachos, etc.) Monday through Thursday. Just off the main lodge area is a small convenience store, a modest fitness center, five meeting rooms, and a business center. Go out the back and you'll find a heated pool, a whirlpool spa, and a tiny basketball court amid attractive landscaping. Grills are available to guests who want to cook out, and nearby is a small but cheerful guest laundry facility with three washers, three dryers, and a folding area. From the lodge you can drive or walk to the 143 suites, divvied up among seven buildings. The smallest suite is a one-bedroom with a king bed plus a sleeper sofa in the living room; the largest suite has two bedrooms and two bathrooms plus a separate kitchen area—ideal for large families or groups. All have full kitchens. Each room has a TV, one with VCR, and both movies and video games are available for a fee. A shuttle offers rides to or from the airport or (depending on availability) destinations within 5 miles of the hotel. Those who hate to grocery-shop will be happy to know there's a free shopping service: Just leave the staff your grocery list in the morning, and the food will be in your fridge that afternoon. Pets (except for cats) are allowed, but the fee is $50 for a short stay. *Note:* Rates drop if you stay five days or longer.

LaQuinta Inn & Suites $–$$
1236 Primacy Parkway
(901) 374–0330, (800) 687–6667
This attractive, pale-peach hotel is across from St. Francis Hospital, just a few blocks off Poplar and close to I–240. Built in 1998,

it won a local beautification award for its well-tended grounds, but its good looks don't stop there. The inviting lobby has high ceilings, a fountain, and Spanish-style architectural elements. It features a small fitness center, a guest laundry facility, a swimming pool, and a whirlpool spa. It offers free shuttle to the airport and nearby destinations as well as free continental breakfast and morning newspaper. The rooms and suites are done up in deep plum, teal, and green and feature movies and video games for an extra charge. The suites also have refrigerators and microwave ovens but no utensils for meals. French doors divide the living area from the bedroom. Pets are allowed at no extra charge.

Marriott Residence Inn $$$–$$$$
6141 Old Poplar Pike
(901) 685–9595, (800) 331–3131
www.residenceinn.com

Discreetly tucked next to a clinic a block off Poplar Avenue, this 105-suite property provides apartment-style living with plenty of hotel-style amenities, including daily housekeeping, free breakfast, and shuttle service to and from the airport or destinations within 5 miles. The large, modern lobby has marble floors that lead to a dining area and meeting rooms in the back and, to the side, a large carpeted sitting area with lots of magazines, a phone, and TV. You'll find a whirlpool bath and a small fitness center indoors, and outdoors, a medium-sized outdoor pool and a basketball court that doubles as a paddle tennis court. The one-bedroom suites are a good 600 square feet, with queen beds in the bedrooms and sleep sofas in the living rooms. You'll find a kitchen with full-sized refrigerator, microwave, stove and oven, toaster, and coffeemaker, as well as the necessary utensils for cooking and serving simple meals. The living-room area and bedrooms are traditionally decorated with teal, plum, and light-mauve fabrics.

The two-bedroom suite can accommodate five people, since the living room sofa pulls out into a bed. One bedroom is off the living room, whereas the second bedroom is upstairs in a loft (both have queen beds). The unit has two full bathrooms, one of which has a separate shower stall and an oversized tub with whirlpool. Curiously, the bedrooms in the suites aren't that private, as only a curtain separates them from the living room and the loft bedroom is open to the living room below. All rooms have pay-per-view movies, and some have working fireplaces. Other amenities include a guest laundry facility, grocery shopping service, and a social hour during the week that includes free appetizers, wine, beer, and soft drinks. Pets are allowed for a $100 fee. The property is next to the railroad track, so if you're a light sleeper, ask for a room on the other side. *Note:* The entrance is on Poplar. Watch for the sign just east of Ridgeway and cut through a small shopping-center parking lot to reach the hotel.

The Ridgeway Inn $$$
5679 Poplar Avenue
(901) 766–4000, (800) 822–3360

Owned and operated by the Peabody Hotel Group, The Ridgeway Inn is situated between the eastbound and westbound lanes of Poplar at I–240. First opened in the 1960s, it recently underwent a $6-million renovation that increased the size of its 155 guest rooms, replaced in-room furnishings, and spruced up the exterior of the building in an effort to attract more business travelers and fewer soccer teams. Also new is butler service, which is available on each floor. A stay on the hotel's concierge floor includes free continental breakfast and happy-hour cocktails and appetizers, as well as access to a communal lounge and a business center. For all its guest, the hotel has a comfortable cocktail lounge with bar, fireplace, equestrian art, and overstuffed furniture, as well as a good-sized outdoor swimming pool and meeting space that includes a 4,000-square-foot ballroom. What really distinguishes the Ridgeway Inn from the other Poplar/I–240 hotels is Café Expresso, an East Memphis favorite that serves a delectable array of desserts from The Peabody, a lavish Sunday brunch, and American cuisine for all three meals in a cheerful tiled setting. Morning coffee and transportation to and from the airport are free, and there's no charge for extra occupants in rooms. A small workout room and free pass to a nearby health club are also available.

Southeast Memphis

Best Suites $–$$
2575 Thousand Oaks Cove
(901) 365–2575, (800) BESTINN
www.bestinn.com

Built in 1999, this all-suites hotel operates next to I-240 behind Memphis Marriott East. To get there you take a circuitous route after turning off Perkins near American Way, a factor that effectively buffers the property from the surrounding neighborhood. Best Suites has a bright lobby and offers a number of amenities, including free hot-breakfast buffet, free drinks and snacks in the evenings, convenience store, and guest laundry. The indoor pool and whirlpool spa are in a greenhouse-type structure on one side of the hotel. The 111 suites range in price depending on the features, which can include in-room whirlpool baths. Some of the units are the company's Evergreen suites, featuring a premium air-purification system, a separate water supply comparable to bottled water, and soft-water showers. The property is designed for long stays, and the price drops if you're there for at least a week.

Fairfield Inn $
4760 Showcase Boulevard
(901) 795–1900, (800) 228–2800
www.fairfieldinn.com

Fairfield Inn, built in 1998, offers clean rooms decorated in calm mauve tones. Although less buffered from the surrounding area than neighboring Memphis Marriott East, Hampton Inn, and Best Suites, it's still a good bet. Guests are offered standard amenities plus free continental breakfast and access to an outdoor pool, a whirlpool, a small fitness center, and a guest laundry. The property has a small lobby with separate breakfast room and 89 rooms with either two double beds or a king plus sleeper sofa.

Hampton Inn—Perkins Road $
2700 Perkins
(901) 367–1234, (800) HAMPTON
www.hampton-inn.com

This 132-room hotel, next to the Memphis Marriott East, is across Perkins from the Mall of Memphis, one of the city's largest enclosed malls, and surrounding shopping centers. Built in 1994, it has a modest lobby with a big dining room area, where a free continental breakfast is served. The rooms, which have either two double beds or one king bed, are decorated in a traditional style and offer pay-per-view movies. There's an outdoor pool. Guests get free passes to a nearby health club. Children are free only up to 12 years of age.

Holiday Inn–Mt. Moriah $$
2490 Mt. Moriah
(901) 362–8010, (800) 477–5519
www.holiday-inn.com

Located just off the Mt. Moriah exit of I-240, this 197-room property was converted to a Holiday Inn in 1993 and has since had a $2.5-million interior renovation. The hotel has a small lobby with a tiny sitting area. A short hallway leads to the 5,300 square feet of meeting space and the restaurant, which provides three meals a day and room service. There's also a small lounge with a full bar and a small jukebox. The attractive swimming-pool area, in a

Insiders' Tip

If you're nervous about catching an early morning flight, or if you experience a long flight delay, remember there's a modest hotel in the Memphis International Airport terminal. The Skyport Inn (901-345-3220) has 44 rooms, ranging from $40 for a small single room to $74 for a king or double room. It's in Terminal A, right across from the Delta Air Lines ticket counter.

large courtyard that's protected from the street noise, is surrounded by flower beds. The pool is large and has bright blue umbrellas over the tables; indoors there's a small, but very clean fitness center. The rooms are traditional, with dark wood furniture that includes an oversized work desk, and the usual amenities, including a 25-inch TV. A free shuttle is available both to and from the airport and destinations within 5 miles. The hotel sits right at the beginning of a string of car dealerships, so if you want to buy a new car or get yours fixed, you're in the right place.

Memphis Marriott East $$$$
2625 Thousand Oaks Boulevard
(901) 362–6200, (800) 627–3587
www.marriotthotels.com/memtn

Opened in 1986 and renovated to the tune of $5 million in 1999, this upscale, full-service hotel is just off I-240 at Perkins Road and across the street from the Mall of Memphis and several shopping centers. With 14 stories and 320 rooms, the Marriott is one of the city's largest hotels. The bright, spacious lobby, with beige and maroon marble on the floors and touches of rich wood paneling on the walls, has plenty of small sitting areas with red-and-gold striped armchairs, tables, and brocade sofas. To the rear the Blue Shoe Bar & Grill serves American and Southern specialties for all three meals amid lively decor that features Cubist-style painting, upholstered booths, and Art Deco light fixtures. The guest rooms, though, are traditional, with floral bedspreads, kelly-green carpeting, and cream-color brocade draperies. The rooms have either two double beds or one king bed plus a pullout sofa. The bathrooms are bigger than most, with the sink and vanity in a separate dressing room. Amenities include Internet, movies, and video games available on room TVs for an extra fee. The hotel also has 14,000 square feet of meeting space with a business center, an outdoor pool (on the ground floor but buffered from the outside world), and a fitness area with workout room, sauna, indoor pool, and whirlpool spa. The 12th and 14th floors are concierge floors, featuring a staffed lounge, free continental breakfast, drinks

and appetizers in the evenings, and some in-room extras such as terry-cloth robes.

Wilson World Hotel & Suites $$
2715 Cherry Road
(901) 366–1000, (800) WILSONS
www.wilsonhotels.com

The two boxy pink hotels near the Mall of Memphis are home to Wilson World Hotel & Suites and its sister property, Wilson Inn & Suites. The interior of Wilson World is nicer than you'd expect from outward appearances. The atrium lobby, with its tan brick flooring and cream stucco walls, features a sunken cocktail lounge plus an indoor swimming pool and a whirlpool spa right there next to the escalator. The 178 rooms also have cream stucco walls, with dark-mauve carpeting, either a king bed or two double beds, a wet bar, a minirefrigerator, a coffeemaker, a hair dryer, and both movies and video games (for an extra charge). It's clean and friendly, even if it's not the freshest, newest hotel in town. Other amenities include free airport shuttle, meeting space with business center, snack shop, and on-site restaurant. Its sister property, with 108 rooms at $65.95, is not bad but not as nice as Wilson World or the comparably priced, newer Fairfield Inn and Best Suites close to the Memphis Marriott East on the other side of Mall of Memphis, a large regional shopping mall.

South Memphis/Airport

Days Inn at Graceland $
3839 Elvis Presley Boulevard
(901) 346–5500, (800) DAYS INN

This modest 61-room hotel, just a stone's throw from Graceland and other Elvis attractions, features free nonstop Elvis movies in your room, a guitar-shaped swimming pool, free continental breakfast, and airport shuttle. It's a favorite during Elvis International Tribute Week, when it is filled with regulars, some of whom have stayed at the hotel every year since Graceland opened. The rooms are standard, with in-room safes and well-worn bathrooms, but the lobby and exterior of the hotel are festooned with Elvis memorabilia and artwork.

Elvis Presley's Heartbreak Hotel™   **$–$$**
3677 Elvis Presley Boulevard
(901) 332–1000, (877) 777–0606
www.heartbreakhotel.net

This 128-room hotel was purchased by Elvis Presley Enterprises and was lavishly renovated into a stylish 128-room hotel that takes you back to the 1950s. It's a great choice for Elvis fans, because it's across the street from Graceland and a few blocks from the other Elvis attractions and related restaurants and shops. It's set back from seedy Elvis Presley Boulevard, with a guarded gate for security. The lobby features plush retro furniture, and a '50s-style TV that plays Elvis movies. The theme continues in the lounge and restaurant, with animal prints and bright colors—and in the patio, where you'll find a heart-shaped swimming pool. The rooms have most of the usual amenities, plus a free in-house TV channel of around-the-clock Elvis videos, a minifridge and microwave.

The rooms, although brightened up with blue-and-gold harlequin bedspreads, are pretty standard, but the real dazzlers are the hotel's four themed suites, including the Burning Love Suite (use your imagination) and the Graceland Suite, complete with "jungle room" den. Each of them is almost 1,100 square feet, with two sitting areas, two bedrooms, and two baths. Other hotel amenities include free deluxe continental breakfast, a fitness center, and a free shuttle to the airport, to Elvis Presley's restaurant on Beale Street, Sun Studios, and the Memphis Rock 'n' Soul Museum. Ask about packages that might include Graceland-tour reservations and dinner at the Beale Street restaurant.

Holiday Inn Select Memphis Airport $$
2240 Democrat Road
(901) 332–1130, (800) 300–5491
www.holiday-inn.com

A $7-million renovation in 2000 transformed the former Four Points Sheraton ITT into this sleek, handsome hotel. Its 374 rooms, 33,000 square feet of meeting space, and its proximity to the airport make it very popular for conferences,

meetings, and other functions. The lobby is a huge lofty atrium with sand-color tiles, with a few islands of navy-blue carpet with tables and chairs, a lobby bar, and a Java Coast coffee kiosk that's always humming in the mornings. The registration desk is to the right, with a gift shop on one side and a business center on the other. Down one level from the lobby a restaurant serves all three meals and provides room service. The hotel actually consists of two buildings with a hallway connector. The smaller, quieter building is called the executive center, and features a little house within its atrium that's home to a large fitness center with separate saunas for men and women. The guest rooms are decorated traditionally, with ergonomically correct chairs, and the TVs feature Internet access, movies, and video games for extra fees. Other amenities include guest laundry facilities and free airport shuttle.

Radisson Inn Memphis Airport $$
2411 Winchester Road
(901) 332–2370, (800) 333–3333
www.radisson.com

This 210-room hotel is literally at Memphis International Airport—you turn into the parking lot just a few blocks before you reach the terminal's arrivals and departures ramps. The hotel's two tennis courts are so close to one of the taxiways that you could make eye contact with passengers as their planes roll past. The smallish pink lobby has a business center near the front desk and 5,500 square feet of meeting space in the back. There's also a restaurant, which serves three meals a day (buffets for breakfast and lunch) and provides room service. A separate lounge/bar and a small fitness center with shower are also available. The swimming pool, on the lower level, is surrounded by the hotel on three sides and enough shrubbery on the fourth side to buffer it from all the airport noise, although you can't get away from the sound of aircraft arriving and departing. The traditional rooms include standard amenities including pay-per-view movies and video games in the rooms. A free airport shuttle is available.

Bed-and-Breakfasts and Country Inns

Bonne Terre Country Inn and Café $$$$
4715 Church Road West
Nesbit, Miss.
(662) 781–5100
www.bonneterre.com

Situated on 100 acres of Mississippi countryside, Bonne Terre is such a quiet, perfect place to get away from it all you might forget you're 15 miles from Memphis. The colorful rooms have pretty chintz curtains, antiques, and other decorations that make them feel quaint, even though the buildings were constructed fairly recently. All the guest rooms have a private bath, fresh flowers, down comforters, and other amenities that might include a fireplace, balcony, or whirlpool bath. Some of the rooms are a bit small, however, so you might want to ask about that when making your reservations.

One of the best parts about staying at Bonne Terre is eating at its cafe, which serves great French country cuisine in pretty, relaxed dining rooms. (See Restaurants chapter for details.) Breakfast is included with the room, but you will probably want to eat at least one other meal there.

Bonne Terre is a great spot for relaxing or strolling, with its woodsy location and small lakes; there's also swimming in summer and horseback riding (which can be arranged by management). Don't be surprised if you see a wedding party during your stay: With its event rooms, newly built reception hall, and chapel, Bonne Terre has become a very popular place for weddings, corporate events, and other gatherings. Although children are allowed, Bonne Terre is more oriented toward adult guests.

The Bridgewater House $$
7015 Raleigh LaGrange Road
(901) 384–0080
www.bbonline.com/tn/bridgewater

Formerly a schoolhouse, The Bridgewater House has been restored into a Greek Revival home with high ceilings, original hardwood floors, leaded-glass windows, and a 250-year-old Adams mantel in the living room.

Owners Steve and Katherine Mistilis take good care of their guests, cooking breakfast that might include Belgian waffles or their personal version of eggs Benedict (eggs Bridgewater). There are two large guest rooms, each with private bath, antiques, down comforters, and robes. The Bridgewater is about a mile from Shelby Farms, a large city park where horseback riding, hiking, and other activities are available. The inn is a good 20-minute drive from Memphis and the attractions there.

Children are not allowed, and smoking is allowed only on the porch or patio.

Shellcrest $$$$
669 Jefferson Avenue
(901) 523–0226
www.shellcrest.com

The Shellcrest is a beautifully restored Victorian Italianate town house, located just east of downtown Memphis. The house is furnished with antiques and has two large one-bedroom apartments, each with a parlor, morning room, and full kitchen. Guests have access to a private garden, covered porches, and washer and dryer, and they can take advantage of free grocery delivery and a private-car service. Shellcrest, so named for the shell motif incorporated into the design, caters primarily to long-term visits but, depending on availability, is available to bed-and-breakfast guests for short visits. Breakfast is included for short-term guests only. No children are allowed, and smoking is allowed only on the veranda or covered porches.

RV Parks

Note: T.O. Fuller and Meeman–Shelby Forest State Parks also have RV access. See Parks and Recreation chapter for contact information.

Agricenter International
7777 Walnut Grove Road
(901) 754–6528

Set well off busy Walnut Grove Road on the Agricenter's extensive grounds, this RV park has 500 sites for RVs and campers only. Each site has water and electricity hookups, but no sewer hookups, although a dump station is available. When you arrive, go to the Agricenter main building or the farmer's market, which operates in a bright-red barn. If neither is open when you arrive, you can pay at the self-pay box on the south side of the farmer's market building. The cost is $18 a night, $15 a night for seniors. The RV park doesn't take reservations except during the busy periods of May and June, so be sure to call ahead if you want to stay there at that time of year.

Memphis Graceland KOA
3691 Elvis Presley Boulevard
(901) 396–7125, (800) 562–9386
www.koa.com

Tucked behind Heartbreak Hotel and across the boulevard from Graceland, this RV park has sites for RVs and tents. The biggest attraction is that it's within walking distance of the Mansion and other Elvis-themed restaurants and shops. The KOA has 72 sites with full hookups (water, electricity, and sewer) at $33.95 a night, 19 sites with water and electricity for $30.95 a night, and tent sites for $21.95 ($26.95 with water and electricity). After you stay six nights, the seventh night is free. The owners take major credit cards except for American Express and have a rule limiting guests' Internet time in the evenings. Amenities include laundry facility, bathhouse with showers, small convenience store, and swimming pool. Pets are allowed, but they must be leashed and cleaned up after. Owners Mary and Jim Parks live on the premises, maintain a secure facility, and are into the spirit of things. In front of their trailer is a sign that reads: ELVIS FANS ONLY/VIOLATORS WILL BE ALL SHOOK UP. Open year-round.

Mississippi River RV Park
870 Cotton Gin Place
(901) 946–1993

Tucked away near the National Ornamental Metals museum and very close to downtown Memphis, this RV park is owned and operated by French-born Huguette Buford, who runs a tight ship. There are sites for 32 RVs, costing $22–$24 for each concrete pad with electricity, water, and sewer hookups. The rates are for two adults. Children under 10 are free, but it's $1.00 a night for each extra person. Amenities include a laundry facility and a bathhouse with showers. Sites are available for tents, too, and it's a popular camping spot during the Memphis in May music fest. It's open year-round. Ask directions before you come, as it's tricky to find the place. Dogs are allowed, but only if you clean up after them.

Tom Sawyer's Mississippi River RV Park
1286 South Eighth
West Memphis, Ark.
(870) 735–9779

This lush, green, spacious RV park is on the Arkansas side of the Mississippi, with views of the river from some sites. To get there from Memphis, follow I-55 into Arkansas and take exit 278. Follow the signs, and don't be alarmed as you zigzag through industrial areas and some depressing residential areas. When you cross the levee, you leave all that behind and go down a country road lined with huge trees. The park has 55 pull-through sites with full hookups (water, electricity, and sewer) for $20–$22 a night, plus plenty of room for tents. Amenities include a free laundry facility, a bathhouse with showers, fishing in the river or pond, and a large field for sports. If you stay six nights, the seventh night is free. Pets are allowed, but no rottweilers or pit bulls. The management is curmudgeonly and strict about the rules.

Youth Hostel

Memphis Hostel $
340 West Illinois Avenue
(901) 948–9005

For travelers hell-bent on staying in a hostel while in Memphis, the first and sixth floors of this Days Inn Riverbluff property have been converted into a hostel that offers dormitory-style accommodations for $15 a night and rooms with double beds for $20 per person. It's in a quiet pocket off I-55, where you'll also find the National

Ornamental Metals Museum. Memphis Hostel is on the dingy side, but $15 gets you a bunk with air mattress in a room shared with three other people with its own bathroom, shower, and minifridge. Guests also get free morning coffee and donuts in the lobby and have access to a swimming pool, a workout room, coin-operated laundry facilities, and a common room with full kitchen and TV. Free transportation is available to and from the airport, Central Station and Greyhound Bus Station; transportation to Beale Street or downtown Memphis is $3.00 per person.

Insiders' Tip

The Memphis Convention & Visitors Bureau's excellent Web site includes an extensive and frequently updated listing of hotels. You can even book a room on-line at some Memphis hotels. The Web address is www.memphistravel.com.

Restaurants

Downtown
Midtown
East Memphis
Winchester/Hickory
   Hill/South Memphis
Collierville
Germantown/Cordova
Raleigh
Mississippi Suburbs

Memphis is famous for its ribs and other pork barbecue, and although you'll find dozens of 'cue restaurants, they're not the only culinary show in town.

The city boasts some outstanding restaurants with national reputations, including Chez Philippe at The Peabody, where French-born José Gutierrez works his magic, and Erling Jensen, where the Danish-born chef of the same name turns out remarkable dishes. Many of the city's top chefs are native Memphians, including Richard Farmer at Jarrett's, Alex Grisanti and Judd Grisanti of Ronnie Grisanti and Sons, and Karen Blockman Carrier of Automatic Slim's. All of them have attracted the attention of the prestigious Beard House in New York City, where they were invited to cook special dinners. Koto and Cielo are examples of dazzling, sophisticated restaurants that just happen to be in Memphis.

You'll find a remarkable number of good restaurants for a city this size, and new ones are opening every year. Among the more promising newcomers are Felicia Suzanne's in downtown Memphis, operated by a former protégé of Emeril Lagasse, and Christopher's, an East Memphis bistro. Memphians are doggedly devoted to Southern home cooking, so you'll find plate-lunch restaurants all over the city that feature fried chicken, corn bread, and generous vegetable choices that include mashed potatoes, casseroles, black-eyed peas, and peculiarly Southern vegetables such as congealed salad and macaroni and cheese. Many restaurants that specialize in other fare also serve these hearty lunches at midday. (See the Close-up on Southern Home-Cooking Restaurants for more information.)

Memphis, like other American cities, is also rich in ethnic restaurants as the population becomes more diversified and diners more open-minded to trying new things. Here you'll find authentic Mexican, Vietnamese, Thai, Japanese, even Ethiopian and Russian restaurants. The city is rich in Italian restaurants, many of them operated by Memphis families of Italian descent for more than 20 years.

We would be remiss, however, if we didn't say a little more about barbecue. Memphis has evolved into the pork barbecue capital of the world, and if you don't believe it, check out the World Championship Barbecue Cooking Contest that takes place here every May (see Annual Events chapter for more details). During barbecue-fest weekend, some 300 cooking teams set up operations at Tom Lee Park as they compete for prizes on barbecued pork ribs, whole hog, and pork shoulder. Even on an ordinary weekend, smokers and grills are going all over the city as Memphians perfect their own secret recipes. Of course, the city has great barbecue restaurants, so be sure and sample some barbecue ribs (wet or dry) and a savory pork-shoulder sandwich during your stay. (See the Close-up on barbecue in this chapter for more information.)

Finally, if you prefer the familiar, you'll find every kind of chain restaurant in Memphis. Fast-food options include Wendy's, McDonald's, Papa John's Pizza, Taco Bell, and many, many more. Other chain restaurants include Outback Steakhouse, Olive Garden, Bahama Breeze, and Applebee's. On the more upscale end, there's Ruth's Chris Steak House and Benihana.

The listings in this chapter focus mainly on local restaurants and are organized according to geographic location: Downtown, Midtown, East Memphis, Winchester/Hickory Hill/South Memphis, Collierville, Germantown/Cordova, Raleigh, and Mississippi Suburbs. Within each section we list the restaurants in alphabetical order.

Most restaurants accept major credit cards (MasterCard and Visa always, and usually American Express and others) and are wheelchair accessible. We note the exceptions in individual write-ups. Most places accommodate both smokers and nonsmokers, although some ban smoking entirely. Unless otherwise noted, smoking is allowed, and all restaurants by law are required to have nonsmoking sections.

Restaurants in Memphis tend to have full bars, so unless we specify no alcohol, beer only, or just beer and wine, you can expect to find a well-stocked bar with wine and beer as well. In restaurants where there's no liquor or just beer, it's standard procedure to bring your own wine if you like, but you may pay a modest "corkage" fee. You can usually bring a special bottle to restaurants that serve wines, but plan on paying a possibly heftier corkage fee.

If you have specific questions or concerns, such as whether the kitchen can accommodate vegetarians or special diets, feel free to call the restaurant. It's never a bad idea to call ahead anyway, because restaurants can sometimes close, change their days and hours of operation, or change the type of cuisine they serve.

Price Code

The price code in this chapter is based on the cost of dinner for two, without appetizers, desserts, drinks, tax, or tip. Your bill may vary, depending on what you order and fluctuating restaurant prices. Prices are for dinner, so keep in mind that lunch at the same restaurant often costs less.

$	Less than $20
$$	$21 to $40
$$$	$41 to $60
$$$$	$61 and higher

Downtown

Amber Palace $–$$
97 South Second Street
(901) 578-9800
This Indian restaurant in downtown Memphis is operated by the same efficient management as India Palace in midtown and serves a very similar menu as well as a popular all-you-can-eat buffet for lunch. If you're new to Indian cuisine, try the tender tandoori chicken and warm flat-bread. (See the write-up on India Palace in this chapter for more details about the cuisine.) Parking can be found on the street or in a nearby parking lot or garage.

The Arcade $
540 South Main Street
(901) 526-5757
This casual restaurant, arguably the oldest eatery in the city (it dates back to 1919), is a step back in time since the proprietors—the grandson of the founder and his wife—have kept the original diner decor intact. The Arcade serves breakfast all day as well as pizzas, sandwiches, salads, and daily

plate lunch specials. It's a favorite hangout both for neighborhood residents and visitors in the popular South Main district. Open for lunch and dinner.

Automatic Slim's Tonga Club $$–$$$
83 South Second Street
(901) 525-7948
This hip downtown restaurant, the brainchild of Memphis-born chef and artist Karen Blockman Carrier, never goes out of style. Named for a character in the well-known blues tune "Wang Dang Doodle," the restaurant reflects Carrier's love for the bright cuisine and colors of the Caribbean and Southwest and always has intriguing artwork on the walls. The menu combines Asian, American, Caribbean, and Southwestern cuisines, resulting in eclectic, flavorful dishes such as coconut mango shrimp, voodoo stew (an exotic cousin to bouillabaisse), whole red snapper, and imaginative sandwiches and salads. The bar is a hangout for the smartly dressed crowd, who are particular about their martinis. Automatic Slim's frequently plays host to in-the-know film crews when there's a movie being shot in town. Open for lunch Monday through Friday and for dinner Monday through Saturday. Reservations recommended.

Blues City Café $$
138 Beale Street
(901) 526-3637
If you're going to eat on Beale Street, this is a wise choice, with its tasty food and experienced servers. They usually serve until well after midnight, and sometimes famous musicians hang out here and even jam with the house band after their gigs at other Beale Street clubs. The steaks here

are really special—up to six pounds, they're served family-style with drippings ladled back over the meat, and the prices include enough fries or potatoes and salads for everybody joining in. Musicians play every night, and truly memorable performances happen here often. The local jazz/jam band Freeworld has ruled this stage for more than a decade on Sunday nights. Open every day for lunch and dinner.

Bogie's Downtown Deli $
80 Monroe Street
(901) 525-6764

The downtown branch of the popular locally owned deli that features Boar's Head meats and excellent prepared salads. See listing in East Memphis section for more information.

The Butcher Shop Steak House $$-$$$
101 South Front Street
(901) 521-0856

The Butcher Shop has been a fixture in downtown Memphis for more than 20 years. The big attraction at this casual steak restaurant, situated amid the lofty cotton companies on Cotton Row, is that you can pick out your own steak and even cook it yourself if you like. You can order salmon or marinated chicken if you don't want steak. Open seven days a week for dinner. Park in the street or at a nearby lot or garage.

There's also a Germantown branch, which operates near the intersection of Germantown Parkway and Walnut Grove, at 107 South Germantown Parkway (901-757-4244).

Café Samovar $$-$$$
83 Union Avenue
(901) 529-9607

The Sadetsky family emigrated from the Ukraine and somehow ended up in Memphis, which is great news for the downtown culinary scene. Café Samovar proudly presents Russian classics such as pirogi, blinis, and borscht as well as outstanding soups and salads including its picturesque *salade niçoise*. Lunch is very popular here among the downtown executive set, with excellent salads, blini, chicken kiev, and sandwiches. The lunch prices are half those of dinner.

The more substantive dinner fare features items such as classic Russian shish kabobs and pork tenderloin with bacon-mango sauce. As a starter at dinner, try the generous Taste of Russia appetizer platter. The interior is very cheery with its Christmas colors, and on pleasant days you can sit out on Samovar's deck to enjoy people-watching with your meal. There's also belly dancing on weekends and a good vodka menu. The restaurant serves lunch and dinner, Monday through Friday, and dinner only on Saturday. It's a good idea to call ahead for dinner during the week.

Capriccio $$-$$$
149 Union Avenue
(901) 529-4000

Capriccio, which opened in mid-2002 at The Peabody hotel, serves a menu of Italian specialties including Tuscan-style crepes stuffed with ricotta and spinach, oven-roasted chicken, and veal scaloppini with mushrooms and marsala sauce. It's the mid-priced restaurant at the grand hotel and features a large bar and waiting area. Open seven days a week for lunch and dinner.

Chez Philippe $$$-$$$$
149 Union Avenue
(901) 529-4188
www.peabodymemphis.com

One of the most elegant dining experiences in Memphis can be had at Chez Philippe, The Peabody hotel's flagship restaurant. It always receives high marks from readers of *Memphis* magazine for its romantic ambiance, its gifted chef, and its attentive service. You enter the restaurant from the grand lobby through gilded wrought-iron gates into an opulent dining room The lavish decor, with velvet draperies, crystal chandeliers, and gilded finishes, make you feel like royalty, as does the white-gloved service. The dining room is arranged as three levels, which helps to create an intimate feeling. José Gutierrez, an acclaimed Master Chef born and trained in France, dazzles diners with a menu of contemporary French cuisine with Southern elements. Dishes such as cornmeal hush puppies stuffed with shrimp provençale and smoked pork tenderloin brushed with

Capriccio, located at The Peabody, serves Northern Italian cuisine. DRAWING: THE PEABODY MEMPHIS

Jack Daniel's mustard and sage on grits couscous demonstrate José's creative blending of these two culinary traditions. You can order a fixed menu or a la carte; for brunch, the buffet here is one of the most elaborate in town. Open for dinner Tuesday through Saturday and for brunch on Sunday. Reservations are recommended, and jackets are required for men. No smoking is allowed. Parking is free if you park at The Peabody and bring your ticket in for validation, and valet parking is available.

Cielo $$$
679 Adams
(901) 524–1886

This Memphis original is historic Victorian house on the outside and an extravaganza of gold leaf, faux finishes, funky lamps, and intriguing artwork on the inside. The result is an upscale restaurant that feels magical, romantic, and fun with food that's as dazzling as the decor. It's the creation of Karen Blockman Carrier, who also owns Automatic Slim's restaurant. The food is just as intriguing, with entrees such as kefir lime oil seared ahi, Peking style duck, and beef tenderloin with skewered lobster club sandwich. The

dining rooms are intimate and inviting, and the upstairs bar is a stylish spot for a glass of wine and appetizer. The adjacent lounge is cozy, and cigar smokers are welcome. There's live piano music on weekends. Open for dinner Tuesday through Saturday. Reservations recommended.

Denny's $
166 Union Avenue
(901) 522–9938

This unit of the well-known breakfast chain is noteworthy because it's the only place downtown where you can get breakfast, lunch, or dinner 24 hours a day. Here you'll find Denny's Original Grand Slam and other familiar breakfast combos in addition to sandwiches and other fare. The restaurant is situated inside the Benchmark Hotel. You can park in a nearby lot or garage. No alcohol served.

Dyers Burgers $
205 Beale Street
(901) 527–DYER

Dyers has the most famous grease in town. When the restaurant moved to Beale in 1998, the cooking grease was carefully loaded onto a flatbed truck and whisked to

Cielo, a one-of-a-kind Memphis restaurant, is housed in this historic Victorian mansion.
PHOTO: MEMPHIS CONVENTION AND VISITORS BUREAU

its new home under police escort. Legend has it that it's the original grease Elmer Dyer first used in 1912. (Actually, the grease recycles itself, as the cooking burgers add new grease to the pot.) Don't be put off by this tale of grease, because the Dyer burger (which is deep-fried, not grilled) is actually one of the best you'll ever have, thin and delicious. The decor is nouveau-retro diner with booths, neon, and a stainless steel eat-at counter. Dyers is open all day for lunch and dinner and at least until midnight for late-night munchies.

Erika's $-$$
52 Second Street
(901) 526-5522

If you were to get caught in the pouring rain, you could find no better refuge than Erika's. Comfort food with a German accent, featuring specialties such as wiener schnitzel, bratwurst, and flavorful sauerkraut, is cooked up by Erika Seipel, who has operated this restaurant for more than 25 years. Don't miss the substantial yeast rolls, but be forewarned that

eating more than one may mean no room for dinner. The decor has changed little over the years at this homey eatery, which continues to be a popular lunch spot for downtown power brokers. Erika's serves beer, but you can bring your own wine. Open for lunch Tuesday through Friday and for dinner on Friday and Saturday.

Felicia Suzanne's $$$
80 Monroe Street
(901) 523-0877

Opened in spring 2002, this fine-dining restaurant is the creation of Felicia Willett, a mid-Southerner who worked closely with New Orleans culinary superstar Emeril Lagasse for many years. The menu features dishes with a Southern accent, such as fresh crab salad with fried green tomatoes and crispy fried oysters with New Orleans barbecue sauce over grits. The decor features lavender hues and 25-foot ceilings. The restaurant can be found in the lobby of the Brinkley Plaza office building at Main Street. Open Tuesday through Saturday for dinner.

Front Street Delicatessen $
77 South Front Street
(901) 522-8943
This friendly, small takeout place serves breakfasts featuring country ham and homemade biscuits as well as sandwiches and a few plate-lunch choices every day. Tom Cruise hung out here while filming the movie of the John Grisham book *The Firm*. There are a few seats inside, and a few tables set up outside during good weather. Open for breakfast and lunch Monday through Friday.

Gordon Biersch Brewery $-$$
145 South Main Street
(901) 543-3330
www.gordonbiersch.com
This brewpub serves a great menu and offers a warm ambiance inside and a popular patio outside. Gordon Biersch, a mainly West Coast chain that brews its own beers, is a local favorite for its outdoor patio right on Main Street, which allows for great people-watching and taking in the downtown scene.

  The menu features grilled skewers, sweet-and-sour cashew chicken stir fry, homemade pizzas baked in wood-fired ovens, and salads as well as peppered ahi tuna for dinner and sandwiches plus meatloaf with garlic mashed potatoes for lunch. Open daily for lunch and dinner, with a late-night menu available on weekends. You can park in a nearby lot or garage or on the street.

Gus's Fried Chicken World Famous $
510 South Front Street
(901) 527-4877
A pair of Memphis entrepreneurs has brought Gus's legendary fried chicken to Memphis from Mason, Tennessee, where it has been winning kudos from GQ magazine and elsewhere. The Front Street restaurant, a franchise of the original, retains a casual atmosphere as well as the menu, which includes 40-ounce bottles of beer, slaw, French fries, and last but not least, some of the best fried chicken on the planet. With its mahogany crust and tender meat, Southern-fried chicken doesn't get better than

this. Gus's serves beer only, so BYOB if you're drinking something else. Open seven days a week for lunch and dinner. For the full Gus's experience, visit Mason, Tennessee, the home of the original establishment. The first structure that housed the restaurant burned recently but was rehabilitated to mimic the unforgettable shotgun-shack atmosphere. (See the Day Trips chapter for more details.) You'll find plenty of street parking.

Harry's Detour South Main $-$$
106 South Main Street
(901) 523-9070
The downtown location of Harry's, featuring fine dining in an ultra-casual atmosphere. See listing in Midtown section for more information.

Huey's $
77 South Second Street
(901) 527-2700
A casual restaurant with great hamburgers and live music on Sunday, with locations throughout the city. See listing in Midtown section for more information.

Isaac Hayes Music Food Passion $$
150 Peabody Place
(901) 529-9222
The main attraction is ambiance and nightly live music at this restaurant/club, a partnership between the great Memphis soul star (also the voice for the *South Park* character Chef) and a Memphis-based restaurant development company. It features Famous Dave's barbecue from Minneapolis, Yankee barbecue that doesn't get much respect in these parts but is tasty nonetheless. The atmosphere of this spacious restaurant resembles an old-fashioned supper club and features the upbeat music of Memphis R&B master Preston Shannon (a real class act!) as well as the occasional appearance by Mr. Hayes himself. The restaurant, in addition to barbecue, serves roasted chicken, sandwiches, steaks, and side dishes that include excellent potato salad. Open every day for lunch and dinner. There's parking in nearby lots and garages.

McEwen's On Monroe $$–$$$
122 Monroe
(901) 527–7085

As soon as it opened a few years ago, this urbane newcomer to the downtown bistro scene became wildly popular with food lovers, who continue to stampede to this place for McEwen's consistently outstanding food, great wine list, and especially the hospitality of owner Mac Edwards. Chef de cuisine Jennifer Dickerson oversees the kitchen, turning out such delectable dishes as poppy-seed-encrusted tuna seared to perfection, maple-and-soy–glazed salmon, and smoked fried chicken. If you like bananas and pie, check out the banana cream pie. The bar, with its exposed-brick walls and uptown ambiance, is a great spot for a martini or, better yet, a glass of wine, since as a knowledgeable former wine rep, Edwards maintains one of the best selections around. A menu of appetizers is available at the moderate-sized bar as well. The dining room, with its warm green colors and bright paintings, is inviting and comfortable. Reservations are a must for dinner at this special eatery, but the bar is first come, first served. Open for lunch Monday through Friday and for dinner Tuesday through Saturday.

Sawaddii $–$$
121 Union Avenue
(901) 529–1818

This stylish downtown restaurant delivers lively Thai specialties such as satays, spicy beef noodles, and red-curry dishes at reasonable prices. It's already known by Memphians and visitors alike but doesn't take reservations, so you may have to wait for a table. In terms of alcoholic beverages, Sawaddii serves beer and wine only, so if you want harder stuff, ask for directions to a nearby liquor store. Check out the large photograph over the bar of a young Elvis Presley (during his army days) hanging out with Siamese royalty. Sawaddii (a variation on the Thai word for "how are you," incidentally) is open for lunch Monday through Friday and for dinner every evening. No smoking except in the bar/lobby area.

Sekisui Downtown/Union Café $–$$
160 Union Avenue
(901) 523–0001

A key advantage of the downtown location of Sekisui is that anyone in your party who doesn't like seafood or Japanese food can order a burger, salad, or clam chowder from the American menu of Union Café. The restaurant, in the lobby of the Holiday Inn Select, has a good sushi bar, and the location promotes good people-watching through the big windows along Union Avenue. (For more details about Sekisui, see the write-up in the East Memphis section of this chapter.) Open for lunch Monday through Friday and every day for dinner.

Zanzibar $–$$$
412 South Main Street
(901) 543–9646

This restaurant/cafe is a hipster South Main Street hangout, where you can get coffee, a meal, dessert or a glass of wine. It's an urbane, cheerful place, with concrete floors and walls painted in bright hues of orange, yellow, and purple. The small but wide-ranging menu features such options as good ceviche, a new-fangled Cobb salad, roasted pork empanadas, and grilled Angus beef fillet. Favorites among the desserts are the many cheesecakes and the chocolate torte. The place is packed on the last Friday night in the month, when art-loving Memphians descend into the area for the Art Trolley Tour. (See The Arts chapter for more information on both the tour and the galleries in the area.) Zanzibar is owned by Nigerian-born painter Ephraim Urevbu, whose work adorns the tabletops as well as the canvases on the walls. Open for lunch and dinner Tuesday through Saturday and for brunch on Sunday.

Midtown

Abyssinia Ethiopian Restaurant $
2600 Poplar Avenue
(901) 321–0082

This family-run, simply decorated midtown restaurant serves up Ethiopian specialties on spongy, flat bread called injera. You can go for the exotic by sitting on short stools around a basket holding a communal platter, eating with your hands by scooping up the stewed meats and veggies with pieces of injera. Or you can sit at conventional tables and eating the unusually spiced food with utensils. You don't have to be a vegetarian to enjoy the vegetable platter, one of the more varied platters on the menu, or try the meat dishes with lamb, beef, or chicken with varying degrees of heat. For a new and different twist on java, try the traditional Ethiopian coffee, said to ensure your return! The cook actually roasts the coffee beans on the stove for each order. Beer is available, but bring your own wine if you don't want the Paul Masson jug version they serve as house wine. Open for lunch and dinner Monday through Saturday.

Anderton's $$
1901 Madison Avenue
(901) 726–4010
This old-fashioned seafood restaurant has been a Memphis institution since 1945, back when this midtown location was considered East Memphis. The exterior facade is the original, done in sea-green ceramic tile with a nautical theme that continues inside the restaurant. The restaurant serves all kinds of seafood, including its famous stuffed pompano en papillote and its baby lobster dainties (small lobster tails imported from Denmark). Anderton's also has seafood platters, as well as hand-cut steaks, the most popular of which is the tenderloin. Open for lunch Monday through Friday and for dinner Monday through Saturday.

Blue Moon Restaurant & Tropical Bar
$$–$$$
3092 Poplar Avenue
(901) 324–4131
This lively fine-dining restaurant features European-Asian fusion cooking in the kitchen and tropical drinks at the bar. Among the favorites are grilled quail with goat cheese quenelles, duck and shiitake spring rolls, crabcakes, and osso bucco Milanese. To find the restaurant go to Chickasaw Oaks Plaza shopping center

and walk inside. Some of the tables are on a deck that looks out into the shopping area, whereas others are in colorful, pretty dining rooms. Open for lunch and dinner every day except Sunday and for dinner on Monday. Reservations recommended.

Bogie's Delicatessen Midtown $
2098 LaSalle Place
(901) 272–0022
The midtown location of this popular locally owned deli has a great covered deck for sitting outside. See listing in East Memphis section for more information.

Boscos Squared $–$$$
2120 Madison Avenue
(901) 432–2222
The midtown branch of the local brewpub and restaurant, a happening nightspot with its own beer, Midtown Brown. See listing in Germantown/Cordova section for more information.

Brother Juniper's $
3519 Walker Avenue
(901) 324–0144
Brother Juniper's, a popular restaurant near University of Memphis, is one of the best places in the city for breakfast. Expect a wait on Saturdays, when people flock there for omelets, homemade breads and biscuits, and other breakfast favorites. The lunch menu consists mainly of sandwiches, homemade soups, and potato casseroles as well as items from the breakfast menu. The service is friendly and down to earth at this casual cafe, which feels like a bit of a throwback to U of M's hippy days. Closed on Mondays and Sundays. No credit cards. Smoking is not allowed inside the restaurant. Although the dining room is wheelchair accessible, the rest rooms are not. There's a second location at the Pink Palace Museum at 3050 Central Avenue (901–320–6320), which also serves dinner.

The Brushmark $–$$
1934 Poplar Avenue
(901) 544–6225
Situated inside the Memphis Brooks Museum in Overton Square, The Brushmark

serves a lunch menu of salads, sandwiches, pastas, its crepe du jour, and grilled salmon as well as its specialty, African peanut soup. This bright and attractive restaurant features a covered deck overlooking the park, a great place to lunch al fresco during nice weather. For dessert don't miss the gooey, scrumptious caramel-fudge pecan cake. Lunch only is served Tuesday through Sunday.

Café Ole $–$$
959 South Cooper Street
(901) 274–1504

This casual, hip restaurant/bar in the Cooper-Young neighborhood is a fun place to have a meal or drink margaritas at the bar, and its outdoor patio is very popular during nice weather. It's long on atmosphere, and although it may not serve the most authentic Mexican food on the planet, its quesadillas, fajitas, enchiladas, and other fare are filling and savory. Monday evenings, when there's $1.00 off all margaritas, is particularly lively. Open for lunch and dinner seven days a week.

Café Palladio $
2169 Central Avenue
(901) 276–3804

This upbeat lunch spot is tucked back amid displays of antiques at Palladio International Antique Mall in Midtown, making it a great place to eat and shop at the same time. The menu is no antique, with imaginative sandwiches such as smoked turkey and green apple, roast veggies, and rare roast beef with brie. Soups, salads, and homemade baked goods also grace the menu, under the able hand of Adrienne Hertz, a Memphis native who's brought her culinary talents back home after working in the Southwest. Check out the cozy brick patio during nice weather. Open for lunch only Monday through Saturday.

Café Society $$–$$$
212 North Evergreen
(901) 722–2177

This is the classic little French restaurant around the corner for many Memphians, some of whom have been dining here for years. Café Society skillfully prepares a French continental menu that includes French onion soup, bacon-wrapped shrimp, sautéed veal tenderloin, and seafood bisque served in a bowl that's actually a scooped-out round French loaf. The restaurant has a warm ambiance and reliable service, and the bar is a great place for a glass of wine and an appetizer. In summer you can sit outside at a sidewalk table. Open for lunch Monday through Friday and for dinner every night. Reservations recommended.

Dino's $
645 North McLean
(901) 278–9127

The decor is nothing fancy, but for some 30 years midtowners have come here for the home cooking and down-home warmth of Dino's. The friendly family restaurant serves up great homemade Italian specialties and southern-style meats and vegetables, both for lunch and dinner. This is a great place to get spaghetti and meatballs, lasagne, Italian salad, or homemade comfort food such as turkey and dressing or fried-chicken dinners. Breakfast, served beginning at 7:00 A.M., includes eggs, bacon, pancakes, waffles, and other breakfast basics. Beer is served here, and you can bring your own wine.

Fino's from the Hill $
1853 Madison Avenue
(901) 272–3466

Midtowners inundate this little Italian deli to get the crusty, oversized sandwiches and hearty pasta specials. The owners bring in authentic Italian meats, cheeses, olives, and other goodies from the Hill, St. Louis's Little Italy, which they pile onto fresh-baked French bread for the sandwiches. These ingredients also find their way into saucy pasta dishes and salads. You can also get Italian desserts, or buy olives, meats, and Italian grocery items to take home. It's extremely casual, down to the paper plates and bus-your-own-table policy. Order at the counter, find a table, and wait for your name to be called, which is when you pick up your food and pay. You can get your order to go and take it to nearby Overton Park for a picnic on a nice day. Fino's is on the bottom floor of an apartment building called The Gilmore, where there's a parking lot in the back. Open for lunch and early dinner Tuesday through Saturday. No liquor.

Harry's Detour $–$$
532 S Cooper Street
(901) 276–7623

Located in a renovated former residence, this midtown restaurant features the imaginative cooking of Harry Nicholas, a Memphis eccentric who also owned (and later sold) On Teur. Harry's features lots of pecan-smoked dishes, including its delectable mahi Redondo spread, and also serves bacon-wrapped sea bass, fiery chaurice sausage, and scallops in a rich cream sauce. Take note that spicy dishes are often fiery indeed, so ask. Don't skip dessert here, where the warm bread pudding and homemade truffles are magnificent! The restaurant also serves an excellent Sunday brunch, and there's an outdoor deck that's nice during pleasant weather. You'll probably want to park on the street, as the minuscule parking lot is generally full. Harry's serves beer, but BYOB if you're drinking wine. Open for lunch and dinner every day except Monday.

Hattley's Garage $
1761 Madison Avenue
(901) 726–3815

This former midtown gas station and garage has been converted into a laidback little restaurant and cafe that serves healthy fare, including smoothies, as well as plenty of choices for vegetarians. The focal point of the menu is Hattley's inventive sandwiches, such as the Asian turkey burger or the garbanzo-bean-and-tahini burger. You can sit at the bar, which feels like a vintage lunch counter, or at one of the tables and chairs in the back. During nice weather there's seating outside. Hattley's also serves espresso and coffee drinks as well as beer. Open Tuesday through Saturday for lunch and dinner. Smoking at the bar only.

Huey's $
1927 Madison Avenue
(901) 726–4372
77 South Second Street

Huey's, with its hefty burgers and Sunday evenings of free live music, has become a Memphis institution since it was first started by a member of the Box Tops, a local 1960s garage band who had a hit called "The Letter." Memphians from all walks of life seek out the comfort-food familiarity of Huey burgers, thick hot fries, and potato soup. Kids love the baskets of chicken fingers and the traditions of writing on the walls (so bring a permanent marker) and blowing frill picks into the soft ceiling through drinking straws. The kitchen makes a delightful grilled-fish sandwich and salads, and there's a full bar. The midtown Huey's on Madison Avenue is the original and by far the favorite, although now it's a small chain, with each location almost exactly the same inside. Huey's is also, perhaps surprisingly, one of the city's best bets for live blues and jazz. (See Nightlife for more details about the music.) Open for lunch and dinner seven days a week.

India Palace $–$$
1720 Poplar Avenue
(901) 278–1199

With its colorful jungle murals, polite service, and daily lunch buffet, local fans of Indian cooking fill this spot up, particularly on tight lunch hours. The menu is easy to understand and has all the usual suspects, such as tandoori chicken, biryani, curries, masalas, and 11 types of Indian bread. Try one of the complete dinners, such as the vegetarian dinner, if want to sample lots of different dishes. The kitchen is usually very careful about keeping the hot spices in check, so have a chat with your server if you want a full allotment of heat. The restaurant also has a full bar and comfortable booths as well as tables. Even though there are white tablecloths, it's pretty casual. India Palace is open for lunch, when you can choose from the menu or the all-you-can-eat buffet, and for dinner daily.

KoTo $$$
22 South Cooper Street
(901) 722–2244

This polished jewel of a fine-dining

restaurant is a partnership between two top Memphis restaurateurs, Japanese-born Jimmy Ishii (owner of Sekisui and others), and Danish-born Erling Jensen. Named for the capitals of their respective homelands (Ko for Copenhagen, To for Tokyo), the restaurant offers East-West fusion cooking, which, in the hands of chefs Karen and Jorge Noriega, means dishes such as kushiyaki–style beef filet skewered with green onions and roasted garlic as well as seared tuna with Japanese spices served over white bean cassoulet. Its small but handsome dining room features lipstick red walls, black-and-white photos, and white tablecloths. Ask about KoTo's monthly sake and wine-tasting dinners. Situated in Overton Square just south of Madison, with parking available in lots across Cooper, KoTo is open for lunch Monday through Friday, and for dinner every night. Reservations are recommended. No smoking is allowed.

Kwik Check Food Store $
2013 Madison Avenue
(901) 274–9293

This is not a restaurant at all, but a midtown convenience store that happens to have some of the most inventive, scrumptious sandwiches in town. You order at the back counter, choosing from muffalettas, spicy meat loaf, vegetarian, falafel, roast beef, and turkey sandwiches, or Kwik Check's own concoctions. Among them: the Hey Zeus, made from roast beef, turkey, feta, and lemon-herb dressing wrapped in pita bread, and the spicy Yippe Kai Yai Yay. You probably want to get your order to go, but there is a small counter at the front of the store if you want to eat your sandwich there. Open every day for lunch and dinner.

La Montagne $–$$
3550 Park Avenue
(901) 458–1060

La Montagne is longtime-standard among Memphians for its international menu that highlights, but isn't limited to, vegetarian cooking, and the comfortable ambiance. The dining room has a quaint European feel with a fireplace that's very soothing, especially during winter months. Dishes include baked encrusted salmon on a bed of brown and wild rice, pesto pasta primavera, and a portabella mushroom stuffed with spinach, feta, and pine nuts. After a healthy dinner you can splurge on chocolate mousse in puff pastry or the more moderate bananas La Montagne, prepared with maple sugar a la bananas Foster. Open for dinner Tuesday through Sunday, for lunch Tuesday through Saturday, and for brunch on Sunday.

La Tourelle $$–$$$$
2146 Monroe
(901) 726–5771

La Tourelle, which opened in 1977 as one of the city's first fine-dining establishments, is still among the best, cherished among romantics and gourmands alike. With creamy-apricot walls, lace curtains, and colorful French posters, it was voted the city's most romantic restaurant by readers of *Memphis* magazine. What's more, the food shines under the direction of chef de cuisine Justin Young, the latest in a long line of gifted chefs that has included Erling Jensen. The dishes are simply prepared, with flavorful demiglace and reduction sauces, incorporating foie gras, ultra-fresh fish, steaks, and other meats with vegetable combinations so delicious and substantive they could stand alone. Its wine list has won kudos from *Wine Spectator.* One of the best-kept secrets in town is The Tower, a casual sister restaurant that operates upstairs in the same house on weekends. It serves a smaller menu that includes the same food as La Tourelle at half the price, with wines to match. Both restaurants are open every night for dinner, and La Tourelle is open for lunch on Fridays and Sundays. Reservations recommended.

Le Chardonnay $–$$
5 Overton Square Lane
(901) 725–1375

Le Chardonnay is Memphis's original wine bar. Many people love the dark ambiance (you practically need a flashlight to see the menu), the great wine list, and accompaniments such as the handmade pizzas and baked Brie at this longtime midtown hideout. Le Chardonnay, however, is an excellent choice for a full meal, with its fancy lunchtime sandwiches, outstanding fresh salads, and scallops carbonara. In the evenings its wood-burning oven is fired up, producing some of the best gourmet pizzas in town. It's a great spot for a romantic glass of wine or dinner. In addition to the tables, there are couches and overstuffed chairs that get snapped up quickly. Open for lunch Monday through Friday and for dinner every night.

Lilly's Dim Sum, Then Some $$
903 South Cooper Street
(901) 276–9300

This restaurant, situated in an old home in midtown's Cooper-Young neighborhood, features potstickers, noodles, and other Asian specialties, served dim-sum style in small dishes. You can order as many of these small dishes as you like, which means you can taste an array of dishes at one sitting. A good deal is the $13.95 all-you-can-eat dim sum special on Sundays. It's very well known, so you might want to go in mid-afternoon when it's not so crowded. Open every day for lunch and dinner, with the same menu for both.

Marena's $$–$$$
1545 Overton Park
(901) 278–9774

This colorful neighborhood restaurant in midtown is tailor-made for special nights, with its romantic atmosphere, rich Italian cuisine, and attentive service. Marena's recently added a list of Italian wines and focused its menu on specialties from northern Italy. You'll find choices such as jumbo shrimp and scallops on pasta with a white-wine sauce, and grilled rack of lamb with a marsala-wine sauce. Dessert lovers will be very happy with Marena's signature crème caramel and meringue cake with chocolate sauce, longtime favorites of Memphis diners. Open for dinner Tuesday through Saturday. The restaurant serves beer and wine only, and smoking is not allowed. A classical guitarist plays during dinner.

Melange $$–$$$
948 South Cooper
(901) 276–0002

This stylish Cooper-Young restaurant garners rave reviews for its fresh, well-prepared European-Asian cuisine. Melange is actually two places: the swank, quiet dining room with no smoking, and a bar with a menu of tapas (plates of "little bites," served with cocktails in the Spanish tradition), with late hours and smoking. The tapas include such delectables as steamed black mussels, house-smoked salmon, and grilled vegetable terrine, which you can eat at the bar or at a table. You can order from the restaurant dessert menu as well. Pass through the double doors into "The Dining Room at Melange," and it's a different world, with bleached wood, green plants, fresh flowers, and white linen tablecloths. Among its signature dishes is roast lamb ribeye with goat cheese and a zinfandel reduction, caramelized escolar, and hot Grand Marnier soufflé, although the menu changes seasonally. The service is professional, and the wine list, which won kudos from *Wine Spectator* in 2001, is one of the best in the city even though Melange has been open only since 2000.

Melange is open for dinner seven nights. Even after the dining room closes, you can order from the tapas menu until the wee hours.

Melos Taverna $–$$
2021 Madison Avenue
(901) 725–1863

Quietly busy for many years, this intimate family-run restaurant serves a menu of Greek specialties including dolmades, moussaka, roasted lamb, and souvlaki, brought to your table with loving care by Melos's longtime servers. The generous Grecian-feast platters in the back of the menu are the best deal, because you can try lots of different items in one meal. If earlier diners haven't already snapped all of it up, be sure to try the marinated-octopus appetizer. Most dinner portions are quite generous, so ask your server what's reasonable for your party. Often one dinner plus appetizers is plenty for two people, and the platters are big enough to feed a herd. The restaurant is cozy and dark, with candles in wine bottles and checked tablecloths. The short and modest wine

Kid-Friendly Dining

The challenge to eating out with kids is to find a restaurant that welcomes kids but also has good food for adults. These restaurants are winners on both fronts, and each has a casual, laid-back atmosphere. (Turn to the Kidstuff chapter for more details about these restaurants.)

Dyer's Burgers
205 Beale Street
(901) 527–DYER
Great burgers and stuff. (See the write-up in the Downtown section of this chapter.)

El Porton
Poplar and Highland
(901) 452–7330
A kid-friendly midtown Mexican restaurant.

Fino's from the Hill
1853 Madison Avenue
(901) 272–3466
A great place to buy picnic fare. (See write-up in the Midtown section of this chapter.)

Garibaldi's
3530 Walker Avenue
(901) 327–6111
Kids love the combination of pizza and game arcade.

Hard Rock Café
315 Beale Street
(901) 529–0007
Popular for older kids.

Huey's
77 South Second Street
(901) 527–2700
Good burgers anytime and live music on Sundays. Other locations around town.

(See the write-up in Midtown section of this chapter.)

Kwik Chek #10
2013 Madison Avenue
(901) 274–9293
Another good bet for picnic fare, particularly for parents. (See the write-up in Midtown section of this chapter.)

The Peanut Shoppe
24 Main Street
(901) 525–1115
Fresh-roasted peanuts and other treats.

Sekisui Downtown
160 Union Avenue
(901) 523–0001
Has something for everyone, with a Japanese and an American menu. The Midtown location appeals to kids as well. (See the write-up in Downtown section of this chapter.)

Spaghetti Warehouse
40 West Huling Street
(901) 521–0907
You can get spaghetti and other Italian dishes at this family-oriented restaurant.

Sean's Deli and Smooth Moves
75 South Main Street
(901) 529–1000
Hot sandwiches and cold fruit smoothies.

list includes a number of Greek wines. Melos is a good deal for families, as children under 6 eat free and those 6 to 12 get a price break. Open for dinner Tuesday through Saturday.

Memphis Pizza Café $
2087 Madison Avenue
(901) 726–5343
5061 Park Avenue
(901) 684–1306

With its cracker-crisp thin crust and fresh toppings, the pizza at this trio of ultra-casual restaurants has been embraced by locals since the first cafe opened in 1994. Pizzas of note are the Café Supreme with seven meat and veggie toppings, Veggie Supreme with eight toppings, and the Alternative, a white pizza with no sauce but plenty of mozzarella and garlic. The menu also includes calzone, a few salads, and sandwiches, and there's beer and a few wines by the glass. During the nice weather, check out the back deck. Open every day for lunch and dinner.

Mojo's Greek and Mediterranean $–$$
775 South Highland
(901) 458–0030
This nondescript student hangout near the University of Memphis serves good Middle Eastern fare, including roast lamb and hen stuffed with rice and ground beef. Lighter fare includes falafel, hummus, and sandwiches that are easy on the wallet. Mojo's serves beer only. The restaurant is wheelchair accessible, but the rest rooms are not. Open for lunch and dinner Monday through Saturday.

Molly's La Casita $–$$
2006 Madison Avenue
(901) 726–1873
Housed in a bright-pink building near Overton Square, this longtime midtown business serves up a great Tex-Mex menu that includes all the usual suspects such as fajitas, chiles rellenos, quesadillas, and burritos. One of the oldest restaurants in midtown, Molly's has been open for more than 20 years. It's a very popular spot and has tons of regulars, who are often on a first-name basis with the servers. Open seven days a week for lunch and dinner. There's a parking lot behind the restaurant.

Morocco Café $$
786 Echles
(901) 324–6688
Eating at this modest restaurant, situated on a quiet street near the University of Memphis, makes you feel as though you're taking a trip to exotic lands. Morocco Café serves a savory mosaic of Middle Eastern specialties including couscous with lamb, roasted chicken, hummus, falafel, and kabobs. The owner, a native of Jerusalem, is friendly and happy to answer any questions you might have about the food. Open for lunch and dinner every day except Sunday. The restaurant does not have a liquor or beer license, so be sure to bring your own if you're drinking.

Obadiah's Café $
1553 Madison Avenue
(901) 722–2266
Right in the middle of this former bakery belonging to local musical-instruments retailer Strings and Things, Obadiah's serves sandwiches, salads, and homemade soups as well as a decadent array of desserts. Order at the counter, then choose a table in the lofty, sunlit dining room to enjoy your lunch or sweet. The cafe also serves espresso drinks, which makes it a perfect place to enjoy coffee and dessert, which includes a sinful carrot cake, a variety of cheesecakes, and that ultimate Southern comfort food, banana pudding. No beer or liquor is sold here, however. Closed on Sundays and Mondays. There's a covered parking garage that's part of the building, a welcome amenity on rainy days. No smoking allowed.

On Teur $–$$
2015 Madison Avenue
(901) 725–6059
This breezy, hip eatery near Overton Square in midtown has gained a huge following of Memphians and Rhodes College students for scallops Henri, steak Saigon, and other delicious, flavorfully sauced dishes. There's the tiny dining room, where you can watch the chefs at work, or the tented deck area strewn with pinlights. (It's enclosed and climate controlled, except during nice weather, when the sides are removed.) On Teur is a Midtown institution, and the food speaks for itself. *Note:* Pay attention if a dish is described as hot, because they aren't kidding. Your server can give you the skinny about the heat. On Teur serves beer but not wine or liquor. Bring your own, or get directions to the

liquor store just down the street. Open daily for lunch and dinner.

Paulette's $$–$$$
2110 Madison Avenue
(901) 726–5128

This pretty, charming restaurant in Overton Square is a tried-and-true Memphis "cornerstone" restaurant for an elegant lunch or Sunday brunch, not to mention a romantic dinner for two. It's decorated like a quaint French country inn, with stucco walls and dark, exposed beams, and has live piano music on weekends. As for the food, Paulette's serves up its traditional standards, such as fillet Paulette and Louisiana shrimp crepes, and is famous for the hot, freshly made popovers served at every meal. You'll find plenty of crepes, salads, and other choices, including elegant variations on eggs Benedict for brunch, as well as luscious desserts. There's piano music on weekends. Open for lunch Monday through Saturday, dinner every day, and for Sunday brunch. Reservations recommended.

Pho Pasteur $–$$
38 North Cleveland
(901) 728–4711

This Vietnamese pho restaurant specializes in savory noodle soups that can be ordered many different ways, depending on your tastes. Pho Pasteur also has an extensive menu of Vietnamese and Chinese dishes like Vietnamese fried chicken, chow mein, and all kinds of stir-fry dishes. If you have a sweet tooth, check out the pineapple freezes. Closed on Tuesday. The clean and bright restaurant has its beer license, and although the dining room is wheelchair accessible, the rest room is not.

Ronnie Grisanti & Sons $$–$$$
2855 Poplar Avenue
(901) 323–0007

This is one of the city's outstanding restaurants, featuring the cuisine of Tuscany as well as traditional Italian dishes such as handmade ravioli and manicotti, for which the Grisanti family is known. The kitchen is in the hands of fourth-generation sons Alex and Judd Grisanti, who learned their trade both inside and outside the family and who travel to Tuscany each year to gather new ideas. The result is a menu that's sophisticated, varied, and dazzling enough to be featured in *Food Arts* magazine. Nightly specials are always worth a try, particularly the fish. Always tasty dishes like steak stuffed with gorgonzola, veal chops, and pumpkin ravioli are pleasers. As tempting as these options may be, you'll be glad you saved room for the restaurant's grand desserts, naturally all made on the premises. Ronnie's, as locals call the restaurant, is wildly popular, and because it doesn't take reservations except for large groups, expect to wait for a table, especially on the weekends. Open for dinner Monday through Saturday.

Sabor Tropical $–$$
2617 Poplar Avenue
(901) 323–2600

The midtown location of this authentic Cuban restaurant. See listing in Winchester/Hickory Hill/South Memphis section for more information.

Saigon Le $–$$
51 North Cleveland
(901) 276–5326

The food at this family-run Vietnamese restaurant is bright, fresh, and so flavorful you'll want to try everything. Try the fresh spring rolls, deep-fried Saigon egg rolls, noodle dishes, and soups of all kinds. Start with an order of the delicious green-shell mussels with French butter sauce. The decor is nothing special, but it's comfortable and clean. This restaurant has a loyal following of Memphis regulars, including families. Saigon Le is situated on Cleveland between Madison and Poplar. Unless you're drinking beer or nonalcoholic beverages, bring your own bottle. Open for lunch and dinner Monday through Saturday; closes at 9:00 P.M. The restaurant is wheelchair accessible but the rest rooms are not.

Sekisui Midtown $–$$
25 South Belvedere Boulevard
(901) 735–0005

A Japanese restaurant/sushi bar with several locations around town, the midtown location is a favorite for its sushi happy hour during the week. See listing in East Memphis section for more information.

Side Street Grill $–$$
31 South Florence Street
(901) 274-8955

This Overton Square bar, popular for its martinis, serves dinners at great prices and a limited menu until the wee hours. The dinner menu includes steaks for under $15, which, with potato or vegetable and salad, makes for a filling dinner, as well as pastas and a popular grilled-salmon fillet. For nice weather there's a great patio in the front that faces a quiet street. Open seven days a week for dinner.

Tsunami $$–$$$
928 South Cooper
(901) 274-2556

This hip eatery, which operates in midtown's Cooper-Young neighborhood, serves up wonderfully prepared fish and seafood dishes as well as soups and salads with an Asian flair. The sake-steamed mussels and crispy calamari are standouts among the appetizers, and any entree that's served with black Thai rice is a must. Roast sea bass with soy beurre blanc is Tsunami's signature dish, but you won't go wrong with other options, which might include spice-crusted tuna and hot and pungent shrimp with coconut milk. Open Monday through Saturday for dinner.

Zinnie's East $–$$
1718 Madison Avenue
(901) 274-7101

Zinnie's East has been a laid-back hangout in Midtown Memphis for more than 15 years. It serves a menu of sandwiches, salads, and entrees that include grilled brochette, steaks, and shrimp. The offbeat "Zinnie-loney" sandwich is a thick hand-cut slice of blackened baloney—not healthy, but very good! It serves a Sunday brunch, and for lunch a menu of sandwiches and plate lunches. A good reason to eat at Zinnie's is the great front deck, where you can watch the world go by during nice weather. Zinnie's is also a popular nightspot. Open every day for lunch and dinner.

East Memphis

Asian Palace Express $–$$
4978 Park Avenue
(901) 761-7888

The East Memphis takeout branch of this excellent Chinese restaurant. See listing in Raleigh section for more information.

Blue Plate Café $
5469 Poplar Avenue
(901) 761-9696

Just off the I-240 exit and convenient to many East Memphis hotels, this bright yellow house is one of the few places in Memphis where you can get a big old-fashioned breakfast, complete with pancakes. It's packed on the weekends, and in addition to serving breakfast all day, Blue Plate also serves plate lunches. Open every day for all meals except Sunday dinner.

Bogie's Delicatessen $
715 S. Mendenhall Road
(901) 761-5846

This unpretentious deli makes great sandwiches, which feature Boar's Head deli meats and cheeses, as well as salads and soups. The homemade prepared salads are outstanding, particularly the potato salad and the fresh shrimp salad, available only on Fridays. Order the salad-sampler platter if you want to try them all. For some reason Bogie's has red, ripe tomatoes all year round, a nice touch on both salads and sandwiches. You order at the counter, and they'll bring your food to your table. Open for lunch Monday through Saturday; hours vary by location.

Bravo! Ristorante $$–$$$
939 Ridge Lake Boulevard
(901) 684-6664

During dinner at Bravo the waiters and waitresses dish up not only your entrees, but also arias and show tunes. The live music makes this hotel restaurant, tucked on the lower level of the Adam's Mark Hotel, a nice place to celebrate a festive occasion or a big business deal. The kitchen fixes pastas, seafood, and steak, including such favorites as fried calamari, a seafood medley over pasta, and beef tenderloin with gorgonzola cheese and portabella mushrooms. The restaurant also serves breakfast and lunch, but without the music. Open seven days a week.

Brontë $
387 Perkins Extended
(901) 374–0881

This bistro is frequented by book lovers as well as people who have never heard of the Brontë sisters. Although most bookstore cafes in Memphis offer mainly coffee, sweets, and sandwiches, Brontë, situated inside Davis-Kidd Booksellers in Laurelwood shopping center, has a large menu with all kinds of entrees, salads, and other fare. The walnut-spinach and roasted-garlic linguine is a big seller, as is the chicken-wonton salad, served on greens with crisp wontons. This is a great place for dessert, especially the blueberry pie, an entire ¼ pie, served with ice cream if you like. It's open for lunch and supper and serves light brunch fare most days. Open seven days a week, closing early on Sundays. Beer and wine are available, but smoking is not allowed.

Brooklyn Bridge Italian Restaurant $$
1779 Kirby Parkway
(901) 755–7413

This family-owned Italian restaurant features lasagne Amalfitano, manicotti, and other pastas as well as entrees like veal and shrimp scampi. The Correale family's homemade sauce goes on the specialty of the house: Brooklyn Bridge's well-known pizza. This is New York–style Italian food served in an attractive place with friendly service. What could be better? Open for dinner Monday through Saturday.

Café Orleans $
919 South Yates
(901) 888–6836

This casual East Memphis lunch place, operated by the same folks who run Owen Brennan's restaurant, serves up great New Orleans style fare, including po'boys, muffalettas, crawfish étoufée, and gumbo, to name a few. There's a good selection of prepared dinners, which you can pick out yourself from the huge refrigerated glass case that lines an entire wall of the restaurant. Although the sandwiches are worth waiting for, this is probably not the place to eat if you're on a tight schedule, for the service can be slow if it's crowded. Consider phoning in your order in advance. Open for lunch only Monday through Friday.

Christopher's $$–$$$
712 West Brookhaven Circle
(901) 682–5202

This elegant fine-dining restaurant features the culinary artistry of Memphis chef Christopher Lee, who serves an American eclectic menu with dishes such as sea scallops in Rockefeller sauce, pepper-seared tuna carpaccio, and medallions of veal Chateaubriand. The service and ambiance make this an excellent choice for a special-occasion dinner. Two desserts that are always first-rate are the Grand Marnier crème brûlée and the walnut-bread French toast with caramelized bananas and ginger ice cream. Open for dinner only, Tuesday through Saturday. Reservations recommended.

Ciao Bella da Guglielmo $–$$
522 South Mendenhall, Suite 300
(901) 205–2500

This tiny neighborhood restaurant features handmade pizzas, pastas, and other Italian specialties served in a bustling, casual atmosphere. Situated next to a Kroger supermarket (oddly enough), it's a great favorite among Memphians for its fresh, well-prepared dishes. Open for lunch Monday through Friday and for dinner every night.

City Bread Company $
575 South Mendenhall
(901) 682–3500

This cheerful East Memphis bakery serves sandwiches, soup, and other light fare for lunch as well as coffee and pastries in the mornings. Among the favorite sandwiches are smoked turkey with sliced apples, curried-chicken salad, and homemade pimento cheese. No beer or liquor. Open Monday through Saturday for lunch.

Erling Jensen, The Restaurant $$$–$$$$
1044 South Yates
(901) 763–3700
www.ejensen.com

The culinary artistry of Danish-born Erling Jensen is the centerpiece of this top-echelon East Memphis restaurant, which along with its chef has been voted the city's best by readers of *Memphis* magazine each year since 1997. The simple exterior of this pale-yellow house near busy Poplar Avenue and its mellow but elegant interior don't prepare you for the plates of food, visual works of art that are scrumptious beyond belief. Chilean sea bass with shellfish and spiced lemongrass broth, wild-boar rack with cherry sauce, lobster pancakes with wild mushrooms, and chilled lobster and crabmeat salad with truffle vinaigrette—these are just a few examples as Erling incorporates global elements into a foundation of traditional French cooking. The portions are so generous that dessert may seem impossible, but it's worth making room for the likes of roasted pineapple with caramelized coconut and crème fraiche, the soufflé du jour, and crème brûlée. The menu changes often but always includes some salads, black Angus steaks, and other items for less fanciful tastes. The wine list, which includes some modestly priced choices, is a worthy companion to the food. Erling Jensen is definitely one of the priciest places in town, but it's money well spent for lavish portions of sublime and beautifully-presented food, for service that's professional, friendly, but not stuffy, and for the ambiance. Open nightly for dinner. Reservations recommended and a jacket for men recommended but not required. Valet parking available.

Folk's Folly $$–$$$$
551 South Mendenhall
(901) 762–8200

This pricey steakhouse packs in the expense-account crowd and plenty of loyal regulars, who return here for hand-cut aged steaks, Maine lobster, grilled Scottish salmon, and other delectables. Started by businessman Humphrey Folk in 1977, it continues to please lots of diners. The wine list here is one of the city's most extensive and has earned The *Wine Spectator* Award of Excellence. Many Memphians swear by the restaurant's butcher shop, where you can buy the same steaks and seafood served at the restaurant to take home and cook yourself. There's also a lounge and piano bar called The Cellar. Open every day for dinner; free valet parking is available. Reservations recommended.

Frank Grisanti's Italian Restaurant $$–$$$
1022 Shady Grove
(901) 761–9462

This handsome Italian restaurant is owned and operated by Frank Grisanti, who's part of the third generation of this renowned local restaurant family. It's inside the Embassy Suites Hotel next to Regalia shopping center, and hotel guests there or at the neighboring Hampton Inn can get room service from the restaurant. Some of the many Italian specialties are seafood fra Diavolo, angel-hair primavera, manicotti, ravioli, and a family tradition, Elfo Special, a buttery shrimp and spaghetti dish. Frank Grisanti's also serves steaks, including its 16-ounce New York strip and rib-eye Toscano, and several veal and fish entrees. You can eat in the wood-paneled dining rooms or at one of the tables outside the restaurant in the lofty atrium of the Embassy Suites Hotel.

The Grove Grill $$–$$$
4550 Poplar Avenue
(901) 818–9951

This lively and hopping East Memphis restaurant, tucked away in the back of Laurelwood shopping center, attracts big crowds of East Memphis residents. They love the warm atmosphere, the fresh oysters, and Southern-accented menu with dishes like hickory-smoked pork chops, black Angus New York strip with béarnaise, and low-country style shrimp and grits. Open every day for lunch and dinner. Reservations recommended.

The Half Shell $–$$
688 South Mendenhall
(901) 682–3966

This unpretentious East Memphis watering hole looks as if it could be on the beach

Southern Home-Cooking Restaurants

Around Memphis hearty, home-cooked meals are usually called plate lunches, although you do hear them called meat-and-threes, because you generally get a choice of three vegetables with fried chicken, meat loaf, or other meat. Of course, in the deep South, macaroni and cheese, congealed salad, and cottage cheese all count as vegetables. The tradition of a big midday meal dates back to the days before air-conditioning, when in order to keep the house cool, Southern families cooked the main meal in the mornings, then served cool leftovers for supper. Plate lunches are served with cornbread and rolls, and locals order "sweet tea"—the authentic stuff is strong iced tea with a TNT blast of sugar. These restaurants usually have a different menu every day, and regulars have their favorites—chicken-fried steak day at Yellow Rose or pot-roast day at Little Tea Shop. Plate lunches are also served in restaurants and bars all over town, including Dino's Grill in midtown, Patrick's in East Memphis, and Mister B's in Germantown. Plate lunches rarely cost more than $8.00 per person, including drink and tax.

Alcenia's Desserts & Preserves Shop
317 North Main Street
(901) 523–0200
This cheery eatery, with its bright table-cloths, pink walls, and black-and-white linoleum, serves soul-food favorites such as catfish, fried chicken, turnip greens, and fried green tomatoes. You'll receive a warm welcome from owner BJ Chester-Tamayo, who uses her mother's recipes and knows many of her customers by name. All the meats are cooked to order, so that's about a 20-minute extra wait for the fried chicken or other entree that arrives at your table piping hot. The desserts are sumptuous: Don't miss the buttery, pecan-encrusted bread pudding or the German chocolate cake. Alcenia's also serves breakfast on Saturday mornings, with specialties that include salmon croquettes, fried green tomatoes, pancakes, and omelets. Open for lunch Tuesday through Friday, with early dinner hours on nights when there's a Memphis Grizzlies game or other special event.

Buntyn Café
4972 Park
(901) 844–2233
1725 Appling Road, Cordova
(901) 380–1725
The Wiggins family has been serving up home-cooked meals since 1946, including homemade yeast rolls the size of Big Macs. Pricier than most lunch places, the Buntyn serves huge portions in an atmosphere that's more dressed up than most. Favorites include its signature vegetable-beef soup (with or without a grilled-cheese sandwich), batter-fried chicken, cobbler of the day, and homemade icebox pie. Until 1998 Buntyn operated in midtown across the street from the railroad, where at one time passengers and railroad workers were frequent customers, but its loyal clientele has followed to East Memphis (Park) and the suburbs (Cordova) locations. Open for lunch and dinner Monday through Friday, for Saturday dinner, and Sunday lunch. Smoking is not allowed at either restaurant.

Cupboard Restaurant
1400 Union Avenue
(901) 276–8015
www.cupboardmemphis.com
149 Madison Avenue
(901) 527–9111
At their hugely popular downtown and midtown restaurants, the Cavallo family serves huge portions of fresh vegetables and casseroles, including turnip greens, corn pudding, fried green tomatoes, and spiced beets, meat (including meat loaf and fried chicken on various days) optional. You could easily make a meal on one or two of the vegetables. In summer Cup-

board gets plentiful supplies of flavorful Ripley, Tennessee, homegrown tomatoes. If you still have room, the desserts include lemon and chocolate icebox pies as well as fruit cobblers. The downtown location is a block east of Main Street and opens for weekday lunch only. The midtown location, which has plenty of parking in the back lot, opens for lunch and dinner during the week and lunch only on Sundays.

Ellen's Soul Food
601 South Parkway East
(901) 942–4888
This south Memphis family restaurant is as basic as it gets, with its bare-bones decor and handwritten menus, but you can't beat the fried chicken, meat loaf, and baked chicken that come out of the kitchen. With your meat entree you'll get a choice of two vegetables (be sure to try the greens if they're on the menu that day) and a plate of piping-hot johnnycakes (thick cornmeal pancakes), which by themselves are worth the price of admission. Ellen's serves a traditional breakfast and, for lunch and early dinner, its soul food menu, Tuesday through Saturday. No credit cards.

Little Tea Shop
69 Monroe Avenue
(901) 525–6000
This friendly plate-lunch restaurant has been serving up homemade favorites since 1918. Under the careful management of Suhair Lauck, the Tea Shop attracts a who's who of downtown Memphis business executives and lawyers. Once at your table, you mark your choices on a long menu sheet that serves as your bill. The menu changes every day, with rotating favorites such as fried chicken, corn beef, and chicken pot pie. Don't miss the buttery cornbread sticks here, and this is a great place to try turnip greens cooked Southern style. If you're not in the mood for meat and vegetables, try the chicken or tuna salad, which arrive on a pretty plateful of fruit. Open for lunch only Monday through Friday. Despite its name it's not open for afternoon tea.

Woman's Exchange
88 Racine Street
(901) 327–5681
Established in 1885 and tucked away in a small midtown house off Poplar, Woman's Exchange volunteers operate a tearoom where you can get an old-fashioned Southern ladies' luncheon, complete with homemade rolls and congealed salad. The menu is limited to a few selections, which change every day, and sometimes include seafood gumbo, chicken salad, and beef tenderloin. While you're there, browse through the gift shop, where you'll find pricey, exquisite handmade children's clothing and other gifts. Open for lunch only Monday through Friday and occasionally for afternoon tea. No smoking.

Yellow Rose
56 North Main Street
(901) 527–5692
Joe Keating's popular downtown lunch restaurant serves up hot, fresh homemade rolls, crunchy chicken-fried steak, fluffy mashed potatoes, and other plate-lunch basics that keep it packed with customers, most of them regulars who work nearby. Keating faxes each day's menu to downtown offices, which results in a lively take-out business as well as reminders of which favorites are being offered that day. The friendly waitresses have been there for years and have their jobs down to a science. Tucked into the corner of the Lincoln American building on Main Street next to Court Square, it's worth overlooking the drab decor for the food, including some of the best yeast rolls on the Memphis lunch circuit. Yellow Rose also serves breakfast until 10:00 A.M. Open Monday through Friday for breakfast and lunch.

somewhere, with its cypress-wood and lanai feel. Specialties of the house are whatever fresh fish has been flown into Memphis that day, along with seafood gumbo, pasta, steaks, and shrimp. This place qualifies as a local landmark, having been in business at the same corner for many years. Later in the evening a cocktail crowd develops, as the 30-something and 40-something set prowl the bar. The Half Shell is open from lunch through late night dinner seven days a week.

Houston's $–$$$
5000 Poplar Avenue
(901) 683–0915

The restaurant may be part of a chain, but the friendly, attentive service and dependably good food make it a local award winner year after year. The restaurant stays busy with patrons who come for both the royal treatment and for prime rib, grilled fish, hearty salads, and sandwiches. The dark wood helps to create an intimate ambiance. The restaurant is situated back from Poplar, west of Wild Oats food market. Expect to wait for a table during the most popular mealtimes, particularly on weekends, when it can take as long as 45 minutes to get seated. Open every day for lunch and dinner.

Jarrett's $$–$$$
5689 Quince Road
(901) 763–2254
www.jarretts.com

Don't let the modesty of its location in an East Memphis shopping center fool you. This warm and lively bistro is where Memphis-born chef Richard Farmer works wonders in the kitchen. Readers of *Memphis* magazine voted Jarrett's (named for the Farmers' son) the most underrated restaurant in town, while voting Farmer, who has cooked at the James Beard House in New York, as one of the city's best chefs. Jarrett's serves a creative American regional menu featuring mushroom-and-cheese strudel, smoked-trout ravioli with Arkansas caviar, horseradish-encrusted grouper, and pecan barbecue rack of lamb. Lots of pride is taken in the wine list, which features California and French vintages, and wine tastings are held at the restaurant almost every Monday. Open for dinner Monday through Saturday. Look for the restaurant at Yorkshire shopping center on Quince, just a few blocks west of Ridgeway.

Jason's Deli $
1199 Ridgeway
(901) 685–3333
www.jasonsdeli.com

This large, cheerful deli with red-leatherette booths may be another chain restaurant, but it has definitely won over the hearts of Memphians, who love the extensive salad bar (perhaps the best in town), muffalettas, and other hot sandwiches. You place your order at the counter and pay, and servers bring you your food. The menu, which is quite long, includes healthy-heart selections, fine soups, and stuffed baked potatoes. The free soft ice cream is a nice, friendly touch. Jason's is packed at lunchtime, so expect a line during the busiest times. Open every day for lunch and dinner.

Jim's Place $$–$$$
5560 Shelby Oaks
(901) 388–7200

Jim's Place, family owned and operated, is one of the city's oldest restaurants, having moved from downtown Memphis to its current location in the 1970s. It's situated off the beaten path on a woodsy lot amid warehouses and other commercial businesses off Summer Avenue. This large and beloved Memphis establishment is chopped up into smaller, cozy dining rooms nicely decorated in different styles, with views of the grounds particularly attractive in spring and summer. Greek specialties such as pork tenderloin or beef kabobs grace the menu, as well as shrimp stuffed with lump crabmeat, grouper Pontchartrain, and excellent steaks. Jim's Place is a wonderful setting in which to celebrate a birthday or other special occasion. Open for lunch Monday through Friday and for dinner Monday through Saturday. Reservations accepted during the week and on weekends only for large parties.

Lulu Grille $$–$$$
565 Erin
(901) 763–3677

Every neighborhood should have a place like this around the corner. This bistro has a loyal East Memphis following, as regulars have been swarming here for 10 years for such favorites as shrimp and lump crabmeat with bow-tie pasta, grilled lamb loin, and grilled ruby-red trout. The desserts are to die for here, and you certainly wouldn't want to pass up the coconut cake or chocolate-mousse cake. The ambiance is cozy and romantic, and the food is consistently wonderful. You may have to hunt for the restaurant, which is tucked in the back of White Station Plaza shopping center. Open for lunch and dinner Monday through Saturday. Reservations recommended.

Mantia's $-$$
4856 Poplar Avenue
(901) 762-8560
Mantia's, a bustling East Memphis gourmet shop, is also a restaurant, serving up sandwiches, salads, and pastas for lunch and a smaller menu of somewhat more substantial fare for dinner. Among sandwiches the homemade chicken salad, pimento cheese, and panini caprese are always smart picks; salad choices include an Oriental chicken salad with mandarin oranges and a club salad. The evening menu is heavy on pastas, such as rosemary chicken ravioli and pasta primavera. Wine and beer are available. Open for lunch Monday through Saturday and for dinner Tuesday through Friday. You can't see Mantia's from Poplar, because it's hidden behind the liquor store on the north side of the street, but it's back there. (See the Shopping chapter for details on the gourmet shop.)

Mikasa Japan $$-$$$
6150 Poplar Avenue
(901) 683-0000
Tucked in the Regalia shopping center, Mikasa is a favorite among many local aficionados of Japanese cuisine. It features traditional dishes with an emphasis on seafood, with shrimp tempura, chicken teriyaki, and sushi. Open for dinner every day; lunch Monday through Friday.

Napa Café $$-$$$
5101 Sanderlin Avenue
(901) 683-0441
This fine-dining restaurant, a sister to Paulette's in midtown and Three Oaks Grill in Germantown, features eclectic American favorites such as rack of lamb and sesame-encrusted salmon. It's situated inside Sanderlin Center shopping center, located just east of the East Memphis Hilton. Open for lunch weekdays and dinner Monday through Saturday. Closed Sunday.

Owen Brennan's $$
6150 Poplar Avenue
(901) 761-0990
This festive restaurant brings a taste of New Orleans to Memphis with its Big Easy ambiance, authentic Creole specialties, and live jazz on weekends. Although not run by the Brennan family of restaurants in New Orleans, Owen Brennan's serves up very authentic po'boys, shrimp Creole, jambalaya, and other specialties. For a festive occasion order the bananas Foster, which will be flambéed and served at your table. The main dining room, with its ultra-high ceilings, is festooned with Mardi Gras decor, and there are smaller, more intimate rooms available as well as an enclosed patio area. The brunch is extremely popular here, featuring eggs Sardou and other dishes off the menu as well as a lavish buffet. Open for lunch and dinner Monday through Saturday and for brunch on Sunday.

Pete and Sam's $$
3886 Park Avenue
(901) 458-0694
This family-owned and operated Italian restaurant is a true Memphis institution and one of the city's most loved restaurants. Here they serve up an array of Italian specialties, including homemade lasagne, spaghetti and meatballs, and Italian spinach. Believe it or not, the steaks are awesome, too! The standout for many diners is the handmade pizzas, which feature such toppings as roasted peppers and barbecue chicken. It looks like the decor hasn't changed a bit in 50 years, although it was completely remodeled a few years ago. Beer is available. Reservations are recommended

Memphis Barbecue

Memphis doesn't fancy itself the capital of pork barbecue for nothing. Dozens of restaurants of all sizes practice the art and science of cooking smoky, flavorful pork ribs and shoulder, as well as other barbecued meats such as beef, poultry, and shrimp.

First, here's a quick primer on Memphis barbecue:

Memphis-style barbecue differs from its counterparts in Texas and elsewhere in that it's mostly pork (unlike Texas barbecue, which is usually beef). The sauce is a tomato-based sauce with varying degrees of heat (unlike that in the Carolinas, where the sauce is vinegar-based).

In Memphis ribs are served in two styles, dry and wet. Dry ribs are cooked without sauce; instead they are rubbed with a mixture of dried spices and herbs before cooking for flavoring. Some restaurants sprinkle on more of the seasoning on ribs before serving. Wet ribs are cooked in sauce and arrive at the table generously doused with sauce. You eat them with your hands, so don't even try to be neat about it.

Pork shoulder is served on a plate or on a bun, usually with sauce and always with a mustardy coleslaw as its only dressing. The pork is usually pulled (that is, pieces of meat are pulled off the bone by hand) but can be ordered sliced or chopped as well.

Barbecue is usually served with coleslaw and beans, although other options include potato salad or barbecue spaghetti, a peculiarly Memphis concoction consisting of spaghetti tossed with bits of meat and barbecue sauce. If you aren't ordering a sandwich, you'll find that at many places your order will arrive with "edible napkins," aka slices of white bread.

Proprietors of Memphis barbecue restaurants are happy for you to purchase some of their sauce or seasoning (and these make great gifts for the folks back home), but don't count on being able to pry loose any secret recipes.

Enjoying great Memphis barbecue won't break the bank: Prices generally run from $4.00 or less for a sandwich to $10–$14 for a large order of ribs.

If you want to really see people go crazy over perfecting pork barbecue, don't miss the World Championship Barbecue Cook Contest that takes place in Memphis each May. (See the Annual Events chapter for more information.)

Big S Grill & Lounge
1179 Dunnavant Street
(901) 775–9127

The kitchen in this small white building in South Memphis serves up great barbecue pork-shoulder sandwiches on toasted buns and rib sandwiches as well as great French fries and burgers. (Specify hot or mild, and believe it when they say "hot.") The pitmaster is J. C. Hardaway, a longtime Memphis barbecue man who was featured in the book and film Smokestack Lightning. Big S has a lounge atmosphere, a jukebox with blues and R&B standards, and a bar, where you can get your beer in a can, long-neck bottle, or quart bottle. This is an excursion for the barbecue adventurer, and one that can be tied in with a visit to the nearby Stax Museum of American Music. To get there from Union Avenue, turn south onto Bellevue, go about a mile and a half and turn left onto McLemore. Turn right onto Dunnavant just before the railroad tracks. Exercise caution, since this is not a great neighborhood. Open seven days a week for lunch and dinner (until 7:00 or 8:00 P.M.), then stays open later as a lounge.

Corky's Ribs & BBQ
5259 Poplar Avenue
(901) 685–9744
www.corkysbbq.com
1740 North Germantown Parkway, Cordova
(901) 737–1988
743 West Poplar Avenue, Collierville
(901) 405–4999

Corky's serves up some of the most popular ribs and pork shoulder in town at its three suburban restaurants. The meats are slow-cooked over hickory wood and charcoal, and you can order the ribs in both dry and wet styles. The restaurants are casual, rustic-style places, where you can expect to wait for a table during peak dinner hours, because they don't take reservations. All three have a drive-through window, so you can get your barbecue to go. Corky's also does a huge mail-order business (see the Web site for more information) and sells its meats (frozen), sauce, and seasoning at supermarkets. It has been voted the best ribs restaurant in Memphis for more than 15 years by readers of *Memphis* magazine. The Cordova and Poplar Avenue restaurants serve beer, but no liquor or wine. Open every day except Thanksgiving and Christmas. *Note:* You will see Corky's franchises in other parts of the South, but the Memphis locations are operated hands-on by the Pelts family, the original owners.

Cozy Corner Restaurant
745 North Parkway
(901) 527–9158

Situated east of downtown at Parkway and Manassas, this modest family operation cooks up fabulous barbecue, including some of Memphis's finest ribs, sliced pork or beef sandwiches with slaw, and delectable barbecued baloney sandwiches (no kidding). But the pièce de résistance is the barbecued Cornish hen, pink with smoked flavor and just the right size for one person, which even impressed Julia Child during a visit in the 1980s. Everything can be ordered either hot or mild (and mind you, mild still packs plenty of flavor). You line up at the counter to place your order, then settle in at a formica-topped table to wait for your number to be called. Cozy Corner was started in 1977 by Ray Robinson Sr., who held court at a front table until his death in 2001. At present his family is carrying on the tradition in splendid fashion. Open for lunch Tuesday–Saturday, but if your heart is set on sampling the Cornish hens, get there early, because they often sell out before the 5:00 P.M. closing time. No beer or alcoholic beverages.

The Germantown Commissary
2290 South Germantown Road, Germantown
(901) 754–5540

This rustic barbecue shack, steeped with hickory smoke and situated near the railroad tracks, certainly looks the part. It has operated for more than 20 years and has many regular customers and fans. In 2001, when the *Wall Street Journal* tested mail-order barbecue in its Weekend section, Germantown Commissary was the only Memphis-area purveyor of 'cue to make their list of favorites. The Commissary serves up excellent ribs (sort of in between wet and dry), barbecue shrimp, and sandwiches as well as variations on the traditional such as barbecue nachos and a barbecue salad. Beer is available. Don't forget the homemade lemon, coconut, and chocolate pies, that is, if you have any room left. Open every day for lunch and dinner; reservations for groups of 12 or more only.

Interstate Bar-B-Q & Restaurant
2265 South Third Street
(901) 775–2304

So named because it's near where the interstate crosses Third Street, Interstate is operated by Jim Neely, widely considered the godfather of Memphis barbecue. This casual, bustling restaurant serves up great pulled-pork sandwiches and generously cut ribs, but the sauce is a real standout: dark, thick, rich, smoky, and sweet but not too sweet. This is a good place to try that Memphis concoction, barbecue spaghetti. Interstate has a drive-through as well. Because Third Street becomes Highway 61, this is the road you'll be taking to the casinos and other Mississippi Delta destinations, so you might want to stop off at Interstate for a "pig samich" for the road. Open Monday through Saturday for lunch and dinner.

Neely's Bar-B-Q
670 Jefferson
(901) 521–9798, (888) 780–7427
www.memphisbarbecue.com
5700 Mt. Moriah
(901) 795–4177

Neely's Bar-B-Q is owned and operated by the four Neely brothers, who as nephews of Jim Neely spent many years working closely with their uncle at Interstate Bar-B-Que. They learned their lessons well: Neely's does great pork shoulder and both wet and dry pork ribs as well as beef brisket and ribs, unusual for a non-Texan barbecue place. The sandwich menu includes not just pork shoulder but also sliced smoked turkey, smoked sausage, and chopped or sliced barbecue beef, and Neely's barbecue spaghetti is also popular. The atmosphere is homey and casual, but calmer and a bit nicer than most Memphis barbecue joints. Takeout orders are available, too. The Jefferson location is just a few blocks from downtown, once you cross the overpass. Draft beer is available. When the Memphis Grizzlies play, Neely's offers all-you-can-eat barbecue for $11.50 and a free shuttle to the game. Open Monday through Saturday for lunch and dinner.

Payne's Bar-B-Q
1762 Lamar Avenue
(901) 272–1523
1393 Elvis Presley Boulevard
(901) 942–7433
You'll find one of the best lunch deals in

town at Payne's, where you can get a first-rate sliced or chopped barbecue sandwich with homemade slaw for about $3.00. The Lamar Avenue location is housed in a former gas station; the dining room is painted apricot on the inside and lined with tables (you can see where the bays used to be). You place your order at the counter from Payne's all-pig menu (not for vegetarians; even the beans have bits of barbecue pork), where you can hear them chop the meat for your sandwich. The meat is subtly smoky, with pieces of jerkylike outside crust and not as salty as its counterparts elsewhere in town. No credit cards; no beer or alcoholic beverages. Payne's is on Lamar Avenue, just west of McLean Boulevard. It's open Monday through Saturday for lunch, serving all afternoon. Three nights a week it stays open for supper. The Elvis Presley location is open Monday through Saturday for lunch and dinner.

The Rendezvous
52 South Second Street, Rear
(901) 523–2746
www.hogsfly.com

You can literally follow your nose to this

A waiter at The Rendezvous serves up famous Memphis barbecue.
PHOTO: MEMPHIS CONVENTION AND VISITORS BUREAU

famous Memphis institution, which permeates downtown with its smoky fragrance. Make your way down General Washburn alley (between the Holiday Inn Select and Best Western on Union, just across the street from the Peabody); then go downstairs. You'll find a rowdy, crowded eatery staffed by sassy, wise-cracking waiters. A visit to the Rendezvous, opened in 1948 by Charlie Vergos and still operated by the family, is a must for visitors and a favorite for Memphians seeking the occasional 'cue fix. OK, there's better barbecue in this town, but nobody can match the scene here, with its festive crowd, red-checked tablecloths, memorabilia on the walls, and the constant parade of waiters bearing giant trays of barbecue ribs and other specialties. Rendezvous is famous for its dry ribs, but you can get them wet, or you can try the lean pork loin or chicken if you're limiting your fat intake. Start with a cheese-and-sausage plate, and don't be surprised if you get a free sample of red beans and rice. You can get beer or wine with your dinner. The place gets packed on weekends, so expect a wait. Alternatively, try to go early, say around 5:00 P.M., or get your order to go. Rendezvous also does a significant mail-order business (888–464–7359). Open for dinner Tuesday through Saturday, and for lunch on Friday and Saturday.

Tops Bar-B-Q
Various locations
(901) 363–4007 (main office)

Tops Bar-B-Q serves up a fast-food version of Memphis barbecue, which is really pretty good, especially the shoulder sandwich. There are at least 12 locations throughout the city, including ones at 1286 Union Avenue, 3353 Summer, and 4183 Summer. The menu is available to eat in or to take out, either from the counter inside or the drive-through window.

on weekends. Open for dinner only, seven nights a week. The dining room is wheelchair accessible, but not the rest rooms.

Salsa $–$$
6150 Poplar Avenue
(901) 683–6325

Tucked away in the corner of Regalia, an upscale shopping center, you'll find Salsa, a restaurant that serves Mexican with a California flair in a lively, festive atmosphere. Specialties include fajitas, pollo chipolte, and other straightforward, flavorful dishes. Salsa also has wine tastings, which are very popular among locals. Open for lunch and dinner Monday through Saturday.

Sekisui of Japan $–$$
50 Humphreys Boulevard
(901) 747–0001

Memphis is lucky to have a group of outstanding sushi restaurants despite its inland location, thanks to Japanese-born restaurateur Jimmy Ishii. Sekisui serves great sushi as well as a complete menu of other Japanese dishes, including tempura, kushiyaki dinners, and teriyaki. The Humphreys Boulevard location is the best looking, with its East-meets-California feng-shui ambiance, rice-paper panels, and tiny indoor brook. It features a robata menu and a weekend brunch. Open seven days a week.

Sekisui Pacific Rim & Sushi Bistro $$–$$$
4724 Poplar Avenue
(901) 767–7770

This sleek, harmonious restaurant is a treat for those who like imaginative East-West flavor combinations. As the Pan Asian restaurant in Japanese-born entrepreneur Jimmy Ishii's portfolio, Pacific Rim serves up dishes such as soba noodles with seafood in soy broth, kiwi-glazed duck breast with red-curry reduction, various fish tartars, tataki (seared fish or beef), and salads. The menu is heavy on appetizers, so this is a good place to order lots of small dishes to taste. There's also a full sushi menu and a good-looking sushi bar. The restaurant has a good selection of sake (Japanese rice wine), and the traditional wine list includes a generous selection by the glass. Open for lunch Monday through Friday and for dinner every night.

Shu's
3588 Ridgeway
(901) 366–9760

Shu's gets rave reviews from aficionados of dim sum for the quality and selection of its weekend dim sum. Its Chinese buffet, which it serves for lunch, is also a great favorite. Shu's serves not only Chinese food but also Thai specialties and sushi. Its menu includes Peking duck, sesame chicken, and other Oriental dishes. Open every day for lunch and dinner.

Taqueria Guadalupana $–$$
4818 Summer Avenue
(901) 685–6857

The friendly management, truly authentic Mexican cooking, and low prices make this modest-looking restaurant a big hit with gringos and Hispanics alike. Enchiladas, burritos, refried beans, and other Mexican standards are outstanding here, but the Cornish hen—cut up, deep fried, and served with tortillas, beans, and rice— is to die for. Also sublime is the shrimp cocktail: 10 or 12 big fresh shrimp served in a tall glass with fresh salsa and avocado. The atmosphere is clean and austere and decidedly casual except on Sundays, when T-shirts mix with Sunday best. There's no liquor license, so bring your own bottle. Open for lunch and dinner every day.

Wally Joe $$–$$$
5040 Sanderlin Avenue
(901) 818–0821

The chef who created the award-winning KC's Restaurant in Cleveland, Mississippi, brought his considerable culinary talents and wine expertise to East Memphis in 2002. Wally Joe, which operates in a small shopping center at Sanderlin and Mendenhall, features modern American dishes with Asian and Southern influences. Try the soy ginger marinated sea bass with soba noodles, shitaki mushrooms, and ginger shoots or the smoked pork loin over goat cheese grits. The wine list is sure to build up over time. That's something to watch, considering that Wally Joe's original restaurant won recognition from *Wine Spectator* magazine for its outstanding list. The decor, with its open kitchen and sleek dining room, is dazzling.

Winchester/Hickory Hill/ South Memphis

The Emerald $
5699 Mt. Moriah
(901) 367–2827

This family-run restaurant is the city's original Thai restaurant, serving an authentic menu of pad thai, red-curry dishes, and traditional soups and more. The servings are generous, and at lunch you can order from the menu or sample the all-you-can-eat lunch buffet that's enjoyed by those who work in the area. The Emerald serves lunch Monday through Saturday, and dinner every night.

Huey's $
2858 Hickory Hill
(901) 375–4373

A casual restaurant with great hamburgers and live music on Sunday, with locations throughout the city. See listing in Midtown section for more information.

Marlowe's Ribs and Restaurant $–$$
4381 Elvis Presley Boulevard
(901) 332–4159

You'll get a warm welcome at this super-friendly, family-run restaurant just a mile and a half from Graceland. In business since 1974, it's the kind of place that opens on Christmas to take care of its regulars and delights in greeting newcomers as well. The wide-ranging casual menu includes barbecue, which you can order as ribs, a sandwich, on a pizza, on nachos, or in a salad. Other choices include steaks, burgers, catfish, and homemade lasagne. If you're staying in an area hotel, Marlowe's will deliver food to your hotel or give you a ride to and from the restaurant in its shuttle bus. Open every day for lunch and dinner.

Sabor Tropical $–$$
3999 Lamar Avenue
(901) 566–0960

If you're homesick for fried plantains, strong Cuban coffee, and a sandwich Cubano, make an excursion to the Hispana Plaza shopping center and check out Sabor Tropical. Situated in an industrial part of Memphis, this bright, no-frills Cuban place has become a regular stop for its hearty platefuls of roasted meat or seafood and black beans and rice, all served with plantains. Save room for dessert; you'll be the envy of the table if you order the creamy, caramelized flan. Bring your own beer or wine, as they don't have a liquor license. Open every day for lunch and dinner.

Tycoon $
3307 Kirby Parkway
(901) 362–8788
This restaurant features all types of Asian cuisine, including Chinese, Malaysian, Thai, and Hong Kong. The menu has lots of noodle dishes and soups. Popular dishes include spicy garlic shrimp, tom yum soup, Malaysian noodles, and coconut-curry chicken. The restaurant, situated on Kirby between Winchester and Knight Arnold, serves beer only, so bring your own bottle if you're drinking wine. Open for lunch and dinner Monday through Saturday.

Collierville

Huey's $
2130 West Poplar Avenue
(901) 854–4455
A casual restaurant with great hamburgers and live Sunday evening music, with locations throughout the city. See listing in Midtown section for more information.

Ja Ja's Cuisine of Thailand $
192 Washington Avenue
(901) 850–5222
Situated a block east of the historic town square of suburban Collierville, this is an unlikely spot for such a gem of an ethnic restaurant. Ja Ja is the nickname of Thai native Pen Fryer, who moved here with her American husband in 1979. Ja Ja runs the kitchen with delectable results, turning out first-rate Thai spring rolls, sticky rice, and pad thai and spicier dishes, such as curries, goy, and lemongrass chicken,

which can be as hot (or mild) as you like. The servers know the menu, and can give you as much or as little information as you like. It's family friendly, with a kid's menu that features corn dogs and chicken nuggets, and a gift shop with Thai foods and imported gifts. It's a nonsmoking restaurant, open Monday through Saturday for lunch and dinner.

White Church Tea Room $–$$
196 North Main
(901) 854–6433
Formerly a 19th-century church, with its colorful stained-glass windows, the building provides an inspiring atmosphere for enjoying such specialties as maple pecan chicken salad, house-cured salmon, and herb-crusted rack of lamb. The restaurant has a country French feeling and features a wine bar. The old church is at the corner of West Poplar and North Main near the Collierville town square. Open for lunch and dinner Tuesday through Saturday.

Germantown/Cordova

Bol A Pasta $–$$
2200 North Germantown Parkway, Cordova
(901) 384–7988
3160 Village Shops Drive, Germantown
(901) 757–5609
This family-friendly restaurant, another one operated by the Grisanti family, serves all kinds of pasta as well as other specialties such as steaks, shrimp scampi, and seafood entrees. An often-requested dish is the sirloin steak carbonara with pasta alfredo. Parents and kids alike are at home at these casual restaurants, decorated with colorful original murals. Open every day for lunch and dinner.

Boscos $–$$$
7615 West Farmington, Germantown
(901) 756–7310
www.boscosbeer.com
Fresh-baked pizzas from its wood-burning oven are the focal point of Boscos menu, but these brewpub restaurants also serve salads, sandwiches, and entrees such as wood-oven planked salmon and rosemary grilled

chicken. The restaurant's original German-town location, in the Saddle Creek shopping center at Farmington and Poplar, has an uptown feel and an outdoor patio area for catching rays and people-watching while you enjoy your beer and pizza. This was Tennessee's first brewpub, featuring award-winning handmade beers and a changing menu of seasonal beers. There's also a full bar and wine list if you're not a beer drinker. A jazz brunch menu featuring omelets, Benedict dishes, and Belgian waffles is served on Sunday. (Check out the Nightlife chapter under Brewpubs for more details.) Open every day for lunch and dinner.

The Butcher Shop Steak House $$–$$$
107 South Germantown Parkway, Germantown
(901) 757–4244
The suburban branch of the downtown steak restaurant. See listing in Downtown section for more details.

EJ's Brasserie $–$$
1884 North Germantown Parkway, Cordova
(901) 751–1150
This casual, European-style restaurant is a less-pricey sister to Erling Jensen. The restaurant, open with an eye to adding a Scandinavian flair to American cooking, features a very creative menu, with the likes of EJ's shrimp tower (made from layers of poached shrimp, tomatoes, and greens), pecan-coated chicken breast, filet of beef, and salmon on bowtie pasta. The interior is warmed with lots of teak wood and a mural of Copenhagen. The restaurant serves specialty beers and wine. Open for lunch Monday through Friday, for dinner every night, and for brunch on Sunday. No smoking allowed.

Equestria $$–$$$
3165 Forest Hill-Irene Road, Germantown
(901) 869–2663
Locals love the decor of this equestrian-theme restaurant, with its beautiful wood finishes, candlelight, and other elegant touches. As far as the menu goes, steaks, rack of lamb, and sea bass are favorites. The restaurant takes great pride in its prime beef served with herb butter. Open for dinner Monday through Saturday.

Huey's $
1771 North Germantown Parkway, Cordova
(901) 754–3885
A casual restaurant with great hamburgers and live Sunday evening music, with locations throughout the city. See listing in Midtown section for more information.

Jason's Deli $
1575 Chickering Lane, Cordova
(901) 844–1840
The Cordova location of this popular lunchtime spot. See listing in East Memphis section for more information.

Mister B's $$–$$$
6655 Poplar Avenue, Germantown
(901) 751–5262
Tucked away in The Carrefour shopping center, this New Orleans–style seafood kitchen is well liked by Memphis suburbanites, who come here for fried oysters, shrimp Creole, and po'boys as well as for steaks. That's the dinner menu; for lunch Mister B's serves hearty plate lunches featuring country-fried steak, meat loaf, and the like. Even though the address is Poplar Avenue, to find Mister B's, drive to the back of the shopping center, where you'll find it just west of Borders bookstore. Open for lunch Monday through Friday and for dinner Monday through Saturday.

Three Oaks Grill $$–$$$
2285 Germantown Road South, Germantown
(901) 757–8225
Three Oaks Grill, owned and operated by the owner of Paulette's, is a fine-dining venue convenient to persons who live and work in Germantown. Like its midtown sister this restaurant delivers great atmosphere, service, and delectable continental cuisine with a French accent. Among the favorites on the menu are ginger-roasted salmon, rack of lamb, and filet mignon. Situated in the town's historic district across from the old train depot, the restaurant has an elegant yet cozy atmosphere. Open for lunch Monday through Friday, for dinner every night, and for brunch on Sunday.

YiaYia's Eurocafe $-$$
7615 West Farmington, Germantown
(901) 756-4004

This trendy eatery, with its lodgelike warm wood and stone interior, offers a menu of what it calls "homestyle Mediterranean" cuisine, including such dishes as crab risotto cakes, wood-roasted salmon salad, oak-fired pizzas, and whole oven-roasted fish. There's also an all-you-can-eat brunch buffet on Sundays, where you can sample some of everything. Open for lunch and dinner every day. YiaYia's bar is also an alluring nightspot for area yuppies, especially on Wednesday and Friday nights, both for happy hour and later.

Raleigh

Asian Palace $-$$
2920 Covington Pike
(901) 388-3883

You can get fried rice and egg rolls at many places around town, but Asian Palace is generally considered the best Chinese restaurant in town, given its huge menu and consistent quality. Situated off the beaten path near Covington Pike's Auto Row, this large restaurant has everything from cold jellyfish and potstickers to scallops, Peking duck, and shrimp with walnuts and oysters, with a good selection of seafood dishes amid predictable Chinese restaurant decor. Their wonton soup is a standout version of this old standard. The restaurant serves beer and wine. Open for lunch and dinner.

Jasmine Chinese & Thai Restaurant $-$$
3024 Covington Pike
(901) 386-2974

Venture beyond the row of car dealerships on Covington Pike, and you'll find Jasmine about a mile down. This family-run restaurant serves Thai and Chinese specialties, with plenty of vegetarian dishes. Among the most popular are crispy fried vegetables with tofu, curry chicken, and pad thai. The restaurant serves beer only, so bring your own if you plan on drinking wine. Jasmine is open Tuesday through Sunday for lunch and dinner.

Mississippi Suburbs

Bonne Terre Café $$$
4715 Church Road West, Nesbit
(662) 781-5100

This gem of a restaurant is worth an excursion into Mississippi to enjoy the warm country French ambiance and outstanding cuisine. Be prepared to splurge, as the restaurant requires you to order a three-course dinner for $45 or a four-course dinner for $55. The menu includes such delectables as lobster bisque, seared foie gras on truffle polenta, chicken Wellington, and roast rack of lamb. The dazzler on the dessert menu is its bread-and-butter pudding with cherries. Open Tuesday through Thursday for lunch, Monday through Saturday for dinner, and for its terrific jazz brunch on the first Sunday of each month. Beer and wine are served, but smoking is not allowed. Ask about limousine service, or expect about a 20-30 minute drive from Memphis. To get there take I-55 to Nesbit, then the Church Road exit, and go 4.4 miles on Church. Reservations are recommended. (For more information about Bonne Terre Country Inn, see the Accommodations chapter.)

Olive Branch Catfish Company $
9659 Old Highway 78, Olive Branch
(662) 895-9494

This homey catfish restaurant has been here for years, long before Olive Branch became as suburban as it is today. The decor is nothing special, but the excellent fried catfish certainly is and keeps the customers coming back for more. You can also get catfish grilled or blackened, or if you're really hungry, a platter that includes all three. Steaks, chicken, shrimp, and sandwiches are also served here. The restaurant serves beer. Open for lunch and dinner seven days a week.

Memphis Music

For the past century Memphis has been the world's signature musical city. Cleveland may be home to the Rock and Roll Hall of Fame, and Nashville, with its country glitz and major record label offices, may be Music City USA. Other American cities—notably, New Orleans, St. Louis, Chicago, Detroit, and New York—may boast incredible music legacies. But nowhere else did music hit as hard, or mean as much, as it did in Memphis.

Of the three major music earthquakes that took place in Memphis—in blues, rock and roll, and soul—certainly the birth of rock and roll here in the 1950s ranks as one of the very few true, geographically specific music explosions over the last 100 years. Others include cultural eruptions such as Jamaican ska and reggae in the 1960s and 1970s, hip-hop's New York–based birth and development in the late 1970s and 1980s, and England's Beatles and Stones–fueled "invasion" in the mid-1960s.

In addition to giving birth to rock and roll in the 1950s, this de facto capital of the Mississippi Delta witnessed the nation's most vibrant blues scene in the first half of the 20th century, as the music moved from the cotton-field juke joints into Beale Street clubs and recording studios. In the 1960s Memphis became the mecca of Southern soul. Why Memphis, a relatively small city surrounded by farmland? The reason seems to be the city's unique mix of black and white, rural and urban, Northern and Southern, which formed the demographic catalyst for these successive musical earthquakes.

Memphis is currently enjoying the most vibrant music scene it has experienced since the late soul era of Al Green and Isaac Hayes in the 1970s, with its musicians making big contributions to the national scene in hip-hop, hard rock, gospel, and, of course, the blues. The fact is, however, that most music lovers are drawn to Memphis by the mystique of its musical past, a legacy that gives credence to the city's official slogan, "The Home of the Blues and the Birthplace of Rock and Roll."

In this chapter you'll find the story of Memphis music, of how musical earthquakes and some other major rumbles changed American music forever. Then we'll bring you into the present, with a portrait of what's happening today. Who knows: When it's all said and done, maybe Memphis could write another chapter in the history of American music.

Finally, we list the Memphis attractions you can visit to see where it all happened (see Close-up on page 102). Don't forget to check out the Nightlife chapter, to find out where you can hear the best of Memphis music.

W.C. Handy, Beale Street, and the "Birth" of the Blues

Memphis's first real claim on music history came early in the 20th century, when Beale Street had become the center of black culture and commerce under the guidance of Robert Church, the South's first black millionaire.

Beale at that time was a wild place, with Pee Wee's Saloon as the street's signature nightspot and with ragtime piano booming from the windows of brothels on nearby Gayoso Street. Its mix of prostitution, drugs, and organized crime made Beale Street so rough that in 1918 a statistician for Prudential Insurance determined that Memphis was the murder capital of the United States, with most of the action centered on Beale.

Memphis's first contribution to the

This tiny storefront houses the legendary Sun Studios, where Elvis recorded his first hit.
PHOTO: MEMPHIS CONVENTION AND VISITORS BUREAU

national music consciousness came through the work of William Christopher Handy, known as "the father of the blues." Handy didn't invent the music, of course, but during his years in Memphis he was the first to transcribe and arrange the existing music. Handy still has his critics in blues circles, but the fact remains that Handy's popularization of the blues form was crucial to the genre's success.

The son of a former slave, Handy was a well-traveled and well-educated musician who specialized in jazz and ragtime. In 1902 he settled in the nearby Delta town of Clarksdale, Mississippi, where he "discovered" the local music known as the blues. Handy moved his family to Memphis soon thereafter to pursue regular work in the Beale Street clubs.

In 1912 Handy put out "Memphis Blues," one of the first published blues songs (in the era before recordings, sheet music was the primary means through which music was purchased and enjoyed at home). "St. Louis Blues" followed soon after, then, in 1916, "Beale Street Blues." These songs were a huge success for Handy, who soon moved his orchestra to New York's Tin Pan Alley but never again matched the success he'd had during his Beale Street years.

Though the first recordings were introduced in 1900 and Handy's blues songs were successful a decade later, black acts weren't recorded until the 1920s. The first recorded blues stars were largely women, and Memphis had a small role in these early successes. The most prominent early blues star, Bessie Smith, performed regularly on Beale during the 1920s, and Memphian Alberta Hunter wrote one of her biggest hits with "Down Home Blues."

Memphis Jug Bands

Though more obscure now than the solo bluesmen of the era, Memphis's greatest post-Handy contribution to the blues was the jug bands. Encompassing a variety of instruments—though almost always the jug, blown across the mouth to produce basslike sounds, and stringed instruments such as guitar, banjo, or fiddle—jug bands featured such delightful ensemble playing and drew from such a wide variety of genres (blues, jazz, ragtime, hillbilly,

Sun Studio

In 1950 Sam Phillips, a young engineer and deejay at WREC radio, opened his own business, Memphis Recording Service, in a small building at 706 Union Avenue. His motto: "We Record Anything—Anywhere—Anytime." Phillips also developed his own record label, Sun Records, and over the next nine years, this tiny three-room studio would be the site of recording sessions so important to the development of music that, at present, 706 Union is a musical holy land.

It's difficult to fathom the musical history that was made in the quaint, cramped little room. Here a whole generation of postwar Delta bluesmen—B.B. King, Junior Parker, Little Milton, Howlin' Wolf—cut their teeth. Here in 1951 Jackie Brenston and the Delta Cats, with a teenage Ike Turner on piano, recorded "Rocket 88," widely considered the first rock-and-roll song. Here also, in 1953, an 18-year-old truck driver with a dime-store guitar stumbled in to record a vanity demo: This Memphis teenager, Elvis Presley, would come back a year later for the most famous recording session in history.

During that session in Phillips's studio, Presley joined a couple of local country musicians, Bill Black and Scotty Moore, to record the Arthur Crudup blues number "That's All Right, Mama" and Bill Monroe's bluegrass "Blue Moon of Kentucky." Later dubbed "the great wedding ceremony" for marrying black blues to white country, the session changed American music forever and launched one of the greatest musical careers in history.

After Elvis came the flood—Carl Perkins, Johnny Cash, Jerry Lee Lewis, and Roy Orbison—leading a generation of musical revolutionaries through Sun's doors. In 1956 Presley, by then signed to RCA and a major national star, dropped by the studio and sat in with Cash, Perkins, and Lewis for an impromptu recording session and gabfest that would be released three decades later as *The Million Dollar Quartet*.

Sam Phillips's magic at the tiny studio wouldn't last into the 1960s, however. In 1959 Phillips had his last major hit for Sun, Charlie Rich's "Lonely Weekends." He closed the small studio and moved Memphis Recording Service to a larger space a few blocks away on Madison Avenue.

Sun Studio would disappear for a quarter of a century, although during that time the building that housed Sun would be home to a barbershop and a scuba-equipment store.

Then in the mid-1980s, Sun Studio experienced a rebirth as a music entity. After helping to restore the building, Phillips oversaw a modern update of *The Million Dollar Quartet*, with Roy Orbison filling in for the late Presley. The resulting album was *The Class of '55*. In 1986 the building was purchased by entrepreneur Gary Hardy, who maintained it as a fully functioning recording studio that's still in use and converted it into a full-time tourist attraction.

Sun Studio is arguably the most essential stop in any music-lover's trip to Memphis, and it attracts more than 100,000 visitors a year. When you visit, it's worth taking the 30-minute tour that's free with admission, conducted by knowledgeable tour guides who use vintage props and audio clips to re-create the Sun experience.

One of the best things about Sun Studio is that it still feels like 1954 inside: The shabby, poorly lit space has the same linoleum and acoustic-friendly tile it had during the studio's heyday. Also still there is much of the equipment used at the time, including the microphone Elvis sang into when he recorded "That's All Right, Mama."

At night after the tourists leave, Sun is a busy recording hub and in recent years has drawn such prominent artists as U2, Beck, Ringo Starr, Def Leppard, Bonnie Raitt, and Tom Petty.

and novelty songs) that they are as much proto-rock and roll as any early American pop music.

The style is said to have originated in Louisville and was popular elsewhere, but Memphis was where jug bands had the most success. The most prominent was the Memphis Jug Band, formed in the mid-1920s. In 1927 the New York–based Victor label came to Memphis for a recording field trip. Its taping of the Memphis Jug Band in downtown Memphis was the first commercial recording ever made in Tennessee. The MJB had a rotating lineup that sometimes used great female blues singers Hattie Hart and Memphis Minnie. Over a seven-year recording career, the group cut 75 sides for Victor and Columbia/OKeh, but lasted as a live unit well into the 1940s.

Other local jug bands were the Beale Street Sheiks and Cannon's Jug Stompers, whose leader, Gus Cannon, composed "Walk Right In," which The Rooftop Singers would make a number-one pop hit in 1963.

Victor, the record label that had recorded the Memphis Jug Band, returned in 1928 for a second session. This time, Victor captured the first recordings by Delta bluesman Tommy Johnson, in addition to more jug-band music. The flamboyant Johnson is generally considered one of the three most important first-generation Delta bluesmen, along with Charley Patton and Son House, who had less direct connection to Memphis.

The same year the OKeh label set up in Memphis for a recording trip, capturing the first recorded work of the Mississippi gentle blues giant John Hurt. He would become a major star of the 1960s blues revival, when he was rediscovered by dedicated fans. Other significant early bluesmen who were prominent on the Memphis scene included Robert Wilkins and Sleepy John Estes.

This first burst of Memphis blues activity soon ended with the onslaught of the Great Depression, drought, and the boll weevil. Record companies stopped making trips to Memphis.

Early Memphis Blues Singers

Memphis produced several prominent blues singers during the 1920s, the first decade that the music was recorded, although Beale Street decreed they were not polished enough to play inside the clubs. Products of a Delta lifestyle where sharecropping encouraged large families and then subsequent urban migrations, several of the Delta's most prominent early blues artists ended up in Memphis.

Walter "Furry" Lewis, who worked with the Memphis Jug Band and Cannon's Jug Stompers at medicine and tent shows, is probably most synonymous with the city's blues heritage to native Memphians. Lewis first recorded in 1927 in Chicago for Vocalion and ended up cutting 20 sides in all from 1927 through 1929. Lewis then disappeared from the public eye until resurfacing in 1959 during the blues/folk revival and returned to active recording until his death in 1981.

Crossroads: Robert Johnson and the Post-Depression Blues

The most important of the post-Depression blues artists was undoubtedly Robert Johnson, who spent virtually his whole life in the area around Memphis. Johnson died under mysterious circumstances in 1938 at the age of 27 and had only had three recording sessions totaling only a few dozen songs. Yet despite such a small body of work and brief career span, Johnson stands as one of the most important figures in all of American music. The 1990 CD debut of his complete recordings became the first blues recordings to ever sell one million copies.

Johnson's "crossroads" legend that he sold his soul to the devil in order to acquire his otherworldly skills has become American music's most evocative myth, but the truest account of Johnson's life can probably be found in music journalist Peter Guralnick's 1988 book, *Searching for Robert Johnson.*

Presently, Johnson dwarfs his contemporaries in the public imagination, but he wasn't the only prominent blues musician this area produced during the post-Depression era. Others included pianist Peter Chatman (aka Memphis Slim), who was a Beale regular in the 1930s, as well as Washboard Sam, the original Sonny Boy Williamson, and Robert Johnson associate Johnny Shines.

Key area bluesmen who emerged in the 1940s included Howlin' Wolf and Sonny Boy Williamson II, who was becoming a star with his "King Biscuit Time" radio show in Helena, Arkansas. The Delta also produced Muddy Waters, the major star of the Chicago blues scene who was first recorded in nearby Clarksdale by the Library of Congress's Alan Lomax.

Radio and Recording: The Memphis Fifties' Explosion

Memphis's second great music explosion had its roots in radio. In 1948 the owners of downtown station WDIA gambled and made it the nation's first all-black-staffed radio station. By broadcasting black music—largely the postwar blues hybrid dubbed "rhythm and blues"—in 1949 to a primarily black audience, WDIA became a massive success, tapping a previously ignored market and billing itself as the "Mother Station of the Negroes." The station also boasted Nat D. Williams and future star Rufus Thomas as part of its broadcasting team and gave Riley King, an aspiring blues musician from Indianola, Mississippi, his big break with a 15-minute slot on the station. King was dubbed the "Beale Street Blues Boy," the "blues boy" part later giving way to the snappier "B.B."

Due to the peculiarities of the station's license, it wasn't allowed to broadcast after sunset, leaving room for another station, WHBQ, to move in and pick up WDIA's audience at night. WHBQ hired a white deejay—the brash Dewey Phillips—to spin black blues and R&B records. Phillips's show, called "Red Hot & Blue," debuted in 1949. Phillips would later become the first broadcaster to play an Elvis Presley song over the air, thus becoming a key player in the birth of rock and roll.

This Beale Street statue salutes the contribution of W.C. Handy, who lived in Memphis when he became the father of the blues.

PHOTO: MEMPHIS CONVENTION AND VISITORS BUREAU

While WDIA and WHBQ were changing the sonic landscape of the city's airwaves, another local radio employee, WREC engineer Sam Phillips, was making moves that would forever change recording in the city. In 1950 Phillips renovated a small building just east of downtown Memphis and turned it into Memphis Recording Service. Phillips's endeavor soon became the first significant local recording since the Victor and OKeh sessions. (See Close-up on Sun Studio in this chapter.)

Phillips began to capture a new generation of postwar bluesmen. Ike Turner of Clarksdale brought his band to record and, in 1951, with sax player Jackie Brenston playing lead, Phillips cut the group's "Rocket 88," which has since been widely cited as the first rock-and-roll song. Released under the name Jackie Brenston and the Delta Cats, the song went all the way to number one. Turner soon became Phillips's session leader and talent scout, helping to bring a succession of soon-to-be-historic bluesmen into the tiny studio. Among the major blues figures who recorded with Sam Phillips in the early 1950s were B.B. King, Howlin' Wolf, Walter Horton, Little Milton, and Junior Parker.

Around this time WDIA also began recording artists, including King, Roscoe Gordon, Bobby Bland, and Johnny Ace, on program director David James Mathis's Duke label, which later relocated to Houston.

By 1952 Phillips was growing tired of recording his artists for other labels and decided to form his own record label, Sun. The label's first big hit came with WDIA deejay Rufus Thomas' "Bear Cat," an answer record to Big Mama Thornton's hit "Hound Dog."

Elvis Presley and the Rockabilly Era

Elvis Presley may have seemed like an anomaly to most of Middle America when he burst onto television sets in the mid-1950s, but the young man with the startling voice and overactive hips didn't come out of nowhere. He came out of Memphis. With radio bringing R&B directly to white teenagers, with Beale Street making the music an around-the-corner inevitability, and Sam Phillips providing a forum, the stage was set in Memphis for someone to break out and fulfill Phillips's famous plea: "If I could find a white singer with the Negro sound and the Negro feel, I could make a million dollars."

Cultural forces—including a postwar economic and technology boom that helped turn Elvis's rock-and-roll revolution from regional subculture into teen-driven mass culture—are one big reason for the rise of Elvis Presley. No one, however, could have expected Phillips's find to be such a genius singer or to exude such overwhelming charisma. Cultural forces may be enough to explain a Carl Perkins,

the great rockabilly singer who followed Elvis to Sun, but Elvis Presley is another matter entirely. (See Close-up in this chapter and the Attractions chapter.)

A teenage Presley first entered Memphis Recording Service in 1953 to cut a souvenir disk. Phillips brought the young Presley back the next year and paired him with a couple of veteran Memphis country musicians, guitarist Scotty Moore and bassist Bill Black. Things clicked at that freewheeling and now-historic recording session, producing what would become Elvis's first single, with a silky cover of the Arthur Crudup blues song "That's All Right (Mama)" on the "A" side and a raucous version of the Bill Monroe bluegrass classic "Blue Moon of Kentucky" on the "B" side. Sam Phillips hustled an acetate of the single over to his friend Dewey Phillips at WHBQ, who debuted the song, and the new artist, on Red Hot and Blue. The response was deafening, and soon Elvis, and Sun, were on their way. Presley's first major concert followed a few weeks later at Memphis's Overton Park Shell.

Elvis rapidly spread from a local to a regional phenomenon, landing a spot on the popular country radio show "The Louisiana Hayride." Elvis's performance there drew the attention of Colonel Tom Parker, then managing country stars Hank Snow and Eddy Arnold. He signed Elvis in August 1955. The Colonel engineered Phillips's sale of Elvis's contract to New York's RCA that November. The RCA deal and subsequent national television appearances on *The Ed Sullivan Show* and other shows turned Elvis into a national star. In January 1956 Elvis released "Heartbreak Hotel," his first million seller, and in August of that year he made his first movie, *Love Me Tender*. The rest is history.

Elvis would return to Sun Studio to record only one more time, in December of 1956 as part of an informal jam session with then-current Sun artists Jerry Lee Lewis, Johnny Cash, and Carl Perkins, which was dubbed "The Million Dollar Quartet."

It may seem crazy in retrospect for Sam Phillips to have sold Elvis's contract to RCA for $35,000, but that seemingly paltry sum was quite a hefty fee at the time, and it allowed Phillips to keep his little label solvent, thus paving way for the

Elvis: The Musician behind the Legend

"I sing all kinds." That's what a shy teenage Elvis Presley said at his first Sun recording session in 1954 when asked about his repertoire, and he meant it.

In the decades since Elvis's historic rise and sad decline, the King of Rock and Roll has become such a pop-culture icon that it's easy to put aside or even underrate his actual artistic output.

So what made Elvis a great artist? The key lies in that simple statement: "I sing all kinds."

Other first-generation rockers could outdo Elvis in one way or another. Chuck Berry was both rock-and-roll's definitive instrumentalist and greatest writer. Little Richard and Jerry Lee Lewis made records that were far more viscerally powerful than those of Elvis, but no one united the various tributaries of American music with the grace, ease, or originality of Elvis Presley—and no one could sing like him. Presley's vocal gifts and love of vocal pop make him as much the last great interpretive singer—an inheritor of Bing Crosby, Billie Holiday, and Frank Sinatra—as he was the first rock-and-roller.

What Elvis accomplished at Sun was no less than an unleashing of the invisible republic that had long been at the heart of American music. He created a mass-cultural sphere in which gospel, blues, country, and pop-crooning could become part of the same thing. Elvis's music embodied black and white, city and country, urbane sophistication and proletarian vitality. Amazingly, he did all this, with varying degrees of artistic success, throughout his career.

Elvis the icon is everywhere these days, but Elvis the artist exists only in his recordings. His is one of the largest and most continually repackaged bodies of work in recorded history. It is easy to get lost in this ocean of product, but here are seven Elvis records no serious fan of American music should do without:

The Sun Sessions CD: Arguably the most essential rock-and-roll recording of all, this is a complete document of Elvis's Sun recordings. Every master take is now a classic, but "That's All Right" and "Blue Moon of Kentucky" can claim to be the musical definition of rock and roll. "Mystery Train," where Elvis adds a casual air of defiance to a blues dirge, might be the music's philosophical summation. *The Sun Sessions* was trumped by RCA in 1999 with *Sunrise*, a two-disk set that adds 10 tracks of early demos and live cuts to *The Sun Sessions*' 28-song studio set. *The Sun Sessions* is tighter and more essential, but ultimately you need this music in whatever configuration you can find it.

The Million Dollar Quartet: No longer a Sun artist, Elvis dropped by the studio one day in 1956 to hang out. One way or another, then-current Sun stars Carl Perkins, Jerry Lee Lewis, and Johnny Cash were there too, and Sam Phillips was prescient enough to roll tape. You can listen to this for an hour waiting for an actual "jam session" to break out, but the true worth of this lazy, relaxed little song-and-story swap comes from the sheer, loving range of material covered. It includes two utterly priceless moments: The four rockabillies marveling over Chuck Berry's "Brown-Eyed Handsome Man" and Elvis's appreciatively jealous description of seeing Jackie Wilson do "Hound Dog."

Elvis Presley: Elvis's RCA debut from 1956, before the army and Hollywood. The material and instrumentation are similar to his Sun recordings, and the end result is only slightly less magical. It was the first rock-and-roll album to hit number one on the *Billboard* pop charts.

Elvis Is *Back!*: The conventional wisdom is that Elvis didn't produce much great music between his army induction and his 1968 "comeback." This record, released in 1960 as his first album after the army, is a harsh rebuke to that notion. No one really knew how a two-year absence would affect such a young star in such a young (and still not entirely trusted) medium as rock and roll. But Elvis answered all doubters with this strong, mature, bluesy album. It remains the most under-recognized music of his career.

The Number One Hits: An 18-track collection of every number-one pop hit Elvis ever cut, from "Heartbreak Hotel" to "Suspicious Minds." This is the Elvis most people know and for good reason: There are few more rousing vocal perform-ances than the blistering "Jailhouse Rock" and perhaps none so assured as "Don't Be Cruel."

***Tiger Man*:** Released in 1998, *Tiger Man* presents one entire concert performance from Elvis's 1968 "Comeback Special." In this famous television show Elvis, clad in black leather from head to toe, had something to prove after spending a decade in Hollywood watching rock culture pass him by. The performance's middle stretch—"One Night," "Love Me," "Trying To Get To You," and "Lawdy Miss Clawdy"—may be the wildest and most desperate stretch of music Elvis ever made. The crowd screams alone are worth the cover price.

The Memphis Record: The complete document of Elvis's 1969 sessions at Memphis American Studios, his first official recording sessions back home since he left Sun in the 1950s. The album opens cagily with the apt "Stranger in My Own Home-town." Then it proceeds through blistering versions of soul and country classics like "Only the Strong Survive," "True Love Travels on a Gravel Road," and "Gen-tle on My Mind," moving next to Elvis-identified hits "Suspicious Minds" and "Kentucky Rain." It's maybe the greatest blue-eyed soul collection this side of Van Morrison's best work.

extraordinary flow of artists who followed Elvis into Sun.

Jackson, Tennessee's pure rockabilly sensation, Carl Perkins, was Phillips's next discovery, and his historic "Blue Suede Shoes" would become the first record to ever top the pop, country, and rhythm-and-blues charts at the same time. Arkansas's Johnny Cash was next at Sun, with a coun-try-heavy rockabilly that produced hits such as "I Walk the Line" and "Folsom Prison Blues." But Sun's biggest artist at that time, by far, was Jerry Lee Lewis. This wild man from Ferriday, Louisiana, and "his pounding piano" (as some early records were credited) produced major, still bone-rattling hits such as "Great Balls of Fire" and "Whole Lotta Shakin' Goin' On."

A succession of important minor artists followed at Sun, including Texas crooner

Roy Orbison (who would become a major artist after leaving Sun), and second-tier rockabilly icons Billy Lee Riley, Charlie Feathers, Sonny Burgess, Malcolm Yelving-ton, Warren Smith, and Carl Mann. Sun's last major star was Charlie Rich, a talented pianist from nearby Colt, Arkansas, whose first hit in 1959, "Lonely Weekends," was Sun's last. Sun Records soon closed.

The Memphis Soul Era: Stax and Hi Records

Though Sun's rockabilly eruption was made entirely of white men, many of whom loved black music, the inherent racial inter-action that produced Elvis would directly manifest itself in Memphis's next big thing, the Stax-based soul era.

The roots of Stax lay in banker and part-time fiddle player Jim Stewart, who founded Satellite Records in 1957 and soon upgraded his equipment with money borrowed from sister Estelle Axton. The fledgling label's first success came with "'Cause I Love You," a duet by Rufus Thomas and his 17-year-old daughter, Carla. Carla Thomas followed the song with the sweet "Gee Whiz," becoming the label's first star.

At this time the label began a relationship with Atlantic Records and R&B–loving honcho Jerry Wexler, one that would help the label become a national player without losing its identity or autonomy. The label's first major hit came with an informal instrumental, "Last Night," recorded by a bunch of house musicians and credited to the then fictional group the Markeys. "Last Night" was a top-five hit on both the pop and R&B charts.

Just as the label was becoming prominent nationally, legal troubles with a pre-existing label forced Satellite to change its name in 1961. Combining the names of its two owners, Jim Stewart (St) and Estelle Axton (Ax), the Stax name was born. Soon William Bell's "You Don't Miss Your Water" gave the Stax label a male soul star to rival Carla Thomas.

During this time the Stax house band earned the right to be cited as one of the greatest bands ever. The legendary group coalesced into an interracial, neighborhood-bred rhythm section, consisting of Booker T. Jones on organ, Steve Cropper on guitar, Al Jackson, Jr., on drums, and Lewis Steinberg (later Duck Dunn) on bass. This ensemble, which played over virtually the entirety of the Stax catalog, also became hit makers of their own right. Under the moniker Booker T. and the MGs, they scored a massive hit with "Green Onions," which began a series of instrumental smashes.

Though most of Stax's talent was homegrown, the label's two biggest stars arrived from the outside. Macon, Georgia's Otis Redding had his first hit for Stax in 1962 with the ballad "These Arms of Mine" and quickly became the label's biggest star and most significant artist. But the label's biggest hit makers were the duo Sam and Dave, a Florida-based act sent to Stax by

This is where Southern soul history was made, as Otis Redding, Isaac Hayes, and other soul greats recorded at Stax Records in Memphis.
PHOTO: FANTASY, INC.–STAX ARCHIVES

Wexler. Recording mainly songs written by the emerging in-house songwriting partners David Porter and Isaac Hayes, Sam and Dave scored with songs such as "Hold On, I'm Comin'" (the label's first number-one hit since "Green Onions" and "Soul Man").

The out-of-town talent kept flocking to Stax. Though he never recorded under the Stax imprint, Wilson Pickett came to Stax to write and record classics such as "In the Midnight Hour" and "634-5789." In 1965 soul singer Eddie Floyd recorded "Knock on Wood" for the label.

In 1967 a Wisconsin plane crash took the life of Redding and most of his backup band, the Barkays, bringing an end to Stax's golden age. The label would persevere into the mid-1970s, recording a new generation of soul stars, including the blues-oriented Albert King and Little Milton, the gospel-based Staples Singers, and Johnnie Taylor. The label's breakout star in the 1970s ended up being longtime studio hand Isaac Hayes, who moved in front of the microphone to become "Black Moses," recording a few classic albums and the iconic "Theme from Shaft."

Stax wasn't the only landmark soul music to come out of Memphis in the 1960s. Producer Chips Moman, who was an important part of Stax's early years, ran American studios, which came out with James Carr's soul classic, "The Dark End of the Street." American also produced a variety of local and national acts, including Dusty Springfield and Neil Diamond.

In the 1970s, as Stax was on the way down, another Memphis soul label was on the way up. Hi Records was actually founded as a rockabilly label in the mid-1950s, but in the early 1960s, its way with instrumentals drew Willie Mitchell, a Beale Street bandleader who had had several hits on his own during the 1960s. Hi's glory years began with Mitchell's discovery of Al Green, who became the last great Southern soul singer and, arguably, Memphis's last major musical star. After a few attempts at gruff, Otis Redding–style soul singing, Green found his softer, more intimate sound with 1971's "Tired of Being Alone," a million seller. That breakthrough was followed immediately by Green's signature tune, "Let's Stay Together," which hit number one on both the pop and R&B charts and began a string of 15 top-10 singles over the next five years. Green was the dominant force for Hi, but a string of important second-tier soul stars, most notably Ann Peebles, Syl Johnson, and Otis Clay, also recorded hits there.

Memphis's Final Rock-and-Roll Glory Years

Soul may have been Memphis's major contribution to pop music in the 1960s and 1970s, but rock and roll was far from dead in the city that created it. After years of lucrative but artistically negligible film work, Elvis freed himself from Colonel Parker's grip long enough for a brief but major comeback. Clad in black leather, Elvis thrilled audiences with informal, powerhouse ver-

sions of some of his classic recordings on an NBC television special that aired in December 1968. The next month Elvis returned to Memphis for his first local recording session since leaving Sun. Elvis entered American studios as an icon with a lot to prove, and he delivered. Those Memphis sessions marked Elvis's finest music since his early RCA recordings, spawning the commanding *From Elvis in Memphis* album and the soulful classic "Suspicious Minds."

During the years Elvis had been busy in Hollywood, Memphis was part of the garage-rock "movement," producing a new generation of hit makers heavy on one-hit wonders. Among the Memphis contributions to this national, Brit-invasion-fueled craze were the Gentrys's "Keep on Dancing," the Hombres "Let It Out (Let It All Hang Out)" and Sam the Sham's "Wooly Bully." The biggest garage band was the Box Tops, a product of American Studios fronted by teenage lead singer Alex Chilton. The Box-tops had a string of hits in the late 1960s, including "The Letter" (number one for a solid month in 1967) and "Cry Like a Baby."

Eventually, the Box Tops mutated into Big Star, a Chilton-led band whose twisted but sweet anglophiliac power pop never sold as well as the Box Tops but ended up being much more influential. Big Star recorded three records for new local label Ardent in the mid-1970s, their career petering out with limited distribution and even more limited sales. But a cult would grow up around the band, making them one of the key influences for the indie and alternative-rock movements of the 1980s and 1990s.

For the 15 years or so after Al Green found religion and bid adieu to secular music in the late 1970s, Memphis music took a turn for the mundane. The city produced an occasional notable artist (singer-songwriter Keith Sykes, indie rockers the Grifters) and brought in plenty of out-of-town acts (ZZ Top, John Prine) to record at independent studios such as Ardent. Unfortunately, though, the momentum that had driven the city's music scene for most of the century had dissipated.

It may be forlorn to expect the city to ever again witness musical eruptions as galvanic as the blues, rockabilly, and soul scenes of earlier decades, but the last few

Andrew Love and Wayne Jackson (aka The Memphis Horns) worked at the Stax recording studio with Sam Moore (of Sam & Dave) and Stax-owner Jim Stewart (seated).
PHOTO: FANTASY, INC.–STAX ARCHIVES

years have seen Memphis begin to make a move again, once more becoming a force on the national music scene.

The Current Music Scene

Though locals argue about how much it has to do with the city's storied musical past, everyone seems to agree that the current music scene in Memphis is the strongest it has been in more than 20 years. Memphis music is once again making major inroads into the national music scene, with most of the action thus far concentrated in four areas: hip-hop, hard rock, gospel, and, of course, the blues.

Over the last several years, Memphis has emerged as one of the leading markets in the country for rap/hip-hop, both in terms of consumption and production. Leading the way has been Three-6 Mafia, a "gangsta rap" collective who, along with group off-shoots such as Gangsta Boo and Project Pat, have released a string of gold and platinum albums—the first Memphis-based artists to have such massive and sustained success since Isaac Hayes and Al Green. The Three-

6 contingent is merely at the forefront of a large local and regional scene that is likely to produce other national stars in the near future. Another promising Memphis talent is Gangsta Blac, a local rapper with the major record label Koch.

Hard-rock scenes have been bubbling up all over the country in the last few years, as metal has returned as the most commercially viable rock music. Memphis boasts one of the country's hottest hard-rock scenes, led by Saliva, the rap-metal band that had been at the forefront of Memphis metal for several years. Saliva signed to major label Island-Def Jam in the late 1990s, releasing their major label debut, *Every Six Seconds,* in early 2001. With strong promotion behind them, Saliva emerged as one of rock music's breakout national stars, and their signing sparked a wave of other local hard-rock bands inking major-label contracts, including Dust for Life, Breaking Point, and Primer 55. These bands are products of a fertile local scene centered at the New Daisy Theatre, a large rock club on the east end of Beale Street.

Gospel music is huge in Memphis, though the local scene's national impact largely rests on the work of the late O'Landa Draper and his choir, the Associates. Draper formed the group while still a college student and led them to Grammy-winning success until his death from kidney failure in 1998. The Associates have continued since Draper's death under the name O'Landa Draper's Associates.

As for the blues, it remains the city's largest tourist draw and largest local scene, but the last few years have seen the city produce a few blues artists of national renown. The North Mississippi Allstars, an interracial blues rock band from nearby Coldwater, Mississippi, has become a critical cause célèbre and commercial force, especially as a concert draw. Led by the two sons of long-time local producer and musical raconteur Jim Dickinson, the band has drawn comparisons to the Allman Brothers while selling records to jam-band aficionados and alternative-rock fans alike. Along the way they've garnered fawning press coverage in national publications such as *Rolling Stone* and *The New York Times.*

Another major blues artist that has come out of Memphis is Alvin Youngblood Hart, an internationally known star on the blues circuit whose stylistically ambitious take on the blues tradition marks him as an inheritor of Taj Mahal.

Memphis can also claim the last decade's most aesthetically influential blues scene in the form of the droning hill-country blues captured by nearby Oxford, Mississippi, label Fat Possum. Fat Possum artists such as R.L. Burnside and the late Junior Kimbrough were among the most respected blues artists to emerge in the 1990s, and their sound, with its droning, hypnotic guitar riffs and guttural vocals, is equally popular among blues, rock, and punk fans.

Two of the city's very best blues/jazz performers—Di Anne Price and Richard Johnston—float from club to club. They can be found on Beale occasionally, but they are both well worth searching for at more out-of-the-way, and more intimate, local clubs. Johnston is a young, white blues player of sublime skill and surprising restraint. His one-man-band attack recently won him the grand prize at the Blues Foundation's International Blues Challenge amateur contest. The unjustly unknown Price might be as close as you can come to a Bessie Smith or Ella Fitzgerald in this day and time—a widely acknowledged local treasure.

Some of the most dynamic blues performers in the city can be found on Beale Street. B.B. King's Blues Club has the street's deepest and finest roster of house acts in the form of diva Ruby Wilson and blues player Little Jimmy King. Up the street Rum Boogie Café boasts regular performances from Beale stalwarts James Govan and the Boogie Blues Band.

Other performers include the Daddy Mack Blues Band and legendary local barrelhouse-piano player Mose Vinson, who perform regularly at the Center for Southern Folklore, a funky downtown space devoted solely to preserving the city's cultural heritage. Hollywood Allstars might be the finest blues band in the city, but to hear them you'll have to go to Wild Bill's juke joint in North Memphis, an excursion that's only for the brave of heart.

The city's local rock scene—outside of hard rock and metal—is a rich mix heavy

You can still hear Memphis sounds on Beale, both in the street and in the clubs.

PHOTO: MEMPHIS CONVENTION AND VISITORS BUREAU

Music Attractions

If you are an aficionado of Memphis music specifically or rock and roll or soul music in general, you won't want to miss these attractions. (See the Attractions chapter for more details and information on each one.)

Gibson Guitar Factory
145 Lt. George W. Lee Avenue
(901) 543–0800
Here you can take a tour and watch guitars being made by hand. The Memphis Rock 'n' Soul Museum is located in the same building.

Graceland Mansion
Elvis Presley Boulevard
(901) 332–3322, (800) 238–2000
www.elvis.com
This is the home of Elvis Presley, where you can tour the house and see all of Elvis's gold records and other memorabilia.

The Lewis Ranch
1595 Malone Road, Nesbit, Miss.
(662) 429–1290
This is Jerry Lee Lewis's home, which is open to tours. Call ahead, as hours vary.

Memphis Rock 'n' Soul Museum
145 Lt. George W. Lee Avenue
(901) 543–0800
www.memphisrocknsoul.org
This museum tells how Memphis played a key role in the development of rock and roll, soul, and other American music.

Stax Museum of American Soul Music
926 East McLemore Street
(901) 946–2535
www.soulsvilleusa.com
Built on the site of the former Stax Records studio, the museum tells the story of this famed studio, where Otis Redding, Isaac Hayes, and other Southern soul stars recorded, as well as the development of soul in Detroit, Philadelphia, and other American cities.

Sun Studio
706 Union Avenue
(901) 521–0664, (800) 441–6249
www.sunstudio.com
This tiny studio produced musical giants, including Elvis Presley, Jerry Lee Lewis, and Johnny Cash, as well as the first rock and roll recording.

W. C. Handy House
352 Beale Street
(901) 522–1556
This modest house is where W. C. Handy lived in Memphis at the time he "discovered" the blues.

Books about Memphis Music

There have been plenty of books written about Memphis music. Here are some of the best ones out there:

It Came from Memphis by Robert Gordon, Pocket Books, 2001.

Last Train to Memphis: The Rise of Elvis Presley by Peter Guralnick, Little Brown & Co., 1994.

Careless Love: The Unmaking of Elvis Presley by Peter Guralnick, Little Brown & Co., 1999.

Sweet Soul Music by Peter Guralnick, Little Brown & Co., 1999.

Deep Blues by Robert Palmer, Viking Press, 1995.

The Land Where the Blues Began by Alan Lomax, New Press, 2002.

on garage rock and roots-rock. Memphis has always been one of the country's biggest garage-rock cities, dating back to a 1960s heyday that produced the likes of the Box Tops, Sam the Sham, and the Gentrys. Now it's more of an underground scene, but garage bands such as the Reigning Sound, the Tearjerkers, the Subteens, and Eighty Katie are among the city's most popular local acts.

Equally big on the city's club scene in recent years is alternative-country-oriented bands. The North Mississippi Allstars protégés Lucero are one of the city's most highly regarded acts, and singer-songwriter Cory Branan is widely regarded as one of the city's most important emerging talents.

Ready to check out some music? Turn to the Nightlife chapter for its listing of clubs and other music venues.

As a current music-industry center, Memphis pales in comparison to its cross-state rival, Nashville. One reason is that although Nashville is the center for one genre of music—country, of course— Memphis's music heritage, much like its population, is considerably more diverse, with blues, rock and roll, jazz, soul, and gospel all sharing the city's attention. A more important reason for the industry gap may be the disparate temperaments of the two cities' most important musical entrepreneurs. Nashville—sometimes to its credit,

sometimes not—is a town of company men. Those who built up the Grand Ole Opry and the city's recording infrastructure were eager to join the music establishment. Memphis, on the other hand, has always been a city of mavericks and independent record labels, with the iconoclastic Sam Phillips as a model.

That said, Memphis still boasts a stronger music-industry infrastructure than most cities. Local recording studios continue to draw national talent, particularly Ardent Studios, which has been home to mainstream rock artists such as 3 Doors Down and Sister Hazel and contemporary blues performers such as Deborah Coleman. Easley Studios is one of the most popular recording homes for indie and punk bands, such as Pavement and the White Stripes.

Memphis also boasts one of the country's most active chapters of the National Association of Recording Arts and Sciences, serving as head of a regional branch that includes St. Louis and New Orleans. The Blues Foundation, the world's blues-related organization, calls Memphis home and hosts the Handy Awards (the blues' version of the Grammys) in Memphis every year. And recently, the city and county government formed the Memphis and Shelby County Music Commission, a body formed to promote what the city considers its greatest natural resource.

Nightlife

Bars and Clubs

Brewpubs

Coffeehouses

Concert Venues

Country-and-Western
Clubs/Bars

Dance Clubs

Gay Bars

Juke Joints

Movies

Sports Bars

Wine Bars

Memphis nightlife is centered on historic Beale Street, a 3-block stretch of clubs where music can be heard well into the wee hours seven days a week. The west end of Beale is one of the most lively blues centers you'll find anywhere in the country, although there are also some chain clubs and bars such as Hard Rock Café and Wet Willie's daiquiri bar.

Anchoring the street is B.B. King's Blues Club, which consistently brings in first-rate and high-profile national blues and roots acts, in addition to having the strip's best house acts, including diva Ruby Wilson.

Other choice Beale venues are Rum Boogie Café, which boasts regular performances from Beale stalwarts James Govan and the Boogie Blues Band; King's Palace Café where you can find dynamic jazz singer/pianist Charlie Wood most nights. Elvis Presley's Memphis features rockabilly amid décor fit for The King.

On Beale between Second and Fourth Streets, the clubs have sidewalk bars, and you can buy drinks there and carry them around with you. The bars can serve until 5:00 A.M. on weekends, although they rarely do. On Fridays and other nights, you can buy a wristband for $15 (or more on special nights), which gets you into many of the clubs on those 2 blocks of Beale.

Things change regularly on Beale Street, so you might want to check local newspapers or log onto www.bealestreet.com for the latest information on the street. One thing to look for: Pat O'Brien's, the New Orleans bar famous for its Hurricane cocktail, is scheduled to open in late 2002.

The local blues scene, however, isn't restricted to Beale Street. The finest venue for Memphis roots music may be the Center for Southern Folklore, an intimate club and folk-art gallery located in the Pembroke Square building just north of Beale Street. (See the Attractions chapter for more information about CSF.)

Inside the Gibson Guitar plant directly south of Beale, you'll find The Lounge, which offers a good lineup of live music amid sophisticated uptown decor. Then, for the brave of heart, there are the juke joints, Delta remnants that still litter the city. Wild Bill's in North Memphis has become a hip spot in recent years and boasts a house band, the Hollywood Allstars, which might be the city's most authentic blues band.

The local rock scene is anchored by a handful of clubs in the midtown and downtown areas. The New Daisy Theatre on Beale Street books prominent national club acts as well as lots of local hard rock. Also downtown is the tiny Map Room, a hipster bar that's home to local indie and punk bands, with a few national acts of the same stripe. The club also does occasional jazz shows that are among the city's best-kept musical secrets.

In midtown, the Hi-Tone Café specializes in roots-rock and Americana acts and books a more consistently interesting lineup of national acts than any other small club in town. The Hi-Tone is also a favorite spot for local punk, garage, and roots bands. The Young Avenue Deli, also in Midtown, books many of the same local bands as the Hi-Tone, as well as an uneven, if often impressive, lineup of national acts that tend more toward college-oriented jam bands and alternative rock. The Blue Monkey near Overton Square features a diverse lineup of local acts and occasional national ones that appeal to a more upscale, and more adult, crowd. The other major rock club in Memphis is Newby's, the cornerstone of the University of Memphis–based Highland Strip, where the club books rock, roots, and blues acts that appeal to their largely collegiate clientele.

Bluesman B.B. King's namesake club anchors the west end of Beale Street.
PHOTO: MEMPHIS CONVENTION AND VISITORS BUREAU

For something a little different, visitors can look to a couple of coffeehouses: Precious Cargo Exchange downtown for jazz, reggae, and hip-hop and Otherlands in midtown for acoustic music.

Memphis also has its share of the usual nightlife suspects, including sports bars, gay bars, and dance clubs. There are a few country-and-western bars as well, not surprising for a city that sits between the country-music capital of the world (Nashville) and Texas.

A glitzy alternative to the Memphis nightlife scene lies 30 miles south in Tunica County, Mississippi, where you'll find the third-largest gaming resort between Atlantic City and Las Vegas. There, the action goes 24 hours a day at 10 world-class Las Vegas–style casinos, each with hundreds of slot machines as well as dozens of game tables featuring black jack, craps, and other gaming staples. All of them have good-quality restaurants and their own hotels, and many feature live entertainment. (For more details, check out the Casinos chapter.)

In terms of concerts Memphis gets major acts each year that have included the Rolling Stones, Bob Dylan, and Pearl Jam. The city's prime concert venue is the downtown Pyramid Arena, but there are also shows at the Mid-South Coliseum, The Orpheum Theater, and Mud Island Amphitheater. For country and bluegrass the Lucy Opry at Bartlett Performing Arts Center in the suburbs is the prime venue, although the suburban Germantown Performing Arts Center also books bluegrass and New Age acts in addition to a first-rate cast of classical performances.

The city's concert scene is augmented by a great collection of music festivals, including the Beale Street Music Festival, a three-day May event packed with national and local music acts that has grown into one of the nation's leading music events. On a much smaller scale is the Memphis Music and Heritage Festival, a definitive celebration of local and regional artists held downtown each Labor Day weekend. See the Annual Events chapter for more details on these and other festivals, and check local newspapers for smaller events that might be taking place during your visit.

As de facto capital of the Mississippi Delta, Memphis is also close to a legion of small-town blues festivals, the best of which is likely the King Biscuit Blues Festival in nearby Helena, Arkansas. Others include the Delta Blues Festival in Greenville, Mississippi, and the Sunflower River and Gospel Festival in Clarksdale, Mississippi. (For more information see the Day Trips chapter.)

If you party in Memphis, you should be aware of the drunk-driving laws, which are severe. You are considered to be driving under the influence if your blood-alcohol level reaches .10 (this will likely be reduced to .8 at some point), and carrying open containers of alcoholic beverages in cars is illegal. It's best to have a designated driver in your party (the bartender may well give them their soft drinks for free), or to stay within walking distance of Beale or wherever you plan to drink. All Memphis bars are required to serve food, even if it's only a microwave burrito. Most places do a lot better than that, however, offering a decent selection of pub grub such as hot wings, nachos, and sandwiches.

Bars and Clubs

Beale Street

Alfred's
197 Beale Street
(901) 525-3711
With its prime location at the corner of Beale and Third Street and a huge, two-story outdoor patio, Alfred's is the prime people-watching spot on Beale. The night-time crowds tend toward the young and the yuppie, and you won't hear any of the street's trademark blues among the club's regular musical stable, which ranges from pop to salsa to "classic-rock" covers. There's also a dance floor.

B.B. King's Blues Club
143 Beale Street
(901) 524-5464
Blues legend B.B. King doesn't actually own this club—Beale's cornerstone venue, both

literally and figuratively—but he does play here at least once a year. The club's regular stable of performers—most recently including Beale diva Ruby Wilson—may be the street's best. But what makes B.B.'s special is that it may be the only club on the street that regularly draws A-list touring-blues talent, with artists such as Marcia Ball, Clarence "Gatemouth" Brown, and Chubby Carrier regular visitors. Most Thursdays the club also hosts tapings of *Beale Street Caravan,* a Memphis-based, internationally syndicated public-radio program that is the most widely heard blues radio show in the world.

Black Diamond
153 Beale Street
(901) 521–0800

Perhaps the most intimate and least touristy blues club on Beale, the Black Diamond has live music most nights, usually from local artists. The club also hosts events with the Beale Street Blues Society and has recently been the host of Keith Sykes Songwriter's Night, a monthly singer-songwriter revue hosted by Sykes, one of the city's most successful songwriters. Through a side door you can visit Tater Red's Mojos, a voodoo and T-shirt shop with all kinds of funky stuff.

Blues City Café
138 Beale Street
(901) 526–3637

With a large kitchen and dining area connected to the music side, the ultra-casual Blues City Café is the best spot on Beale for late-night dining, with steaks, ribs, shrimp, and catfish available into the wee hours. The musical lineup is mostly local. Sunday nights feature FreeWorld, a local jazz and jam band that has been together longer than just about any other local act. Sometimes well-known musicians or Beale Street regulars will sit in for a set.

Elvis Presley's Memphis
126 Beale Street
(901) 527–6900

Owned by Elvis Presley Enterprises (aka Graceland), this haven for Elvis fans is housed in the building that once boasted Lansky Brothers, the clothing shop where Elvis bought his hip threads. There's plenty of Elvis memorabilia to gawk at, including a pool table where Elvis once played Paul McCartney. The bar design is as irresistibly gaudy as The King himself, and its live-wire house band, the Dempseys, is actually the city's finest rockabilly act. And, yes, you can order Elvis's favorite, a fried peanut-butter-and-banana sandwich.

Hard Rock Café
315 Beale Street
(901) 529–0007

Hard Rock is a relatively recent addition to Beale, so you probably know what to expect from this celebrated chain—loads of choice rock memorabilia, overpriced burgers, and plenty of T-shirts in the souvenir shop. The Hard Rock's music bookings are mostly local bands and, befitting the name, mostly hard rock.

King's Palace Café
162 Beale Street
(901) 521–1851

One of the older clubs on Beale, King's Palace features a New Orleans–oriented menu that's considered one of the strip's most reliable dining options. As for music, local jazz keyboard player and vocalist Charlie Wood plays at King's Palace almost every night. Often compared to Mose Allison, Wood is one of the city's finest acts.

Rum Boogie Café
182 Beale Street
(901) 528–0150

Rum Boogie is the longest-running bar on Beale, which begins serving up blues to appreciative crowds way before urban renewal transformed the rest of the strip. Now the Boogie is a well-worn respite on a street marked by neon newness. James Govan and the Blues Boogie Band can be heard here most nights and may be the best house band on Beale. Govan is more soul than blues and is equally talented at pleasing tourists with sing-alongs like "Mustang Sally" and showing off his deep-soul vocal chops with strong renditions of classics like Sam Cooke's "Bring It on Home to Me."

You'll find live music and a good time at Rum Boogie's on Beale Street every night.

PHOTO: MEMPHIS CONVENTION AND VISITORS BUREAU

Silky O'Sullivan's
181 Beale Street
(901) 522–9596

A standard rite of passage for area fraternity and sorority types is the "Diver" at Silky's Billed as "a gallon of Southern fun," the Diver is a big yellow plastic bucket filled with some type of alcoholic concoction and multiple straws. You can see tipsy young things lugging Divers up and down Beale on most nights. Inside, Silky's is more a social hangout than a serious blues club. A crowd-participation-friendly dueling pianos act is the most common entertainment. Silky's also has a huge outdoor patio where you can party with the bar's pet goat.

Downtown

Automatic Slim's Tonga Club
83 South Second Street
(901) 525–7948

With a great location right across the street from The Peabody hotel, chic decor, and a polished, adventurous menu, Slim's is one of downtown's finest restaurants. Its bar is also one of downtown's prime

"see-and-be-seen" locales, where dress is a step above casual and the drinks of choice tend toward martinis and cosmopolitans.

Center for Southern Folklore
119 South Main Street
(901) 525–3655
www.southernfolklore.com

This large, brightly painted venue lives up to its name—promoting Southern culture from music to folk art to food. The music, which focuses on but isn't at all relegated to blues, is a cut above Beale in terms of authenticity. This funky space features live music most nights, including regular performances by the Daddy Mack Blues Band and legendary local barrelhouse-piano player Mose Vinson. Once the jewel of Beale Street, the nonprofit center moved but continues to function as a nightclub, tourist attraction, cafe, and unofficial welcome center. Most weekdays the center serves lunch alongside performances from a fine batch of local musicians. Check out the artwork too, especially the great folk art in the center's "Sofo" gallery. There's usually a modest cover charge during performances. It's in the lower level of the Pembroke Building, so look for the sign on Main Street.

Dan McGuinness Irish Pub
150 Peabody Place
(901) 527–8500
The best meet-and-drink spot in the downtown Peabody Place entertainment complex, Dan McGuinness boasts a full Irish menu and first-rate service. The bar also features a popular pub quiz every Tuesday night and the friendly management style of Jo Delahunty, an Irish lass who's a great favorite among Memphians. Despite the Peabody Place address, the pub faces Second Street.

Earnestine & Hazel's
531 South Main Street
(901) 523–9754
This one-time brothel is one of the hot spots in downtown's recently resurgent South Main neighborhood. A funky two-story bar with loads of character, Earnestine & Hazel's is a favorite spot for young, hip Memphians to wind up a night of partying, dancing to tunes on the bar's first-rate jukebox and a downing a "soulburger," one of the city's most heralded late-night snacks. The bar has also begun booking punk and alternative-rock bands on some nights.

Flying Saucer Draught Emporium
130 Peabody Place
(901) 523–7468
Located just a block off Beale, this beer palace is prime real estate and a popular place for downtown professionals to grab a postwork drink. During the warm months, which is most of them, the large bar's open windows let a breeze in and the music out. The music is mostly local and usually not too exciting, but the Saucer has probably the largest beer menu in the city, both on tap and in bottles. It's a yuppie mob scene on Friday and Saturday nights.

High Point Pinch
111 Jackson Avenue
(901) 525–4444
This popular late-night dive is one of the cornerstone bars of the north downtown

Memphis area known as the Pinch District. Located just a couple of blocks east of the downtown basketball/entertainment arena The Pyramid, the Pinch is a prime spot for a postevent brew or two. The bar also features live music most nights—usually blues and classic-rock locals—though music seems to be secondary to hanging out at the Pinch. The other cornerstone is The North End, situated just across Jackson from High Point Pinch.

Huey's
77 South Second Street
(901) 527–2700
The downtown location of the popular local burger chain, offering live blues and jazz on Sunday afternoons and evenings. (See the Midtown listing in this chapter for more details on music and the Restaurant chapter for more details on food.)

Jillian's
150 Peabody Place
(901) 543–8800
This massive chain-entertainment complex is a three-story fun house for adults located within downtown's Peabody Place mall. Jillian's has a full bowling alley, a state-of-the-art arcade, several pool tables, and huge banks of big-screen TVs for sports viewing. It has been accurately described around town as "Chuck E. Cheese for grownups." The bar/restaurant is on the ground floor. Kids are allowed until 10:00 P.M.; after that, you have to be 21 to enter.

Kudzu's
603 Monroe Avenue
(901) 525–4924
Though it may call itself "a neighborhood bar looking for a neighborhood," Kudzu's really is the place in Memphis where everybody knows your name. Located in an off-the-beaten path, slightly industrial part of downtown, Kudzu's is an intimate, no-frills bar that's a popular hangout for local reporters, midtowners, and downtowners. At night, Kudzu's offers a diverse array of entertainment, from singer-songwriter nights to magic shows to improv comedy to the occasional touring band. The bar's Wednesday-night pub quiz is a Memphis staple.

The Lounge
Second Street and George W. Lee Avenue
(901) 544–7998, ext. 4070
This spacious club, with its comfortable leather chairs and sofas, feels like an urbane, updated take on Manhattan supper clubs of the 1950s. It's tucked inside the Gibson Guitar Factory and has a great menu of appetizers. The drinks can be expensive, and there's usually a cover charge for the live music.

The Map Room
2 South Main Street
(901) 543–8686
Downtown is also home to the tiny Map Room, a hipster bar that features local indie and punk bands with a few national acts of the same stripe. The club also does occasional jazz shows that are among the city's best-kept musical secrets. The atmosphere is comfortable and homey, with upholstered chairs and couches as well as tables and chairs, and Map Room has its beer license.

The Peabody Hotel Lobby Bar
149 Union Avenue
(901) 529–4000
It's been said that the Delta begins in the lobby of this grand old hotel, and there may be no better place to spot celebrities and other high-rollers than by sipping a pricey cocktail at The Peabody's lobby bar and spending an evening people-watching. The hotel's usually open rooftop is a choice spot to hang out and get a glimpse of downtown from above, and on Thursday nights during summer, it's the site of a massive party featuring live music and plenty of singles action.

Sleep Out Louie's
88 Union Avenue
(901) 527–5337
This downtown watering hole, which makes its home in a former fire station, has one of the best happy hours in town, attracting a range of professionals who work and live in the area. It's also got a great patio for sitting outdoors on nice days, with service even in December if there's an unexpected heat wave. If you're

hungry, there's a full menu of pub grub, too. Sleep Out's is a great place to party before Pyramid Arena events, baseball games, or other downtown happenings, especially University of Memphis Tigers and Grizzlies games, as there's a free shuttle bus to the games.

Midtown

Alex's Tavern
1445 Jackson Avenue
(901) 278–9086
A favorite hangout for the students at nearby Rhodes College, Alex's is a tiny bar with a big local reputation, frequently cited as a favorite bar, late-night dive, and jukebox spot by locals of all ages. Locals swear by the hamburgers here.

Hi-Tone Café
1913 Poplar Avenue
(901) 278–8663
This midtown bar, located right across the street from Overton Park, is actually one of the city's finest music venues. The sound is good, the room is cozy, and the bartenders are friendly. The city's best local rock and roots acts play here regularly, and the club boasts an uneven, if occasionally spectacular, mix of similar national acts for a small club. Some recent bookings have included The Itals and Marshall Crenshaw. The crowd is hip and very casual, with most patrons in their 20s and 30s. The club has a side room with pool tables and a dartboard, too. *Note to Elvis fans:* Guess who took karate lessons in this building years ago?

Huey's
1927 Madison Avenue
(901) 726–4372
This local burger chain, owned and operated by a member of local '60s garage-rock band the Box Tops, is a true Memphis staple, with Huey burgers one of the city's ultimate comfort foods. The midtown location is the original. On Sunday afternoons and evenings, it's also one of the city's best bets for live blues and jazz. All Huey's locations offer intelligently and lovingly booked live

music on Sundays for no cover. The midtown and downtown locations usually offer the choicest music options, but it's rare for any Huey's to offer music that isn't authentic roots music that's easy on the ears. (See the Restaurant chapter for more details on food.)

Newby's
539 South Highland Street
(901) 435-8408

Newby's is the signature club on the University of Memphis area Highland Strip and second only to the New Daisy on Beale among local rock clubs for the size of its music hall. Newby's caters to regional jam bands and college rock bands to appeal to nearby University of Memphis students. Newby's back patio sometimes has live acoustic music as well.

The P&H Café
1532 Madison Avenue
(901) 726-0906

The quintessential midtown bar, the P&H (aka "Poor and Hungry"), seems to be everybody's most beloved watering hole, with idiosyncratic local cartoons, photos, and such lining the walls and ceilings. There's also first-rate people-watching, cheap beer, and pub grub, and the bar's outrageous proprietress, local celebrity Wanda Wilson. The P&H is the favorite hangout of the local theater crowd and has live local music on an irregular basis. No liquor is served here; it's strictly a beer joint.

Side Street Grill
31 South Florence
(901) 274-8955

This bar in midtown's Overton Square neighborhood specializes in martinis and other festive cocktails and features a nice outdoor patio with umbrellas, wrought iron, and magnolia trees. Side Street is cigar-friendly and employs a powerful fan to keep the indoor air relatively clean. If you're hungry, you can get a tasty and substantial steak or salmon dinner here for less than $15. Appetizers also are served from 4:00 P.M. to 3:00 A.M.

Young Avenue Deli
2119 Young Avenue
(901) 278-0034

This large bar/restaurant/club in the bohemian Cooper-Young neighborhood rivals the Hi-Tone as midtown's best music venue. The sound isn't as good and the atmosphere not as intimate as its crosstown rival, but the bar is bigger and better-stocked, the music lineup, both in terms of local and national acts, is similar, and the pool tables are more plentiful at what Memphians just refer to as "the Deli." The crowd at the Deli tends to be fairly college-oriented, and the bar has a reputation as a choice, laid-back meat market even when there isn't a band playing. The Deli also serves up outstanding French fries and a menu of filling sandwiches.

East Memphis and the Suburbs

Bottom Line
1817 Kirby Parkway
(901) 755-2481

This no-frills local hangout, north of Poplar, which has been around for 25 years, caters to a yuppie crowd in their 20s, 30s, and 40s. There's live music most nights. Lunch and dinner are served, and a happy hour goes from 2:00 to 7:00 P.M. It's a good place to take in a University of Memphis basketball game or just hang out amid the dark wood and memorabilia.

The Grove Grill
4550 Poplar Avenue
(901) 818-9951

The bar at The Grove Grill, attracting well-dressed professionals of all ages, is one of the hippest places in East Memphis to get a martini or other cocktail. Happy hour is very popular, and you can order the usual array of cocktails and beer as well as fine single-malt scotch and wines from the restaurant's wine list. It's a good-looking cherry-wood bar, with walls painted in soothing colors. It can get crowded, though, with a combination of bar customers and people waiting for tables at the restaurant. You don't have to go to the restaurant to sample Grove

Grill's well-regarded cuisine. Just order fresh oysters, appetizers, or other delectables at the bar. It's situated in the back of Laurelwood shopping center near Davis-Kidd Booksellers.

Huey's
2858 Hickory Hill
(901) 375–4373
1771 North Germantown Parkway, Cordova
(901) 754–3885
2130 West Poplar Avenue, Collierville
(901) 854–4455
The popular local burger chain offers live blues and jazz on Sunday afternoons and evenings. (See the Midtown listing in this chapter for more details on music and the Restaurant chapter for more details on food.)

Patrick's
4698 Spottswood Avenue
(901) 682–2853
This casual East Memphis restaurant/bar, situated in Audubon shopping center, packs them in for lunch, happy hour, and evenings. Happy hour usually attracts an older crowd of bankers, stockbrokers, and other professionals, but later the crowd is the 30s and 40s set. There's live music on weekends and Wednesday nights, too. With its dark wood and checkered tablecloths, this favorite hangout serves plate lunches at midday and until 8:00 P.M., as well as steaks, burgers, and other fare.

The Stage Stop
2951 Cela Street, Raleigh
(901) 382–1576
If you want to party way off the beaten path, this is the place. Those county-fair, long-hair-and-metal days of yore never went out of vogue at the Stage Stop, a metal-and-proud-of-it rock venue in the working-class suburb of Raleigh. Check this place out on a weekend night and see why it has inspired Memphians to lovingly refer to the neighborhood as "Rockin' Raleigh."

T.J. Mulligan's Cordova
8071 Trinity Road, Cordova
(901) 756–4480
This locally owned Irish–style pub is very popular among the yuppie set, although the crowd can range from college age to 40s,

T.J. Mulligan's is one of the many nightspots where you can enjoy live music and a lively bar scene.
PHOTO: MEMPHIS CONVENTION AND VISITORS BUREAU

depending on the band that's playing that night. Mulligan's is busy all evening from happy hour through the wee hours, and local bands play on Tuesdays and on weekends. Mulligan's is open from 11:00 A.M. to 3:00 A.M. daily, serving plate lunches at midday and a menu of burgers, chicken sandwiches, and other fare until 2:30 A.M. It looks and feels like a big Irish nouveau pub, despite the fact it's tucked behind the Exxon at Trinity Road off Germantown Parkway. You'll also find T.J. Mulligan's at 362 North Main Street (901-523-1453) and at Quince and Kirby in East Memphis (901-753-8056).

Brewpubs

Boscos
7615 West Farmington, Germantown
(901) 756–7310
www.boscosbeer.com

Boscos considers itself Tennessee's original brewpub and makes its own award-winning beers. Here, you can try a number of handmade beers, including its Flaming Stone beer and Germantown Alt as well as seasonal beers. There's also a full bar. The original Boscos is situated in Saddle Creek shopping center just off Poplar Avenue, where you can sit on the outdoor patio or inside, where brickwork, blonde tones, and a colorful wall mural make for a comfortable environment. The food is great, especially the handmade pizzas baked in a wood-burning oven. (See Restaurants chapter for details.)

Boscos Squared
2120 Madison Avenue
(901) 432–2222
www.boscosbeer.com

Boscos Overton Square location is a popular nightspot, where midtowners gather to enjoy handmade beers or cocktails as well as fresh-made pizzas, appetizers including fried artichoke hearts and calamari, and entrees ranging from salads to steak. The beer menu includes Midtown Brown, an English-style nut-brown ale, Boscos classics such as Flaming Stone and Ed's Porter, and seasonal beers. Boscos also has a very popular jazz brunch.

Gordon Biersch
141 South Main Street
(901) 543–3330
www.gordonbiersch.com

Gordon Biersch may be a chain (mostly West Coast), but it's definitely worth a visit for its brewed-on-the-premises beers, handsome decor, and good food. During nice weather Gordon Biersch's patio is probably the best place to take in the downtown street scene, for it's situated right on the pedestrian portion of Main Street for optimal people-watching. The German-style beers, which include a blonde bock and pilsner as well as seasonal beers, are brewed on the premises, and you see the operation through a glass wall in the back of the restaurant. The menu has an Asian flavor and includes favorites such as fried calamari, grilled skewers, and potstickers. Open daily for lunch and dinner and serves a late-night menu until around midnight.

Coffeehouses

Borders
6685 Poplar Avenue, Germantown
(901) 754–0770

The cafe at Borders draws a crowd that's as diverse as the bookstore and music store clientele and includes all ages as well as families. The cafe serves all kinds of coffee drinks, other beverages, pastries, and light food items such as sandwiches. Despite being part of a national chain, the Borders cafe brings in plenty of local musical acts, including bluegrass and folk acoustic musicians, who perform on many weekends. You can pick up a Borders newsletter in the store or cafe for details about music and other in-store events. The café provides a nonsmoking, nonalcoholic environment and operates whenever the store is open. The cafe is open until 10:00 P.M. Monday through Thursday, 11:00 P.M. on Fridays and Saturdays, and 9:00 P.M. on Sundays.

Café Expresso at the Ridgeway Inn
5679 Poplar Avenue
(901) 763–3888

This suburban East Memphis coffee shop isn't the hippest place in town, but it does serve great homemade desserts, including cheesecakes, some sinful chocolate concoctions, and key lime pie. You can also get coffee and espresso drinks as well as sandwiches and brunch fare. The atmosphere is cheerful, with lots of tile design.

Café Francisco
400 North Main
(901) 578–8002
Owned and operated by a homesick San Franciscan, this lofty coffeehouse feels as though it belongs in that urbane California city. There are booths in the front, but at the back of the store, there are loads of antiques and collectibles you can browse while you're waiting for your order. The cafe roasts its own coffee and also serves beer and wine as well as pastries, bagels, and a menu of excellent sandwiches and salads. Local acoustic musicians play here sometimes, both in the evenings and during lunchtime. Café Francisco is open every day for lunch and dinner but closes early on Sundays. Strictly nonsmoking.

Deliberate Literate
1997 Union Avenue
(901) 276–0174
The cafe at this midtown bookstore, Café Literati, is a popular hangout during the day and early-evening hours. There are comfortable sofas and overstuffed chairs throughout the shop, where you can relax with a book or magazine or chat with a friend or associate, as well as cafe tables outdoors to be enjoyed during nice weather. Literati serves Seattle's Best coffee, pastries, and a light menu of sandwiches and homemade soups. Open Monday through Saturday until 7:00 P.M. (See Shopping chapter for details about the bookstore.)

Java Cabana
2170 Young Avenue
(901) 272–7210
This homey, bohemian hangout in midtown's Cooper-Young neighborhood has been around since 1993, with live music on many evenings and a comfortable atmosphere for reading and conversation. Every Thursday night at 8:00 P.M. there's an open-mike poetry reading, featuring local writers and sometimes visiting poets, a Java Cabana fixture since it first opened. Wednesday nights there's live jazz and, on weekends, live folk, jazz, or flamenco music. Java Cabana serves up coffee and espresso drinks as well as homemade desserts and sandwiches. Smoking is not allowed at the cafe. Closed Monday; open until 10:00 P.M. during the week and until midnight on weekends. Not wheelchair accessible.

Otherlands Coffee Bar
641 South Cooper Street
(901) 278–4994
This friendly, bohemian midtown coffee shop attracts all kinds of customers, from yuppies grabbing their morning joe on the way to work, to the students, self-employed locals, and others drifting in throughout the day to the after-work and after-school crowd. Otherlands serves a big menu of coffees and coffee drinks, as well as H&H bagels, pastries, soups, quiches, sandwiches, and vegan fare. In addition to the tables, chairs, and couches indoors, there's an outdoor deck in the back. Otherlands also has an ecletic gift shop that features cards, jewelry, and all kinds of gifts. The coffee shop is open from early in the morning to 8:00 P.M., but Thursdays it's open to about 11:00 P.M., and features live music and beer. Strictly nonsmoking at all times.

The Precious Cargo Exchange
381 North Main Street
(901) 578–8446
There's something going on just about every night at this colorful, artsy north Main Street cafe, from poetry readings on Mondays and Fridays and comedy on Wednesdays to reggae on Saturdays and jazz on Sundays. The cafe's owners see this as a haven for visual and performing artists and for people who enjoy their work. Situated at the corner of Overton Street near the Pyramid, Precious Cargo serves coffees and espresso drinks as well as a menu of salads, desserts, and its special Jamaican jerk chicken. The colorfully painted walls are hung with local artists' work, and there's a chess game going most of the

time. Precious Cargo serves beer, but it's BYOB for harder stuff. Open until midnight every night, with extended hours on weekends.

Starbucks Coffee

Memphis has not been immune to the ubiquity of Starbucks, and you can find them all over the city and at the airport. They have all the familiar coffee and tea drinks, and most have both attractive seating areas and drive-through windows for to-go orders. For the location nearest you, check the phone book. If you're looking for Starbucks downtown, it's hidden away in Peabody Place Mall at 150 Peabody Place.

Concert Venues

Bartlett Performing Arts and Conference Center
3663 Appling Road, Bartlett
(901) 385–6440
www.bpacc.org
Built in 1998, this suburban venue sponsors a seasonal lineup that has featured such artists as singer/songwriter Iris DeMent, the Cashore Marionettes, and the Nashville Mandolin Ensemble. This is also home to the Lucy Opry, the area's prime venue for country and bluegrass music.

Germantown Performing Arts Center
1801 Exeter Road, Germantown
(901) 757–7256
www.gpac.com
This acoustically perfect theater, which opened in 1994, provides an intimate venue for performances of all kinds, including jazz and bluegrass. G-Pac, as locals call it, hosts a series of popular performances that have included artists such as Dave Brubeck, Doc Watson, and Alison Kraus.

Mud Island Amphitheater
125 North Front Street
(901) 576–6595
Although this outdoor venue isn't used as much as it formerly was, when there is a performance here, you can enjoy a river view along with the entertainment on the stage. From the entrance on Front Street, you take the tram across the river to Mud Island.

The New Daisy Theatre
330 Beale Street
(901) 525–8979
Anchoring the east end of Beale Street, this converted movie theater is the city's largest rock club, with a 1,000-person capacity and balcony seating above a large, open standing section. It's really a venue, though, because it's only active when there's a show. Almost all the club's local bookings and a good deal of its touring shows are hard rock and metal, but the club also books a surprising amount of jazz and other acts that are too big for small clubs, too small for the Pyramid. Recent bookings have included Lucinda Williams, Ani DiFranco, and Iggy Pop. Most shows are general admission, and you can buy tickets in advance from the box office.

The Orpheum Theater
203 South Main Street
(901) 525–7800
www.orpheum-memphis.com
The lavish Orpheum Theater, built in 1928 as a venue primarily for vaudeville, holds court at the foot of Beale Street in downtown Memphis. At present, in addition to hosting touring Broadway shows and other performing-arts productions, the Orpheum gets upscale, adult-oriented concerts by performers who have included Lyle Lovett and Natalie Merchant. The Orpheum sells tickets at the theater's box office or at a satellite box office at Davis-Kidd Booksellers.

The Pyramid Arena
1 Auction Avenue
(901) 521–7909
www.pyramidarena.com
Major touring acts, including Aerosmith, the Dixie Chicks, and Pearl Jam, perform here when they're in town. This arena is a 32-story, stainless-steel pyramid, with seating capacity for 21,000 people for concerts. Its management likes to boast that this is the third-largest pyramid in the world, taller than the Statue of Liberty. The Pyramid ticket office is open Monday through Friday, or you can get tickets through Ticketmaster (901–525-1515 or www.ticketmaster.com).

Country-and-Western Clubs/Bars

Denim and Diamonds
5353 Mendenhall
(901) 365-3633
www.denimanddiamonds.com

This cavernous country-and-western club is a three-ring circus of action on Thursday, Friday, and Saturday nights, with a large dance floor, three bars including a $1.00 shooter bar, eight pool tables, a mechanical bull, a 20-foot screen of country-and-western videos, and, of course, plenty of country-and-western dance music. Thursdays feature dance lessons and free admission for ladies until midnight. On Sundays Denim and Diamonds shifts gears for soul night, when it becomes a soul club featuring live music. Cover is $5.00 if you're 21 or over, $15.00 if you're under 21. There's also another dance club at the same location, The Mine, which features Top-40 dance music with some rap and hip-hop (see Dance Clubs.) Denim and Diamonds is at Mendenhall and Winchester, about 2 miles from the Mt. Moriah exit of I-240. Closed Monday through Wednesday.

Dance Clubs

The Mine
5353 Mendenhall
(901) 365-3633
www.denimanddiamonds.com

This dance club, situated inside the country-and-western club Denim and Diamonds, features Top-40 dance music as well as some rap and hip-hop. The club features a continual light show as well as a 16-set video wall, three dance floors, and two bars, one of which is a $1.00 shooter bar. Cover is $5.00 if you're 21 or over, $15.00 if you're under 21. The Mine is at the corner of Mendenhall and Winchester. Open Thursday through Saturday nights.

Raiford's
115 Vance Avenue
(901) 528-0150

Situated a couple of blocks south of Beale Street downtown, Raiford's used to be a neighborhood dance hall but in recent years has become one of the city's trendiest hangouts as a younger, more upscale crowd has flocked here. It's definitely the place for a shot of funkiness—beer served only in 40-ounce bottles and classic soul and contemporary R&B spun deep into the night by the club's irrepressible owner, Robert Raiford. The beloved sign out front reads NO DISCRIMINATION—and Raiford's means that, unless you try to come in wearing sneakers, a definite no-no.

Gay Bars

Backstreet
2018 Court Avenue
(901) 276-5522

This gay bar for men is definitely a late-night place, which doesn't crank up until about midnight. It features a show bar with cabaret performances as well as a lounge area with pool tables and a dance floor. There's also a patio. Backstreet serves beer only, so BYOB if you're drinking liquor or wine. To get to this midtown bar, take Madison and turn onto Morrison past The Blue Monkey. You'll see the club to the right across the street from the back of the milk plant.

Crossroads
111 North Claybrook and 1278 Jefferson Avenue
(901) 276-1882

This gay bar for men, at the corner of Jefferson, is actually two bars: a show bar that features a DJ, as well as cabaret shows and karaoke on various nights, and a neighborhood-style bar with a country flavor, pool tables, and a jukebox. In the back is a huge patio and yard. Crossroads is a beer bar, so BYOB if you're drinking wine or liquor. There's a modest cover charge on Friday and Saturday nights. The show bar is open at night, Thursday through Sunday, and the other bar is open seven days a week starting at noon. Both sections are open until 3:00 A.M.

J. Wag's
268 Madison Avenue
(901) 725–1909
This gay bar for men, which has been operating for more than 20 years across Madison from the Southern College of Optometry, is a fixture on the city's gay scene. J. Wag's is open 24 hours a day, and patrons describe it as a gay bar all day and a bigger gay bar at night. There are some cabaret shows, as well as a jukebox that has everything from country to disco. The bar serves beer, as well as a menu of burgers and sandwiches, but bring your own wine or liquor. The club generally charges a cover on weekends.

The Madison Flame
1588 Madison Avenue
(901) 278–9839
The Madison Flame, a gay bar for women, makes its home at a locally famous Memphis club address—the punk/New Wave club The Antenna operated here for many years. The Flame is a dance bar with DJ on Friday and Saturdays and features karaoke on Wednesdays and Sundays. It's a casual bar, with darts and other bar games, and a large variety of beers. Occasionally, there's live music. The Madison Flame is open only at night on Wednesday, Friday, Saturday, and Sunday. There's a cover on Saturdays.

One More
2117 Peabody Avenue
(901) 278–6673
This gay bar for women is situated on Peabody just off Cooper Street. Open seven days a week, One More is a neighborhood-style bar that serves beer as well as a menu of pizza, burgers, and other fare.

There's a jukebox, and there's live music on Wednesdays and Sundays. One More is packed on weekends. Open all day and until 3:00 A.M. every day. No cover.

The Pumping Station
1382 Poplar Avenue
(901) 272–7600
This gay bar for men, formerly The Pipeline, features a DJ on weekend nights and videos after 10:00 P.M. It's casual (drag attire not allowed), with pool tables and darts, an outside patio and deck, and a beer menu with 50 different brews (BYOB if you're drinking harder stuff). The Pumping Station has special nights, including local leather night and local bears night, as well as special events such as its Sunday beer bust and buffet and pool and dart tournaments. No cover.

Juke Joints

Wild Bill's
1580 Vollintine Avenue
(901) 726–5473
Never mind Beale Street. If you really want to hear the down-home blues upon which the city's music foundation was built, you have to go to this packed north-Memphis dive. The "club" itself is one small, unadorned room, the cover is usually $5.00, the beer is served only in 40-ounce bottles (if you want any other kind of alcohol, feel free to bring it yourself; Bill's will be happy to set you up), and the house band, the Hollywood Allstars, serves up the city's finest blues—bar none—on Friday and Saturday nights from 11:00 P.M. until well into the next morning. Expect a clientele that's about 75 percent older African Americans from the bar's working-class neighborhood and 25 percent 20-something white kids, with a smattering of European tourists and slumming rich folks thrown in for good measure. This is an essential Memphis experience.

Movies

Studio on the Square
2105 Court Street
(901) 725–7151
www.overtonsquare.com

Malco's Studio on the Square, unlike the city's other movie houses, has lounge areas and tables and serves specialty coffees, beer, wine, desserts, and light appetizers. It's a great place to hang around before or after the movies. This Overton Square theater has four screens that play the latest in foreign and independent films as well as some mainstream movies.

Sports Bars

Fox & Hound English Tavern
5101 Sanderlin Avenue
(901) 763–2013
847 Exocet Drive, Germantown
(901) 624–9060

These popular watering holes are less like English taverns and more like large American sports bars, with plenty of pool tables and big screens, where you can catch the big games of the moment. There's a good selection of beers, servers are very attentive, and its pub fare is better than most. Fox & Hound draws a good, yuppie-ish crowd both for happy hour and later in the evening. The Sanderlin location is in Sanderlin shopping center, next to the East Memphis Hilton, whereas the Exocet location is near the intersection of Germantown Parkway and Fischer Steel Road.

Sports Pub
5012 Park Avenue
(901) 767–8632

This locally owned hangout for sports enthusiasts doesn't look like much from the outside—it's tucked in behind the Firestone Tire place—but inside, this cozy pub has 16 screens of sporting events, a small stage that sometimes features live music, a decent beer list, and a menu of pub grub. The clientele of mostly 20-somethings gather here for Monday-night football, college basketball, or whatever big game is being aired. Open seven days a week starting at lunchtime.

Wine Bars

Le Chardonnay
5 Overton Square Lane
(901) 725–1375

The dark ambiance, great wine list, and wood-burning oven make this wine bar a romantic favorite among Memphians. You can get a table, sit at the bar, or nestle into one of the overstuffed chairs or couches. The wine list, which is heavy on domestic wines from California, Washington state, and elsewhere, has more than 100 choices, about equally divided between red and white. About 40 of these are available by the glass. There are also Australian, French, and Italian wines. Le Chardonnay also has a great menu that includes handmade pizzas, excellent salads, and appetizers that include baked Brie. Le Chardonnay is on the small street that runs parallel to and just south of Madison Avenue, between Cooper and Florence Streets.

Attractions

Memphis is rich with interesting, fun attractions of all kinds, including Graceland Mansion, the home of the late Elvis Presley and the king of area tourist attractions. Some 700,000 people tour the mansion each year, making it one of the most visited homes in America. A visit to Memphis is not complete without venturing over to The Peabody hotel lobby to see the famous ducks, who march (to the tune of John Philip Sousa music) to their fancy marble fountain for a day of swimming. A Memphis Queen Line cruise is a relaxing way to appreciate the grandeur of the Mississippi River and to get views of the city. You'll also find one-of-a-kind ornamental-metals museum perched on a bluff overlooking the river, the state's largest fine-arts museum, a handful of beautifully restored Victorian homes, and a working vineyard, just to name a few possibilities.

You won't want to miss the Memphis Rock 'n' Soul Museum or Sun Studio, where Elvis made his first record. Kids of all ages will enjoy the Memphis Zoo, not to mention Pink Palace Museum, with its IMAX theater and exhibits that include a replica of the world's first supermarket (Memphis's own Piggly Wiggly). You can learn about the courageous Memphis black sanitation workers and leaders such as Dr. Martin Luther King, Jr., at the National Civil Rights Museum, and see a farmhouse (Burkle House/Slavehaven) that, according to local legend, was a stop for slaves trying to escape up north to freedom.

We've divided the city's attractions into five categories: General Attractions, Museums, Memphis History, Memphis Music, and African American Heritage. If you're traveling with kids, be sure to check out the Kidstuff chapter, where we've singled out the attractions that appeal most to children. You will probably also want to read the History, Memphis Music, and African American Heritage chapters for background on many of these sights.

We list the hours of operation in effect during the busy summer season, but they sometimes change at other times of the year. It's never a bad idea to call an attraction or check its Web site in advance of your visit, to double-check hours and admission prices, which are subject to change, and to scope out information on temporary exhibitions. The Memphis Convention and Visitors Bureau at (901) 543-5300 or www.memphis-travel.com also has up-to-date information on its Web site, or you can pick up a free *Memphis Travel Guide & City Map* brochure from one of the information racks you'll find all over town at hotels and attractions. It's updated every year.

So don't forget your sunglasses, your camera, and your adventurous spirit—it's time to see the town.

General Attractions

A. Schwab
163 Beale Street
(901) 523–9782
A. Schwab is the oldest establishment on Beale. It was founded in 1876 by Abraham Schwab, an immigrant from Alsace, France, whose descendants still mind the store. A trip to Schwab's is like a trip back

in time, when stores had wooden floors and old-fashioned cash registers.

The first floor is full of tourist trinkets like Memphis bumper stickers, key rings, souvenir license plates, and more. The other two floors carry, well, everything. The store's motto is: "If you can't find it at Schwab's, you're better off without it." You can find straight razors, cast-iron griddles, ladies' bloomers, lye soap, and men's pants up to size 74. Upstairs are vintage signs, cash registers, and other memorabilia—on display, not for sale. Hours are 9:00 A.M. to 5:00 P.M. Monday through Saturday.

Beale Street
Downtown Memphis between Lt. George W. Lee Avenue and Peabody Place
www.bealestreet.com

This is the most visited street in America after New Orleans's Bourbon Street and is Tennessee's most-visited attraction. The street has a rich history, good souvenir shopping, and plenty of places to eat and party, with most of the action between Second and Fourth Streets. Points of interest include the W. C. Handy house and Memphis Police Museum. (See additional write-ups on Beale elsewhere in this chapter.)

Center for Southern Folklore & Cafe
119 South Main Street
(901) 525-3655
www.southernfolklore.com

Center for Southern Folklore is devoted to keeping the South's music, crafts, and other traditions alive. One of the biggest draws is live music performances that feature such legends as the Fieldstones, barrelhouse-musician Mose Vinson, and Blind Mississippi Morris. Contact the center for a schedule.

The center also features works by many African American artists, both in the small gallery that highlights the artists and in the gift shop, and it maintains extensive archives that are available to scholars. CSF has done films about Southern folklore, which the staff will show to interested visitors. It's also a cafe that serves beer, coffee, and other beverages as well as some food.

The center, which has moved around quite a bit over the years, now has a permanent home inside the Pembroke Square Building on Main Street at Gayoso. To get to the center, enter through the double doors nearest to Gayoso and go to the back of the lobby. (For more information about the center, see the Nightlife chapter.)

Cordova Cellars Winery
9050 Macon Road, Cordova
(901) 754-3442

This working winery offers tours of its wine-making operation as well as free samples of its wines. You go down into the basement of the main building to see casks, fermenters, crushers, and other equipment used in the process. Don't look for any grapevines, however. Cordova Cellars originally had its own vineyard but had to pull up the damaged vines in 1998. Instead, fruit is shipped in, 75 percent of it from outside Tennessee—Washington, Arkansas, and elsewhere—for its wines. In business since 1989, in 2001 the winery won bronze awards from the International Eastern Wine Competition for two of its wines, a 2000 Chardonnay and a Gewürztraminer made from Washington-state grapes. From April through October the winery has lawn concerts from 3:00 to 5:00 P.M. on Sundays featuring jazz, bluegrass, and other types of music. One of the performers in past years is cellist Joan Jenrenaud, sister of winery-owner Mary Dutcher Birks, who has appeared solo and with the group Kronos. The winery sells bottles of chilled wine at the concerts but nothing else, so remember to bring your own picnic, other beverages, blankets, or lawn chairs. To get to the winery, turn east onto Macon from Germantown Parkway and go about 3 miles. Macon is curvy, so stick with the twists and turns until you see the sign on the left.

The winery is open Tuesday through Saturday from 10:00 A.M. to 5:00 P.M. and Sunday from 1:00 to 5:00 P.M. Admission to the winery is free, but admission to the Sunday lawn concerts is $5.00 per person.

Graceland Mansion
3734 Elvis Presley Boulevard
(901) 332-3322, (800) 238-2000
www.elvis.com

If you visit only one attraction while in Memphis, Graceland Mansion should be it, even if you're not necessarily an Elvis fan. It's one of the most visited homes in America and is as American as the American dream that Elvis personifies to much of the world.

Graceland is the home that a 22-year-old Elvis Presley bought for $100,000 in 1957 for himself and his parents after his meteoric rise to superstardom and the place where he sought refuge, with family and friends, throughout his life. In those days it was situated in the best neighborhood in Memphis, and the 13.5-acre grounds kept the fans at bay and provided room for Elvis and his buddies to race golf carts around and indulge in other entertainments.

At present cars aren't allowed on the grounds of the mansion, but you can drive to the complex across the street, which resembles a big shopping mall, where you can park in the huge lot ($2.00 per car) and follow the signs into the main building, where you buy your tickets and queue up for a bus to take you across the street to the mansion. (Plenty of souvenir shops, additional attractions, and a few restaurants are available to visit before or after you see the mansion.) You get an audiotape gizmo, with a running narration that includes Lisa Marie Presley talking about her childhood memories of Elvis in the house.

When you walk through the front door, you see the living room, dining room, and his parents' bedroom, all done up in 1970s kitsch—white shag carpeting, mirrors, bright blues and purples in the decor. Truly one of a kind are the blue and bright yellow TV room, with Elvis's stereo and record collection, as well as three TVs, and the Jungle Room, with green shag carpet on floor and ceiling and Polynesian-style furniture. The story is that Elvis himself picked out the furniture at a Memphis retailer because it reminded him of Hawaii. The kitchen looks like, well, a normal 1970s kitchen but on the large side, where old-fashioned home-cooked meals as well as Elvis's favorite, fried peanut-butter-and-banana sandwiches, were turned out at all hours.

A recent addition to the tour is the garage, converted into a gallery that features furniture and clothing that belonged to Elvis. A highlight is the round, white fake-fur bed, with a stereo and mirrors built into a headboard that curves over the bed.

Although the home tells you about the man, including the fact that he loved to read and collected guns, the Trophy Room, housed in a separate building, is where you learn about his amazing career. Here the displays tell the Elvis story: his

Insiders' Tip

Several attractions allow you to make your visit a musical one, by putting on outdoor concerts during summer. Call ahead to the Dixon Gallery & Gardens, Cordova Cellars Winery, and Memphis Botanic Garden for information about performances by the Memphis Symphony Orchestra, Memphis musicians such as soprano Kallen Esperian, or soul man Isaac Hayes and others.

first records, his famous TV appearances, and press accounts that include an October 1956 Variety announcing how Elvis had become a millionaire in less than a year. You learn about his years in the army, his movie career, during which he made 33 films, his 1968 TV appearance known today as his "Comeback Special," and the Las Vegas performances. These include a gold lamé suit from 1957, posters and props from his movies, and all kinds of the Elvis-theme merchandise: billfolds, shoes, I LIKE ELVIS buttons, I HATE ELVIS buttons.

Even the most world-weary visitor can't help being dazzled by the dozens of gold and platinum records as well as the plaques that recognize his 14 Grammy nominations (with three wins, all for gospel), adulation from fan clubs and gratitude from the charities he supported. Elvis is one of the best-selling artists of all time, with gold, platinum, or multiplatinum records for more than 130 albums and singles. The collection is so big it spills over into another building.

The tour ends in the Meditation Garden, where Elvis and family members are

Getting Married in Memphis

Thinking about getting married during your trip to Memphis? If you're a U.S. citizen age 22 or older, all you need is your social security number and $32 for the marriage license. There's no waiting period, and the license is good (only in the state of Tennessee) for 30 days. If you're not a U.S. citizen, the same criteria apply, except you need to present your passport rather than social security number. If you are 19–21 years old and a U.S. citizen, you need to present your birth certificate, and you do not need parental consent.

You can get your marriage license at the Memphis County Clerk's Office at 150 Washington Street in downtown Memphis. Justices of the peace are not readily available to perform marriages, so you must make prior arrangements for a justice of the peace or other official/clergyman to perform the ceremony.

You'll find several wedding chapels that can accommodate small weddings, including The Wedding Chapel in Germantown (901–755–9885 or 800–755–9885) and For Your Special Moment Wedding Chapel (901–396–3723).

For something truly unique, contact the Center for Southern Folklore (901–525–3655). Someone can arrange for you to be married at the center in front of the First Church of the Elvis Impersonator, a one-of-a-kind mechanized Elvis shrine.

For a more conventional preplanned wedding, there are many options, ranging from the Chapel in the Woods at Graceland to the Memphis Queen Line to the National Ornamental Metals Museum. For more information get a copy of Mid-South Bride (901–521–9000 or www.midsouthbride.com), an annual magazine that's a gold mine of information about where to find everything you need for weddings and receptions.

buried. The graves are adorned with flower arrangements and other embellishments that fans continually send even 25 years after his death.

Once back across the street, you can check out Elvis's two private jets, the *Lisa Marie* and *Hound Dog II,* which aren't that impressive beyond the gold seatbelt buckles and gaudy bathrooms aboard the *Lisa Marie.*

More interesting is the Elvis Presley Automobile Museum, which you won't want to miss if you're a car buff. You'll see the 1960 red MG convertible from the movie *Blue Hawaii,* several Stutz Black Hawks and, of course, the 1957 Pink Cadillac, called Gladys's car because even though Elvis's mother, Gladys, didn't drive, it was her favorite. There are also a few motorcycles and a collection of golf carts and other vehicles that Elvis and his buddies used to drive around the grounds of Graceland.

The Sincerely Elvis Museum houses Elvis's personal effects, including his records and sneakers.

Graceland and related attractions are open Monday through Saturday from 9:00 A.M. to 5:00 P.M. and on Sunday from 10:00 A.M. to 4:00 P.M. Admission to Graceland mansion is $16 for adults, $14.40 for seniors and students, $6.00 for children 7–12. The Platinum Tour Package gets you into the mansion, Automobile Museum, airplanes, and Sincerely Elvis Museum. Cost is $25 for adults, $22.50 for seniors and students, and $12 for children 7–12. Reservations can be made 24 hours in advance, a good bet during the summer months if your time is limited.

Lichterman Nature Center
5992 Quince Road
(901) 767-7322

Lichterman Nature Center provides 65 acres of preserved forest and lake habitat in the middle of East Memphis. Roomy, paved paths wind through the forest and across the meadows. Along the paths, different species of trees and plants as well as birds, insects, and small creatures are identified so that you can fully appreciate what you see. Lichterman's lush preserve is a wonderful place to slow down, take a quiet walk, and enjoy wildlife. In short, it lives up to its description of itself as "a home for wildlife and a haven for humans." Various kids' camps and workshops are offered throughout the year. *Note:* This is a great spot for adults, but unless they're participating in a camp or workshop, kids tend to become bored after a short while.

Open 9:00 A.M. to 4:00 P.M. Monday through Thursday, 9:00 A.M. to 5:00 P.M. on Friday and Saturday, and noon to 5:00 P.M. on Sunday. Admission is $6.00 for adults, $5.50 for youth and seniors 60+, $4.50 for children 3–12, and free for children 2 and under.

Main Street Trolley
Main Street, various stops
(901) 274–6282

Riding the Main Street Trolley is great for getting to places downtown so that you can take a break from the car. And for 60 cents a ride, it's the best entertainment value in town. The train runs along Main Street and up Madison Avenue but also loops around for a great view of the Mississippi River. (See Getting Around chapter for more information about the Main Street Trolley and other transportation.)

Tickets are 60 cents per ride for all ages, except seniors and disabled persons, who pay 30 cents. You can also get a $2.50 daylong pass or a $6.00 three-day pass. Exact change is required.

Memphis Belle Pavilion
125 North Front Street
(901) 576–7241

The legendary bomber *Memphis Belle,* a proud survivor of World War II, is displayed on Mud Island. You can reach the *Memphis Belle* by entering at Front Street, then taking the pedestrian bridge or tram to Mud Island, or by driving across the Auction Street bridge to Mud Island, turning left, and asking the guard for directions. Admission is free. The *Memphis Belle* is scheduled to move to a new home at Forest Hill–Irene Road and Bill Morris Parkway in Germantown in late 2003. Call

ahead or check with the Tennessee Welcome Center for more information. (See Memphis History section in this chapter for more details.)

Memphis Botanic Garden
750 Cherry Road
(901) 685–1566
www.memphisbotanicgarden.com

Situated in the heart of East Memphis in Audubon Park, Memphis Botanic Garden consists of 96 acres planted with all kinds of flowering plants, trees, and other flora. Starting in late February, when tens of thousands of daffodils begin flowering on Daffodil Hill, you'll find something in bloom every time you visit until the first frost (usually October or November). Cherry trees become clouds of pink blooms in March, dogwoods flower in April, and, for much of the summer, roses, daylilies, and cactus are spectacular. Also notable are the Tennessee Bicentennial Iris Garden, which celebrates the state flower, and a Japanese tranquillity garden open year-round. A number of these gardens date back to the 1950s and 1960s.

The botanic garden is a popular spot for picnics and strolls for everyone, and gardening enthusiasts can take advantage of its extensive education program. The main building, Hardin Hall, is a popular place for parties, weddings, meetings, and other events and also has a small gift shop. A series of evening concerts in summer and other events take place on the grounds.

Admission is $4.00 for adults, $3.00 for seniors and students, and $2.00 for children 6–17. It's open Monday through Saturday from 9:00 A.M. to 6:00 P.M. and Sunday from 11:00 A.M. to 6:00 P.M. The museum is free after 12:30 on Tuesdays.

Memphis Queen Riverboats
45 Riverside Drive (at the foot of Monroe Avenue)
(901) 527–5694 or (800) 221–6197
www.memphisqueen.com

Don't miss your chance for an up-close-and-personal experience of the Mississippi River. The Memphis Queen Line's riverboats, complete with paddlewheels, have daily cruises, dinner cruises, and all kinds of special trips. Plan to arrive 30 minutes

A cruise on the Memphis Queen Line is probably the best way for visitors to appreciate Old Man River.
PHOTO: MEMPHIS QUEEN RIVERBOATS

before departure to enjoy the calliope music and to get your picture taken as a souvenir. Once everyone is aboard, the captain gives a tour, complete with historical facts and important sites on the river. There's also a piano player and a snack bar on board, but the main attraction is the view of the river and the city. Cruises are available daily at 2:30 P.M. and 5:30 P.M. Ticket prices are $12.50 for adults (18–59), $11.50 for seniors, and $9.00 for children. Children ages 3 and under go free with their parents. Be sure to ask about dinner cruises and special events. (See Kidstuff chapter for more details.)

Memphis Zoo
2000 Galloway
(901) 725-3452
www.memphiszoo.org

This excellent zoo, with its Egyptian decorations, exhibits such as Cat Country and Animals of the Night, and very likely its own giant pandas, is the city attraction that locals like to brag about. More than 400 species of animals from all over the world reside in renovated natural habi-

tats. A favorite event is seal feeding, which takes place at 2:30 P.M. every day.

Hours are 9:00 A.M. to 6:00 P.M. Admission is $9.50 for adults, $7.50 for seniors, and $5.50 for children 2 to 11. *Note:* If you have a large family, it might be more economical to purchase a Memphis Zoological Society membership. (For more information about the zoo, see the Kidstuff chapter.)

Mud Island River Park
125 North Front Street
(901) 576-7241, (800) 507-6507
www.mudisland.com

This attraction, although geared more toward kids, is full of interesting information about Old Man River. One of the main draws is a detailed replica of the Mississippi River, which flows through the park. For a detailed chronology of the history and culture along the great river, visit the Mississippi River Museum. You can see a reconstructed 19th-century steamboat, witness a battle aboard a Civil War gunboat, and listen to the river hollers and work songs of the river roustabouts. Guided tours are available.

To get to Mud Island, go to the ticket office on Front Street; then either walk across the pedestrian bridge or take the monorail across the Mississippi to the island. The *Memphis Belle* (see above) is also on Mud Island.

Open daily from 10:00 A.M. to 8:00 P.M. Last admission is one hour before closing time. The park is free, but the museum is $8.00 for adults, $6.00 for seniors and children ages 5–17, and free to children 4 and under. Parking is available near the Front Street side of the monorail for $2.00 to $3.00.

The Peabody Ducks
149 Union Avenue
(901) 529–4000

In the lobby of The Peabody hotel, you'll find one of Memphis's most popular attractions, the famous Peabody ducks. Every day at 11:00 A.M., five mallard ducks march down a red carpet from the elevator to the lobby's fountain, to music by John Philip Sousa. Then, at 5:00 P.M. the carpet is unrolled again, and these lucky ducks—after a strenuous day of swimming in an Italian marble fountain—march back to the elevator, then up to their penthouse home on the hotel's roof. (For more about the Peabody Ducks, see the Close-up in the Accommodations chapter.)

Wonders: The Memphis International Cultural Series
255 North Main Street
(901) 521–2644, (800) 2MEMPHIS
www.wonders.org

Organizing blockbuster exhibitions for Memphis audiences and/or bringing them to Memphis from other cities is the mission of Wonders, which was established after a 1987 exhibit of artifacts surrounding the rule of Rameses the Great drew some 675,000 visitors to downtown Memphis. With proof that if you build it, they will come, Wonders has continued to produce exhibitions, ranging from a show of Egyptian artifacts from the British Museum to *Titanic:* The Exhibition, featuring relics brought up from wreckage of the mighty ship.

The exhibits typically run from April through September, usually at the Mem-phis Cook Convention Center, which has now been renovated with an eye to providing a permanent home to the series.

If there's a Wonders exhibition open during your trip to Memphis, chances are you won't want to miss it. Call Wonders or check out its Web site when you plan your trip. It's usually advisable to make reservations, as the tickets are sold for entry at a particular day and hour. During the popular shows it's tough to get tickets for the same day, but it's worth checking if you didn't plan ahead. The gift shop is worth a look, as the operators usually do a good job of selecting merchandise that appeals to shoppers of all ages and pocketbooks of all sizes.

Hours and admission prices vary.

Museums

Art Museum of the University of Memphis
3750 Norriswood Street
(901) 678–2224
www.amum.org

Tucked away in a quiet corner of the University of Memphis Communication and Fine Arts Building, the museum features two small but excellent permanent exhibitions as well as shows of contemporary work that change frequently. Its Egyptian art, from the university's Institute of Egyptian Art and Archaeology, includes sculpture, religious and funerary objects, jewelry and other items, some of it excavated at a cemetery near Memphis, the city on the Nile for which the city on the Mississippi River is named. An authentic mummy is displayed under glass, with his feet and face exposed so that you can see how well preserved the body is (teeth and some toenails are still intact after several thousand years). There are also tiny snake mummies, which priests once sold to be used as votives to the gods. A painted wood model of a boat, which includes stiff-armed figures of servants standing onboard, is in remarkably good shape, considering that it dates back to at least the 18th century B.C.

The other permanent exhibit is Spirit of Africa, which displays masks, figurines, and other items from West Africa. Particularly interesting are the forest-spirit masks, donned for special ceremonies in the belief that the wearers would become the spirits represented by the mask.

The museum is open Monday through Saturday from 9:00 A.M. to 5:00 P.M. but is closed during university holidays and while exhibitions are being changed over. Admission is free. It's best to stop at the university's information office, a small, round building at Central Avenue and Patterson, to get directions to the museum. You can get a permit to park free, or you can pay at the parking garage next to the museum.

The Children's Museum of Memphis
2525 Central Avenue
(901) 458–2678, (901) 320–3170 for recorded information
www.cmom.com

Memphis has an excellent children's museum that allows kids to pretend to drive, shop in a grocery store, to be firefighters racing to a fire, and to participate in other interactive entertainment. There's also a vertical maze and other activities. The museum has a $6-million expansion with 8,000 square feet of exhibition space, more activities for children ages 10 to 12, and more computerized activities.

Open 9:00 A.M. to 5:00 P.M. Tuesday through Saturday and noon to 5:00 P.M. on Sunday. Admission is $7.00 for adults and teens, $6.00 for seniors and children 1–12. Free parking is available. (For more information see the Kidstuff chapter.)

The Dixon Gallery and Gardens
4339 Park Avenue
(901) 761–2409
www.dixon.org

The Dixon, as Memphians call this small museum, is a pretty, quiet oasis compared with its busy Park Avenue surroundings. Once a private estate, the museum features a Georgian-style mansion, with traditionally furnished galleries, as well as pleasant gardens and a lawn used for performances and other events. Most notable, though, are special exhibitions, which in the past have ranged from the Painters of Normandy, an exhibition of French paintings, to the art of Dr. Seuss. This privately funded museum also has a number of permanent collections, including French

The Dixon Gallery and Gardens offer beautiful grounds outside and interesting art exhibits inside.
PHOTO: MEMPHIS CONVENTION AND VISITORS BUREAU

The museum, housed in a 1910 firehouse that at one time housed fire horses, tells the story of how fire fighting developed, complete with early fire engines on display. You can also learn important fire-safety information, and uniformed firefighters are on hand to answer questions.

Open from 9:00 A.M. to 5:00 P.M. Tuesday through Saturday and from 1:00 to 5:00 P.M. on Sunday. Admission is $5.00 for adults and teens, $4.00 for seniors and children 3 to 12. There is no parking available at the museum, so look for a space in a nearby lot or take the trolley, which stops a block west of the museum on Main. (For more information see the Kidstuff chapter.)

Insiders' Tip

If you are love Victoriana or need to get into the holiday spirit, don't miss the Victorian Holiday Walk in downtown Memphis's Victorian Village the first Sunday in December. The Mallory-Neely House, the Woodruff-Fontaine House, and the more modest Magevney House, as well as private homes that are usually closed to the public, are all lavishly decorated for Christmas and open to tourists and locals alike.

Memphis Brooks Museum of Art
1934 Poplar Avenue
(901) 544–6200
www.brooksmuseum.org

The state's largest and oldest fine-arts museum, the Brooks (as locals call it) was originally built in 1916 in the Beaux-Arts style. Since then it has been expanded three times, with the final addition (1989) including a rotunda and first-rate amenities such as a restaurant and auditorium. In summer the distinctive white structure stands out from its lush green Overton Park setting, well back from the street and close to both the Memphis College of Art and Memphis Zoo.

The museum has three levels, where it displays items from its own extensive collection as well as traveling exhibitions. The ground-floor galleries feature 17th-, 18th-, and 19th-century items from the permanent collection, much of it British and American furniture plus paintings by Anthony Van Dyck, Winslow Homer, and Gilbert Stuart, among others. You get a sense of how Italian painting styles developed from the Brooks display of medieval religious art and works from the High Renaissance and Baroque periods. Look for special exhibits on the ground floor or lower level. The museum has had an incredible variety of exhibits, with works ranging from segregation-era and civil-rights period photographs by Memphian Ernest Withers to originals used in Absolut vodka advertisements to jewels of Russia's Romanov Dynasty. Don't miss the upper level, where

and American Impressionist and Postimpressionist paintings donated by the Dixon family as well as one of the most extensive collections of decorative pewter pieces in the world.

The gardens are particularly nice in spring, when the azaleas are in bloom, adding bright splashes of color and white all around the museum and its grounds. The south lawn is a popular spot among Memphians, who flock there to enjoy concerts, plays, and the Dixons' annual family picnic.

Admission is $5.00 for adults, $4.00 for seniors, $3.00 for students, and $1.00 for children under 12. The museum is open from 10:00 A.M. to 5:00 P.M. Tuesday through Saturday and from 1:00 to 5:00 P.M. on Sundays. On Mondays, when the galleries are closed, you can pay half price and enjoy the gardens.

Fire Museum of Memphis
118 Adams
(901) 320–5650
www.firemuseum.com

At the Memphis Brooks Museum, you can see an array of paintings, sculpture, and decorative objects as well as special exhibits. PHOTO: MEMPHIS CONVENTION AND VISITORS BUREAU

the Global Galleries include beautiful African masks and sculptures, a Roman head of Nero from 50 A.D., Chinese figures from the Han and Tang dynasties, and a reconstructed suit of jade squares dating back to the Han era. You'll also find a tiny collection of French Impressionist and Postimpressionist paintings by Camille Pissarro, Eugène Boudin, and others.

Off the rotunda where you enter the museum, you'll find a first-rate restaurant, the Brushmark, which serves lunch every day except Monday, and a great museum shop with all kinds of imaginative, funky objects in addition to the usual art books and note cards. Admission is $5.00 for adults, $2.00 for children and students, and $4.00 for seniors. The museum is open Tuesday through Friday from 10:00 A.M. to 4:00 P.M., Saturday from 10:00 A.M. to 5:00 P.M., and Sunday from 11:30 A.M. to 5:00 P.M. The museum is open until 8:00 P.M. the first Wednesday of each month and closed on Monday and major holidays.

The museum has an extensive program of film, art classes, and other stuff, so just ask.

Memphis Police Museum
159 Beale Street
(901) 528-2370
At the Memphis Police Museum, which is also a working police station, you can see an actual jail cell, confiscated weapons, and old newspaper clippings relating how Machine Gun Kelly was captured in Memphis in 1933 and how crowds were controlled at Elvis Presley's funeral.

Open 11:00 A.M. to midnight Sunday through Thursday and "until the crowd leaves Beale Street" on Friday and Saturday. Admission is free. (For more information see the Kidstuff chapter.)

National Civil Rights Museum
450 Mulberry
(901) 521-9699
www.civilrightsmuseum.org
The National Civil Rights Museum, which celebrated its 10th anniversary in 2001, provides a realistic and thoughtful look at the struggle to bring about racial equality and how that continues all over the world. *USA Weekend*, a magazine supplement of *USA Today*, recently named the

museum as one of the top-10 places to visit to gain a better understanding of our country. It's housed at the Lorraine Motel, where Dr. Martin Luther King, Jr., was killed, and at the building across the street, from which the shot was fired.

Open 9:00 A.M. to 6:00 P.M. Monday through Saturday and 1:00 to 6:00 P.M. on Sunday. Admission is $8.50 for adults, $7.50 for seniors and students, and $6.50 for children 4–12. Parking is free. (For more information see the African American Heritage section of this chapter.)

National Ornamental Metal Museum
374 Metal Museum Drive
(901) 774–6380
www.metalmuseum.org

This small, offbeat museum is the only institution in the United States dedicated exclusively to the collection and exhibition of fine metalwork, such as iron gates, swords, and other items. You'll find it in a quiet pocket of land overlooking the Mississippi River, which seems a step back in time. Across the street are Native American ceremonial mounds, converted into bunkers during the Civil War. Local legend has it that this is the spot where explorer Hernando DeSoto first saw the great river. The museum is housed in the former 1930s nurses' dormitory of the U.S. Marine Hospital, and although it has its own collection, it usually offers temporary exhibits such as a 2001 display of swords ranging from bronze-age weapons to a World War II Japanese officer's sword. Consult the museum Web site or call ahead for details. When you visit, check out the museum gift shop for unusual jewelry and other metal items. Don't miss an opportunity to stroll the grounds, a great spot for a picture that features a spectacular view of the river. Check out the working blacksmith shop, which once restored Graceland's famous gates. Picnickers should bring their own everything (including bug spray!), as there are no restaurants or food stores in the area. The museum is open Tuesday through Saturday from 10:00 A.M. to 5:00 P.M. and on Sunday from noon to 5:00 P.M. Admission is $4.00 for adults, $3.00 for seniors, $2.00 for children over 5 and students, and free

for children under 5. (Maximum family admission is $10.)

Note: Finding the museum can be tricky. From downtown take Riverside going north (left if you're facing the river) and turn onto the I-55 North exit. Take the first right off the ramp (you'll see a sign); then follow the signs to the museum.

Peabody Place Museum
119 South Main Street
(901) 523–2787
www.belz.com

You have to hunt for this museum, located in the basement of the Pembroke Building on Main Street, but it's worth it for its collection of Chinese sculptures, mostly 19th-century (Ching Dynasty) works of jade, ivory, and agate. Intricately carved, often from one piece of stone, the works include dragon boats and a 10-story pagoda with 1,000 carved figures on the various levels. Don't miss the colorful two-by-two lineup of horses, camels, tigers, and other creatures—all the size of carousel animals—or the large gilt bronze temple lions. These artifacts, which include other items such as Mongolian silver and interesting rock formations, come from the collection of Memphis developer Jack Belz, who spearheaded the redevelopment of downtown Memphis. The museum includes five large galleries and provides a cool, peaceful respite if you want to take a break from sightseeing.

Open Tuesday through Friday from 10:00 A.M. to 5:30 P.M. and Saturday and Sunday from noon to 5:00 P.M. Admission is $5.00 for adults, $4.50 for seniors, and $4.00 for students and children 12 and over.

The Pink Palace
3050 Central Avenue
(901) 320–6362
www.memphismuseums.org

The Pink Palace is actually three attractions housed in one large pink mansion: The Pink Palace Museum, the Union Planters IMAX Theater, and the Sharpe Planetarium. The lavish mansion dates back to the 1920s, when it was built of pink marble for Clarence Sanders, a Memphian who opened the world's first supermarket and founded the Piggly-Wiggly grocery chain.

Sadly, Sanders went bankrupt, and no one ever lived in his pink marble palace.

You can buy a ticket separately for each attraction, but a combination ticket is a far better value. See below.

Pink Palace Museum: The permanent exhibition of The Pink Palace traces the natural history of the Mid-South region from prehistoric dinosaurs to the present. The artifacts are diverse, ranging from fossils and dinosaur bones found in the area to Indian artifacts to life-sized dioramas illustrating the life of the early European settlers. Along the way you will learn about Memphis's connection with the Trail of Tears, the Civil War, Elvis and rock and roll, the modern chain supermarket as we know it, and much more. Don't miss the Clyde Park Miniature Circus. Mr. Park spent 50 years carving and motorizing this circus replica before donating it to the museum. The circus is turned on each day at 10:30 A.M. Ask about temporary exhibits, too.

Union Planters IMAX Theater: At an IMAX theater, instead of watching a movie, you experience it on a screen four stories high and five stories wide while actually feeling the vibrations from the sound system.

The IMAX allows you to swim with dolphins, scream with the others as the most outrageous roller coaster tests your thrill tolerance, or descend to the depths of the ocean in search of the *Titanic*. Films change constantly, so call (901-763-IMAX) for updated listings and show times.

Sharpe Planetarium: The Sharpe Planetarium allows you to glorify in the beauty and bounty of the constellations as you have never seen them before. Pointing with a laser light, guides explain the stories and history behind the stars and other astrological discoveries. Right before your eyes, the sky changes with the seasons so that you can see the movement of the stars. Lying back in a reclining chair, you will be amazed by the vastness and mystery of our galaxy. Call ahead for show times and ticket information.

The Pink Palace, IMAX theater, and planetarium are open Monday through Thursday 9:00 A.M. to 4:00 P.M., Friday 9:00 A.M. to 9:00 P.M., and Sunday noon to 6:00 P.M. Check for show times for IMAX and the planetarium. The combination ticket for all three attractions is $12.50 for adults, $11.50

for seniors, and $8.50 for children ages 3–12. Admission to the museum is $7.00 for adults, $6.50 for seniors, and $4.50 for children 3–12. IMAX tickets are $6.50 for adults, $6.00 for seniors, and $5.00 for children 3–12. Tickets for the planetarium are $3.50 for adults and $3.00 for seniors and for children 3–12.

Wonders: The Memphis International Cultural Series
255 North Main Street
(901) 521–2644, (800) 2MEMPHIS
www.wonders.org

We include Wonders here because its exhibitions are always of museum quality. Wonders produces blockbuster exhibitions that have ranged from a show of Egyptian artifacts from the British Museum to *Titanic:* The Exhibition, featuring relics brought up from wreckage of the mighty ship.

If there's a Wonders exhibition open during your trip to Memphis, chances are you won't want to miss it. Call Wonders or check out its Web site when you plan your trip. It's usually advisable to make reservations. Hours and admission prices vary. (For more information see the General Attractions listings in this chapter.)

Memphis History

Chucalissa Archaeological Museum
1987 Indian Village Drive
(901) 785–3160

In 1939, while excavating the site to develop a city park, workers discovered the ruins of a Choctaw Indian village. They named the village Chucalissa, which means "abandoned house." The park is dedicated to educating visitors about the Choctaw Indians who populated this area before European settlers arrived. A museum and reconstructed village have been developed over the years from the information and artifacts that archaeologists discovered on the site. On-site demonstrations of traditional dancing, food, and crafts help visitors imagine the village as it was when the Choctaw lived there. If you are interested in Native American history and archaeology, Chucalissa is worth a visit.

Graceland: Shrine to the King

Each year, hundreds of thousands of people flock to Memphis to visit Graceland, and on the anniversary of Elvis's death in August, thousands—including fans from all over the world—participate in the Candlelight Vigil, many of them passing through the gates of Graceland to Elvis's grave to pay their respects. (See the Annual Events chapter for details on this and other events of Elvis Week.)

Clearly, Elvis has grown into something larger than the simple man from Memphis. He changed modern music forever, earned more than 130 gold and platinum records, and sold out some 837 shows in Las Vegas. More than that, he is one of the most enduring icons of the 20th century, and like Marilyn Monroe, John F. Kennedy, and James Dean, he appeals to devoted fans as well as ordinary people. At present more than 500 recognized Elvis Presley fan clubs flourish in 44 states and 45 different countries, despite the fact that their idol has been dead for more than 25 years. Thousands of Elvis impersonators throughout the world keep the image alive in their own personal way.

What's the appeal? Fans speak of the Elvis world, in which everybody belongs, drawn by their love of one man. They admire his rags-to-riches rise, his charm and good looks, his generosity, his humble attitude, and how much he gave to his fans, even though his success may ultimately have destroyed him. They say they feel as though they've met him, that they know him.

Of course, others simply love Elvis's music, whereas still others like to poke fun of the kitschy, gaudy elements that were popular in the 1970s: the white jumpsuits, the sideburns, the flamboyant Jungle Room with its carpeted ceiling.

You'll learn plenty about Elvis at Graceland, the home where he sought refuge from fans and the rigors of performing. Fans should also check out Sun Studio, where he made his first record, and Beale Street, where he hung out to hear R&B. There's also his high school (Humes High School), his early homes, the church he attended (First Assembly of God Church), and the shop where he bought records (Poplar Tunes). You can also drive 100 miles to Tupelo, Mississippi, to see Elvis's birthplace and other related sights. (See the Day Trips chapter for more information on Tupelo.)

For a tour of these and other Elvis-related sights, see the sidebar on Offbeat Tours of Memphis in this chapter.

To get there from downtown, take Riverside Drive (which turns into I-55 South). Take the Third Street exit and go south. Turn right onto Mitchell (you should see a sign) and follow the signs. It's about a 30-minute drive from downtown.

Chucalissa is open Tuesday through Saturday from 9:00 A.M. to 4:00 P.M. Admission is $5.00 for adults, $4.00 for seniors, and $3.00 for children ages 4 to 11.

While in the area, you might want to check out Interstate Bar-B-Q & Restaurant, one of the city's best for a sit-down meal or drive-through order. It's at 2265 South Third Street, just on the other side of the Interstate (hence its name). (See Restaurants chapter for more information.)

Davies Manor Plantation House
9336 Davies Plantation
(901) 386-0715

This is the oldest log house in Shelby County, built by an Indian chief in the early 1800s. In 1851 the Davies family bought the house, expanding it into a country farmhouse that sits on a 2,000-acre plantation. The construction is log-and-chink, and the interior is outfitted with early family furnishings.

Insiders' Tip

Elvis fans who want to pay their respects to The King and his family in the Meditation Garden at Graceland Mansion can visit in the early mornings before the tours begin. Graceland opens its gates from 7:00 to 8:30 A.M., with free admission to the grounds. Graceland is generally less crowded at that time than during the mansion tour. Call ahead (901-332-3322), as the hours sometimes vary.

Open Tuesday through Saturday from noon to 3:00 P.M. or at other times by appointment for tour groups. Admission is $4.00 for adults and $2.00 for children.

Historic Elmwood Cemetery
824 South Dudley Street
(901) 774-3212
www.elmwoodcemetery.org

Historic Elmwood Cemetery, which opened in 1852, covers 88 acres and includes a large collection of Victorian funeral sculpture and many beautiful old trees. The real attraction, though, is the past, since a tour of Elmwood is a tour of Memphis history. Buried in the cemetery are 12 Civil War generals (including two from the Union side), a madam who maintained a "resort of commercial affection," governors, senators and E. H. Crump, the man who dominated Memphis politics for much of the 20th century. Some 5,000 people interred here died in the three yellow-fever epidemics that plagued Memphis, including many who came to Memphis to nurse the sick and others who stayed behind to care for loved ones. University of Tennessee maintains a plot for people who've donated their bodies to science. Confederate General Nathan Bedford Forrest was buried here, but later was moved to a park created in his honor near downtown Memphis.

Both blacks and whites are buried at Elmwood, so you'll find the graves of many African Americans, including many of the city's most important leaders. The most visible is the mausoleum in which Robert Church and his family are entombed. He was the South's first black millionaire, and he established Beale Street as a mecca for African Americans. There are also the graves of Beale Street blues singer Ma Rainey II; the Martin brothers, doctors who owned the Red Sox Negro Baseball League team; and Rev. Samuel Augustus Owen, founder of what is now LeMoyne Owen College in Memphis. About 300 slaves were buried here between 1857 and 1865, most of them marked with such designations as NEGRO MAN instead of names.

Admission to the cemetery is free, and for $5.00 you can rent an hour-long recorded tour to play in your car as you drive through. A detailed map and informational brochure ($5.00) will direct you to the graves of the more prominent and colorful people who are buried here.

The Magevney House
198 Adams Avenue
(901) 526-4464

While millionaires lived in mansions such as the Mallory-Neely and Woodruff-Fontaine houses up the street, this pre–Civil war home shows how the middle class lived. It was built sometime before 1837, the year Eugene Magevney, a schoolteacher who emigrated from Ireland to the United States, bought it and later added on. The home looks tiny from the street but has a large backyard, at one time home to the kitchen, privy, stables, and slave quarters. Decorated with furniture and reproduction wallpaper typical of about 1850, it houses some of the family's possessions, including portraits of the owner and his family as well as a mahogany desk that served as an altar in the city's first Catholic Mass. Magevney eventually became wealthy from real-estate holdings but continued to live in this house until his death from yellow fever in 1889.

Open Tuesday through Saturday from 10:00 A.M. to 4:00 P.M. Admission is free, but donations (suggested: $2.00 for adults, $1.00 for children) are appreciated.

The Mallory-Neely House
652 Adams Avenue
(901) 523-1484

This mansion, built in 1852 by insurance executive Isaac Kirtland and redecorated in high Victorian style in the 1890s, was home to two prominent Memphis families. The last resident was Daisy Mallory, who died in 1969 after living there for 86 years, leaving instructions that the house was to be a museum. Most of the furnishings are original to the house, including stained-glass windows, a Chinese prayer chest bought at the St. Louis World Fair, and two beautiful crystal chandeliers in the parlor, each with 12 lights and 250 prisms.

The exterior of this three-story house has elements of Italian Villa architectural style, including arched windows and a stucco facade designed to look as if it were made from stone blocks. A porch runs along the front of the house.

Inside, the house has colorful, ornate hand-stenciled walls and parquet flooring downstairs, with ceiling paintings, ornate plaster moldings, and other frills. These have been restored carefully to remove years of dirt and soot, and a few untouched spots allow you to see how the house was decorated differently over the years.

Open Tuesday through Saturday from 10:00 A.M. to 4:00 P.M. and on Sunday from 1:00 to 4:00 P.M., with the last tour at 3:30. (Ticket office and gift shop are in the carriage house behind the mansion.) Admission is $5.00 for adults, $3.50 for children, and $4.00 for seniors. (On days that both are open, for $9.00 per adult, you can tour both this home and the Woodruff-Fontaine House two doors down.)

Memphis Belle Pavilion
125 North Front Street
Mud Island (901) 576-7241

The legendary *Memphis Belle*, under a parachute-like canopy on Mud Island, sits as a

Many of the furnishings of Mallory-Neely House are original to this Victorian house, built in 1852 and open to visitors. PHOTO: MEMPHIS PINK PALACE MUSEUM

Offbeat Tours of Memphis

See the town in style by riding in a 1955 pink Cadillac or a horse-drawn carriage, or by taking a helicopter tour. These are all options for visitors who are looking for a little something special for their tour of Memphis. Of course, you can always opt for a bus tour of Memphis attractions from operators that include Blues City Tours (901–522–9229) and Gray Line of Memphis (901–382–6366 or 800–222–0089).

American Dream Safari
(901) 274–1997
www.americandreamsafari.com
Tad Pierson can take you on a three-hour tour of the city, a gospel church tour, or a daylong excursion to the Mississippi Delta to explore the roots of the blues. Best of all, you ride in a 1955 pink Cadillac, just like the one Elvis drove. This is very popular, especially during summer months, so book ahead.

Carriage Tours of Memphis
(901) 527–7542
You can find horse-drawn carriages lined up in front of The Peabody on Union Avenue, some of them with lavish decor and all of them with canine mascots. Each carriage can accommodate four adults or two adults and up to four children.

Memphis Explorations
(901) 761–1838
www.elvistyle.com
Mike Freeman and Cindy Hazen literally wrote the book about Elvis's Memphis (Memphis Elvis–style), so who better to show you where The King lived, worked, and played. They offer a driving tour as well as a walking tour that meets at the Elvis statue on Beale Street. They can also show you Elvis's Tupelo, or the homes, studios, and hangouts of other Memphis musicians. If you want to know every little thing about Elvis, this tour's for you. Reservations are required.

proud survivor of World War II. Pilot Robert Morgan named his B-17 bomber after his Memphis sweetheart, Margaret Polk. He had her likeness painted on the side of his plane as good luck, and good luck she was. The *Memphis Belle*, the most famous airplane of World War II, had a distinguished combat record, completing its quota of 25 missions over Nazi-occupied territory.

To reach the *Memphis Belle*, enter at Front Street; then take the pedestrian bridge or tram to Mud Island. Alternatively, you can drive across the Auction Street bridge to Mud Island, turn left, and ask the guard for directions. Admission is free.

Note: The *Memphis Belle* is scheduled to move to a new home at Forest Hill–Irene Road and Bill Morris Parkway in Germantown in late 2003. Call ahead or check with the Tennessee Welcome Center for more information.

Woodruff-Fontaine House
680 Adams Avenue
(901) 526–1469

This gem of a Victorian house, which dates back to the days when Adams Street was the city's "Millionaires' Row," has a mansard-roofed tower, from which its merchant owner could watch boats come in from the river. The house has its original hardwood floors and ceiling paintings as well as floor-to-ceiling windows that helped to cool homes in the days before air-conditioning. The house is outfitted mostly with Victorian furniture donated by Memphis's elite, including a Wooten desk and courtship chairs designed to keep a courting couple from getting too close. Original to the house is a stained-glass fanlight over the front door that depicts a bird's nest with four eggs, a reference to the fact that the owner had four children. Don't miss the pretty playhouses in the back and the garden area, complete with fountain, a popular place for summer weddings. Check out the small gift shop, which has jewelry, cut-glass vases and other items culled from local estate sales by a volunteer, at good prices.

The house is closed Tuesday but open 10:00 A.M. to 4:00 P.M. Monday and Wednesday through Saturday. It's open from 1:00 to 4:00 P.M. on Sundays. Admission is $5.00 for adults, $3.50 for children, and $4.00 for seniors. On days that both are open, for $9.00 per adult, you can tour both this home and the Mallory-Neely House just two doors down.

Memphis Music

Beale Street
Downtown Memphis, between Lt. George W.
Lee Avenue and Peabody Place
www.bealestreet.com
Musical history was made on this famous street several times over, and you'll find historical markers along the street that tell part of the story as well as statues of W. C. Handy in Handy Park and of Elvis Presley (across the street from Elvis Presley's Memphis, near Second). (Check out the Memphis Music chapter for the whole story.) At night you can check out all the neon signs, enjoy people-watching, and hear the music Beale Street made famous at the clubs. (See the Nightlife chapter for details.) During the day you can visit shops, restaurants, and attractions that include the W. C. Handy Performing Arts Center at Handy Park and Memphis Police Museum, but otherwise, you'll learn a lot more about Memphis's

musical history by visiting the Memphis Rock 'n' Soul Museum a block south of Beale. (For more information on the museum, see the write-up in this section.)

Center for Southern Folklore & Cafe
119 South Main Street
(901) 525-3655
www.southernfolklore.com
Center for Southern Folklore is devoted to keeping the South's music, crafts, and other traditions alive. One of the biggest draws is live music performances that feature such legends as the Fieldstones, barrelhouse-musician Mose Vinson, and Blind Mississippi Morris. Contact the center for a schedule.

The center also features works by many African American artists, both in the small gallery that highlights the artists and in the gift shop; it also maintains extensive archives that are available to scholars. CSF has done films about Southern folklore, which the staff will show to interested visitors. It's also a cafe that serves beer, coffee, and other beverages as well as some food.

The center, which has moved around quite a bit over the years, now has a permanent home inside the Pembroke Square

Insiders' Tip

During the third week in October, the National Ornamental Metal Museum has its annual repair days, when you can bring your silver, bronze, or other metal items to the expert craftsmen at the blacksmith shop to be fixed. The estimate is free, and if you opt to get the work done, your repair receipt gets you into the museum for free.

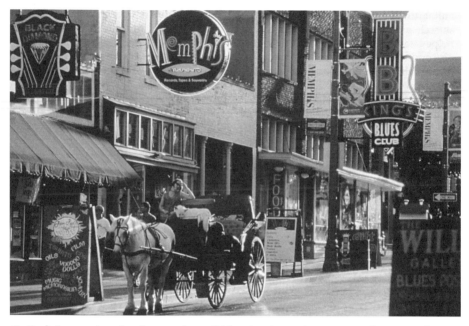

On Beale Street and nearby, there are plenty of sights, shopping, and restaurants to keep visitors busy.
PHOTO: MEMPHIS CONVENTION AND VISITORS BUREAU

Building on Main Street at Gayoso. To get to the center, enter through the double doors facing Main Street and nearest to Gayoso, and go to the back of the lobby. (For more information about the center, see the Nightlife chapter.)

Full Gospel Tabernacle
787 Hale Road
(901) 396-9192

This small brick church, located south of Graceland Mansion in the Whitehaven area, is well known for its famous pastor, soul legend Al Green. He has led the church for more than 25 years, following an incredibly successful recording career during the late 1960s and early 1970s that resulted in 16 top-10 hits. Services are held here at 11:00 A.M. every Sunday, and when he's in town, Reverend Green preaches and fronts for the Full Gospel Tabernacle choir. It's an electrifying and joyful experience to hear Green's charismatic preaching, if you are lucky enough to visit when he's in the pulpit. Visitors are welcome, but be aware that this is a

church, not a tourist attraction, so behave with respect (no cameras).

Gibson Guitar Factory
145 Lt. George W. Lee Avenue
(901) 543-0800

Drawn by the mystique of Memphis music, Gibson Guitar opened a factory here just a block from Beale Street. Gibson makes electric guitars here, including custom-made instruments for B.B. King, Prince, and others. It also makes the bright Beale Street Blue guitar, a special-edition instrument that commemorates this location. You can take a 25-minute tour of the Memphis Gibson Guitar Factory, and watch as the musical instruments are crafted by hand at various workstations throughout the factory. You see each step, as wood forms are transformed into about 100 finished musical instruments each day, ready to ship to guitar stores all over the world. Because the groups are limited, you might want to call ahead for reservations; otherwise, factory operations are closed to the public. You can buy a guitar at the Gibson

Guitar shop as well as a T-shirt or other souvenir. Check out The Lounge, a bar that features uptown atmosphere and great live music in the evenings. The building is also home the Memphis Rock 'n' Soul Museum. Cost of the Gibson guitar tour is $10 per person, age 12 or older. Younger children are not allowed on the factory tour.

Graceland Mansion
Elvis Presley Boulevard
(901) 332–3322, (800) 238–2000
www.elvis.com

This was the home of Elvis Presley, the young Memphis man who bought the mansion in 1957 after his first hits had made him a millionaire and an international superstar. The mansion itself sheds some interesting light on the man behind the legend, but music fans shouldn't miss the impressive collection of more than 130 gold and platinum records as well as memorabilia from every phase of Elvis's career. Most of the collection is in the Trophy Room, but some of it spills over into the nearby racquetball-court building. (For more information on Graceland, see the General Attractions section of this chapter.)

Ask at the guest services counter about the free shuttle service from Graceland to Sun Studio, the Memphis Rock 'n' Soul Museum, and the Stax Museum of American Music.

Open Monday through Saturday from 9:00 A.M. to 5:00 P.M. and on Sunday from 10:00 A.M. to 4:00 P.M. Admission to Graceland mansion is $16 for adults, $14.40 for seniors and students, and $6.00 for children 7-12. The Platinum Tour Package gets you into the mansion, automobile museum, the two custom airplanes and the "Sincerely Elvis" memorabilia museum. Cost is $25.00 for adults, $22.50 for seniors and students, and $12.00 for children 7-12.

The Lewis Ranch
1595 Malone Road, Nesbit, Miss.
(662) 429–1290

This is the home of Jerry Lee Lewis, the piano-pounding rockabilly legend nicknamed "The Killer." Here you can see his pianos, his piano-shaped swimming pool,

car collection, gold records, and memorabilia, although Jerry Lee himself isn't part of the tour. The house is about 20 minutes from Memphis but worth the trip for Jerry Lee fans. Call ahead for directions and to ask about the hours, which can vary. Admission is $15.00 for adults and $7.50 for children under 10.

Memphis Rock 'n' Soul Museum
145 Lt. George W. Lee Avenue
(901) 543–0800
www.memphisrocknsoul.org

Housed in the Gibson Guitar Factory just south of Beale, the Rock 'n' Soul Museum is a great introduction to Memphis music and a good first stop before seeing Sun Studio and other music-related attractions. (There's a Sun Studio shuttle that will take you there, to Graceland, and to the Stax Museum.) The exhibits tell the story of how the musical traditions drifted from the cotton fields and hills around Memphis into local recording studios and finally into America's musical mainstream as rock and roll, rhythm and blues, and soul. A short video sets the stage and features interviews with Carl Perkins, B.B. King, and Sam Phillips, who first recorded Perkins, Elvis, and others. The early part of the exhibition shows how the rural people, black and white, lived, before many of them left the farm for the city as part of the great migration that cut the rural population of Tennessee, Mississippi, and Arkansas from 3.7 million in 1930 to less than a million by 1969. The rest of the exhibition shows what happened when they got to Memphis, the importance of Beale Street as the heart of black Memphis, and the role of early radio. Much of the exhibit is devoted to the record labels that brought these musicians into the mainstream, first Sun Studio with the rock and roll of the 1950s. You learn plenty as well about the Memphis soul sound that emanated from here in the 1960s, as Hi Records first recorded Al Green and Ann Peebles and Stax Records recorded soul greats Otis Redding, Isaac Hayes, and Sam and Dave. The experience is enhanced by a portable CD player, free with admission, which in addition to providing a running narrative also allows you to listen to full-length recordings of the music you're learning about.

The museum is open daily from 10:00 A.M. to 6:00 P.M. Admission is $8.50 for adults, $5.00 for children 5 years and older, and $7.50 for seniors.

Stax Museum of American Soul Music
926 East McLemore Street
(901) 946–2535
www.soulsvilleusa.com

This is hallowed ground indeed, where Otis Redding, Sam and Dave, Booker T. & the MGs, Isaac Hayes, and numerous other soul artists recorded on the Stax label. The museum, set to open in 2002 at the same address where Stax made musical history, is designed to provide an interactive experience as visitors hear the story of how this legendary recording studio came to be, learn about the music makers, and, most important, enjoy the music that topped the charts then and still remains popular.

The museum is being designed as a replica of the Capitol Theater, the former movie house where Jim Stewart and Estelle Axton started Stax Records. The museum also includes a 500-seat auditorium, facilities for the LeMoyne-Owen College music department, and a music academy for school-age children.

The museum is part of a larger revitalization program for this South Memphis neighborhood, known as Soulsville USA. (For more information go to the African American Heritage chapter.)

The museum hours are 9:00 A.M. to 5:00 P.M. Monday through Saturday, 1:00 to 5:00 P.M. Sunday. Admission is $9.00 for adults, $8.00 for seniors and military, $6.00 for children 7 to 12, and free for children under 7 years old, as long as they accompany an admission-paying adult.

Note: The Sun Studio shuttle stops at the museum, located just south of downtown Memphis.

Sun Studio
706 Union Avenue
(901) 521–0664, (800) 441–6249
www.sunstudio.com

It's hard to believe so much musical his-tory was made in this small, simple studio, but that's what makes Sun Studio fascinating. This is where African American music crossed over into the mainstream, changing music forever. Elvis was discovered here, the first rock-and-roll song ("Rocket 88") was recorded, and a legendary roster of rockabilly and blues musicians made records here. They include Jerry Lee Lewis, Carl Perkins, Johnny Cash, B.B. King, Howlin' Wolf, Little Milton, and many others. (For more information see the Close-up on Sun Studio in the Memphis Music chapter.)

Buy your tickets (and refreshments too, if you like) in Sun Studio Café on the corner; then wait for the next tour. A gift shop upstairs has all kinds of merchandise with the famous Sun logo as well as other souvenirs, CDs, and books.

Open daily from 10:00 A.M. to 6:00 P.M. Admission is $8.50 for adults and free for children under 12. Tours start every hour on the half hour. Free parking is available behind the studio.

W. C. Handy House
352 Beale Street
(901) 522–1556

The tiny house you see set back from Beale Street was home to the blues giant W. C. Handy. He didn't invent the blues, but because he was the first to write down the music so the world could enjoy it, he has gone down in musical history as the "Father of the Blues." He lived here with his family from 1905 to about 1918, when he moved to New York to further his career. Moved from its original location to Beale Street in 1985, this was his home when he wrote "Memphis Blues," "Street Louis Blues," and "Beale Street Blues." While in Memphis, Handy started his own music-publishing company, Handy & Pace, at 392 Beale Street, which still exists in the form of New York–based Handy & Brothers. The house contains memorabilia and photographs as well as furnishings and musical instruments of the period. Open Tuesday through Saturday from 10:00 A.M. to 5:00 P.M. and on Sunday from 1:00 to 5:00 P.M. Admission is $2.00 for adults and $1.00 for children.

African American Heritage

Beale Street
Downtown Memphis between Lt. George W.
Lee Avenue and Peabody Place

Beale Street was the center of African American cultural and commercial activity during the segregated era that took up most of the 20th century. You'll find historic markers with information about important black Memphians, including Ida Wells, Nat D. Williams, and Robert Church. You can also see the oldest brick-constructed, multi-story church for blacks (now First Baptist Beale Street), and Church Park and the Old Daisy Theatre. (See the African American Heritage chapter for more information about Beale, and the important people and places that made history.)

Burkle House/Slavehaven
826 North Second Street
(901) 527-3427

This five-room house, the home of Jacob Burkle, was a stop on the Underground Railroad, the path by which runaway slaves escaped to the North. Burkle, a German immigrant who owned a thriving stockyard, built the house in the 1850s just a few blocks from the Mississippi River in what was then the countryside. The basement of the house, which has a secret door, is where the slaves are said to have hidden as they rested during their long journey, with easy access to the river. The house, decorated with furnishings from the period, also has displays about the realities of slavery: the hardship of traveling by boat from Africa, the lifestyle they were forced to lead, and even shackles once used to prevent slaves from escaping. Particularly intriguing are handmade quilts, with patterns that were actually coded directions for fellow slaves on how to make their way north. Purists say there's no documentation that Burkle hid slaves here, although Burkle's descendants have confirmed the story of this activity, and it stands to reason he would have avoided the risk of writing about it. Still, it's a compelling story, especially when paired with displays that remind the viewer of the realities that drove slaves to escape.

> ## Insiders' Tip
> A number of Memphis museums have Free Days, including the National Civil Rights Museum (Mondays, 3:00 to 5:00 P.M.), the Pink Palace Museum (Tuesdays, 1:00 to 4:00 P.M.), Memphis Zoo (Tuesdays, 2:00 to 5:00 P.M.), Memphis Brooks Museum of Art (Wednesdays, all day), Lichterman Nature Center (Tuesdays, 1:00 to 4:00 P.M.), and Memphis Botanic Garden (Tuesdays, noon to 6:00 P.M.).

To get there go north on Third to Chelsea; turn left and then right onto Second. It's best to drive rather than to walk from downtown, because it's not a great neighborhood.

Open Monday through Saturday 10:00 A.M. to 4:00 P.M. Admission is $5.00 for adults and $3.00 for children 5 to 17.

Mason Temple
930 Mason Street
(901) 578-3800

This is the church where Dr. King gave his final address, the famous "I've Been to the Mountaintop" speech, the night before he was gunned down at the Lorraine Motel. Mason Temple is also the international headquarters of the Church of God in Christ, a denomination with more than four million members worldwide. A historic marker in front of the temple gives further details.

National Civil Rights Museum
450 Mulberry
(901) 521-9699
www.civilrightsmuseum.org

Opened in 1991, the National Civil Rights Museum focuses on the major events of the civil rights movement, including events surrounding the integration of Central High School in Little Rock and the march on Selma. *USA Weekend*, a magazine supplement of *USA Today*, in 2001 named the museum as one of the top-10 places to visit to gain a better understanding of our country.

The museum is housed in the Lorraine Motel, where Dr. Martin Luther King, Jr., was shot in 1968, and in the building across the street from which the shot was fired. The assassination of Dr. King and the Memphis sanitation-workers strike that brought him here are also a focal point. (For background on Dr. King and the strike, see the African American Heritage chapter.)

The museum features photos, documents and descriptions, as well as interactive experiences to illustrate civil rights history. An audiotape tour, narrated by actors Ozzie Davis and Ruby Dee, helps to keep up the tempo and to put a human face on what you're seeing. There's also a separate audiotape for children. (See Kidstuff chapter for details.)

The main museum exhibit briefly describes developments from the 1600s, when slaves were first brought to this country, through the first half of the 1900s. The main focus, though, is on major events of the civil rights movement, from the *Brown* v. *Board of Education* decision that outlawed segregation in public schools in 1954, to Dr. King's assassination in Memphis in 1968. There are pictures, photos, and descriptions, as well as interactive experiences, to illustrate events surrounding the integration of Central High School in Little Rock, the Montgomery, Alabama, bus boycott and the 1964 Freedom Summer's black-voter registration drive in Mississippi. You can sit on a bus with a seated statue of Rosa Parks, whose refusal to give up her seat sparked the Montgomery bus boycott. You feel firsthand what it's like to be ordered to the back of the bus.

The Lorraine Motel, where Dr. Martin Luther King, Jr., was assassinated, is now home to the National Civil Rights Museum. PHOTO: NATIONAL CIVIL RIGHTS MUSEUM

In 2002 the museum opened its Exploring the Legacy annex in the building from which the fatal bullet was fired at Dr. King. Here, the museum details what happened after the assassination, including the investigation of the murder and the trial of James Earl Ray, who was convicted of killing Dr. King. Other exhibits focus on civil rights struggles outside the United States, including events in South Africa.

Open 9:00 A.M. to 6:00 P.M. Monday through Saturday and 1:00 to 6:00 P.M. on Sunday. Admission is $8.50 for adults, $7.50 for seniors and students, and $6.50 for children 4–12. Parking is free.

Stax Museum of American Soul Music
926 East McLemore Street
(901) 946–253
www.soulsvilleusa.com
This is the site of the legendary Stax Records, which turned out hits by Otis Redding, Carla Thomas, Isaac Hayes, and others in the 1960s and 1970s. By 1974 Stax was the fifth-largest black-owned business in the country, according to *Black Enterprise* magazine. There's also information about Memphis's Hi Records and soul music produced in other cities.

The museum hours are 9:00 A.M. to 5:00 P.M. Monday through Saturday, 1:00 to 5:00 P.M. Sunday. Admission is $9.00 for adults, $8.00 for seniors and military, $6.00 for children 7 to 12, and free for children under 7 years old, as long as they accompany an admission-paying adult.

Note: The Sun Studio shuttle stops at the museum, located just south of downtown Memphis. To reach by car take the South Parkway exit off I-240 or, from downtown, go east on Union, turn right onto Bellevue, then right onto McLemore. (For more details see the Memphis Music section of this chapter.)

W. C. Handy House
352 Beale Street
(901) 522–1556
This tiny two-room house is where W. C. Handy, considered the "Father of the Blues," lived with his family from 1905 to 1918. Open Tuesday through Saturday from 10:00 A.M. to 5:00 P.M., and on Sunday from 1:00 to 5:00 P.M. Admission is $2.00 for adults and $1.00 for children 5 to 17. (See the Memphis Music section of this chapter for details.)

The Arts

Memphis has a very active arts scene for a city its size, with a range that takes you from the classics to a funky, homegrown alternative scene energized by the presence of a major art school, Memphis College of Art. The symphony, ballet, and opera are all represented by major professional companies, and, in fact, there are two symphonies currently performing in the city. Local theater, which is very strong, dates back to at least 1920, when Front Street Theater (now Theater Memphis) began featuring local stage talent. The historic Orpheum Theater and other venues bring in a steady stream of Broadway shows and other national acts, something that has been a tradition in this river-port town throughout its history. Visual arts can be enjoyed at local museums, most notably, the Memphis Brooks Museum and Dixon Gallery & Gardens, and galleries range from snob to funk.

Filmgoers will want to catch the city's two independent film festivals each year and may recognize Memphis as the backdrop in several movies, as it has become a popular place to shoot films. Among those filmed here are the movies made from the John Grisham novels *The Firm* and *The Client* and Jim Jarmusch's cult film *Mystery Train*. A few of the city's independent filmmakers have received national recognition, including Craig Brewer for *The Poor and Hungry*, and self-styled exploitation auteur John Michael McCarty, director of *Teenage Tupelo* and *Elvis Meets the Beatles*. During summer moviegoers can see classic movies such as *Gone with the Wind* on the big screen at the Orpheum.

A number of actors and actresses have come from Memphis. Some, including Kathy Bates and Cybill Shepherd, grew up here and developed their careers elsewhere, whereas Michael Jeter (TV's *Evening Shade*) and Chris Ellis got their start in local theater. A major claim to fame is that Tennessee Williams wrote his first play, *Cairo! Shanghai! Bombay!*, in the 1930s while visiting his grandparents at their home near what is now Rhodes College.

Theater continues to be strong, with Playhouse on the Square (the city's professional company) and Theater Memphis putting on more mainstream productions that have included *A Chorus Line* and *Deathtrap*. Circuit Playhouse focuses on off-Broadway fare, and Theater Works provides a stage for several smaller theater companies, the best of which is Memphis Black Repertory Theater, started in 1997. Other small independent theater companies bubbling up around the city include Sleeping Cat Studio, which produces dramas.

Memphis is rich in other performing arts and currently supports two symphonies. Memphis Symphony Orchestra, an excellent regional symphony, gives 80 performances a year and will be at home at the Cannon Performing Arts Center downtown starting in 2003. IRIS, a chamber orchestra formed in 2000, performs six times a year and brings in stars that have included cellist Yo Yo Ma. The conductor is Michael Stern, an internationally known musician who's also the son of the late violinist Isaac Stern. Opera Memphis, under the direction of savvy American composer Michael Ching, produces three or four operas a year that have included *Aida* and new compositions as well. Internationally known soprano Kallen Esperian makes her home in Memphis and occasionally makes guest appearances in Opera Memphis productions.

Ballet Memphis is a professional dance company that performs full-length classical works and a yearly production of *The Nutcracker*. There are also some smaller companies that present more cutting-edge works.

For visual arts South Main Street, a historic district once home to the hustle and bustle of the city's major train station, has become a mecca for art galleries. The most festive way to check out these galleries is the Art Trolley Tour, which takes place on the last Friday of every month. From 6:00 to 9:00 P.M. you can ride the Main Street trolley for free between the Orpheum Theater at Beale and Central Station at G.E. Patterson and enjoy complimentary champagne. The galleries, shops, and stained-glass manufacturers are open, so you can browse the artwork and sip a glass of wine. This is a favorite party spot among the Memphis artsy set, so people turn up as much to see and be seen as they do to enjoy the artwork.

In East Memphis you'll find many of the city's serious galleries, those that represent artists from the region with national recognition. Many feature changing exhibits and opening receptions for the artists that are open to the public (usually Friday nights). Others are open by appointment only. Among the artists with national and international reputations are painters Burton Callicott and Brenda Joysmith, well known for her pastels and prints of daily life among African Americans. Two legendary photographers hail from Memphis: William Eggleston, whose color photographs have been shown at the Museum of Modern Art, and Ernest Withers, whose black-and-white photographs chronicle the civil rights movement in Memphis as well as life on Beale Street during segregation.

The more avant-garde arts scene is centered on Marshall Avenue near Sun Studio, sometimes called "the edge" because it's on the eastern edge of downtown. The area is home to 25–30 artists' studios and two galleries that feature the work of neighborhood artists and others. Memphis College of Art shows the work of its students and faculty mainly. The city is home to dozens of working artists—painters, potters, sculptors, and others—many of them graduates of the art college.

Remember that in Memphis visual art isn't limited to galleries and museums. Artwork can be found in restaurants, shops, theater lobbies, and office buildings all over town, and often it's for sale.

Arts groups in Memphis, no matter what the discipline, usually incorporate a strong educational element into their programs, offering lessons (and sometimes scholarships) and performing in schools for students. And speaking of education, don't forget that University of Memphis, Rhodes College, and other colleges have strong programs in the arts, which include theater productions, concerts, and art shows by their students and faculty as well as programs that bring in important nationally known artists. These are usually listed in local newspapers.

As is the case in any city, the Memphis arts scene changes, as established arts groups shift gears and newer ones emerge. Be sure and check out the listings in the *Commercial Appeal* "Playbook" section or *The Memphis Flyer* for general information as well as the ticket information, hours, and other specifics on current performances and art shows.

Galleries

South Main/Downtown

Art Village Gallery
410 South Main Street
(901) 521–0782
This gallery, a sister business to the trendy cafe Zanzibar, is the permanent home for the work of Ephraim Urevbu, a Nigerian-born artist who has been in Memphis for many years. Urevbu's contemporary abstract paints are afire with bright colors, and you can see more of them on the walls of Zanz-

ibar. The gallery also features exhibitions of work by other artists. Art Village Gallery is open Tuesday through Saturday from 11:00 A.M. to 5:00 P.M., or by appointment.

Center for Southern Folklore
119 South Main Street
(901) 525–3655
www.southernfolklore.com
The center's "SoFo" gallery features folk art and other pieces by Southern artists. The center, which is also a cafe, music venue, and all-around friendly place, can be found on the lower level of the Pembroke Building, so look for the sign on Main Street.

Durden Gallery
509 South Main
(901) 543-0340
www.durdengallery.com
Durden Gallery focuses on emerging artists, some of them local, some regional, some national. Among the artists shown here are Priscilla Cunningham, a Memphis native who paints landscapes and flowers in an Impressionistic style, as well as Nashville painter Streater Spencer and Steve Griffith, an Arkansas painter of still life and landscape works. The gallery is open Tuesday through Sunday, or by appointment.

Jay Elkin Gallery
409 South Main Street
(901) 543-0035
www.jayetkin.com
When New York–born Jay Etkin moved his gallery from the Cooper-Young historic district to South Main in 2000, it was a big boost to the downtown arts scene. You could say that this is the flagship gallery in the area, given the many artists and the variety of styles represented. Etkin is considered a major player, and at any given time this two-story, Soho-style space is filled with the work of at least a dozen different artists, which sometimes includes local sculptor Roy Tamboli and painters Annabelle Meacham and Pam Cobb. The gallery also handles the work of New York artist Tim Rollins & K.O.S. and others to Memphis market, not to mention Etkin's own abstract paintings and conceptual art. Jay Etkin Gallery is open Tuesday through Saturday or by appointment.

Joysmith Gallery
46 Huling Street
(901) 543-0505
www.joysmith.com
This gallery, situated between South Main and Front Streets, features the work of African American artist Brenda Joysmith, who moved from her studio from northern California with her husband, Robert Bain, to her hometown of Memphis in 2000. Joysmith, one of the artists credited with creating the market for African American art during the 1980s, sells her work all over the world. One of her paintings even hung on the walls of the Huxtable home on TV's *Cosby Show*. The gallery features Joysmith's works, both limited and open editions, as well as works by other black artists, who have included painter Claude Clark, Sr. Joysmith Gallery is open Tuesday through Sunday or by appointment.

Mariposa Art Space
505 South Main
(901) 543-8535
www.mariposaartspace.com
This crowded, friendly South Main gallery focuses on works that it considers to be of good quality, fun, and affordable. About 32 artists are represented, working in glass, painting, photography, sculpture, and other media. Among the artists is Les Waite, whose paintings feature primary colors and jigsaw puzzle design, and Leslie Baron, who creates whimsical, abstract still-life works. Owner Kennedi Benjamin also shows her own work, abstract pieces that feature Picasso-esque faces as well as ones that represent aspects of nature. The gallery is open Thursday through Sunday or by appointment.

Second Street Contemporary
431 South Main Street
(901) 521-1514
This second-floor alternative space holds four to six shows a year, featuring mostly local artists. Past exhibitions have included the work of Hamlett Dobbins, who paints large, abstract oils; Greeley Myatt, who creates a variety of sculpture and installations, and Terri Jones, a conceptual artist who does installations. The gallery is open Monday through Friday.

Willis Gallery
156 Beale Street
(901) 526-3162
This gallery has operated on Beale Street since 1989, featuring artwork that's the visual counterpart of the blues and other music you hear at the clubs. Willis features original works, prints, and posters by local Southern artists, including George Hunt, Don Allen, Danny Broadway, and the Twins. Closed on Tuesdays.

Marshall Avenue

ArtFarm Gallery
652 Marshall Avenue
(901) 859-3135
www.memphisartfarm.com

This nontraditional coop gallery was started in 1999 by artists with studios in the area, who felt a need for a place where artists could show their work without compromise. The gallery rents the space to artists for exhibitions ranging from wild student group shows to established local artists that include Hamlet Dobbin and Diane Hoffman, as well as artists from other cities in the South. ArtFarm also has a gallery in which it shows the works of artists who work in the Marshall Arts area. Open Saturday afternoons or by appointment.

Delta Axis at Marshall Arts
639 Marshall Avenue
(901) 458-4207
www.deltaaxis.com

Established in 1992 as a nonprofit, contemporary visual-arts organization, Delta Axis stages its local art shows at Marshall Arts, an artists' workspace the organization started to support the city's working artists. The focus is on new and emerging artists from this region, as well as artists from other parts of the country. Examples include a show of artist sketch books, a group show of artists from Arkansas State University at Jonesboro, and Ghosts, an exhibit that involved taking works by out-of-town artists out of the gallery and positioning them in various places around the South Main Street district. The gallery is usually open Monday through Friday, but call (901) 522-9483, because hours can be sporadic.

Midtown/East Memphis

Albers Fine Art Gallery
1102 Brookfield Road
(901) 683-2256
www.albersgallery.com

This East Memphis gallery was established in 1984 by Kathy Albers, a respected art dealer, and features both two- and three-dimensional works by artists from the Southeast as well as a few with national reputations. Among the artists represented are Ann Kobdish, a Texan who paints tranquil landscapes, and Michael Barringer, a painter who often used mixed media on paper. William Morris is a maker of glass vessels and scupture, with works at the Metropolitan Museum of Art, widely considered one of the foremost glass artists of the 20th century. The gallery has 10 shows a year and is open Tuesday through Friday or by appointment.

Carole Thompson Fine Art
1515 Central Avenue
(901) 278-2741
www.southernphoto.com

Carole Thompson specializes in selling museum-quality works of art mostly to corporate clients, with a particular emphasis on Southern artists and French 19th-century work. Examples of the work found here include photographs of Memphis photographer William Eggleston, early 19th-century photographer Lewis W. Hine, sculpture by Degas, and works by Mississippi painter Walter Anderson. It's open by appointment only.

Insiders' Tip

In Memphis you can enjoy theater even if you're on a budget. For each of their productions, Circuit Playhouse, Theatre Memphis, and Playhouse on the Square have a "pay what you can" performance, where you can pay any sum for a ticket. For more information call the theater box office.

David Lusk Gallery
4540 Poplar Avenue
(901) 767-3800
www.davidluskgallery.com
Situated in Laurelwood Shopping Center near Grove Grill restaurant, this gallery was established in 1995 by Memphis art dealer David Lusk. The gallery specializes in the work of established regional and Southeastern artists with national recognition. Among them is Carroll Cloar, the late painter whose realism is compared with Edward Hopper's, and Memphis-born photographer Huger Foote, whose work is featured in magazines such as *Interview* and in his book, *My Friend from Memphis.* (Incidentally, he's the son of Shelby Foote, the Civil War historian who lives in Memphis.) Other painters include Robert Rector and Mary Sims. David Lusk Gallery is open Tuesday through Saturday or by appointment.

Lisa Kurts Gallery
766 South White Station
(901) 683-6200
www.lisakurts.com
Lisa Kurts Gallery prides itself on being the city's oldest, established in 1979, and represents some 30 artists from the United States and Canada. The gallery has 10 to 12 shows each year, featuring artists such as landscape-painter Wade Hoefer, sculptor Anita Huffington, and Marcia Myers, New Mexico painter influenced by works found in Pompeii and other excavation sites in Italy. Although the focus has traditionally been on Memphis artists, presently the focus is moving away from the city and to Impressionist works. A propos of that, the gallery has one Impressionist painting show each year and operates Lisa Kurts Ltd., a business that advises collectors of late 19th-century and early 20th-century paintings. The gallery is open Monday through Saturday.

Memphis College of Art
1930 Poplar Avenue
(901) 272-5100
www.mca.edu
The gallery at Memphis College of Art mainly exhibits the work of its students

and faculty but also exhibits other work, which has included a show of black-velvet art by local artists. Here you can get a fix on what the next generation of artists is up to. The gallery is open Monday through Friday. For more information about the college, check out the Education chapter.

Perry Nicole Fine Art
3092 Poplar Avenue
(901) 405-6000
www.perrynicole.com
Tucked away in the Village at Chickasaw Oaks shopping center in midtown, this gallery was opened in 1999 by Nicole Haney and David Smith, alumni of Lisa Kurts Gallery. The focus of this gallery is to find artists who have already had shows in markets similar to the Memphis market such as those in New Orleans and St. Louis, and to market their works here. Among the artists represented are Seattle abstract-painter Adele Sypesteyn, New Orleans glass-artist Mitchell Gaudet, and Lisa Weiss, a Nashville artist who paints oils on aluminum. Perry Nicole has a new show each month. The gallery is open Monday through Saturday or by appointment.

Art Museums

Art Museum of the University of Memphis
3750 Norriswood Avenue
(901) 678-2224
www.amum.org
This quiet museum in the University of Memphis Communication and Fine Arts building houses a gallery displaying works by students, faculty, and other artists as well as an excellent small exhibition of Egyptian artifacts. (For more details see the write-up in the Attractions chapter.)

Dixon Gallery & Gardens
4339 Park Avenue
(901) 761-2409
www.dixon.org
The Dixon is a former private estate with a small permanent collection of Impressionist art and decorative arts as well as temporary exhibitions that range from the

Painters of Normandy to Dr. Seuss. (For more information check out the longer write-up in the Attractions chapter.)

Memphis Brooks Museum of Art
1934 Poplar Avenue
(901) 544–6200
www.brooksmuseum.org
The state's largest and oldest fine-arts museum, the Brooks displays works from its own extensive collection as well as temporary exhibitions that range from Russian Romanov jewels to the art of Warner Brothers cartoons. Situated in Overton Park, this Beaux Arts style palace also hosts lectures, musical performances, and other events. (For details check out the Attractions chapter.)

National Ornamental Metal Museum
374 Metal Museum Drive
(901) 774–6380
www.metalmuseum.org
This small, offbeat museum is the only institution in the United States dedicated exclusively to the collection and exhibition of fine metalwork, such as iron gates, swords, and other items. On display you'll find exhibitions on some type of ornamental metals, such as its 2001 display of swords from the Bronze Age through World War II. (For more information see the Attractions chapter.)

Peabody Place Museum
119 South Main Street
(901) 523–2787
www.belz.com
Tucked away on the lower level of the Pembroke Building on Main Street, this museum has an extensive collection of Chinese sculptures, mostly 19th-century (Ching Dynasty) works of jade, ivory, and agate. (For more information see the Attractions chapter.)

Wonders: The Memphis International Cultural Series
255 N. Main Street
(901) 521–2644, (800) 2MEMPHIS
www.wonders.org
It's always worth checking to see if there's a Wonder exhibition coinciding with your visit. This group organizes blockbuster exhibits that have included Catherine the

The Memphis Brooks Museum has something to interest art lovers of all ages.
PHOTO: MEMPHIS CONVENTION AND VISITORS BUREAU

Great of Russia and a show of Egyptian artifacts from the British Museum. (See the Attractions chapter for more details about this series.)

Dance

Ballet Memphis
7950 Trinity Road
(901) 737-7322
www.balletmemphis.org

This 24-member professional company performs full-length classical works such as *Giselle* and *Swan Lake* as well as modern ballet by top choreographers. Ballet Memphis was started in 1985 by Dorothy Gun-

Ballet Memphis performances feature exquisite dancing as well as beautiful costumes and scenery. PHOTO: MEMPHIS CONVENTION AND VISITORS BUREAU

ther Pugh, who remains its artistic director, and presently has a season of four major productions in Memphis at the Orpheum Theater, in addition to participating in local arts festivals and touring. In 2001 the company received national exposure when it traveled to New York to perform at the Kaye Playhouse as one of nine dance companies. Its yearly performance of the holiday classic *Nutcracker Suite* is always a favorite among Memphians. Ballet Memphis also reaches out into schools and teaches 500 adults and children each year at all levels.

Memphis Dance Group
60 Perkins Road Extended
(901) 537-1483, (901) 537-1486 (box office)

This small dance company presents ballet as well as modern, jazz, and latino dance at the Buckman Center for Performing and Fine Arts at St. Mary's Episcopal School. The dance group features two main stage performances a year, which have included El Beso, a blend of ballet and flamenco, as well as community outreach performances.

Project: Motion
2085 Monroe Avenue
(901) 272-0344

This local, nontraditional modern-dance company, founded in the mid-1980s, puts on two concerts a year as well as performances in schools and other educational outreach. The works are usually collaborative efforts choreographed by local artists and generally include other disciplines such as visual arts, performance, and music. Project: Motion makes its home at TheatreWorks in Midtown Memphis.

Film

Indie Memphis
639 Marshall Avenue
(901) 458-4207
www.indiememphis.com

Indie Memphis was started by a University of Memphis film student in 1998 to provide a voice and forum for the local film community. The group sponsors a juried competition each year entitled The Indie Memphis Film Festival: The Soul of Southern Film, focusing on films made in Shelby County and in the surrounding Delta area. The four-day event, which takes place in June, includes screenings, symposiums, and other events, with the action centered around The Orpheum Theater downtown. Through partnerships with the arts group Delta Axis and the Memphis Brooks Museum, Indie Memphis works to promote film as artistic expression.

Memphis Film Forum
3475 Central Avenue
(901) 452-2151, ext. 116
www.memphisfilmforum.org

This nonprofit organization is dedicated to promoting cinema arts, most visibly with the Memphis International Film Festival it launched in 2000. The festival, held every spring, features independent films made in the South as well as works with international scope, including shorts, animation, documentaries, experimental films, and foreign films. In 2001 the festival featured the Oscar-nominated short film *By Courier* as well as *Marine Life*, starring Memphis-born actress Cybill Shepherd, who made an appearance at the festival to discuss the film. The film forum also sponsors the Spike and Mike Animation Festival in the fall, featuring animated short films and other events, such as special premiers, throughout the year.

The Orpheum Classic Movie Series
203 South Main Street
(901) 525-7800
www.orpheum-memphis.com

Every summer this historic theater presents a series of classic films on Friday nights, including such favorites as *Gone with the Wind*, *North by Northwest*, and *One Flew over the Cuckoo's Nest*. The films are shown on the big screen and usually include a concert of organ music from the silent-movie era.

Studio on the Square
2105 Court Street
(901) 725-7151
www.overtonsquare.com

Opened in 2000 at Overton Square entertainment district in midtown, Malco's Studio on the Square generated great excitement by bringing the movies back to midtown. The theater caters to film buffs who prefer independent and foreign films to the latest commercial blockbuster. Unlike the city's other movie houses, Studio on the Square, in addition to its four screens, also has lounge areas and tables and serves specialty coffees, beer, wine, desserts, and light appetizers. The theater gets involved with the local film scene, sponsoring special events promoting *Poor & Hungry*, a film by Memphis filmmaker Craig Brewer, and festival screenings.

Summer Quartet Drive-In
5310 Summer Avenue
(901) 767-4320

Okay, maybe this isn't high art, but Summer Quartet is one of the few drive-in theaters left in the country. Here, you can pretend it's the fifties as you park, get refreshments, and take in a double feature. For parents of young children, it's a great way to get to the movies, because the kids usually crash in the back seat pretty early in the evening.

Classical Music

Calvary and the Arts
102 North Second Street
(901) 525-6602
www.calvaryjc.org

Every fall Calvary Episcopal Church presents a concert and lunch series, featuring free musical performances and a $5.00 lunch prepared by downtown chefs. Among those who have performed are the Navy Band Mid-South and blues-and-rock artist Kirk Smithhart. Most years the series includes performances by soprano Kallen Esperian, who makes her home in Memphis when not performing in New York or abroad, and the O'Landa Draper Associates gospel group. Calvary has other musical events throughout the year, including a holiday performance of Handel's *Messiah*.

Insiders' Tip

The Beethoven Club, which dates back to 1888, brings together music lovers of all ages to listen to classical-music performances, usually by local musicians. You can learn more about the club, which welcomes new members, by calling (901) 274-2504.

Concerts International
Harris Concert Hall
3775 Central Avenue
(901) 527-3067
home.midsouth.rr.com/webs/Concerts International

For more than 30 years, Concerts International has been bringing in internationally acclaimed chamber music to Memphis through its annual concert series. The performances usually take place at Harris Concert Hall on the University of Memphis campus. The series has included performances by the Street Petersburg String Quartet and the Jacques Thibaud String Trio.

IRIS: The Orchestra
Germantown Performing Arts Center
1801 Exeter, Germantown
(901) 757-7256

During the time that Memphis Symphony Orchestra was performing at a local church while waiting for its sleek, new concert hall to open downtown, this young upstart chamber orchestra burst onto the scene in 2000. With internationally known conductor Michael Stern at the podium and guests such as cellist Yo Yo Ma, IRIS immediately attracted sellout crowds. It's smaller than MSO and is composed mostly of out-of-town musicians. Six or seven performances are given each year at

the Germantown Performing Arts Center. Local music lovers are hoping that there's room in this town for both orchestras.

Memphis Chamber Music Society
Various locations
(901) 758-0150

Some of the city's most beautiful and historic private homes open their doors to aficionados of chamber music for a series of nine yearly concerts. The concerts range from duos to 12 musicians, and although most of the performers are local musicians, there are sometimes out-of-town guests. Subscriptions and single tickets both sell out quickly, as audiences are limited to about 100 people. The performances are at 3:00 P.M. Sundays, followed by a reception.

Memphis Symphony Orchestra
3100 Walnut Grove Road
(901) 324-3627
www.memphissymphony.org

Founded in 1952, the Memphis Symphony Orchestra is one of the country's premier regional orchestras, with 85 musicians who present 80 performances each year. Under the leadership of David Loebel, who became musical director and conductor in 1999 after a decade with the Saint Louis Symphony Orchestra, the musicians perform everything from classical masterworks to pops to premiers of original works. Highlights each year include Handel's *Messiah,* a Mad about Mozart program, and outdoor performances at the Dixon Gallery & Gardens. The orchestra frequently welcomes guest performers, who have included violinist Pamela Frank and the Eroica Trio. Starting in early 2003 MSO is performing in its new home, the Cannon Center for the Performing Arts, an intimate, 2,100-seat concert hall that's part of the newly rebuilt and expanded Memphis Cook Convention Center in downtown Memphis. The orchestra originally performed at the convention center but has been floating among venues during the time the center has been under reconstruction. MSO also sponsors the volunteer Memphis Symphony Chorus as well as Memphis Youth Symphony.

Memphis Vocal Arts Ensemble
Buckman Performing Arts Center
60 Perkins Road Extended
(901) 683–6774

This vocal group has been performing in Memphis for more than 10 years, currently under the directorship of Thomas Machen. The ensemble gives four concerts each season, usually at Buckman Performing Arts Center at St. Mary's Episcopal School in East Memphis. The programs range from Broadway show tunes and popular music to opera and holiday favorites.

Opera Memphis
4821 American Way
(901) 257–3100
www.operamemphis.org

Memphis has a long tradition of opera, dating back to when Jenny Lind sang here in 1851. Formed in 1956, Opera Memphis is the largest opera company in Tennessee, led by general and artistic director Michael Ching, also a well-known composer of operas such as *Buoso's Ghost*. The company features three or four fully-staged productions each season at the Orpheum Theater. These have included classic favorites such as *The Magic Flute* and *Aida* as well as new American works. The operas are usually sung in their original language, with English subtitles, and are accompanied by the Memphis Symphony Orchestra. Renowned soprano Kallen Esperian makes her home in Memphis and sometimes makes guest appearances with Opera Memphis, always a sellout event.

Opera Memphis is building new headquarters at Humphrey Boulevard and Kirby in East Memphis, which will include a 250-seat concert hall for small performances and concerts. It's expected to open in spring 2003.

Theater

Circuit Playhouse
1705 Poplar Avenue
(901) 726–4656
www.playhouseonthesquare.org

Circuit Playhouse is a year-round theater that stages eight different plays each year.

The focus is on off-Broadway and experimental theater, with productions that have included *Miss Evers' Boys, From the Mississippi Delta,* and *Chess*. Its home in midtown since 1979 is a 140-seat theater, although the theater company has been active since 1969. Circuit is also home to A Show of Hands, a troupe of hearing and hearing-impaired actors playing to both hearing and hearing-impaired audiences. Circuit is a sister theater to Playhouse on the Square

Ewing Children's Theater
2635 Avery Avenue
(901) 452–3968

Established in 1949, the Ewing Children's Theater presents eight shows each year, which have included *Charlotte's Web* and *Jungle Book*. The theater's management encourages young people to participate in all aspects of putting on a play, not just acting but also writing, stagecraft, lighting, costume design, and other elements of theater production. The theater also offers drama classes for children aged 5 through 18, which include a talent showcase.

Germantown Community Theatre
3037 Forest Hill Irene Road, Germantown
(901) 754–2680

Considered one of the best small community theaters in the state, this local theater makes its home in a converted turn-of-the-century schoolhouse, where it puts on seven productions a year in its 116-seat theater. Founded in 1972, Germantown Community Theatre has staged performances of *The Glass Menagerie, Deathtrap, Catfish Moon,* and the musical *Pearlie*. Every year the theater puts on *The Best Christmas Pageant Ever,* a favorite among local theatergoers during the holiday season.

Memphis Black Repertory Theatre
2085 Monroe Avenue
(901) 274–7139

Founded in 1997, this professional company of African American actors includes some astonishing local talent. The company performs mostly at Theater Works in midtown, with productions that have included *Black Nativity, Robert Johnson Tricked the Devil,* and original works as well.

Playhouse on the Square
51 South Cooper Street
(901) 726-4656
www.playhouseonthesquare.org

This professional resident year-round theater presents mainstream fare, with performances of such plays as *Hair, You Can't Take It with You,* and *South Pacific.* The company makes its home in the former Memphian Movie Theater in the Overton Square area, which has seating for an audience of 258 people. During the holidays Playhouse on the Square puts on performances of *A Tuna Christmas,* always a favorite among Memphis audiences. A number of Playhouse alumni have gone on to successful acting careers in Hollywood and New York, including Michael Jeter (who won an Emmy for hit work on the TV show *Evening Shade*), Chris Ellis,

This scene is from the play Golf with Alan Shepard, *just one of the many performances at Playhouse on the Square.*

PHOTO: FOWLER PHOTOGRAPHY

and Shannon Cochran (active with Steppenwolf Theater in Chicago).

Sleeping Cat Studio
655 Marshall Avenue
(901) 728-4262

This tiny independent theater company, under the direction of Virginia playwright Jim Esposito, presents works by established dramatists such as David Mamet as well as Esposito's own plays, which are edgy dramas with an element of dark humor.

Theater Works
2085 Monroe Avenue
(901) 274-7139

Here you'll find some of the city's more avant-garde productions.

Situated at Overton Square just around the corner from Playhouse on the Square, this 110-seat theater provides a home to emerging artists and groups who don't have their own performing spaces. Currently, this is home to the Memphis Black Repertory Theater, Playwrights Forum, and several other groups. Built in 1995 by Playhouse on the Square, Theater Works is intended as an artistic incubator for the local performing-arts community.

Theatre Memphis
630 Perkins Extended
(901) 682-8323
www.theatrememphis.org

Theatre Memphis is one of the oldest community theaters in the country, dating back to 1920. Since 1974 it has made its home at an East Memphis facility that has two stages, The Main Stage, with seating for 424, and its Little Theater, with seating for 75-120. The Main Stage features Broadway shows and plays that have included *Mame, A Funny Thing Happened on the Way to the Forum,* and *Deathtrap.* The Little Theater features off-Broadway fare, including *Betrayal* and *Little Shop of Horrors.* In addition, Theatre Memphis's ShoWagon program features a troupe of young professional actors who perform seven or eight shows a year at schools. There's also a kids' program, where kids can audition for plays such as *Charlotte's Web.*

Venues

The theaters and performing-arts centers listed here are where you'll find performances of the orchestra, ballet, opera, traveling Broadway shows, and some popular artists. For more venues that feature popular music, including rock, country, and R&B, refer to the listings in the Nightlife chapter.

Bartlett Performing Arts and Conference Center
3663 Appling Road, Bartlett
(901) 385–6440
www.bpacc.org
Built in 1998, this suburban venue sponsors a regular season lineup that has featured such artists as singer/songwriter Iris DeMent, the Cashore Marionettes, and the Nashville Mandolin Ensemble. This is also home to the Lucy Opry, a regular forum that features bluegrass music.

Buckman Performing and Fine Arts Center
60 Perkins Road Extension
(901) 537–1483, (901) 537–1486 (box office)
www.stmarysschool.org
This 288-seat theater at St. Mary's Episcopal School is where you'll find some of the more diverse performing arts in the city. Through the World Tour Series, the center has presented performances by flamenco dancers from Spain and Russian gypsies as well as Celtic music and Tibetan music and dance. Buckman is also home to the Memphis Dance Group.

Cannon Center for the Performing Arts
255 North Main Street
(901) 576–1200
This 2,100-seat, acoustically superior concert hall is part of the $93-million expansion and renovation of the Memphis Cook Convention Center in downtown Memphis. The performing-arts center is set to open in late 2002 and will be the permanent home for the Memphis Symphony Orchestra. The hall is designed so that the stage extends into the audience, creating an intimate ambiance. It can also be converted into meeting facilities for conventions.

Germantown Performing Arts Center
1801 Exeter Road, Germantown
(901) 757–7256
www.gpac.com
This acoustically perfect theater, which opened in 1994, provides an intimate venue for performances of all kinds. The center, which locals refer to as "G-Pac," hosts a series of popular performances that have included artists such as Dave Brubeck, Alison Kraus, and the Karamozov Brothers. It's also the artistic home to IRIS, the chamber orchestra founded in 2000, and brings in ballet companies and other performers as well. The theater seats 824 people, and no seat is more than 55 feet from the stage.

The Orpheum Theater
203 South Main Street
(901) 525–7800
www.orpheum-memphis.com
The lavish Orpheum Theater, built in 1928 as a venue primarily for vaudeville, holds court at the foot of Beale Street in downtown Memphis. At present the theater hosts performances of Broadway shows, Opera Memphis, and Ballet Memphis as well as other acts that have included singer Natalie Merchant and Garrison Keillor's "Prairie Home Companion." Bedecked with crystal chandeliers, gilded moldings, and brocade draperies, the Orpheum also sponsors a popular film series in summer (for more details see write-up under Film). The theater was renovated in 1983 and 1997, to the tune of $15 million, so now it can accommodate traveling Broadway shows that have included *Miss Saigon* and *Annie Get Your Gun*. The Orpheum sells tickets at the theater's box office or at a satellite box office at Davis-Kidd Booksellers.

Support Groups

Greater Memphis Arts Council
8 South Third Street
(901) 578–2787
www.memphisartscouncil.com
Started in 1963 to foster improvements in the artistic and cultural quality of the area, the Greater Memphis Arts Council administers

the 10th-largest arts-funding program in the United States. During its 2000-2001 fiscal year, the arts council raised more than $3 million in support of 20 local arts groups, about 40 special-arts projects, and its Center for Arts Education. This program brings the arts to 100,000 schoolchildren each year through subsidized tickets for performances, after-school arts programs, and other activities. The council also works with the UrbanArt Commission to develop public artworks in public buildings and outdoor locations. The Memphis/Shelby County Public Library and Information Hub, completed in 2001 with works by local artists inside and out, is a good example. The council depends on gifts from individuals and companies. It recently gave $3.6 million to help fund the construction of the Cannon Performing Arts Center. Although many organizations have their own support groups, such as the Memphis Symphony Orchestra with its Memphis Symphony League, much of the city's arts-support activity is under the Arts Council umbrella.

Germantown Arts Alliance
6685 Quince Street, Germantown
(901) 757-9768

This nonprofit group, whose mission is to develop, support, and strengthen the area's cultural environment, was spun off from the governmental Germantown Commission in 1992. The group's main function is to raise money and give out matching grants to local arts groups as well as to local schools for arts programs. In 2000 the Alliance gave out $51,000 in grants. Among the arts groups it supports are Germantown Community Theatre and the Germantown Symphony Orchestra.

Shopping

Malls and Major Shopping Centers

Antiques

Bookstores

Clothing and Accessories

Farmer's Markets

Flea Market/Thrift Shops

Garden Shops

Gift Shops

Gourmet Stores

Music and Musical Instruments

Outfitters/Sports Stores

Souvenirs, including Elvis-abilia

Memphis has always been a destination for shoppers, as people from surrounding farms and towns come in to buy the latest fashions, home furnishings, books, antiques, gourmet foods, and other merchandise. In more recent years visitors have been more interested in buying guitars, Elvis souvenirs, and hard-to-find CDs and records. You can find a good selection of all of the above in Memphis, not to mention the things you need for your home, your wardrobe, or your lifestyle.

Although there are a few pockets of retail in downtown Memphis, you'll probably have to get in the car for serious shopping, as the malls and the best shopping centers are mostly in suburban areas, whereas many antiques dealers, music stores, and gift shops are scattered around midtown.

Two major department stores operate in the Memphis area, Goldsmith's (part of Federated Department Stores) and Dillard's (a Little Rock–based chain), both with locations in area shopping malls. Both have a good array of merchandise, but Goldsmith's, founded here in 1870, is the hometown favorite. A sister to Rich's in Atlanta, this is where generations of Memphians have been shopping for up-to-date fashions, wedding gifts, and home furnishings. Not only does Goldsmith's tend to be a bit more fashionable, carrying designers such as Eileen Fisher and Dana Buchman, it also has frequent sales.

In Memphis you'll find plenty of the usual chain stores, including Costco, Target, Walgreen's, Sears, J.C. Penney, T.J. Maxx, Marshall's, Toys R Us, Gap, Banana Republic, Ann Taylor, Limited, Victoria's Secret, and Barnes & Noble, just to name a few. Most of these are in suburban malls and shopping centers.

Memphis also has its share of antiques dealers and shops, with the largest concentration on Central Avenue between Cooper Street and East Parkway in midtown. Others are scattered throughout the city, from downtown to the far suburb of Collierville. You'll find all kinds of antique furniture, with plenty of English, French, and American pieces from the 19th and 20th centuries, as well as collectibles of all sorts. There's also a large flea market in the city, as well as a number of thrift shops for those who like to search through secondhand goods for vintage clothing and other treasures.

If you're shopping for clothes, you'll find many options. For women's clothes there's everything from a Nicole Miller Boutique to Holliday's, a locally owned discount retailer where you can try out the latest trend at bargain prices.

Grandparents will delight in the many children's shops, ranging from The Disney Store to Woman's Exchange, with its pricey handmade outfits. Men can choose from two locally owned clothiers, James Davis and Oak Hall, as well as chains that include Jos. A. Banks, Brooks Brothers, U. S. Male, and Eddie Bauer.

One of Memphis's best-kept shopping secrets is the Williams-Sonoma outlet store (see the Gourmet Stores of this chapter for details). The chain maintains a major warehouse in Memphis, and when the season changes or the warehouse gets too full, trucks bring the merchandise to the outlet to sell at a discount. You'll find not just Williams Sonoma merchandise, but also items from its other stores, including Pottery Barn, Hold Everything, and Chambers. (You can go to nearby MailBoxes Etc. to ship your purchase home if it doesn't fit in your suitcase.)

Beale Street and Graceland are both hubs for souvenir shopping, so when you visit the attractions there, be sure to allow time for shopping.

Malls and Major Shopping Centers

Belz Factory Outlet
3536 Canada Road, Lakeland
(901) 386-3180

This factory-outlet mall is situated just off the Canada Road exit of I-40, about eight minutes from the I-240 loop. The mall has a variety of outlets and discount stores, including Bass Company Store, the Rack Room clearance store, Dress Barn and Dress Barn Woman, Van Heusen, Nike Factory Outlet, and Big Dog Sportswear. Anyone looking to outfit a new home on a budget will want to visit Old Time Pottery, which sells dinnerware, cookware, and other items for the home. You'll also find a Samsonite Co. outlet, Perfumania, and Toy Liquidators.

Hickory Ridge Mall
6075 Winchester Road
(901) 367-8045

Situated in the Hickory Hill area of Memphis, this mall has more than 100 stores including Goldsmith's, Dillard's, Gap, Bath and Body Works, and Sam Goody. The focal point of the mall is its famous antique Venetian-style carousel, a favorite among families. There's also a movie theater, a food court, and plentiful parking.

Laurelwood Shopping Center
Poplar Avenue at Perkins Extension
(901) 794-6022

Situated across the street from Oak Court Mall, this East Memphis upscale shopping plaza has a great collection of tony stores, including the clothier James Davis, which sells men's and women's apparel, much of it designer lines including Giorgio Armani. Joseph has beautiful shoes, handbags, apparel, and jewelry as well as top makeup lines including Bobbi Brown; Zoe sells cosmetics, bath goodies, and other potions including the popular Kiehl brand. David Lusk Gallery is one of the city's top art dealers, and Davis-Kidd Booksellers is a great favorite for books, magazines, and gifts. You'll find other options for shopping as well, including

Sears for more middlebrow needs, Talbots, and a Nicole Miller boutique.

Mall of Memphis
I-240 at Perkins Road
(901) 369-9469

This mall is conveniently located for visitors staying at the Memphis Marriott, Wilson World, and other hotels in southeast Memphis. Originally opened with great fanfare as the city's largest mall, unfortunately it has lost its luster in recent years. Specialty stores have been the focus since 2001, when anchors J.C. Penney and Dillard's closed their doors. The mall also is home to the city's only public ice-skating rink, Ice Chalet, which makes it a popular spot for families.

Oak Court Mall
4465 Poplar Avenue
(901) 682-8928

This East Memphis favorite is the closest mall to downtown Memphis and features Goldsmith's and Dillard's as well as dozens of other stores. You'll find Body Shop, Origins, the usual mall suspects such as Limited, Victoria's Secret, Structure, American Eagle, and Starbucks. Plenty of free parking, including covered lots near the Dillard's and Goldsmith's entrances, a food court, and a number of other specialty shops in the immediate area.

Peabody Place
150 Peabody Place
(901) 526-5799

This downtown shopping mall, which includes Ann Taylor Loft, Victoria's Secret, Tower Music, Gap, and other shops, is noteworthy because it marks the return of retail to downtown Memphis in a big way. There's also a movie theater, entertainments such as Jillian's and Putting Edge miniature golf, Starbucks, and a number of restaurants and bars.

Raleigh Springs Mall
3384 Austin Peay Highway
(901) 388-4300

This mall, the city's third largest, has been around for more than 30 years,

Wolfchase Galleria mall in the suburb of Cordova is a favorite shopping spot for Memphians and visitors alike. PHOTO: MEMPHIS CONVENTION AND VISITORS BUREAU

staying vibrant by reinventing itself as a bargain-shopping destination and continually renovating its premises. When glitzy Wolfchase Galleria Mall was built nearby in 1997, the J. C. Penney store at Raleigh Springs became a J. C. Penney Outlet, and more bargain stores were added, such as Holliday's, Simply Fashion, and Payless Shoe Store. You'll also find Goldsmith's, Dillard's, and Sears, plus other mall standards such as Waldenbooks, Bugle Boy, and Lenscrafters. There's plenty of free parking.

The Regalia
Poplar Avenue at I–240
(901) 767–0100
This center, conveniently situated at Poplar off the Expressway, has a number of upscale retailers, including the locally owned men's clothier Oak Hall, Reverie Fine Linens & Down, and Elizabeth Edwards, a high-end women's clothing shop. There are also a number of restaurants, including Owen

Brennan's (a New Orleans–style eatery), Mikasa (Japanese), and Salsa (Mexican). Embassy Suites Hotel and a Hampton Inn are right next to Regalia.

The Shops of Saddle Creek
7615 West Farmington at Poplar Avenue,
Germantown
(901) 761–2571
This posh shopping center in suburban Germantown features a lot of great upscale shops, mostly chains including Williams-Sonoma Grand Cuisine, Ann Taylor, J. Jill, Banana Republic, Gap, Sharper Image, and Apple computer store. Good restaurant/bar bets are Bosco's Brewery & Pub and Yia Yia's EuroCafe, whereas Marble Slab Creamery has good ice cream. Most of the shops are situated north of Poplar, but you'll find Saddle Creek West at 7509 Poplar, with Eddie Bauer Home, Talbots Petites, and Structure. Saddle Creek South is south of Poplar at 2055 West Street, with Talbots, Eddie Bauer, and a few other stores.

Southland Mall
1215 Southland Mall
(901) 346–1210
Situated at the corner of Elvis Presley Boulevard and Shelby Drive in south Memphis, Southland Mall was built in 1966 as the city's first mall. At that time people from Memphis and surrounding areas flocked here to shop. Now much of that crowd shops at the other malls around town, while Southland concentrates on serving its main customer base, residents from the surrounding Whitehaven neighborhood and tour busses from nearby Graceland. The mall is anchored by Goldsmith's and Sears, with specialty shops that include Milano's, Holliday's, Rave, Sam Goody music, and Colberts.

Wolfchase Galleria
2760 North Germantown Parkway
(901) 372–9409
Wolfchase Galleria is the swankiest shopping mall in town and a good-looking one, which is embellished by the work of local artists. It's not only the newest one, built in 1997, it also features stores that you won't find anywhere else in the city, including Brooks Brothers, Abercrombie & Fitch, and Pottery Barn. You can shop at 120 stores, including state-of-the-art Goldsmith's and Dillard's department stores, Sears, Ann Taylor, Harold's, Banana Republic, Disney Store, Gap, Laura Ashley, Inner Self, and The Coach Store. Wolfchase also has a working carousel at the entrance, as well as a food court and an eight-screen movie theater plus plenty of free parking. You'll also find lots of other stores near the mall, including Barnes & Noble bookstore, Toys R Us, and Best Buy.

Antiques

Memphis has dozens and dozens of antiques and secondhand shops and malls with all sorts of furniture, collectibles, and bric-a-brac. The shops along Central Avenue between Cooper and East Parkway in midtown is where you'll find the largest concentration of antiques

shops and dealers, so for an afternoon of antiquing, that's where you'll probably want to spend your time.

Central Avenue Antique District

Consignments
2230 Central Avenue
(901) 278–2131
This consignment shop sells best-quality antiques, including 18th- and 19th-century French and English furniture as well as a good selection of silver, cut glass, and porcelain items. Consignments also gets antiques through its Westport, Connecticut, sister store, which keeps the selection lively.

Flashback
2304 Central Avenue
(901) 272–2304
This funky retro shop, which calls itself the vintage department store, specializes in Art Deco as well as furnishings and collectibles from the 1950s. You can also find new upholstered furniture and chrome dinettes in retro style, as well as vintage furniture from the era, and there's plenty of 1970s merchandise as well. The shop does about half of its business in vintage clothing, which includes recycled blue jeans.

Market Central
2215 Central Avenue
(901) 278–0888
This antique and decorator showroom features country French, French, and English furniture as well as decorative accessories, lamps, and mirrors.

Palladio Antique Market
2169 Central Avenue
(901) 276–3808
www.PalladioAntiques.com
Here you can browse the antiques and decorative arts of some 45 exhibitors at this antiques marketplace, which range from investment-grade antiques to affordable coffee-table items. You can find every type of style, from 17th-century pieces to contemporary accessories. Inside the shop is Café Palladio, where you can enjoy beauti-

fully prepared sandwiches, salads, and other lunch fare.

Second Hand Rose
2288 Central Avenue
(901) 278-3500
This shop specializes in good solid furniture, which it sells in a warehouse atmosphere. Here, you'll find pieces such as pine tables, French armchairs, and chests, mostly from the late 19th century. Second Hand Rose also has a large selection of mostly antique books, oil paintings, and chandeliers. Open Wednesday through Saturday.

Outside the Central Avenue District

Jimmy Graham Interior Design
3092 Poplar Avenue
(901) 323-2322
Tucked away inside Chickasaw Oaks shopping center, Jimmy Graham has a mixture of English and continental furniture and accessories, which changes with every buying trip. The shop, which maintains a comfortable atmosphere, is also home to Graham's interior-design business. While at Chickasaw Oaks, you should also check out Ainsley Hall Antiques, Antiques & All That Jazz, and other shops.

Linda M. Felts Interiors
400 South Main Street
(901) 578-5780
This immense South Main building is filled with all kinds of antiques, vintage furniture and accessories, and architectural pieces as well as some new items and collectibles. In addition to this eclectic selection of merchandise, there's also an interior-design shop complete with a sample room. Open Monday through Friday and on the last Friday evening of the month for the Art Trolley Tour.

Maybee's Antique Center
198 South Center Street, Collierville
(901) 854-0188
Housed in an old lumberyard about half a block from Collierville's historic square,

Insiders' Tip

For a more complete listing of Memphis antiques shops and malls, look for a small, white brochure entitled *Memphis Antique Guide.* It's available at many antiques shops, or call (901) 726-5358.

Maybee's has been in business since 1970, selling mostly American antiques with an emphasis on country and primitive pieces. Maybee's also does restoration, repairs, and can build reproductions of farm tables and other hard-to-find furniture. Open Tuesday through Saturday.

Wellford's Antique Collection
262 South Highland Avenue
(901) 324-1661
This shop operates out of an English cottage-style house, and features 18th- and 19th-century imported English antiques. Here, you'll find drop-leaf dining-room tables, chairs, chests, and other furniture as well as china, some crystal, and a large collection of antique silver—all displayed in rooms that resemble those in an English manor house. There's also a large selection of paintings, including many landscapes. The owner, Karen Wellford, is also an interior designer

Bookstores

Barnes & Noble
Wolfchase Galleria Mall
(901) 386-2468
6385 Winchester Road
(901) 794-9394
Barnes & Noble has everything you could want in a large, modern suburban chain bookstore, including a large selection of

Davis-Kidd Booksellers is one of the city's many excellent bookstores.
PHOTO: MEMPHIS CONVENTION AND VISITORS BUREAU

books and magazines as well as a cafe with specialty coffees, pastries, and such.

Bookstar
3402 Poplar Avenue
(901) 323–9332
Housed inside a restored movie theater at Poplar Plaza shopping center at Poplar near Highland, Bookstar features a decent selection of nonfiction and fiction books. One of the biggest draws is its cafe, where you can linger over Starbucks coffee, pastries, and light fare such as soup and sandwiches amid images of great writers that are painted on the walls. It's a popular midtown meeting spot. There's also a Bookstar in Germantown at 7680 Poplar Avenue (901-757-7858).

Borders
6685 Poplar Avenue, Germantown
(901) 754–0770
Despite being part of a national chain, Borders is a Memphis bookstore and music store in that it has a large selection of books by Memphis writers and Memphis music. Local music also figures into the live music performed at its cafe. Borders prides itself on having the largest selection of books in town, as well as a selection of music and DVDs second only to Tower Records downtown.

Borders is situated in the back of The Carrefour shopping center at Poplar and Kirby near the railroad track.

Burke's Book Store
1719 Poplar Avenue
(901) 278–7484
www.burkesbooks.com
Burke's Book Store, a Memphis institution since 1875, specializes in used and antiquarian books as well as new books. You can find first editions, lots of works by Southern writers, as well as an array of out-of-print and used books at this cozy, family-owned shop. If you are looking for a particular hard-to-find book, Burke's will hunt a copy down for a fee. The store has a number of book signings every year, with appearances of local writers as well as best-selling authors, and it's the only place in town (and one of the few in the country) where novelist John Grisham does book signings.

Davis-Kidd Booksellers
387 Perkins Road Extension
(901) 683–9801
www.daviskidd.com
This cheerful, well-stocked book and music store features all kinds of books, magazines, CDs, and other music, not to mention a good selection of gifts, journals, stationery, and cards. Davis-Kidd has frequent in-store signings, with authors ranging from former president Jimmy Carter to local writers, as well as book clubs and musical events that have featured folk-singer Kate Campbell and the Memphis Youth Symphony. There are also separate areas for magazine browsers to lounge and for children to play and enjoy story hours. The icing on the cake is Brontë, the only full-service bookstore restaurant in town, where you can get pastries, specialty coffees, and other beverages at other times of the day. You'll find Davis-Kidd in the northeast corner of Laurelwood shopping center.

Deliberate Literate
1997 Union Avenue
(901) 276–0174
This locally owned book store is a favorite among midtowners, who flock here to browse the books, gifts, and magazines or to meet with friends and business associates and enjoy coffee and espresso drinks, pastries, and light lunch fare. Deliberate Literate carries a small but eclectic inventory of books, but they'll order any book you want at a 20-percent discount. The homey atmosphere includes plenty of comfortable couches and chairs throughout the shop. Open seven days a week starting early in the morning to accommodate the many people who stop in for a coffee on the way to work.

Clothing and Accessories

Kids' Apparel and Toys

Chocolate Soup
7730 Poplar Avenue, Germantown
(901) 754–7157

Tucked in the Germantown Village Square shopping center at the corner of Poplar Avenue and Germantown Road, Chocolate Soup sells moderately priced children's apparel, including girls' sizes up to 16 and boys' sizes up to 7. As one of 14 shops throughout the South and parts of the West, Chocolate Soup sells both its own designs, featuring hand-sewn appliqués, as well as other labels that include Heart Strings, Kite Strings, French Toast, and smocked dresses by Anavini. The merchandise ranges from dressy party clothes to the latest kid fashions and also includes baby gifts, elegant stuffed animals, and accessories such as pretty little Easter purses. Chocolate Soup has been a Germantown favorite for more than 25 years.

The Country Bunny
408 Perkins Road Extended
(901) 683–6810
Situated in Laurelwood shopping center near Medikow Jewelers, Country Bunny specializes in moderate-to-better children's apparel with classic styling and a touch of fun. Brands include Sweet Potato, Maggie Breene, Monkey Wear, and Susanne Lively.
You'll find mostly girls apparel, because the shop carries boys' sizes up to 24 months and girls' sizes up to size 16 preteen. Country Bunny also sells an array of baby gifts, accessories, and toys that include Groovy Girls.

Little Lambs and Ivy
1227 Ridgeway Road
(901) 767–5262
This little shop, situated in Park Place shopping center at Ridgeway and Park, sells apparel, accessories, shoes and gifts for infants, for girls up to size 16, and for boys up to size 7. The focus is a traditional look, with brands including Anavini, Vive La Fete, Cotton Tail Originals, and Kata Mini. About half of the merchandise consists of baby clothes, bedding, and gifts; shoes range from Keds to European-made brands. There's a separate room for "big girls" apparel, painted in pink and lavender. Prices are in the moderate to better range.

Village Toymaker
4615 Poplar Avenue
(901) 761–1734
7850 Poplar Avenue, Germantown
(901) 755–3309
www.thevillagetoymaker.com
This old-fashioned toy store has a carefully selected array of toys for all ages and price ranges, but the great thing about Village Toymaker is its staff. Tell them the age and interests of the child you're shopping for, and they're great at helping you to find the perfect toy. Gift wrapping is free.

Woman's Exchange
88 Racine Street
(901) 327–5681
Situated in midtown just off Poplar in a modest house, Woman's Exchange is where volunteers run a children's clothing and gift shop as well as a tearoom that's a popular ladies' lunch spot. The handmade christening dresses, flower-girl dresses, baby clothes, and special-occasion dresses and boys' outfits make this shop a grandmother's dream come true. A tradition since 1885, Women's Exchange also has beautiful linens, gifts, quilts, and handcrafted children's tables and chairs. The prices are steep, but gift wrapping is free. Open Monday through Friday.

Men's Apparel

James Davis
400 Grove Park Road
(901) 767–4640
This distinguished East Memphis shop for men and women, situated in Laurelwood shopping center, sells fine apparel in brands that include Giorgio Armani, Burberry, Brioni, and Dolce & Gabbana. It is owned and operated by the Weinberg family, longtime Memphis haberdashers, and it is staffed by knowledgeable salespeople.

Oak Hall
6150 Poplar Avenue
(901) 761–3580
Generations of Memphians have been coming to Oak Hall for blazers, suits, and other high-end, traditional apparel. In business for more than 140 years, the shop

caters both to its old customers as well as their children, with suits by Hickey Freeman, Oxxford, Canale, and Ermenegildo Zegna for men and Ron Leal for women, as well as a full selection of apparel for men and women. Oak Hall also carries the Burberry line as well as ties, scarves, and other accessories by Hermès. The shop is situated in Regalia shopping center at Poplar near I–240.

Women's Apparel/ Boutiques

Joseph
418 South Grove Park Road
(901) 767–1609
This chic women's shop has a great selection of shoes, bags, clothing, jewelry, and cosmetics from some of the best in the business. The apparel is mainly day-to-evening and sportswear in lines that include Armani and Michael Kors. If you love shoes and handbags, Joseph is a paradise, with shoes by Prada, Gucci, Ferragamo, Stuart Weitzman, Calvin Klein, and others. You can find beautiful handbags by Kate Spade, Prada, and Furla. The shop also carries John Hardy, Margaret Ellis, and other lines of fine jewelry, as well as makeup by Bobbi Brown, Trish McEvoy, and others. This retail operation has been in Memphis since 1930, originally as the shoe department of Levy's Department Store. Joseph has a second location in Houston.

Minor Frances
3080 Poplar Avenue
(901) 452–4949
1209 Ridgeway Road
(901) 255–1070
Minor Frances has been a Memphis tradition for more than 30 years, with women's fashions for customers of all ages. One of Minor Frances's particular strengths is special-occasion dresses, so you could find the perfect outfit here both for the mother of the bride and the teenage sister of the bride. The shop carries brands ranging from Trina Turk and Supply & Demand to William Pearson and Barry Bricken. You'll find lots of sportswear as well as office attire and accessories that include Judith

Jack Jewelry. The Poplar store is close to midtown in Chickasaw shopping center; the Ridgeway store is in Park Place shopping center at Ridgeway and Park in East Memphis near Germantown.

Nicole Miller
434 South Grove Park Road
(901) 753-2601
www.nicolemiller.com

This shop, featuring apparel and accessories by trendy designer Nicole Miller, may be part of a chain, but it's still a good place to find great dresses, apparel for going out on the town, and accessories including colorful scarves and purses. These days, special-occasion and bridal dresses are an important focus, so a bride-to-be can find dresses for her bridesmaids as well as her own dresses both for the big day and for parties. You can still find plenty of the feminine little cocktail dresses for which Miller is famous as well as separates and whimsical accessories such as make-up bags and umbrellas.

Timna
5101 Sanderlin Avenue
(901) 683-9369

Situated in Sanderlin Centre shopping center, Timna specializes in apparel, jewelry, accessories, and gift items made by leading American artisans. You won't find anything here that's mass-produced, only handmade items. This is the place for find a hand-woven jacket, and clothing from Babette or Susan's from Berkeley, for example. Gifts, which range in price from $15 to $300, include handblown glass and unusual items for the home.

Farmers' Markets

Agricenter International Farmers' Market
7777 Walnut Grove Road
(901) 757-7790

Housed in a distinctive red barn, the farmers' market features all kinds of locally grown fruits, vegetables, flowers, herbs, and crafts in summer, as well as pumpkins in October. You won't want to miss the famous local tomatoes grown in Ripley, Tennessee, or freshly shelled but-terbeans and other beans in season. The market is particularly lively on Saturdays, when you find the most vendors, the best variety of produce, and more people.

To get there turn onto the Agricenter International property from either Germantown Parkway or Walnut Grove Road, and look for the big red barn. Open April 1 through Halloween.

Flea Markets/Thrift Shops

The Memphis Flea Market—The Big One
955 Maxwell Early Boulevard
(901) 276-3532

This sprawling, huge flea market takes place the third weekend of every month, attracting 800 to 1,000 vendors from all over the region as well as more than 20,000 shoppers. You'll find all kinds of merchandise, used and new, including antiques, collectibles, clothes, jewelry, household goods, even computers, NASCAR items, and produce. The market takes place at the Mid-South Fairgrounds at Central and East Parkway, taking up four buildings and spilling into parking-lot areas as well. Admission is free; parking is $2.00. Although the flea market usually takes place once a month during the third weekend, there are two flea markets in December, and the September date changes to accommodate the Mid-South Fair. Hours are 8:00 A.M. to 6:00 P.M.

Garden Shops

Bayless Greenhouses
6120 Walsh Road, Millington
(901) 353-4721

It's a good drive from most parts of Memphis to Bayless, located near Shelby Forest, but well worth it for the huge selection. Bayless, which has been around for more than 30 years, grows all its own plants (except for large trees and shrubs) and is the largest grower of bedding and potted plants in the area. In spring you'll find thousands of items, including hostas, daylilies, roses, grasses, and lots of other perennials. Be sure to wear your walking shoes, because it's a big place.

Insiders' Tip

Don't forget that you'll find some great shopping at area museums, including the Memphis Brooks Museum and the National Ornamental Metals Museum.

Sam Stringer Nursery and Garden Center
2974 Poplar Avenue
(901) 458–3109

This midtown garden center sells all kinds of plants, pots, accessories, and supplies as well as Christmas trees and greenery during the holiday season. A neighborhood favorite, Stringer's has knowledgeable staffers who can make recommendations and also offers landscaping services. There's also a suburban location at 9495 Poplar Avenue in Germantown (901-754-5700).

Trees by Touliatos
2020 East Brooks Road
(901) 346–8065

This 20-acre family-owned nursery, located well off the beaten path in south Memphis, sells not only trees but also other plants and all kinds of related items. The shop specializes in water gardens and has about 14 water-garden displays. Owners Plato and Sarah Touliatos and their staff probably know more than anyone about what plants do well in this part of the country, and landscaping services are available. Ask about the shop's Saturday gardening seminars, which typically take place from March to November. Touliatos is west of the airport on Brooks near Airways. Open Monday through Saturday.

Urban Gardener
742 Mt. Moriah Road
(901) 374–9964

This shop, although it doesn't sell plants and trees, does have a great collection of fountains, bird baths and feeders, benches, planters, and other items to brighten up gardens of all sizes. The shop is in a pink building, right where Mt. Moriah curves around to meet Poplar.

Gift Shops

Babcock Gifts
4626 Poplar Avenue
(901) 763–0700

This traditional gift shop is a Memphis institution, and no society bride in the city would walk down the aisle without first registering at Babcock. Here, you'll find exquisite things, including fine porcelain by Herend, Raynaud, and Limoges; crystal by Waterford and Baccarat, and flatware by Buccellati as well as all of the traditional sterling lines. The shop also has plenty of gifts for babies, men, and women for all occasions.

Bella Notte
2172 Young Avenue
(901) 726–4131

This chic little shop next to Java Cabana in the hip Cooper-Young district has all kinds of unique gifts, ranging from exquisite baby frocks (for babies up to two years old) and old-fashioned toys to imported soaps and bath products, candles, stationery, writing papers, glassware, picture frames, and handmade jewelry.

Carabella's
99 North Second Street
(901) 525–5500

This downtown favorite has a great selection of classy and fun gifts ranging in price from several dollars to several hundred dollars. The shop has an eclectic mix of decorative accessories, candles, barware, bath products, and gifts for children and pets. Among the lines it carries is Votivo candles and Bloom and Thymes Ltd. line of bath products. The shop, situated on the ground floor of Talbot Heirs Guesthouse across from The Peabody, is open Monday through Saturday.

Carnevale
530 South Main Street
(901) 543–0332

Although primarily a retailer of trendy tableware, Carnevale exhibits artwork by local artists who have included David Nester and Ruth Williams. The merchandise includes porcelain by Dan Levy, Aronson Noon art glass from England, and McCarty pottery reproductions. The selection of both art and tableware is guided by the eye of by John Simmons, a Memphis-based gift-shop owner who in the 1970s had a 40-plus chain of John Simmons shops with stores in Houston, San Francisco, and other cities. Carnevale is open Tuesday through Sunday and during the monthly Art Trolley Tour.

Gourmet Stores

Epicure
208 North Evergreen
(901) 722–2220

At this gorgeous, small gourmet shop, an offshoot of the restaurant Café Society, you can choose from elegant prepared meals, restaurant-quality fresh fish and meats, cheeses, coffees, and a delectable array of sauces, mustards, chutneys, and other grocery items. Epicure is also Memphis's exclusive purveyor of Leonidas Belgian chocolates, which are nirvana for any chocolate lover.

Mantia's
4856 Poplar Avenue
(901) 762–8560

This East Memphis restaurant also has a market that sells gourmet foods, including French sausages and other meats, packaged grocery items including pastas, oils, sauces and sweets, as well as prepared takeout food. Mantia's also has the most extensive selection of domestic and imported cheeses in Memphis, including its own house-made fresh mozzarella. (See the Restaurants chapter for more information.)

Viking Culinary Arts
119 South Main Street
(901) 578–5822

This cooking school/retail store is the prototype for a national chain being developed by Viking Range Corporation, the Greenwood, Mississippi, company famous for its professional-quality stoves and other appliances. Downstairs is a dazzling retail space, stocked with all kinds of professional cooking tools including Viking's own brand of cookware and knives, and a demonstration kitchen in the back. There's also bakeware, kitchen gadgets, gourmet food items, and other merchandise for the kitchen except for Viking appliances (you have to go to an authorized dealer for that purchase). Upstairs is a state-of-the-art demonstration kitchen, with multilevel theater-type seating, where you can get a single cooking lesson or a series. Instructors include celebrated local chefs, visitors who have included Frederic Van Coppernolle of the French Culinary Institute, and Viking Culinary Arts staff.

Williams-Sonoma Outlet
4718 Spottswood Avenue
(901) 763–1500

Tucked away in Audubon Shopping Center is one of the city's great shopping spots. Here Williams-Sonoma sells merchandise from its Memphis warehouse, at discounted prices. You'll find cookware, cappuccino machines and other small appliances, table linens, stemware, holiday items, and gourmet foods, not to mention merchandise from the company's other lines, such as Pottery Barn and Hold Everything. If you're lucky, your visit will coincide with the arrival of a new truckload of merchandise, so you can get first pick.

Music and Musical Instruments

Pop Tunes
308 Poplar Avenue
(901) 525–6348
www.poptunes.com

This is the original Pop Tunes, opened in 1946, where Elvis used to hang out listening to records. At present it's an urban music store that focuses on rap and hip-hop, but Elvis fans can find plenty of Elvis

CDs and memorabilia. Pop Tunes has six other Memphis locations, including East Memphis (4195 Summer, 901-324-3855) and Germantown (7652 Poplar Avenue, 901-255-9404).

River Records
822 South Highland
(901) 324–1757
This shop boasts the city's largest selection of records, with some 300,000 albums and 45s. Situated near University of Memphis, River Records has lots of prewar blues records, 78s, and originals from the 1940s and 1950s. There's also plenty of Elvis, as well as CDs and cassettes. The shop also sells collectible comic books and baseball cards.

Shangri-La Records
1916 Madison Avenue
(901) 274–1916
www.shangri.com
This midtown record shop carries new and used albums and CDs of Memphis music, indie music, Memphis and Delta blues, funk, R&B, and more. It also has its own record label, Shangri-La Records, which has recorded The Grifters and other local bands. If you're into Memphis music, you'll definitely want to drop by. Ask about their '70s museum and live music events, which take place here from time to time. You can also order from their Web site. Shangri-La also publishes its own hipster guide to Memphis, *Kreature Comforts,* available for $2.50.

Strings and Things
1555 Madison Avenue
(901) 278–0500
Strings and Things is a shopping center for musical instruments that makes its home in a former bakery in midtown. Here, you'll find that drums, electric guitars, acoustic guitars, bass guitars, keyboards, pianos, sound equipment, and recording equipment each has its own little shop, with staffers who are knowledgeable about all these instruments. All of them sell new and used instruments as well as strings and other supplies. There's also a mastering studio, lessons available, and a deli/cafe

called Obadiah's. It's a one-stop shopping experience for anyone interested in guitars or other musical instruments.

Tower Records
150 Peabody Place
(901) 526–9210
Opened in 2001 as part of Peabody Place, Tower Records has a huge selection of CDs, magazines, and other music, including a large area devoted to Memphis music. Even though it's a chain, Tower is worth keeping an eye on as it features free, in-store performances by artists who have included Buddy Guy. Tower is on Third Street at the corner of Peabody Place.

Yarborough's Music
6122 Macon Road
(901) 761–0414
This locally owned music store is well known for the bluegrass jam it has put on every Tuesday night for more than 20 years. It's the place to go for acoustic instruments, including guitars as well as bluegrass instruments such as dulcimers, banjos, and mandolins. Yarborough's also has electric guitars, basses, and drums as well as lighting, audio, and recording equipment. The store is at Macon Road at Sycamore View Road.

Outfitters/Sports Stores

Edwin Watts Golf
4625 Poplar Avenue
(901) 767–1244
www.edwinwatts.com
This chain retailer of golf equipment, apparel, and accessories for men and women is the best golf shop in town. Here, you can find the most complete selection of clubs, balls, bags, and all kinds of gifts and accessories, with brands that include Calloway, Titleist, and Taylormade. They also carry golf shoes, golf shirts and other apparel in all the top brands. The professionals at Edwin Watts can help fit you for clubs, too, for a $40 charge that's waived if you purchase the clubs. Club repairs also are available, usually with a 24-hour turnaround.

Outdoors Inc.
833 North Germantown Parkway
(901) 755–2271
www.outdoorsinc.com
5245 Poplar Avenue
(901) 767–6790
1710 Union Avenue
(901) 722–8988
This locally owned outfitter, which has operated here since 1974, prides itself on being the source for outdoor gear, adventure travel, training, and outdoor events. Here, you'll find everything you need for mountain biking, climbing, paddling, backpacking, hiking, camping, and other outdoor activities. The staff, outdoor enthusiasts who test all the equipment themselves, are excellent resources if you're looking for the best places to enjoy canoeing, biking, or other favorite activities. The Germantown location, the largest of the stores and the one with the best selection, also has a rock wall, where you can practice your climbing skills. Brands include North Face, Gary Fisher bikes, Old Town Canoes, and Vass hiking boots. Outdoors Inc. also rents canoes and kayaks and sponsors events that include an annual canoe and kayak race as well as the Tour de Wolf mountain-biking race.

Souvenirs, including Elvis-abilia

A. Schwab
163 Beale Street
(901) 523–9782
This is the oldest store in the city, opened in 1876 by Abraham Schwab, whose family continues to operate the shop. In this old-fashioned general store, you'll find anything and everything from washboards, hunting hats, and size-74 pants to lye soap, straight razors, and candy sold by the pound. Schwab has Elvis souvenirs at reasonable prices, even though the selection is small, and loads of tourist trinkets such as key rings, backscratchers, and bumper stickers. Don't miss the voodoo corner, where you'll find all kinds of special candles, potions, and the like to help you address that big problem in your life, whether it's a wandering spouse or bad luck. Going upstairs you'll go back in time as you check out the old cash registers, signs, and other retail relics. Remember the store motto: "If you can't find it at Schwab's, you're better off without it." Open Monday through Saturday.

Graceland Plaza
3700 block of Elvis Presley Boulevard
(901) 332–3322
The most extensive selection of Elvis-abilia can be found at Graceland Plaza, across the street from Graceland Mansion. On either side of the area where you board the shuttle for the mansion tour, you'll find a number of different shops, including general souvenir shops and those with a specific focus. Gallery Elvis sells pricey objets d'art and collectibles that include a limited-edition replica of Elvis's Gibson J-200 guitar for $5,000 and a 14K gold TCB ring like the one Elvis wore for $1,600. Good Rockin' Tonight sells Elvis CDs, videos, posters, and books, and Elvis Threads sells T-shirts, hats, ties, and jackets with images of The King. You'll find more shopping at Graceland Crossing Shops, just north of the airplane museum, although it's pretty much the same merchandise: mugs, clocks, T-shirts, key chains, and more—all with images of Elvis.

Memphis Music
149 Beale Street
(901) 526–5047
This Beale Street shop has all kinds of souvenirs related to Memphis music—T-shirts, gifts, jewelry, neckties—as well as the music itself on CDs, tapes, and videos. It specializes in the blues, so you can find early blues recordings by Leadbelly, Blind Lemon, and others.

Strange Cargo
172 Beale Street
(901) 525–1516
Here you'll find unusual, more offbeat souvenirs, cards, T-shirts, and gifts as well as the more routine Memphis and Beale Street souvenirs. There are plenty of Elvis

There's something for everyone at A. Schwab, an old-fashioned general store on Beale Street, which sells everything from souvenirs and voodoo products to frying pans.

PHOTO: MEMPHIS CONVENTION AND VISITORS BUREAU

items, from posters and mugs to beach towels and salt-and-pepper shakers, plus a collection of cookie jars with images that include Elvis and Harley Davidson.

Tater Red's Lucky Mojos and Voodoo Healings
153 Beale Street
(901) 578-7234
www.taterredsluckymojos.com
This funky little shop has everything

from voodoo dolls, Ex-Wife Stay Away oil, and Winning Number candles to refrigerator magnets, all kinds of T-shirts, and reproductions of performance posters. There's also Naughty Queen of Camp Betty Page posters, Elvis and Nixon key chains, iron art by Ernest, and, of course, Tater Red's Lucky T-shirts and hats. The shop is tucked in next to The Black Diamond.

Kidstuff

Memphis is a kid-friendly place with plenty of attractions and activities for youngsters of all ages, from IMAX films and skating to the oldest operating wooden roller coaster in North America and the famous Peabody ducks. In addition to visiting a world-class zoo and children's museum, kids can ride a trolley along the Mississippi River or eat at a restaurant that lets you write on the walls and blow toothpicks into the ceiling through a drinking straw.

Traveling with kids has its challenges, and sometimes that's not so much finding interesting stuff as it is locating nearby clean rest rooms, gauging how much more walking a kid can stand before imploding, and finding a restaurant that serves both chicken fingers and arugula. (You'll find tips throughout this chapter on these points.)

The biggest challenge, though, can be the familiar complaints from the back seat: "This is so boring!" or "Not another museum!" and the proverbial "We never get to do anything the kids want to do!" Doing things that offer something for everyone is the secret to pleasing both children and parents. Of course, it never hurts to have an arsenal of kid activities to use as bargaining chips to exchange for what mom and dad want to do. Ice cream and amusement parks can buy a lot of art-museum time.

If your family is relocating to Memphis, these activities and sights will help you get acquainted with the best of what the city has to offer for kids. We list fair-weather options as well as rainy-day options, just in case the weather's not cooperating when you venture out.

For more ideas of things to do and see, check out the chapters on parks and recreation, spectator sports (including Redbirds baseball), and attractions. Also, don't forget about the Memphis Music and African American Heritage chapters, where you'll find more ideas.

The hours listed are in effect during summer months. They may be different at other times of year, so call ahead. Unless otherwise specified, children under three are admitted free.

Attractions

Downtown

If you're centering your visit in downtown Memphis, you'll find it's a happening place for kids, too. In the last few years, this area has been transformed from a desolate, forgotten wasteland to a lively city center. If you only have a few days to explore Memphis culture and history, spend them here.

Carriage Tours of Memphis
393 North Main Street
(901) 527-7542

In the late afternoon horse-drawn carriages line up on Union Avenue in front of The Peabody hotel and on Beale Street at Second Street. Each driver decorates his own carriage, some with gaudy plastic flowers or an all-Elvis theme. All the carriage drivers have their dogs with them atop the driver's seat, so kids are immediately drawn there, giving the drivers a chance to sell you the tour. The usual tour takes you along Main Street (much of which is closed to cars), up to Confederate Park to see the riverboats, and past many other downtown sights. Drivers provide entertaining trivia and stories about Memphis. Tours are especially fun in cold weather, when everyone has to snuggle under blankets.

Most carriages can accommodate two adults and up to four children. For a family expect to pay $30 to $35 for a 30-minute tour, not including the driver's tip.

Fire Museum of Memphis
118 Adams
(901) 320–5650
www.firemuseum.com

The museum, located in a 1910 firehouse that once housed fire horses, is a big hit with children, who often are fascinated with firefighters as real-life heroes. From its authentic stall a talking fire horse narrates film clips about the development of fire fighting during the last century. On display are a horse-drawn steam pumper and two early fire engines, sparkling and shining as if a child's toy fire-truck collection had magically become the real thing. Two modern fire engines and an ambulance are available for kids to climb on, to imagine themselves as firefighters rushing to the biggest fire ever. Uniformed firefighters serve as the museum educators and patiently answer questions.

The most memorable and moving exhibit is the Fire Room, where you experience a fire in real time. Smoke fills the scene and the room becomes uncomfortably hot as the fire rages behind a glass screen. The film lasts only six minutes, but makes a lasting impression of the seriousness and danger of fires. It's so realistic that it could be frightening to some children. Ask museum educators if you're unsure about whether it's right for your kids.

Open from 9:00 A.M. to 5:00 P.M. Tuesday through Saturday and 1:00 to 5:00 P.M. on Sunday. Admission is $5.00 for adults and teens, $4.00 for seniors and children 3 to 12. There is no parking available at the museum, so look for a space in a nearby lot or take the trolley, which stops a block west of the museum on Main.

Main Street Trolley
Main Street, various stops
(901) 274–6282

Riding the Main Street Trolley is great for getting places downtown so that you can take a break from the car. And for 60 cents a ride, it's the best entertainment

value in town. Kids love everything about it—looking down the tracks for a trolley, dropping correct change into the metered coin box, and pulling the cord over their heads to signal your stop. The trolley windows are usually open, and kids always want to hang their heads out to catch the breeze; don't let them, because the driver will quickly scold.

The trolley runs along Main Street but also loops around for a great view of the Mississippi River. Save the Riverfront Loop ride (ask the driver if he's making the loop) for an afternoon when the kids have had enough and could use 45 minutes of down time. Just sitting, looking out the window, taking in the cityscape can revive even the most frazzled child.

Tickets are 60 cents per ride for all ages, except seniors and disabled persons, who pay 30 cents. You can also get a $2.50 daylong pass or a $6.00 three-day pass. Exact change is required.

(See Getting Around chapter for more information about the Main Street Trolley and other transportation.)

Memphis Belle Pavilion
125 North Front Street, Mud Island
(901) 576–7241

The legendary *Memphis Belle*, under a parachute-like canopy on Mud Island, sits as a proud survivor of World War II. Pilot Robert Morgan named his B-17 bomber after his Memphis sweetheart, Margaret Polk. He had her likeness painted on the side of his plane as good luck, and good luck she was. The *Memphis Belle*, the most famous airplane of World War II, had a distinguished combat record, completing its quota of 25 missions over Nazi-occupied territory. Kids are impressed by the vast size and obvious fortitude of the aircraft and enjoy getting an up-close look from all sides. The *Memphis Belle* is visited often by WWII veterans, many of them former pilots with great stories.

You can reach the *Memphis Belle* by entering at Front Street, then taking the pedestrian bridge or tram to Mud Island. Alternatively, you can drive across the Auction Street bridge to Mud Island, turn left, and ask the guard for directions.

Note: The Memphis Belle is scheduled to move to a new home at Forest Hill–Irene Road and Bill Morris Parkway in Germantown in late 2003. Call ahead or check with the Tennessee Welcome Center for more information.

Memphis Queen Riverboats
45 Riverside Drive (at the foot of Monroe)
(901) 527–5694, (800) 221–6197
www.memphisqueen.com

The best place to see the river and the only way to be on the river, other than bringing your own boat, is to take a Memphis Queen Riverboat cruise. As you approach the fleet docked along the historic cobblestones, the music from the calliope transports you back in time. Plan to arrive about 30 minutes before departure and just take in the atmosphere. Upon boarding each group poses for a photo. A 5 x 7 print commemorating your voyage is available after the cruise for $5.00. The photos, actually, are pretty good.

The captain narrates the tour, pointing out historical facts and locations on the river, but kids much prefer rambling around from the top observation deck to the second-level snack bar and down to the first level, where a crew member sings and plays the piano. You'll hear everything from traditional river ballads and blues to Elvis's greatest hits. It may seem unlikely that kids would go for something as laid-back as a 90-minute riverboat ride, but you may be surprised at the impression the piano player, paddlewheel, and view of the river can make.

Cruises leave at 2:30 P.M. and at 5:30 P.M. daily. Ticket prices are $12.50 for adults, $11.50 for seniors, and $9.00 for children 4 through 18. Children ages 3 and under are free.

Mud Island River Park
125 North Front Street
(901) 576–7241, (800) 507–6507
www.mudisland.com

Think you could walk the length of the Mississippi in a day? Of course not, yet that's the main attraction of Mud Island River Park. A detailed replica of the Mississippi River flows through the park. You can take your shoes off and walk in the water as the Mississippi twists and turns on its way to New Orleans, where it pours into the Gulf of Mexico. When you make it to New Orleans, reward yourselves with ice cream or lemonade from the snack bar.

For a detailed chronology of the history and culture along the Mississippi, visit the Mississippi River Museum. Kids can climb aboard a reconstructed 19th-century steamboat, witness a battle aboard a Civil War gunboat, and listen to the river hollers and work songs of the river roustabouts. Guided tours are available.

To get to Mud Island go to the ticket office on Front Street; then either walk across the pedestrian bridge or take the monorail across the Mississippi to the island. The *Memphis Belle* is also on Mud Island.

Open daily from 10:00 A.M. to 8:00 P.M. Last admission is one hour before closing time. The park is free, but the museum is $8.00 for adults, $6.00 for seniors and children ages 5 through 17, and free to children 4 and under. Parking is available

Insiders' Tip

Muvico Theaters in downtown Memphis offers child care (for ages 3 to 8 only) for up to three hours while parents watch a movie. The kids play in a large, cheerful playroom supervised by certified teachers, and parents are given an on-site pager to ensure quick notification in case of an emergency. Cost is $7.00 per hour per child. Call (901) 248-0101 for more information or to make reservations.

near the Front Street side of the monorail for $2.00 to $3.00.

National Civil Rights Museum
450 Mulberry
(901) 521-9699
www.civilrightsmuseum.org

If you are thinking about not visiting the National Civil Rights Museum because your kids won't like it, reconsider. The museum offers an exceptionally engaging audio tour for children, narrated by Linda Rosa Brown, a fictional young girl with a fresh, upbeat voice. She's named for two civil rights figures, Linda Brown of *Brown v. Topeka Board of Education* and Rosa Parks, who helped to spark the movement when she refused to give up her bus seat. Linda Rosa explains the history of the civil rights movement from the perspective of the "commitment, courage, cooperation, and responsibility" of the participants, some of whom were teenagers and children.

The museum is interactive, with exhibits like a real bus to enter and sit in, with a seated sculpture of Rosa Parks and a bridge to march over with the marchers in Selma. The facts and visuals can be disturbing as the kids struggle to understand segregation, but, overall, the museum is positive, powerful, and affirming.

The National Civil Rights Museum offers free parking. This would be a good place to leave your car and use the trolley to reach other downtown locations.

Open 9:00 A.M. to 6:00 P.M. Monday through Saturday and 1:00 to 5:00 P.M. on Sunday.

Admission is $8.50 for adults, $7.50 for seniors and students and $6.50 for children 4–12. (For more information see Attractions and African American History chapters.)

Beale Street

Any trip to Memphis will undoubtedly include Beale Street. It's the second-most-visited street in America after Bourbon Street in New Orleans and is like a calmer Bourbon Street with smoke-filled clubs but no strip joints. With kids the best time to visit Beale is during the day or the early evening. Later in the evening it becomes rowdier, and after 11:00 P.M. no one under 21 is allowed on the street because of city liquor laws.

A. Schwab
163 Beale Street
(901) 523-9782

A. Schwab is the oldest establishment on Beale. It was founded in 1876 by Abraham Schwab, an immigrant from Alsace, France, whose descendants still mind the store.

For kids, Schwab's is a treasure trove. The first floor is full of tourist trinkets like Memphis bumper stickers, key rings, souvenir license plates, and more. Don't miss the Elvis playing cards featuring a different Elvis photo on each card. The other two floors carry, well, everything. The store's motto is: "If you can't find it at Schwab's, you're better off without it." You can find straight razors, cast-iron griddles, ladies' bloomers, lye soap, and men's pants up to size 74. From all ends of the store, kids are saying, "Mom, look at this!" "Mom, what is this?" and "People really used to wear these?" Browsing at A. Schwab is an adventure worth the couple of bucks you'll spend on tourist trinkets or maybe even something useful.

Hours are 9:00 A.M. to 5:00 P.M. Monday through Saturday. (For more information see Attractions and Shopping chapters.)

Beale Street Visitors Center
200 Beale Street
(901) 543-2200

This small store on the edge of Handy Park has all kinds of souvenirs and tourist information, and, most important, large, clean bathrooms. It also sells cold drinks, bottled water, and snacks.

Memphis Police Museum
159 Beale Street
(901) 528-2370

The Memphis Police Museum is small and not sophisticated in its presentation, but kids love the simple displays and the stories about cops and robbers. The museum houses memorabilia that ranges from a collection of guns and other confiscated weapons to period uniforms and an actual jail cell from an old women's prison. Old newspaper clippings highlight events in Memphis history in which police played an important role, such as the riots following the assassination of Dr. Martin Luther King, Jr., and Elvis's funeral. Did you know that the legendary "Machine Gun" Kelly was captured in Memphis? George Kelly Barnes came home to Memphis when he escaped from prison in 1933 and hid out at the home of his wife and mother-in-law. You'll find newspaper articles, mug shots of Kelly, and the scales on which he was weighed after he was arrested--a coveted item among Machine Gun Kelly collectors.

You wouldn't think this place is an actual operating police station, but it is, even if the officer at the tall dispatch desk wears an old-fashioned police uniform. Tucking in here for a look-see is a nice reprieve from the street.

Open 11:00 A.M. to midnight Sunday through Thursday and "until the crowd leaves Beale Street" on Friday and Saturday. Admission is free.

Elsewhere in Memphis

The Children's Museum of Memphis
2525 Central Avenue
(901) 458–2678, (901) 320–3170 (recorded information line)
www.cmom.com

Kids wouldn't call this place a museum because they don't just walk around and look at boring stuff. Instead they get to touch and explore everything in what feels like a kid-size city.

Kids can "drive" the family minivan and even "fill it up" with gas or check out a dismantled car to see how the steering wheel controls the axles. They can set up an account at the bank and immediately withdraw play money to use at the Kid Market, a stocked, kid-sized grocery store where they can pick out grocery items or pretend to be cashiers, actually scanning bar codes.

Elsewhere in the museum there's a real fire engine and a police motorcycle with a working siren. A 40-foot vertical maze called the Skyscraper intrigues kids as they slip through various-size holes to reach the top of the tower. Like any maze, many routes are dead ends, and it requires

Insiders' Tip

Before you come to Memphis, check your hometown zoo and museum memberships. Reciprocal agreements abound, and you may be eligible for free admission at the Memphis Zoo, The Children's Museum of Memphis, and other attractions. Don't forget to bring your membership card to show at the ticket booth.

patience and industrious backtracking to get through it.

An art area with bins full of recycled lids, tubes, and paper awaits budding artists and sculptors. Glue, crayons, scissors, and hole punchers are supplied at each table, and the museum takes care of cleaning up the mess.

A separate enclosed area is especially geared toward toddlers and kids under five. Here, they can enjoy toys and climbers appropriate for their age group, and there are no bigger kids stepping on them.

The museum's $6-million expansion recently added 8,000 square feet of exhibition space. It includes galleries aimed at older children, especially the 'tweeners, ages 10 to 12, who may think they're too old to enjoy the museum. There's a 25-foot slice of the Mississippi River, where visitors can manipulate bridges, dams, and barges. Elsewhere kids can climb into a real aircraft cockpit or a flight simulator. As always, scattered throughout are computer terminals with a variety of games available.

As for parents there are numerous benches, and the open environment makes it easy to sit and keep an eye on your child from a distance. Children can explore freely and independently and enjoy playing with lots of other kids. A new gift shop and a snack area with vending machines are part of the museum expansion, too.

Open 9:00 A.M. to 5:00 P.M. Tuesday through Saturday and noon to 5:00 P.M. on Sunday. Admission is $7.00 for adults and teens, $6.00 for seniors and children 1–12. Free parking is available.

Chucalissa Archaeological Museum
1987 Indian Village Drive
(901) 785–3160

In 1939, while excavating the site to develop a city park, workers discovered the ruins of a Choctaw Indian village. They named the village Chucalissa, which means "abandoned house." The park is dedicated to educating visitors about the Choctaw Indians who populated this area before European settlers arrived. A museum and reconstructed village have been developed over the years from the information and artifacts that archaeologists discovered on the site. On-site demonstrations of traditional dancing, food, and crafts help visitors imagine the village as it was when the Choctaw lived there. If you are interested in native American history and archaeology, Chucalissa is worth a visit.

To get there from Downtown take Riverside Drive (which turns into I-55 South). Take the Third Street exit and go south. Turn right onto Mitchell (you should see a sign) and follow the signs.

Chucalissa is open Tuesday through Saturday from 9:00 A.M. to 4:00 P.M. Admission is $5.00 for adults, $4.00 for seniors and children ages 4 to 11.

Memphis Zoo
2000 Galloway
(901) 725–3452
www.memphiszoo.org

Of all the city's attractions, the Memphis Zoo is the one locals like to brag about. Formerly a plain-Jane zoo with unattractive pens, the Memphis Zoo has reinvented itself over the last few years with spectacular results. It continues to add more animal exhibits, such as its new Animals of the Night building.

The entrance, which incorporates Egyptian decorations borrowed from the

The variety of animals at the Memphis Zoo draws quite a crowd. PHOTO: JACK KENNER

original Memphis that once flourished by the Nile, impresses children with its sheer grandeur. Its exotic look immediately transports you to far-away landscapes where unfamiliar animals roam. You then walk along a promenade flanked by huge sculptures of safari animals. Each statue has signs that clearly ask you not to climb on the animals, but many kids (and even parents) can't resist.

Inside, among Egyptian carvings and sculptures, more than 400 species of animals from all over the world reside in renovated natural habitats. Just left of the entrance is Cat Country, where visitors stroll through overgrown plantings to peer at lions and tigers that surround the pathway. Huge screens of barely visible piano wire are all that separate you from these wild beasts.

At the Animals of the Night exhibition, you'll enter a dark and eerie exhibit hall with nocturnal animals in full motion. Given the darkness, the symphony of animal sounds, the intimidating closeness of the animals to the glass, and the many bats that swoop overhead, you may be glad to see the light of day again. If you have young children, you or another adult should go in first to see whether this exhibit is too intense for them.

Not for the faint-hearted is the Dragon's Lair, home to the world's largest lizards, the deadly Komodo dragons. Also known as dragon lizards, they can grow to a length of 10 feet. They look slow and real creepy but, actually, are quick to attack, and their bite is deadly. They're scary despite the thick glass wall separating them from visitors.

The newest addition is the zoo's China exhibition, a 3-acre area that includes a pagoda and different animals from China. The zoo is working on acquiring giant pandas to take up residence here, although it's unclear when that will happen.

Be sure to check the information board near the main entrance that tells you about the zoo events for the day, which can include snakes or other animals on display for kids to touch and hold. Always fun is the seal feeding at 2:30 P.M. every day, where the sea lions are guided through their tricks, and their trainers tell you all about them.

It's easy and enjoyable to spend a whole day at the zoo, given its beautifully landscaped grounds and plentiful run-around room for kids. Picnic areas are marked, and the pleasant playground outside the Cat House Cafe is always popular with kids. The cafe has hamburgers, old-fashioned soft-custard ice cream, and other kid-friendly treats. Strollers are available for rent, which may come in handy for young children who get tired of walking.

Hours are 9:00 A.M. to 6:00 P.M. Admission is $10.00 for adults, $9.00 for seniors, and $6.00 for children 2 to 11. *Note:* If you have a large family, it might be more economical to purchase a Memphis Zoological Society membership.

The Pink Palace
3050 Central Avenue
(901) 320–6362
www.memphismuseums.org

The Pink Palace is actually three attractions housed in one large pink mansion: The Pink Palace Museum, the Union Planters IMAX Theater, and the Sharpe Planetarium. The lavish mansion dates back to the 1920s, when it was built of pink marble for Clarence Sanders, a Memphian who opened the world's first supermarket and founded the Piggly-Wiggly grocery chain. Sadly, Sanders went bankrupt and no one ever lived in his pink marble palace.

The Pink Palace, IMAX theater, and planetarium are open Monday through Thursday 9:00 A.M. to 4:00 P.M., Friday 9:00 A.M. to 9:00 P.M., and Sunday noon to 6:00 P.M. Check for show times for IMAX and the planetarium. The combination ticket for all three attractions is $12.50 for adults, $11.50 for seniors, and $8.50 for children ages 3 to 12. Admission to the museum is $7.00 for adults, $6.50 for seniors, $4.50 for children 3–12. IMAX tickets are $6.50 for adults, $6.00 for seniors, and $5.00 for children 3 to 12. Tickets for the planetarium are $3.50 for adults, $3 for seniors and children 3 to 12.

Pink Palace Museum: The permanent exhibition of The Pink Palace traces the natural history of the Mid-South region from prehistoric dinosaurs to the present. The artifacts are diverse, ranging from fossils and dinosaur bones found in the area to Indian artifacts to life-sized dioramas illustrating the life of the early European settlers. Along the way you will learn about Memphis's connection with the Trail of Tears, the Civil War, Elvis and rock and roll, the modern chain supermarket as we know it, and much more. One of the kids' favorites is the Clyde Park Miniature Circus. Mr. Park spent 50 years carving and motorizing this circus replica before donating it to the museum. The circus is turned on each day at 10:30, and kids stand on platforms to watch the delightful performance. The coolest (and grossest) thing in the museum is the shrunken head. Don't miss it and be sure to ask how they shrink it. Ask about temporary exhibits, too.

Union Planters IMAX Theater: At an IMAX theater, instead of watching a movie, you experience it on a screen four stories high and five stories wide while actually feeling the vibrations from the sound system.

The IMAX allows you to swim with dolphins, scream with the others as the most outrageous roller coaster tests your thrill tolerance, or descend to the depths of the ocean in search of the Titanic. There are no bad seats in the theater, but kids especially love the extra sensation and excitement of sitting in the thrill seats at the bottom of the screen. Films change constantly, so call (901-763-IMAX) for updated listings and show times.

Sharpe Planetarium: Too many of us are able to see only a few stars in the night sky these days, given air pollution and light in our cities. The Sharpe Planetarium, though, allows you to glorify in the beauty and bounty of the constellations as you have never seen them before. Pointing with a laser light, guides explain the stories and history behind the stars and other astronomical discoveries. Right before your eyes, the sky changes with the seasons so that you can see the movement of the stars. Lying back in a reclining chair, you will be amazed by the vastness and mystery of our galaxy. Call ahead for show times and ticket information.

The Pink Palace is home to an interesting museum, a planetarium, and an IMAX movie house.
PHOTO: MEMPHIS PINK PALACE MUSEUM

The tiny automated circus at Pink Palace Museum is a big hit with children of all ages.

PHOTO: MEMPHIS PINK PALACE MUSEUM

Rainy Day Activities

Don't let a little rain spoil your vacation. Story hours and pottery studios offer great rainy day fun for families who've had their fill of museums, or check out the local movie listings for some big-screen fun.

Story Hours

Many bookstores and libraries in the area host story hours for children. These places also tend to have extensive children's sections and kid-friendly staffs as well. Be sure to call ahead to verify story-hour times because times change throughout the year.

Barnes and Noble Booksellers, 2774 North Germantown Parkway, (901) 386–2468: Saturdays at 2:00 P.M.

Borders Books Music and Cafe, 6685 Poplar, (901) 754–0770: Wednesdays and Saturdays at 11:00 A.M.

Davis-Kidd Booksellers, 387 Perkins Road Extended, (901) 683–9801: Wednesdays at 10:00 A.M., Thursdays and Saturdays at 11:00 A.M.

Memphis/Shelby County Public Library, Central Branch, 3030 Poplar, (901) 725–8819: 10:30 A.M. Wednesdays (for ages 2 to 5)

Memphis/Shelby County Public Library, Highland Branch, 460 South Highland, (901) 452–7341: 10:30 A.M. Wednesdays (for ages 2 to 5)

Pinocchio's Book Store, 688 West Brookhaven Circle, (901) 767–6586: 10:30 Fridays (for ages 2 to 5)

Zany Brainy, Park Place Center, 1211 Ridgeway, (901) 682–9131: 10:30 A.M. Mondays and Wednesdays, 4:00 P.M. Thursdays, and 7:00 P.M. Fridays

Pottery Studios

The Creative Part
3521 Walker Avenue
(901) 458–9345
Located near the University of Memphis, the Creative Part has a wide variety of greenware including Elvis busts and mugs, as well as a potter's wheel and clay sculpting. If mom or dad don't want to participate, there's a wonderful fenced garden in the front for relaxing and people-watching. After the finishing touches on the masterpieces, walk across the street to Book Adventure, a jam-packed used bookstore, or enjoy pizza at Garibaldi's (see Kid-Friendly Dining in this chapter for details).

Paint-a-Piece Pottery
8075 Giacosa Place
(901) 387–3473
Paint-a-Piece is located in Cordova near the Wolfchase Galleria mall. Family members who don't want to paint pottery can check out the many shops, restaurants, and movies in the area.

Seize the Clay
5030 Poplar Avenue
(901) 683–2529
Located in East Memphis, this is a great place to make holiday gifts or dinner plates to use at home. Great fruit and yogurt smoothies for toiling artists are available right next door at Smooth Moves.

Amusements and Activities

Jillian's
Second Street at Peabody Place
(901) 543–8000
Jillian's is sort of an electronic three-story playhouse with something for everyone, even teenagers. On the top floor is the arcade to beat all arcades, with a huge variety of game and virtual experiences. (The games are pricey, something that's not immediately apparent with Jillian's system of buying and spending points.) One of the most popular activities is virtual bowling, with amazingly realistic graphics. For the real thing check out the cosmic bowling on the first floor. The electronic atmosphere of lights, hip music, food, and drink make this cooler than ordinary bowling. For younger kids you can program your lane to sprout bumpers so their experience isn't a continuum of gutter balls. The second floor has big-screen TVs with sports, pool tables, Ping-Pong, and a full-service restaurant.

The best time for younger kids and teens to have maximum access to the games and activities is during the day until about 6:00 P.M. Jillian's is not a good bet for kids later in the evenings.

Libertyland Amusement Park
940 Early Maxwell
(901) 274–1776
This old-fashioned theme park opened on July 4, 1976, in honor of The Bicentennial, thus the name. It's the largest amusement park with the best selection of rides in town and something for all ages. Its two roller coasters offer the best of the old and the new. The Revolution takes only 22 seconds but you spend half of that time upside down. It's one of those rides that is so scary and "thrilling" that you will want to ride it again and again. The Zippin Pippin, the oldest operating wooden roller coaster in North America, may look lame compared with the hi-tech Revolution, but riding it may change your mind. The noise of the cars against the wooden tracks makes you think the whole structure will collapse any second, and as an unintended thrill, the cars' wheels actually leave the tracks a few times as if it were getting a running jump on its grand descents.

Other Libertyland attractions include a spectacular carousel, live stage shows, a playground, and shade provided by the mature landscaped grounds. The Grand Carousel, built in 1909 by the Dentzel Carousel Co., is listed on the National Register of Historic Places.

For hungry families Libertyland offers the best of "fair" food, such as pronto pups and cotton candy, as well as on-site restaurants with sit-down meals and plenty of air-conditioning.

Libertyland is open 10:00 A.M. to 9:00 P.M. Wednesday through Sunday, and on Memorial Day, July 4th, and Labor Day.

This old-fashioned roller coaster is a big attraction at Libertyland, a popular amusement park.
PHOTO: MEMPHIS CONVENTION AND VISITORS BUREAU

Tickets are $20 for adults and children taller than 48 inches, and $10 for kids up to 48 inches. Seniors and children under 3 are free. All tickets include unlimited rides and park shows.

Miniature Golf and Entertainment Centers

An outing to play miniature golf used to be just that, but now, the miniature golf parks have turned into something-for-everyone "entertainment centers." Memphis has three, each with roughly the same activities: miniature golf, bumper boats, go-carts, kiddie rides, batting cages, arcade games, party rooms,

and snack bars. Bogey's and Putt-Putt also have driving ranges, and Putt-Putt also has LaserTron. You can pay for activities a la carte, but the best deal is a wristband for about $20 that gets you into almost all the activities. The arcades at these parks are happenin' and include basics such as air hockey as well as the newer simulator games. All the games give out tickets, which you can exchange for those junk-toy prizes that kids love.

Hours are 8:00 A.M. to 10:00 P.M. Sunday through Thursday and until midnight on weekends.

Bogey's, 7800 Fischer Steel Road, Cordova, (901) 757-2649, www.bogeys.com

Celebration Station, 5970 Macon Cove, (901) 377-6700

Putt-Putt Family Park, 5484 Summer Avenue, (901) 386-2992, www.puttputtmemphis.com

Laser Games

These high-tech war games are good bets if you are trying to amuse teenagers, and each facility also includes an arcade.

Laser Quest, Poplar Avenue at Highland, (901) 324-4800

Lasertron, at Putt-Putt Family Park, 5484 Summer Avenue, (901) 380-8766

Skating

Memphis has one ice-skating rink, three roller-skating rinks and an extremely skate-friendly area at Tom Lee Park (see the Insiders' Tip in this chapter). For more information including hours and cost, as well as details on where you can skateboard, see the Skating section of the Parks and Recreation chapter.

Cordova Skating Center, 7970 Club Center Drive, (901) 755-0221

East End Skating, 5718 Mt. Moriah, (901) 363-7785

Ice Chalet, 4451 American Way (Mall of Memphis), (901) 362–8877

Skateland Summer, 5137 Old Summer Road, (901) 683–6991

Kid-Friendly Dining

The challenge to eating out with kids is to find a restaurant that welcomes kids but also has good food for adults. These restaurants are winners on both fronts, and each has a casual, laid-back atmosphere.

The Arcade
540 South Main Street
(901) 526–5757
One of the oldest restaurants in Memphis, The Arcade has great pizza available by the pie or by the slice. This downtown favorite also serves a good breakfast anytime and has great milkshakes.

Dyer's Burgers
205 Beale Street
(901) 527–DYER
Dyer's is a kid-friendly place to eat on Beale Street, with shiny, 1950s diner decor and hamburgers fried in Memphis's most famous grease. (See Restaurants chapter for the full story.) It's open all afternoon, so take a rest from sightseeing. Try an old-fashioned milkshake or a Coke float, or if you're hungry, have a burger, fries, or chili.

El Porton
Poplar and Highland
(901) 452–7330
This kid-friendly midtown Mexican restaurant, tucked away in Poplar Plaza shopping center, is generous with the chips and has a nice outdoor eating area. It gets crowded especially around happy hour, so go early.

Fino's from the Hill
1853 Madison Avenue
(901) 272–3466
This midtown favorite is a good place to get a take-out picnic, with great sandwiches and other fare to please the parents.

A whole sandwich is so huge it will easily feed two kids, maybe more. You may want to take your picnic to nearby Overton Park.

Garibaldi's
3530 Walker Avenue
(901) 327–6111
Garibaldi's is a little on the grungy side, but kids love the combination of pizza and game arcade. Located in the University of Memphis area between midtown and East Memphis, it's a good tie-in with a trip to The Creative Part pottery studio.

Hard Rock Café
315 Beale Street
(901) 529–0007
If your kids are clamoring for Hard Rock Cafe, you'll find it at Beale and Fourth, with the usual menu, rock memorabilia, and merchandise shop. Incidentally, the chain was started by a Memphis native, Isaac Tigrett, but a Hard Rock didn't open up here until the 1990s.

Insiders' Tip
If you travel with roller blades, Tom Lee Park (downtown, next to the Mississippi River) is the best place to go, with free parking and open, paved pathways. If you cross the footbridge that goes over Riverside Drive, you'll find the Riverbluff Walkway, known locally as Riverwalk. It has smooth sidewalk with some slight hills as well as a fabulous view of the river.

Huey's
77 South Second Street
(901) 527–2700
Look up when you enter. Yes, those are toothpicks in the ceiling. Each has been spit there through a straw—a challenge that appeals to adults and kids alike. Also bring a Sharpie marker to write on the walls, another Huey's tradition. The menu includes great burgers, sandwiches, salads, and a kid's menu that features the ever-popular chicken on a stick. There's also a midtown location at 1927 Madison Avenue, as well as several in the suburbs.

Kwik Chek #10
2013 Madison Avenue
(901) 274–9293
Actually a convenience store in midtown with a great deli, this is another good bet for picnic fare. Parents will be wowed with the creative and zany selection of sandwiches, but there are plainer options for the kids as well as chips, drinks, and sweets. Nearby Overton Park is a good spot for your feast.

The Peanut Shoppe
24 Main Street
(901) 525–1115
Okay, you probably couldn't make a meal here, but hot roasted peanuts, snow cones, and candy are a great treat after riding the trolley or taking in the sights.

Sean's Deli and Smooth Moves
75 South Main Street
(901) 529–1000
This Greek deli serves great gyros, a huge cheeseburger with fries, and a variety of fruit smoothies (be sure to drink them slowly to avoid a brain freeze). There's also a midtown location at 1651 Union Avenue.

Sekisui Downtown
160 Union Avenue
(901) 523–0001
This sushi bar, located in the Holiday Inn Select, is a good compromise play because it has a sushi menu, a Japanese menu, and an American menu. Sushi lovers will be happy, and nonsushi eaters can choose from a menu of great burgers, fries, grilled cheese, and clam chowder. The restaurant's midtown location (901-725-0005) is also a favorite for kids, who love the sumo wrestling on TV and the little boats that bring sushi around—even if they don't like sushi.

Spaghetti Warehouse
40 West Huling Street
(901) 521–0907
The atmosphere of this family-oriented restaurant, where you can eat in a trolley car or a king-sized bed/booth, is big excitement for kids, even if adults may find the food a little dull. You can take the trolley to get here, as it's located next to the tracks.

Parks and Recreation

Those who like to get out and enjoy the outdoors will find many options in Memphis. The city has some 187 parks and 34 walking trails that encompass nearly 6,000 acres, and beyond the city limits there's Shelby Farm, the largest urban park in the United States with more than 4,500 acres. Best of all, because of the area's relatively mild winters, parks, golf courses, and other amenities can be enjoyed year-round.

Parks have been part of city planning since the city fathers first laid out the town of Memphis in 1819, and Memphians have not been afraid to fight to preserve their favorite parks. For example, in the 1960s and 1970s government leaders planned to build an interstate, I-40, right through midtown's Overton Park, but popular opposition, which led to a Supreme Court ruling to block the plans, saved the park. At present conservationists are working to prevent the construction of a major highway through the heart of Shelby Farms.

Local parks offer a variety of amenities and activities, from walking trails and fishing lakes to swimming pools, tennis courts, and golf courses. The parks also have large stately oaks, cottonwoods, and other trees that make the city green and beautiful.

The largest city parks are Overton Park in midtown, M.L. King/Riverside in south Memphis near downtown, and Audubon Park in East Memphis. There are numerous others, ranging in size from a block to more than 300 acres. We can't list them all, but you can get a complete listing or find out which parks are nearest you by calling the Memphis Parks Commission (also known as the City of Memphis division of park services) public information line at (901) 454–5200 or go on-line to www.cityofmemphis.org and click on "Park Services." The suburbs Germantown, Bartlett, and Collierville each maintain parks, services, and recreational activities of their own. Contact the Germantown parks and recreation department at (901) 757-7375 or visit www.ci.germantown.tn.us/gtpark.htm. For more information on Bartlett parks, call (901) 385-5590. Collierville parks details are available by calling (901) 853-0889 or by visiting www.collierville.com.

Just outside the city you'll find two large parks, Meeman-Shelby Forest State Park and Shelby Farms, each with fishing lakes, hiking and bike trails, and a host of other amenities. If you're willing to venture out farther from the city, you'll find a number of state parks where recreation facilities abound. Because Memphis is at the extreme southwest corner of Tennessee, bordering Mississippi and Arkansas, Memphis residents and visitors have access to three state park systems. There are no major national parks in west Tennessee, with the exception of Shiloh National Military Park, which is described in the Day Trips and Weekend Getaways chapter.

As for recreation you'll find many options, both in the city and within an easy drive. Tennis buffs will find a number of tennis complexes operated by the parks commission at Bellevue, Frayser, Riverside, and Audubon parks. The city also operates seven golf courses around the city, and a wide array of daily-fee courses are scattered throughout the metropolitan area and farther.

City community centers are also a part of the park system, and 15 of them have outdoor seasonal pools, whereas the Bickford Aquatic Facility has an indoor pool. Admission to the pools is free, and lessons are available for persons 3 and older. Other activities for young people at community centers include basketball and volleyball, while for senior citizens there are cultural and educational activities.

Organized sports activities are available under the auspices of the Memphis Park Commission. It sponsors amateur adult sports leagues for baseball, softball, basketball, and touch football as well as youth sports programs for baseball, basketball, and volleyball. Other leagues are organized through area churches, and, of course, schools have sports teams.

As for indoor activities you'll find a whole host of options to keep you busy, including skating, bowling, and racquetball. There are also driving ranges, which tend to be family-entertainment centers that also have go-carts, batting cages, and video games on site.

Water sports are also popular, no surprise given the mild climate and the proximity of the Mississippi River. Old Man River can be a dangerous guy, though, given its currents, whirlpools, and the huge waves that towboats leave behind. It's for experienced boaters only, so you may want to opt for one of the lakes in the area, several of which are less than an hour's drive from the city. Check listings for state parks. For canoeing we suggest some rivers in the area that are picture perfect for paddling.

We also list options for fishing and hunting, two popular activities in this part of the country. Finally, we include some information on great places to enjoy hiking and mountain biking.

So get out there and have some fun.

Parks

City Parks

These are the largest of the city parks, each with more than 100 acres and a variety of amenities. Call the Parks Commission at (901) 454-5200 or check out www.cityofmemphis.org for other options. You can click on park locations to find what smaller parks are nearby or on community centers to learn more about activities such as ceramics or martial arts if that's your interest.

Audubon Park
4145 Southern Avenue

When the city bought this land in the late 1940s to establish what is now the second-largest park in Memphis, it was just east of the city limits. At that time it took some vision to believe city leaders' claims that it would rival Overton Park in 25 years. At present, Audubon Park is in the heart of East Memphis, where residents flock to enjoy the walking trails, picnic areas, 18-hole golf course, and large indoor tennis facility. You'll also find a lighted baseball field, an indoor tennis center, a soccer field, and a seven-acre fishing lake, where kids delight in feeding the ducks. The park is also home to Memphis Botanic Garden, which includes the Japanese garden, the municipal rose garden, and others that had been established in the park. Two annual arts-and-crafts fairs are held here every October, and on Sunday mid-afternoons one of the more intriguing sights is the medieval-style jousting by members of the local chapter of the Society for Creative Anachronism, often in costumes of the period.

Kennedy Park
4577 Raleigh–LaGrange Road

The city bought the 310 acres on which to establish Kennedy Park in 1962, but the first order of business was to fill in the gravel pits on the property before developing the amenities. Situated on Raleigh–LaGrange Road just beyond the I-240 loop, the park is set so far back from the street that it's hard to see. Just take the Covington Pike exit from I-240 and turn left on Raleigh–LaGrange Road, and the park is about a mile on the left. Kennedy Park is geared toward softball, with several lighted baseball and softball diamonds. Each of them has stands, and there are concessions during the summer games, which make it a popular place during the season. You'll also find four lighted soccer fields, a junior football field, and plenty of parking near all the fields.

Martin Luther King, Jr., Riverside Park
South Parkway West and Riverside Drive

This is one of the city's oldest large parks, established at the turn of the century when the city acquired 427 acres on a bluff overlooking the river. It's a historic site, and there are indications of burial sites from multiple periods. Originally named Riverside, it was renamed for Dr. King in 1968. Amenities include playground equipment and a baseball field as well as a 9-hole golf course, tennis, nature trails, and boat ramp access to McKellar Lake.

Overton Park
2080 Poplar Avenue

When the Memphis Park Commission was formed in 1899, one of its first major steps was to purchase 300-plus acres in what was then the city's extreme northeast corner for a major park. At present it's the green heart of midtown. Until then, city parks were in downtown Memphis, because that's where most people lived, and tended to be much smaller. At Overton Park the city established its first municipal golf course and, over the years, also added a clubhouse, the Memphis Zoo, the Memphis Brooks Museum of Art, and Overton Park Shell (where a young Elvis Presley gave one of his first performances). All of them are still operating. In the 1960s the state wanted to route Interstate 40 through the park, and city officials were so sure their efforts would succeed that they demolished almost 200 homes to pave the way. But they underestimated local opponents, who fought to preserve the park. The result was a historic U.S. Supreme Court decision against the highway plan. (This decision put Overton Park in the law books, as this decision set a new standard for review of administrative decisions by the court. Unfortunately, it also threw a monkey wrench into plans for I-40, which is to this day still routed onto the northern portion of the I-240 loop.) Finally city officials gave up their efforts. Now visitors can enjoy one of the city's treasures, an old-growth forest that's preserved within the park, with nature trails and a paved path available for hiking, running, skating, or cycling. Amenities include a wide expanse of soccer fields, a baseball field, and a pond, as well as pavilions and other areas for picnics. It's also home to the Memphis College of Art, an outstanding school for aspiring artists.

River Parks

Memphis has a number of parks and trails along the Mississippi River, where you can take in the beauty and majesty of Old Man River. One of the best places to access these parks is at the foot of Union Avenue at Riverside Drive. Cross Riverside Drive and you'll be at the historic cobblestones, where riverboats first landed to unload passengers and goods and to take on bales of cotton bound for European markets. Originally these stones served as ballast in the many boats that plied the river. When a load of goods or people was taken on board, the ballast was lightened and the stones were placed at the landing. As the largest remaining cobblestone landing in the country, it's listed on the National Register of Historic Places. From here go south to reach Tom Lee Park and the Riverbluff Walk or go north to find the Tennessee Welcome Center and Jefferson Davis Park. For views from the bluff, check out Confederate Park on Front Street, or you can cross the Auction Street bridge to Mud Island and walk or jog along the river at Greenbelt.

City leaders are planning to redevelop the Memphis riverfront, with a plan that includes creating a lake and land bridge to the island. In a few years the riverfront might have a whole new look.

Confederate Park
Front Street between Court and Jefferson Streets

This is one of the city's oldest parks, where during the Civil War Memphians came in carriages to watch the Battle of Memphis between Confederate cannon on the bank and Union gunships. It was used as a dump during the latter part of the century, until in 1900 the park commission brought it back to life. This small park offers a great view of the river from atop the bluffs, as well as a statue of Confederacy president Jefferson Davis and cannon from World War I. It's easily accessible on foot to visitors who are exploring downtown Memphis and may not want to take the downhill walk to the cobblestones and other parks adjacent to the river.

Greenbelt Park
Harbortown Road (downtown)
This paved, 1.5-mile walkway along the Mississippi River starts at a convenient parking area just north of the Auction Street bridge and continues north to another parking area at the other end of the peninsula called Mud Island. It's a popular spot for residents of Mud Island houses and apartments, who flock there to walk, jog, skate, ride scooters and bikes, or walk animals. Don't worry about stepping in an unfortunate spot as the City Council just passed a new ordinance requiring pet owners to clean up after their charges. The walkway forms a loop surrounding a long, flat grassy lawn, and you can get a great view of the river from here.

Martin Luther King, Jr., Riverside Park
South Parkway West and Riverside Drive
This 388-acre park, near South Parkway and about 3 miles south of Beale Street, is home to a 9-hole golf course. (See the listing in City Parks, above, for more details.)

Shelby Farms
Germantown Road and Raleigh–LaGrange/
Mullins Station Road
(901) 382–2249
Situated in the middle of Shelby County and overseen by the county government, Shelby Farms is popular with Memphians and county residents seeking an escape from the hustle and bustle of city life. With more than 4,500 acres of land, Shelby Farms is the largest urban park in the United States, far bigger than Central Park in New York City and the Golden Gate Recreational Area in San Francisco put together. The land had been originally used for the county penal farm, where prisoners grew more than 90 percent of their own food and made money selling what they didn't need. The county penal facility is still located near the western edge of the park. In fact, in 1949 the farm was called

a "taxpayers' dream," but by the mid-1960s it was losing money. The county decided to turn over the acreage for public use, and for years politicians, developers, and conservationists debated what to do with the land, finally agreeing on an urban park.

Shelby Farms has several small lakes, a special handicapped-accessible trail, and a 1,000-acre conservation area called Lucius East Burch, Jr., State Natural Area, where hiking, wildlife watching, and cycling are allowed. Elsewhere in the park you can find the largest range of amenities and activities around, including horseback riding (you can rent horses; see the Recreation section below), pistol and rifle ranges, soccer, walking and bike trails, BMX bicycle area, roller-blading, a 10K cross-country running course, exercise trails with 21 exercise stations, and playgrounds. In addition, you can fish, raft, canoe, sail, or windsurf on 60-acre Patriot Lake or the smaller lakes. The paved pathway around Patriot Lake is a very popular exercise loop. Despite all of this activity, there's still plenty more land for hiking, picnicking, or just enjoying nature. The upland part of this park is referred to as Plough Park.

Tom Lee Park
Riverside Drive and Beale Street
Situated below the bluffs and just across Riverside from downtown Memphis, Tom Lee Park offers great views of the Mississippi River. There's plenty of room for picnics, walking, or tossing a Frisbee. During the 1990s the park was expanded to 24 acres, landscaped, and equipped with a parking lot, restrooms, and sidewalks. The park, originally named Astor Park, was renamed in honor of Tom Lee, a black laborer who saved 32 passengers in 1925 when the USS *Norman* sank in the river near Memphis. In May the park is closed to visitors and given over to the events of Memphis in May, which include a music festival and a massive barbecue cooking contest (see Annual Events chapter for more details.) After dark the park morphs into a youth hangout, as parades of cars continually cruise the lot.

State Parks

Here, we list the parks that are within a couple hours' drive of Memphis, but Tennessee, Mississippi, and Arkansas offer many more options if you are amenable to a longer trip. For more information on Tennessee parks, check out www.tennesseeanytime.org or call (888) TENN-PKS, the centralized reservation system; that is the number you must call in order to reserve accommodations at any Tennessee state park. For more on Mississippi's state parks, call (800) GO PARKS or check out www.mdwfp.com. The state of Arkansas also has a number of state parks, but few of them are very close to Memphis. For information about Arkansas state parks, call (800) NATURAL or check out www.arkansas.com. We list a few of these in the Fishing and Canoeing/Paddling sections of this chapter.

Tennessee State Parks

Tennessee has 54 state parks and a handful of national parks, the best known of which is Great Smoky Mountains National Park way over in east Tennessee. We list the parks closest to Memphis, which have fishing lakes, hiking, and other amenities, but here you won't find the mountains that are commonplace in east Tennessee. Those interested in the Civil War may also want to visit Shiloh National Military Park or Ft. Pillow State Park. (Turn to the Day Trips and Weekend Getaways chapter for details on these historic parks.) Be sure to call ahead about the days and hours of operation for all of these state parks, as they can change. In 2001 and 2002, all Tennessee state parks were closed on Mondays and Tuesdays due to state budget cuts. *Note:* Days and hours of operation for Tennessee parks are subject to change, and the state may implement nominal charges for use of some parks.

Big Hill Pond State Park
984 John Howell Road, Pocahontas
(731) 645–7967

This hidden jewel, located about two hours east of Memphis, is small and lightly used.

Thirty miles of hiking trails with overnight shelters line the hills that surround a lake and the Dismal Swamp. A wooden boardwalk 0.8 miles long will take you through the swamp. Only electric motors or paddling are allowed on the 165-acre lake, and fishing is okay. The 14 miles of horse trails invite riders with their own horses; check at the ranger station to find out if mountain bikes are being allowed on these trails, too. In addition to RV and primitive campsites, you'll find a nice bathhouse. To get there go east on Highway 57 for about 80 miles, and about 7 miles past the intersection of Highways 45 and 57, look for the entrance on the right.

Chickasaw State Park
20 Cabin Lane, Henderson
(731) 989–5141

Also known as Chickasaw State Rustic Park, this facility is situated on some of the highest terrain in west Tennessee. The recreation areas take up less than 10 percent of the park's 14,384 acres of timberland, and they include tennis courts, basketball courts, an archery range, a horseshoe pit, volleyball courts, and a lighted baseball field. The park is also a golfer's delight, given the 18-hole championship course designed by Jack Nicklaus (see Golf section, below). There's also a 50-acre lake, hiking trails, and horseback-riding trails (bring your own horse).

As for other amenities the park has a restaurant, with Southern cooking that serves daily lunch and dinner as well as weekend breakfasts, and 13 cabins overlooking the lake. Three campsites offer modern bathhouses, RV hookups or primitive camping. The park is within easy reach of Shiloh National Military Park and is 18 miles south of the city of Jackson, Tennessee.

From Memphis take I-64 east; then turn east onto Highway 100 at Whiteville and follow signs to the park.

Meeman-Shelby Forest State Park
910 Riddick Road, Millington
(901) 876–5215

This 13,500-acre park is just half an hour's drive from Memphis, making it very accessible for a country getaway.

Meeman-Shelby Forest State Park is just a short distance from Memphis, but it feels like another world.
PHOTO: MEMPHIS CONVENTION AND VISITORS BUREAU

Located north of the city on the Mississippi River, two-thirds of the park consists of bottomland hardwood forests of large oak, cypress, and tupelo. The park and its museum/nature center are named for Edward J. Meeman, the conservation editor of Scripps-Howard newspapers who helped establish this park and the Great Smoky Mountains National Park.

The park contains two lakes for boating and fishing and many miles of hiking trails, as well as a boat ramp on the Mississippi River. There's plenty of wildlife here, including deer, turkey, beaver, and about 200 species of birds. You'll find mountain-bike trails, a swimming pool, pavilions and tables for picnics, an 18-hole disk golf course, and playgrounds. The park also has six two-bedroom cabins (800–471–5293 or 888–TENN–PKS for reservations) and a swimming pool that's open during the summer months. Other attractions include a nature center, with exhibits of live snakes, a fish aquarium, a stuffed animal exhibit, a "touch table," and a Native American exhibit. Special programs at the center include making bird feeders and homemade ice cream, watching nature videos, and taking pontoon boat rides. Directions: From I-40, take exit 2-A, go right, and proceed through six stoplights to Watkins Road and turn left. Drive until the road ends, turn left, and then go right at the General Store. The park entrance is 1 mile on the left.

Pickwick Landing State Park
Park Road, Pickwick Dam
(731) 689–3129, (731) 689–3135 (inn)
Many years ago the Tennessee Valley Authority built numerous dams along the Tennessee River in order to bring electricity to an impoverished region. Another benefit was created at the same time: huge lakes made to order for recreation. Pickwick Dam made a 46-mile-long section of the river into a boating paradise. Pickwick Landing Park sits on the site of a former riverboat stop, that is, before the dam was built. TVA operates the dam and lake, which borders Tennessee, Mississippi, and Alabama. This 43,000-acre lake is proba-

bly the number-one watersports destination for Memphians. During Friday afternoons in summer, a steady stream of vehicles towing boats heads east on State Route 57 (Poplar Avenue) toward the big lake, and many folks buy second homes or condos here for weekend getaways. This park includes a great and inexpensive 18-hole golf course, a resort inn and conference center, cabins with central heat and air and fireplaces, camping, a newly renovated marina and free boat ramps, and rental fishing boats. Swimming is encouraged, plus you'll see all types of boats, including sailboats, on this busy lake. Numerous other parks, campgrounds, and conservation areas dot the lake's boundaries in all three states. For complete listings contact the relevant state-park system for the desired area either in Tennessee, Mississippi, or Alabama.

Reelfoot Lake State Park
Route 1, Box 2345, Tiptonville
(731) 253-7756, (800) 250-8617

This shallow, 15,000-acre lake was created in the winter of 1811–1812 as a result of the New Madrid earthquake. This is the famous massive quake, centered in Missouri, that rang church bells in Philadelphia and caused the Mississippi River to flow backwards for 15 minutes as the lake filled. Today its claim to fame is the population of golden and American bald eagles that make their winter home here and in the adjacent Reelfoot National Wildlife Preserve.

You can go bird-watching on your own or make a reservation for a $4.00 eagle bus tour by calling the park. Road biking, a boardwalk, and three hiking trails are popular activities, and the fishing here is excellent, especially for crappie. The lake is shallow, so boating is done slowly so that stumps can be avoided. Amenities in this area are thin, particularly as the park's inn and restaurant were closed in 2001, but there's a boat ramp, a visitors center, and camping. Campsites have RV hookups, showers and toilets, and fish-cleaning areas. Primitive camping is also available. Reelfoot can be very rewarding if you are a bird-watching enthusiast or fisherman. Take Highway 51 north from Memphis, and the park is about 25 miles north of Dyersburg on State Highway 78.

Reelfoot Lake is one of many lakes in the area where anglers can enjoy their sport.
PHOTO: MEMPHIS CONVENTION AND VISITORS BUREAU

T. O. Fuller State Park
1500 Mitchell Road
(901) 543–7581
This state park is also within easy reach, just 11 miles from downtown Memphis. The park is named for Dr. Thomas O. Fuller, a minister, writer, and teacher who spent his life empowering and educating African Americans during the late 1800s and early 1900s. In 1898 he was the only black senator in North Carolina. When Fuller opened in 1942 as Shelby Bluffs State Park, it was the first park for African Americans east of the Mississippi River.

The park has a softball field, basketball and tennis courts, playground equipment, a swimming pool, and an archery range. There's also plenty of open fields for Frisbee and other games, as well as places to hike and camp. One of the best-kept secrets is the T. O. Fuller State Park Golf Course, an 18-hole course that's challenging and a bargain (see the Golf section, below, for details). Also within the park is Chucalissa Indian Village, a reconstructed and partially excavated Native American village with an archaeology museum. (See the Attractions chapter for more details.)

To get to Fuller Park, go south from the Highway 61/Third Street exit from I-55 (north of the I-240/I-55 interchange) and turn right (west) on Mitchell Road in south Memphis. Continue a couple of miles, and the road will go straight into the park.

Mississippi State Parks
If you're looking for a lake or reservoir to enjoy boating, waterskiing, sailing, or fishing, you'll find some excellent options in Mississippi. Many of these parks also have cabins, plenty of birds and wildlife, and other attractions. For more information about Mississippi state parks, call (800) GO–PARKS or visit www.mdwfp.com.

Arkabutla Reservoir
3905 Arkabutla Dam Road, Coldwater
(662) 562–6261
Forty-five minutes south of the city is a recreation lake that can satisfy many outdoor appetites. More than 300 campsites and 420 picnic places grace 13 different recreation areas, swimming is available at three beaches, and nine boat ramps give access to watercraft. Thirty-seven thousand of 57,000 acres of land are open to public hunting, and the remainder is lake or flooded timber. Call (662) 362–9212 for fishing and hunting license info; $2.00 gets your boat ramp fee, and $1.00/person or $3.00/maximum per vehicle covers swimming. There is also a 5-mile mountain-bike trail that is pretty, if a little rooty. To get there take I-55 south to Hernando, then 304 west to Eudora, then South 301 to Pratt Road, and follow the signs.

Chewalla Lake Recreation Area
Holly Springs National Forest
(662) 252–4581
Just 7 miles south of Holly Springs is this nifty and quiet 260-acre lake and campground. A boat ramp, a fishing pier, picnic sites, and tent camping as well as RV hookups await at this wooded location. If you decide to go, be sure and watch the southern sky after dark for a peek at the mysterious and unexplained colored dots of light that are rumored to sometimes flash and jump across the horizon.

John West Kyle State Park
Sardis
(662) 487–1345
This park is centered around 58,500-acre Sardis Reservoir, well suited to boating, jet-skiing, or almost any other water activities you can think of. The Sardis Lower Lake has several beaches for swimming. The park also includes a facility for your large group's activities. If you want to stay overnight and you didn't bring your tent, ask about their cabins. There's also a swimming pool, tennis courts, and a recreation building in the park. The group campsite can hold 150–200 people on Sardis Lower Lake, and there are adjacent swimming beaches and nature trails. John West Kyle State Park is located 9 miles east of Sardis off Highway 315. From Memphis take I-55 south and get off at exit 252.

J.P. Coleman State Park
Iuka
(662) 423-6515
Another nice park on the Tennessee River at huge Pickwick Lake, this is a wonderful place to practice your backstroke, put your boat in the water for some skiing or fishing, or just stroll peacefully along the bank. Cabins are available for overnight stays if you aren't prepared to pitch a tent, and if you'd prefer a pool to the lake, there's one of those here, too. A complete marina is on site to serve you as well, plus miniature golf and a playground for the children. The park is located in the northeast corner of the state, 13 miles north of Iuka. Take U.S. 72 past Corinth, Mississippi, and go north on Route 25.

Wall Doxey State Park
Holly Springs
(662) 252-4231
The 45-acre, spring-fed lake at Wall Doxey State Park is an excellent location for numerous water sports. The park has excellent facilities to accommodate large groups. Within the park visitors will find a small beach with a diving platform, a large activity field, a playground, a nature trail, a visitor's center, and productive fishing spots. Also, there is a new 18-hole disk golf course.

Lodging facilities include a group campsite (which can accommodate 104 people), nine cabins, 64 improved campsites, and 18 tent camping pads. From Memphis take U.S. 78 south, turn right off the Holly Springs exit on Highway 7, and follow the signs to the park 6 miles south.

Recreation

Bowling

You'll find plenty of spots around Memphis to go bowling, most of them open until midnight during the week and into the wee hours on the weekends. All of them rent shoes, and most offer cosmic bowling, so you can play under wild, psychedelic lights during set hours.

Bartlett Lanes
6276 Stage Road, Bartlett
(901) 386-7701
This 32-lane, 25-year-old facility installed all new lanes in 2000. It offers league play at all levels all week and cosmic bowling Friday and Saturday. There's also a cocktail lounge. Bartlett Lanes is big on birthday parties, company parties, and other gatherings and will gladly cater them.

Billy Hardwick's All Star Lanes
1576 White Station Road
(901) 683-2695
For more than 20 years, this East Memphis alley has been the most convenient for people living or staying in midtown and East Memphis. There's league play and open bowling, and All Star Lanes also has hourly specials and group discounts. Amenities include a snack bar, a lounge, and a playroom.

Cordova Bowling Center
7945 Club Center Cove, Cordova
(901) 754-4275
One of the newer alleys in the area, Cordova Bowling Center has 36 lanes of league play Sunday through Thursday. The center features automatic scoring scoreboards, a pizza parlor, and a snack bar. Bowling specials are run weekly.

Cotton Bowl Lanes
9091 Highway 51 North, Southaven
(662) 342-2695 (no area code to call from Memphis)
This 34-lane bowling alley has a snack bar, a lounge, and a game room and features cosmic bowling. In the wee hours on weekends, for a set price you can bowl as much as you want until closing time.

Fun Quest Lanes
440 Highway 72, Collierville
(901) 850-9600
This all-purpose 32-lane facility features leagues most days and neon bowling on weekends. Fun Quest has a pro shop, a snack bar, a lounge, a restaurant, a roller-skating rink, and a game room, as well as meeting and party rooms. It closes earlier than most other bowling alleys around town.

Imperial Bowling Center
4700 Summer Avenue
(901) 683–5224

This is one of the oldest alleys in the city, established in 1958. It's open around the clock, with 48 lanes. There's league play all week from 6:00 to 9:00 P.M., with open bowling the rest of the time at various rates. Imperial also has a snack bar, a game room, and a pro shop.

Winchester Bowl
3703 South Mendenhall
(901) 362–1620

Winchester Bowl features 40 lanes with league play every day, but open bowling is in the afternoons and after 9:00 P.M. There's a pro shop, a snack bar, auto scoring, and on the weekends, cosmic bowling.

Canoeing/Paddling

You can canoe on all the fishing and park lakes, but paddling nearby rivers is often more satisfying for canoe and kayak enthusiasts. An alternative on these rivers is to take it easy and float in an inner tube, which can be arranged at many of them. The Mississippi River is obviously the closest body of flowing water but should only be attempted by experienced veterans. The river can be dangerous, as entire trees frequently float downstream, and it's plied by a constant stream of barges pushing and pulling immense loads of commodities up and down the waterway. The wakes created by some of the tall towboats can add to the already substantial undercurrents, and swimming is highly dangerous. Now that you've been sufficiently warned, you should know that the most complete local outfitter, Outdoors, Inc. (800–370–1224), sponsors a yearly canoe and kayak race on the Mississippi that is part of the Memphis in May festivities. (See the Shopping chapter for more details about Outdoors, Inc.) Every May hundreds of paddlers line up at the starting line, located at the northern parking lot and boat ramp at Mud Island where the Wolf River empties into the Mississippi, and then race downstream to the southern tip of the island. There they turn into the harbor and head for the finish line and cash prizes that await the speediest. All levels of skill and craft size compete in their respective categories, and the competition can be intense! For the very adventurous, watercraft can be launched from access spots farther up the river at Shelby Forest for downstream floats, but as there are no commercial services to help with transportation, you're on your own. Again, Outdoors, Inc. is a great source for information if you want to give it a shot.

These area rivers, excellent for canoeing, are really much more beautiful than the Big Muddy and far less threatening:

Buffalo National River
Jasper, Ark.
Buffalo River Outfitters
(800) 582–2244
www.buffalonationalriver.com

This breathtaking river, also the first National River, comes tumbling out of the Ozark Mountains of north-central Arkansas. It's home to black bear and elk, and you can hear howling coyotes that send chills up your spine. The main attraction, though, is the tall limestone cliffs for which the river is famous and the incredible beauty that's all around. Paddlers will find that sharp bends and fast shoals interrupt the slower stretches, but it's an enjoyable trip. Buffalo River Outfitters in Jasper (800–582–2244) is your best bet for renting a canoe, and the staff can give you directions from Memphis. The drive takes a little more than three hours, but it's worth it because of the beautiful wilderness.

Buffalo River
Flatwoods Canoe Base
Highway 13, Flatwoods, Tenn.
(931) 589–5661
www.flatwoodscanoe.com

This lovely and clean Class I and II river is well suited to beginners and anyone who enjoys a lazy float. Smallmouth bass, catfish, and bluegill are some of the fish to be caught on the 43 miles of river running through Perry County. Holiday weekends during the peak season tend to be busier, so to avoid crowds, consider other times. A one-day canoe rental is $22.00, kayaks $20.00, tubes $7.00.

To get there travel east on I–40 to Jackson, take the Law Road/Highway 152 South exit and go 1 mile to Highway 412. Turn left and go east through Lexington and Parsons, and into Linden. At the four-way stop in Linden, go right onto Highway 13 South. Go 12 miles south and into Flatwoods, and it's on the left. The entire trip is about two and a half hours.

Eleven Point River
9931 Highway 93
Pocahontas, Ark.
(870) 892–9732
Not far from the Spring River in northeast Arkansas is the beautiful Eleven Point River, originating just across the state line in Missouri. Small, spring-fed and quiet, this is a generally peaceful alternative to the Spring River, because far fewer people come here. The wildlife is abundant, especially if you venture into a backwater slough, and fish of all kinds are in the water. The water temperature is cold, which can be welcome during the hot summer. Just about all the property along the river is private and marked, but seldom inhabited, and plenty of sandbars provide places to stop and picnic or just relax. No waterfalls have to be negotiated, and rapids are few, mild, and short, so beginners should be comfortable. Woody's Camp and Canoe Rental near Pocahantas is your best bet if you need a campground and canoe outfitter. Woody rents canoes for about $25.

The Ghost River (Upper Wolf River)
Moscow and La Grange, Tenn.
Wolf River Canoe Rentals
(901) 877–3958
A meandering channel through breathtaking cypress wetlands and a lush lily-pad swamp are just a couple of the habitats to be experienced in the gentle Ghost River section of the upper Wolf River in Fayette County, just a short drive east from Memphis. Virtually unknown to most local paddlers until the 1990s, this peaceful escape is still only lightly trafficked. Wise and vigilant guardians at The Wolf River Conservancy

(901–452–6500, www.wolfriver.org) established the canoe trail in 1990, marked by blue and silver signs at regular intervals. Rated a Class I run, few if any rapids will be encountered. Depths are shallow, and sometimes low water can require that you get out and pull across sandbars or over trees fallen across the route. Occasional motorized fishing boats will navigate the river, and a popular fishing destination is the swamp, rumored to be the favorite local hole for Collierville resident and fishing-superstar Bill Dance! Largemouth bass, crappie, and catfish are some of the resident species.

To get there go east from Memphis on Poplar Avenue (Highway 57); as you approach the city of Moscow, you'll cross a bridge, and to the right is a gravel parking lot and boat ramp. This is the lowermost access point, and depending on which float you decide on, you might want to leave a car here. Continuing into Moscow you'll see Lewis's BBQ, go 2.5 miles farther to Bateman Road and turn south or right. Another 2.5 miles on the left is a small gravel lot and ramp just before the bridge. Putting in here and floating downstream is a two- to three-hour trip through grassy chutes. For a longer float keep going east on Highway 57 about 10 minutes to the small town of La Grange, where there's only one main intersection marked by a flashing light. Turn right and proceed down the steep road less than a mile to the bridge. Before you cross it look for the dirt parking and launch area on the right. The float from here to Bateman Bridge takes roughly six hours and traverses several different kinds of wetlands. For a longer paddle, La Grange to below Moscow takes around nine hours.

Sarah and John Wilburn operate the only nearby outfitter, called Wolf River Canoe Rentals. The six-hour float runs $35, and the three-hour one is $30, including the shuttle ride. If you have your own canoe, they'll be glad to drive your car to the get-out spot for a small fee. Wolf River Canoe Rentals operate from late March until the end of November. Efforts continue to protect the river through land purchases, and if you're going downstream between the La Grange and Bateman points, everything on the left is now public and open! On the right there are parcels still privately held, so no trespassing or camping is advised.

Spring River
Mammoth Spring, Ark.
(870) 856–3451

Located in north-central Arkansas about three hours from Memphis is this very popular river. Summertime sees flocks of youthful partyers, many from Memphis, especially on weekends. A huge spring that wells up out of the ground in Mammoth Spring, Arkansas, feeds the river with millions of gallons of chilly water every hour, and if you have the chance, definitely go there and look at the spectacle. Bass and trout are fished out of these waters. Modest rapids and short falls make paddling pretty easy, and several outfitters service visitors. Many Islands Camp Canoe Rental (870–856–3451) is the biggest company and probably has the best amenities and selection of trips. Canoes are $30.00 per day, kayaks $32.00, and camping $7.00 per person.

To get there from Memphis, cross into Arkansas on either I–40 or I–55, then continue north on I–55 until you reach the Highway 63/Jonesboro exit, and then continue north. About 7 miles north of the town of Hardy, you'll see signs for Many Islands Rentals.

Cycling/Mountain Biking

Because the terrain is as flat as a pancake, road biking can be done anywhere in Memphis. Unfortunately, the city hasn't yet recognized the merits of cycling over automobiles; therefore bike lanes are all but nonexistent. The famous Mississippi River Trail passes through here on its way south to New Orleans and also includes sights like Alex Haley's boyhood home in Henning. Many area roadies prefer the asphalt of Shelby Forest, where traffic is light. An excellent club and an outstanding resource for rides and social events for individuals and families is the Memphis Hightailers Bicycle Club (901–748–2137, www.memphishightailers.com). The club arranges regular weekly rides all year, and you don't have to join the club to ride with them. Founded in the 1960s,

it holds monthly meetings, and there's a monthly newsletter to keep members informed.

Off-road trails in the area range from easy to expert, and every October the sport's biggest stars, like Tinker Juarez, descend on Shelby Farms to compete in Tennessee's biggest mountain-bike event, the Tour de Wolf race, sponsored by Outdoors, Inc. Numerous racing classes fit every skill level and age, and vendors from all the big bike companies set up display booths and tents to showcase their latest innovations. Contact Outdoors, Inc. for registration information or go to www.outdoorsinc.com. You can also ask for more details about the following trails.

Mountain-Biking Trails

Arkabutla Reservoir, Mississippi: Five miles through woods and plenty of charm characterize this trail 45 minutes south of Memphis. Autumn is a good time to enjoy the fall colors around this lake. To get there take I–55 south to Hernando, then take 304 west to Eudora, turn onto South 301 to Pratt Road, and follow the signs. (See the State Parks section of this chapter for more details about Arkabutla Reservoir.)

Herb Parsons State Park: Tucked inside Herb Parsons State Park is this 6.5-mile trail that features abundant tree-crossings as the route takes you around the lake. Be sure to wear long pants, as the poison ivy can be brutal. To get there take Macon Road in East Memphis east past the town of Fisherville, go right on Fisherville Lake Road, and then follow the signs. It's less than an hour's drive.

Shelby Farms: The 5.5 mile trail at Shelby Farms on which the race is held is undoubtedly the most popular in the area. Single track, fire roads, and open prairie with slight elevations make for a fast ride, which favors a "hard-tail" bike. Another section of the park is home to the White Trail, a technical and narrow single-track through the woods. The starting point of this 8-mile trek is under the Walnut Grove bridge on Germantown Road, about 0.5 mile south of the intersection of Walnut Grove and Germantown Road.

Stanky Creek: Only a few years old, this collection of three loops and a cool

Insiders' Tip

Greg Pickett (7948 Winchester, 901-757-1112) is the preeminent golf-club technician to the local pros. He has a shop (laboratory?) that any wizard would be proud of, and he can perform first-class jobs on any club. His specialty is custom-fitting clubs to your swing, and he's proud to feature True-Temper shafts, made right down the road in Olive Branch.

jump area is awesome. The name comes from the bottomlands that the trails occupy, but the smell isn't nearly as bad as the name suggests. This collection of narrow and technical single-tracks in the middle of Bartlett will test all your skills, and all three trails offer jumps and tight twists. Riding these trails when they're wet is nearly impossible because they get really slick. Also, it's easy to get lost without an experienced rider along, so a detailed map of the trails can be found at www.midtownbikeco.com. Directions: From I–40 take the Sycamore View exit north toward Bartlett. A couple miles up and just past Freeman Park (on the left), turn left before the barbecue place and continue past the old town center to the four-way stop sign. Turn left, and the parking lot is about 200 yards on the right.

Fishing

Tennessee Wildlife Resources Agency Lakes

The Mississippi River can be sport fished for monster catfish, but eat 'em at your own risk and don't take a boat out unless you are very familiar with the treacheries of Old Man River. A better bet is one of seventeen TWRA-managed lakes in middle and west Tennessee, open year-round. Some of these lakes are operated by private concessionaires under contract and offer complete services for the fishing public. Lakes open one-half hour before sunrise to one-half hour after sunset, except Garrett Lake, which is open 24 hours a day. Camping may be permitted after obtaining permission from the lake manager and only in designated areas. A daily lake permit of $3.00, in addition to the regular fishing license, is required to fish most of these lakes. All residents 16 through 64 years of age, except holders of a Sportsman License or Lifetime Sportsman License, and all nonresidents (regardless of age) must have this permit, obtainable at the lake office. The lakes are open to fishing all week. Some concessionaire-operated lakes may be closed on Thanksgiving Day and Christmas Day. When the office is closed, deposit the $3.00 permit fee in an envelope just outside the lake office. Speed boating, waterskiing, and swimming are not permitted, nor are houseboats, sailboats, and inboard cruisers. On Bedford, Marrowbone, VFW, and Williamsport lakes, only trolling motors can be used. Boats may be rented for $5.00 per day at many lakes. Mandatory flotation devices and paddles rent for free. Statewide creel and size limits apply with the following exceptions: Only rods and reels, poles and hand-held lines, and jugs may be used. Cast nets are illegal on agency lakes. For more information, call TRWA (731-423-5725) or visit www.state.tn.us/twra and click on "Fishing in Tennessee."

State and County Park Lakes

In addition to the TWRA lakes, nearly every single park and reservoir has at least one fishing lake, if not more. Crappie (pronounced "croppy"), large- and smallmouth bass, catfish, sauger, and other species are plentiful around the Memphis area. You'll need appropriate licenses for whichever state you're fishing in, as well as day-use permits for most state park lakes. (See the State Parks write-ups in this chapter for directions and details.) You can also fish on the Wolf and Buffalo Rivers.

Under River Parks, see Shelby Farms. Under Tennessee State Parks, see Big Hill Pond State Park, Chickasaw State Park, Meeman-Shelby Forest State Park, Pickwick Landing State Park, and Reelfoot Lake State Park. Under Mississippi State Parks, see Arkabutla Reservoir, Chewalla Lake, Sardis Reservoir (see John West Kyle State Park), and Wall Doxey State Park.

Other Fishing Lakes

Horseshoe Lake
Hughes, Ark.

The west-central portion of the state is composed mainly of flat farmland, and most recreational lakes are found well to the west in mid-central Arkansas, like Greer's Ferry Lake north of Little Rock or Lake Hamilton near Hot Springs. If you absolutely must splash around in nearby Arkansas, consider Horseshoe Lake. Situated about 30 minutes south of West Memphis, this big oxbow lake is home to a small community made up largely of weekend places owned by Memphis families. Two thousand five hundred acres of water produce all the standard local varieties of fish, and waterskiing can be popular, along with jet-skiing. Amenities are spare, but at the main entrance to the lake, there's a boat ramp and a fishing dock (small fees) and a homey little country restaurant. The food is good, and the owners and servers are friendly. You can't go wrong when you stop in after a long day on the water, sit at the counter facing the lake, and order a piece of the fresh pie *du jour* with coffee. To get here cross the Mississippi River on I–40 to West Memphis and take exit 271. Pick up Highway 147 South here and follow it all the way to the lake, about 25 miles.

Tunica Lake
Tunica, Mississippi
www.tunicalake.com

Created by the Corps of Engineers for flood control, this large oxbow lake is large enough to support lots of fishermen easily. Although the lake is well known for crappie, lots of other fish lurk these waters, including the toothy alligator gar, and white, yellow, and largemouth bass. With a small chute to the Mississippi River, the lake is able to replenish constantly, so nourishment for fish is abundant. You'll find several places here that operate bait shops and ramps that require a small fee. To get here follow Highway 61 South past the casinos and look for the signs to the lake off to the right. The trip takes about 45 minutes from Memphis.

World-Class Trout Fishing in Arkansas

Avid fly-fishermen in Memphis consider themselves to be extremely fortunate to live so close to the generous streams and rivers of north-central Arkansas, in particular the White River, the North Fork River, and the Little Red River. The current world-record brown trout, weighing in at 40 pounds, 3 ounces, was hauled out of the waters of the Little Red River, located two hours (100 miles) west of Memphis. Thanks to an aggressive trout-stocking program and well-managed rivers, Arkansas is home to some of the best trout fishing in the country. Fish hatcheries grace the Little Red, White, and North Fork Rivers, among others. Brook trout ("brookies"), German Brown, cutthroat, and rainbow trout can all be landed from the same bit of water on a really good day. Most anglers stick to the traditional fly-fishing techniques, but trout caught from the bank with a plain old rod and reel are fun, too! Several dollars at most docks will cover the cost of fishing, but not your license. For a fee guides can be hired to float you down the river in a shallow boat and tell you how to catch 'em. Keep an eye out for grocery stores. They're a good place to get a license and fishing regulations, and you can pick up food at the same time.

Sometimes a good day on the river is defined as a day when the water is slow and shallow, as upstream dams manipulate water flow for electricity generation, and heavy power demand can mean that heavy water flows are needed to turn turbines. Nonetheless, veteran and novice fly fishermen from far and wide descend upon these waters in hopes of tricking wily Mr. Trout into biting a hook. During peak season folks line the middle of the rivers for long stretches, so plan ahead and make reservations if you want to fish holidays or summer weekends.

Caution: Listen for loud blasts from the air horns blown by the dams to warn fishers of impending water releases. Count the number of blasts, and that will tell you how many turbines will be operated and, consequently, how high and fast the water will become. Always know how far you are from the dam because only a few minutes' warning is given, and even for single or double blasts, you'll have to get out of the water fast.

For lists of trout docks and guide services on all the rivers, contact the Arkansas Department of Tourism at (800) NATURAL or go to www.arkansas.com. One favorite place to rent a cabin or hire a guide for a float-fishing trip is Gene's Resort (870-499-5381) in Salesville, on the North Fork River. Just a little south of Mountain Home, Gene's is a neat, clean establishment that is staffed by knowledgeable people. Cabins and RV spots can be rented, but even if you pitch a tent at the park down the road (at the base of the dam), go by Gene's to find out how the fishing's been. By the way, on the other side of the dam is the long and deep Norfork Reservoir, also full of fish, as well as people who are sailing, waterskiing, fishing, sunning, and the likes. To get to Gene's from Memphis, cross the Mississippi River on I-40 and turn north on I-55 on the far side of West Memphis. After roughly 25 minutes look for the Highway 63/Jonesboro exit and continue north on Highway 63 toward Jonesboro. Stay on this road through Jonesboro to Hardy; then take Highway 62/412 West all the way to the city of Mountain Home. From there follow Highway 5 South to Highway 177 and turn left. The Norfork Dam and Gene's are right down the road; just look for the signs.

Golf

Golfers in Memphis are a lucky lot, thanks to an abundance of courses and weather that permits essentially year-round play. Whether you prefer economical municipal courses, the latest name-brand designer links, or something in between, there are choices aplenty.

Memphians are proud of their contributions to the game as well. The late Dr. Cary Middlecoff, winner of 40 PGA tournaments, an early Masters winner and two-time U.S. Open Champion, was a native Memphian. Some active PGA players who call Memphis home are "The Boss of the Moss" Loren Roberts, Doug Barron, Shaun Micheel, and occasional resident John Daly. PGA Tour player and 1999 U.S. Amateur winner David Gossett and 1994 and 2001 Mid-Amateur champion Tim Jackson hail from Germantown. The 1999 Mid-Amateur champ is the colorful Danny Green, who is just down the road in Jackson, Tennessee, when he's not playing on the Walker Cup team.

Every June the PGA Tour stops here for the FedEx/St. Jude Classic. (See Annual Events chapter for more information.) During the week of the tournament, Tour pros can be spotted all over town, and because so many local hackers are at the Classic watching great golf, area courses are wide open and deserted.

Always call ahead before setting out to play, and ask about tee times, specials, and course conditions (especially in summer, when bent-grass greens can suffer from the heat). Virtually all area courses offer an array of discounts for juniors and seniors, and for weekday, winter, and afternoon play.

Memphis Park Services Municipal Golf Courses

"Muni" golf is thriving in the city, thanks to the seven courses operated by Memphis Division of Park Services. Modest in cost and conveniently located, almost all these mature courses are located inside or near the I-240 loop, with the exception of the hilly and tight Davy Crockett course situated about 10 minutes north of the loop in Frayser. All have a good selection of equipment and lessons as well as sandwiches, snacks, sodas, beer, and electric and pull carts. Most of these courses have been open for many years and were built at a time when Bermuda grass was the norm for tees and fairways. Accordingly, some allow metal spikes, but since that policy is subject to change at any time, it's better to call ahead and ask. Several have driving ranges, practice greens, and lessons. It's best to call ahead about the condition of the course, lest you arrive at the course only to find out the greens have just been aerated. Tall, healthy trees line generally wide fairways at many of the facilities, making for moderately challenging holes that are ideal for mid- to high- handicappers and even beginners. Walking will set you back about a buck a hole in summer, and cart riders will pay $30; expect slightly better prices in the off-season. Overton and M.L. King are 9-holers. It would be hard to find two better beginner's layouts, and they cost about half as much as the full-sized layouts. M.L. King (formerly Riverside) sits on the bluffs over McKellar Lake, which we all know was Elvis's favorite lake. The epicenter for Memphis muni golf is Galloway, which hosts more rounds than any other, so definitely call and make sure you can get a tee time! A major overhaul and update were completed in spring 2002, as the holes were redesigned, bunkers and water hazards added, some sick trees eliminated, and a smart looking new clubhouse sits where the old snack bar rested. A great "new" place to begin your Memphis golfing experience!

Audubon, 4160 Park Avenue, (901) 683–6941

Davy Crockett, 4380 Rangeline Road, (901) 358–3375

Fox Meadows, 3064 Clarke Road, (901) 362–0232

Galloway, 3815 Walnut Grove Road, (901) 685–7805

M.L. King, Jr., 465 South Parkway West, (901) 774–4340

Overton, Overton Park (2100 block of Poplar Avenue), (901) 725–9905

Pine Hill, 1005 Alice Avenue, (901) 775–9434

Other Golf Courses

Edmund Orgill Golf Course
9080 Bethuel Road, Millington
(901) 872–3610, (901) 872–7493 for tee times
www.orgillpark.com

This Millington bargain is another very playable muni-type layout, located in a 442-acre park of the same name. The only course operated by Shelby County, it's the site of

regular high school district and regional competitions. Most fairways are wide and accommodating, and the course is generally in good shape. A few holes are next to a magic lake that eats golf balls and spits out catfish! Bermuda greens and fairways mean that this one of the few courses that allows metal spikes. Par is 70, and length is 6,400 yards from the back tees. Rates: $31 with cart included, but ask about junior, senior, and twilight discounts. Lessons are available. There is a driving range and modest clubhouse, and walking 18 holes is common at this course, situated near a naval base. Directions: From downtown take I–40/240 east to the Millington exit and continue north on Highway 51 for 11 miles. At the second light turn right onto Navy Road and proceed 3.3 miles to Bethuel Road and turn left. From there the course is 2.5 miles on the right.

T.O. Fuller State Park Golf Course
1400 Pavilion Drive
(901) 543–7771
www.state.tn.us/environment/parks/tofuller/golf.htm

The only local course run by the state park system can be found at T.O. Fuller State Park in the southwest corner of Shelby County. Another older-style Bermuda course, it's nestled among some hills originally hunted by the Chickasaw Indians centuries ago. Recently, funds were spent here to improve the overall condition, and as a result the course was honored by the state in 1998 as the Best State Park Golf Course. Several holes capitalize on the terrain by running along the tops of ridges, along the dales, or both. One of the hardest par-3s ever conceived is hole number 4, affectionately called "The Volcano." It's 196 yards to a small green, if you hit it! Par is 72 on this 5,986-yard course, and there is a practice green near the first tee, but no driving range. Costs run $16 weekdays and $18 on weekends in summer, and add $11 for a cart. This is a great course to walk for exercise, and pull carts are available for a nominal fee. The clubhouse is home to a modest selection of apparel, balls, gloves, and a few clubs. Nice folks run the snack bar, and they serve a mean cheeseburger and soda, but because it's a state park, no alcoholic beverages of any kind are allowed on the grounds. If you like hilly, frequently deserted golf courses, this is a good spot, and the rates fit many budgets. Directions: Head south on Third Street, either from downtown or I-55, and turn right on Mitchell Road and after a few minutes the road runs straight into the park. Once in the park, take your first right and then bear right at the top of the hill.

Semiprivate Courses

Most Tennessee and Mississippi suburbs boast one, if not several, "daily-fee" golf courses, generally of excellent quality and surrounded by residential developments. These courses frequently offer memberships at a moderate cost (usually worth it if you play two or three rounds a week) in addition to tee times for the nonmember public. Fees are higher than those at municipal courses, and dress codes are stricter; collared shirts are usually required, and cut-off shorts are frowned upon. All these higher-quality facilities offer lessons from PGA professionals and have ranges and putting greens, nice clubhouses, and well-stocked pro shops. Yardages stated are from the back tees, so subtract a bit for regular and ladies' tees. The highest weekend and holiday rates with carts are listed, but expect to pay less if you're walking, playing weekdays or during the off-season (winter). About walking: Most of these places don't allow it on weekends in order to keep the speed of play faster, and all prohibit metal spikes on your shoes.

Cherokee Valley Golf Club
6635 Crumpler Boulevard, Olive Branch, Miss.
(901) 525–4653
www.olivebranchgolf.com

Cherokee is another of the younger courses on the local golf scene, and one of the best. Plenty of time was allowed for the grass to mature before play started, and it shows: The Zoysia fairways are sweet, and the bent-grass greens (like those at Plantation) are area favorites, with lots of tricky, hidden breaks! This is a relatively short course, 6,054 yards, with ample water hazards and bunkers. In fact, there are 78 bunkers scattered around the course, a

tribute to Highway 78, which runs right past a couple of holes. Number 12 is a par-4 dogleg right around a pond to a green with a backdrop of sorts. Confident longer hitters might try to fly the pond to set up an eagle putt. Good luck! A fee of $46.50 will get you on this beautiful course, which can yield some low scores.

The Club at Big Creek
6195 Woodstock Cuba Road, Millington
(901) 353–1654

This semiprivate facility is several miles north of downtown in a community called Woodstock. The greens have recently been upgraded to Champion Bermuda, and the fairways are still Standard Bermuda. Almost 7,100 yards from the tips, the front 9 of this long course is made up of basically flat, pine-lined, wide, back-and-forth holes. The back 9 snakes through wooded hills and requires more precision off the tee. In warm weather bring your bug repellent to thwart monster mosquitoes bred in the nearby creek bottoms. Numerous ponds, traps, and wooded OB's can paste extra strokes to your score, and if the greens happen to be lightning fast, you'd better watch out! Lots of membership packages are offered, and non-member summertime greens fees reach $42 plus tax. To get here ride the I–240 loop to its northwest corner and follow the signs to Highway 51 and Millington. Go north on Thomas Street 5.5 miles and turn left onto Fite Road (across the highway from the DuPont plant). Go straight until the road comes to a T, and turn left. Turn left again soon on Woodstock Hills Road and then immediately right; the course is about 0.25 mile on the right. Affiliated with Big Creek is The Club at North Creek in Southhaven, Mississippi.

The Club at North Creek
8770 North Creek Boulevard, Southaven, Miss.
(901) 280–4653
www.golfmississippi.com

This sister course to Big Creek is still a relative newcomer but has matured over the last few summers. Some holes are open; more are framed by woods and water hazards. Think before you tee off: Lots of the holes require shorter and more precise tee shots than a driver can deliver, and some long hitters could even leave their biggest drivers at home. Play your approach shots with care, too, lest your ball slide off one of the slick greens. Carts come equipped with GPS systems that really help describe the holes and nail down yardages! The completed clubhouse is handsome, with all the standard amenities. Fees are $45.

Fair Oaks Golf Club
220 Fair Oaks Drive, Oakland
(901) 466–1445

Located in the newest, farthest reaches of the ever-expanding metropolitan area, this daily-fee course has generally wide-open Bermuda fairways and modern TifEagle Bermuda greens of generous size. Accuracy keeps the ball out of the rough, but misses aren't penalized too much. Par is 72 on these 6,970 yards, designed by Kevin Tucker of Nashville. John Lisman is the PGA golf professional. He owns the course, and he might just be the one who loads your clubs on the cart, sells you your green fees, tells you where not to hit, and what kinds of sandwiches are on hand. You gotta like that! Plenty of home sites are still vacant, and given how quickly the memberships have sold, buying a home site is the only way remaining to wiggle into a membership. The clubhouse has not yet been built, so operations run from a temporary structure. Daily-fee players trade $40 for a green fee and cart in summer, $35 in winter.

Plantation Golf Club
9425 Plantation Road, Olive Branch, Miss.
(901) 525–2411
www.olivebranchgolf.com

Slightly west of Southaven is the city of Olive Branch, Mississippi, home to Plantation, its sister course Cherokee Valley, and others. Plantation is a long test from the back tees (6,773 yards from the tips) but still a joy to play. Par is 72, and only slight elevation changes interrupt this largely flat layout. Zoysia fairways provide fluffy, upright lies, and water hazards abound. Be sure to enjoy hole number 18. A par 4, it makes a sharp dogleg left over a wide pond

to an elevated and sloping green. One reason this club hosts so many tournaments is that is has one of the best finishing holes in the city. A spacious and airy clubhouse contains one of the better-stocked pro shops. Greens fees are $42.50 including cart during summer weekends. The nice people at this club also operate Cherokee Valley, just a little way down the road.

Quail Ridge Golf Course
4055 Altruria Road, Bartlett
(901) 386–6951

Here is a nifty 18 located northeast of the city in the suburb of Bartlett. Tree-lined fairways (some wide, some narrow) demand careful tee shots because you'll be looking to set up your ever-important approach shots on most of these holes. All the par 3s demand good shot-making, taking advantage of moderate elevation changes that set up large and well-maintained greens. Length from the back tees is only 6,314 yards and par is 71, but this deceiving layout will drive many golfers to overconfidence. It's difficult to put a finger on what exactly makes this spread such a favorite—perhaps the friendly staff, the design? Rates are in line with comparable area courses, at $42 plus tax during busy summer times (includes cart) and $35 plus tax in winter. Memberships are available. The clubhouse at this busy place is attractive and pretty new and includes a snack bar and pro shop.

Stonebridge Golf Club
3049 South Davies Plantation Road, Lakeland
(901) 382–1886
www.stonebridgegolf.com

This 6,743-yard gem is adjacent to I–40, but only a couple of holes abut the interstate, and there is ample vegetation to block most noise. This layout can be quite a challenging test. In winter overseeded rye makes for green fairways, and the bent-grass greens can be deadly fast anytime! Many holes feature water hazards, and a healthy breeze is a frequent adversary. George Cobb is well known for designing "Amen Corner" at Augusta, but not many locals know he did this layout as well. Lots of corporate tournaments are held here, so always call ahead. Being close to the freeway means quick and easy access from most of the city, so that adds to the course's popularity. Weekend rates including cart (w/GPS) run $46.

Wedgewood Golf Club
5206 Tournament Drive, Olive Branch, Miss.
(901) 521–8275

Another Olive Branch spread, and not too far from Plantation, is Wedgewood. The holes here are flat and wide for the most part, but many are adjacent to wide, deep ditches that will devour any ball that enters, so beware! Steep sides and thick kudzu prevent any retrieval whatsoever. Fast bent-grass greens are generally in good condition. The slick green on number 17 is maybe the toughest in the Memphis area, with a steep grade and three tiers. Number 18 features a very narrow fairway lined with trees to keep you honest, and a pond guards the front of a steep two-tiered green. Fees are in line with other similar courses at $45 with cart in summer.

Worthy Golf Outings

Several outstanding layouts are within an hour's drive (give or take) of the city limits. Because they are in the countryside, they offer a more relaxed setting for swinging away without the fear of plunking a golf ball into someone's living room. These include two casino "resort" courses near Tunica, Mississippi.

The Bear Trace at Chickasaw State Park
9555 State Route 100
Henderson, Tenn.
(888) 944–2327
www.beartrace.com

Opened in spring 2000, this Jack Nicklaus design is already building a sterling national reputation. This and four other Nicklaus courses compose Tennessee's Bear Trace "golf trail" of outstanding yet affordable layouts. About 1 hour and 15 minutes away, this is the nearest one to Memphis so far, but there are rumors of one to be built even closer. Carved out of the woods in massive Chickasaw State Park, characteristics include the marshy wetlands of Piney Creek and its tributar-

ies and gentle rolling hills. The gorgeous holes total over 7,100 yards from the tips, with a slope of 134, so this is no cakewalk. The clubhouse, handmade from logs, looks like a mansion where Davy Crockett would be right at home. Bermuda fairways and bent-grass greens stay in good shape, which they should, considering top rates of $57 including cart in summer; however, winter and twilight fees are substantially lower. As with all Bear Trace courses, packages are available.

The Cottonwoods Golf Course
13615 Old Highway 61 North
Robinsonville, Miss.
(800) 946–4946
River Bend Golf Links
205 Nine Lakes Drive
Robinsonville, Miss.
(888) 539–9990
www.riverbendlinks.com

These two courses are owned and operated by the casinos in Tunica County, Mississippi. River Bend's manicured course was created by the collaboration of Harrah's, Hollywood, and Sam's Town. Wide open and without trees, the grass-covered dunes are indeed reminiscent of true Scottish links. Opened in 1998, the architect is Clyde Johnston. Fees run $60 with cart. Cottonwoods is owned by the Grand Casino. A touch longer than River Bend (6,999 yards vs. 6,923 yards), it is a links-style course as well. Hale Irwin designed this resort course, and peak-season fees are $115 for nonguests and $100 for guests. Packages are available through the casinos. (For more information see the Casinos chapter.)

Kirkwood National Golf Club
Highway 4
Holly Springs, Miss.
(662) 252–4888
www.kirkwoodgolf.com

Possibly the most outstanding daily-fee course in this area is Kirkwood National Golf Club, just south of Holly Springs. From the Memphis city limits, it should take about 50 minutes to reach this devilish spread. Use the highway time to polish your mental game because you'll need it. Every hole is a tribute to the game. Take number 4 for example, a long and narrow par-5 with a 90-degree dogleg at the end, where you'll then have to fly a creek and bunkers to reach the elevated two-tier green. Not for the faint of heart! A bit farther on, number 6 is another par 5, this one curving nearly 180 degrees to the left, leaving a short shot to a green surrounded by water on three sides and sand on the fourth side. Champion Bermuda greens welcome well-placed shots from Bermuda fairways at this grand layout. Despite the hearty fairway grass, leave your metal spikes at home, and don't plan on walking this 7,100-yard beast on weekends. The fairly new clubhouse, though not huge, is nicely appointed and can be a great postgame place to soothe your ego with a sandwich, a bubbly beverage, and the understanding words of other golfers. Rates: $35 during the week and $45 weekends, including cart *and* range balls; lessons are extra. There's also a driving range. From I-240 South, take the Lamar Avenue exit south. This road will become Highway 78, so continue south about 30 miles to the Holly Springs/Oxford exit and then turn right, or south, on Highways 7 and 4. Go 1 mile and make a right onto Highway 4 West. From there the course is 1 mile on the left. Check out the Web site for information on rental cottages and cottage rental/green fee specials.

Mallard Pointe Golf Course
John Kyle State Park
Sardis, Miss.
(888) 833–6477
www.mallardpointegc.com
Perfectly situated on hilly land overlooking Sardis Lake, this is the type of course that can lead to severe golf addiction! No pushover, this 7,000-yard Bob Cupp–designed treat wears gloves most of the time. But when the wind blows off the lake, be ready for a test of your game. Number 3 is a moderately long dogleg par 4, easily reachable in two, but the green is nestled up against a pond. There is nothing but shaved grass along the edge, so if your ball hits anywhere near the slope, goodbye! Number 17 is a potentially drivable par 4 for long hitters, but the sheer front face of the elevated green is covered with sand traps that offer only difficult and nearly vertical recovery

shots. The clubhouse is small, with a walkup snack and sandwich window where soda and beer is available, too. Cheerful youngsters bring carts to your car and load your bags for you, the driving range is really nice, and so is the practice chipping green behind it—all of this for only $30 including cart, even on weekends and holidays. Ask about other discounts, and if you want to play a second round it's only $12 more! To get here go south on I-55 to exit 252, which only takes about 50 minutes, and from there head east about 3.5 miles to the park entrance.

Driving Ranges

Bogey's Golf and Family Entertainment Center
7800 Fischer Steel Road
(901) 757–2649
www.bogeys.com
This place is a bit different than Putt Putt in that it's located right off Germantown Parkway about a half mile north of Walnut Grove, smack in the middle of suburbia. The grass-tee area here is smaller, but there's a fun 9-hole par 3 course at the side of the range protected by netting.

Putt Putt Family Park
5484 Summer Avenue
(901) 386–2992
www.puttputtmemphis.com
This entertainment complex has both artificial and grass tees, and the artificial tees are heated in cold weather. There is a pro shop full of goodies and a PGA certified teacher on hand to correct your duck-hook. The range balls are kept fresh, and the cart that retrieves the balls is protected by wire mesh should you *accidentally* hit in that direction. Batting cages, go-carts, miniature golf, and a video arcade round out this facility, located just east of the I-40/I-240 interchange on Summer Avenue.

Hiking

Most state parks have hiking trails that can be enjoyed at all times of the year. See the state parks listings for more information. Alternatively, ask at Outdoors, Inc. (901–755-2271), an outfitter that sells hiking boots and equipment; the staff is knowledgeable and up to date about good places to hike.

Wolf River Bottomlands
Highway 194, Rossville
(901) 452-6500

Eight miles west of Moscow is the town of Rossville, where a new half-mile boardwalk gives walkers access to one of the few remaining cypress-forest swamps that used to characterize the entire Mississippi Basin. It's the work of the Wolf River Conservancy. To get there from Memphis, follow Poplar Avenue (Highway 57) East to tiny Rossville and turn left at the local bank onto Highway 194. Just a little bit north of the city limits is the parking lot for the boardwalk.

Horseback Riding

Shelby Farms Park
(901) 382-4250

The place to ride horses is at Shelby Farms, the large park east of Memphis. You can rent horses for all types of riders and ride over 450 acres of land for $15 an hour for riders aged nine and older, and younger kids can ride the ponies. The stables are open from 8:00 A.M. until 5:00 P.M. seven days a week, and because no reservations are taken, it's first come, first served.

Hunting and Shooting

Hunting

The Tennessee Wildlife Resources Agency (731-423-5725 or www.state.tn.us/twra) assures equal access to publicly held land for all uses, including hunting, and they can tell you what to do to gain access to the best public-hunting areas. Because there aren't enough public-land permits to go around, drawings are held in order to select recipients. The applications are available from TWRA or can be downloaded from their Web site. Remember, Memphis is in the middle of the Mississippi River Flyway, so the surrounding area has some of the best waterfowl hunting in the country, and lots of public land is located in Mississippi and Arkansas, too. Numerous private landowners outside the city operate hunting resorts for all kinds of game, not just waterfowl. In fact, hunting leases have become a signifi-

cant source of income for cash-strapped farmers. The classified ads in the local newspaper include a hunting/fishing section, and there are almost always ads offering land for lease, clubs looking for members, and offers for guided or "pay" hunts and full-service hunting resorts. One good bet is to contact the knowledgeable staff at the local hunting store Tommy Bronson Sporting Goods (901-458-5458) for a recommendation or look over the pamphlets pinned to the big bulletin board at Buck & Bass Sports Centre (901-660-3515).

Shooting Ranges

Venues for honing your shooting skills are plentiful around town, and the local government even operates one for the general public at Shelby Farms. The Memphis Sport Shooting Association, which used to be called Memphis Rifle and Revolver Association, was incorporated in 1936. Their 185-acre facility, which is just outside town in Arlington at 9428 Old Brownsville Road, includes several pistol-range and rifle-firing points, five skeet and trap fields, two sporting clay courses, and more. Call (901) 867-8277 for current membership fees and requirements. Here are some other shooting options:

Range Master
2611 South Mendenhall
(901) 370-5600
www.rangemaster.com

This indoor, full-service pistol range offers classes, information for getting permits, memberships, and more. The range is open to nonmembers for $15; memberships, which start at $149 a year, will reduce the usage fee.

Shelby Farms Public Shooting Range
6791 Walnut Grove Road
(901) 377-4635

This is an outdoor facility run by the local government on park property, but it's across the street from the main park area. It features rifle and pistol ranges, as well as muzzle-loading, trap, and archery areas. The cost to fire a gun is $10, but senior discounts may apply. Eye and ear protection is mandatory, and the range is closed Monday and Tuesday.

Top Brass Sports
4788 Navy Road, Millington
(901) 873-2264
www.top-brass.com
In addition to their indoor handgun range, this place also sells and even rents firearms for use at their facility. No membership is needed, training is available, and range rates are only $8.00.

The Willows Sporting Clays
Grand Casino
Tunica, Miss.
(800) 946-4946
This fast-growing sport, sometimes described as golf with a shotgun, is available at Grand Casino in Tunica. The game, conducted in a controlled atmosphere, simulates a hunting environment, providing players a variety of targets. It's a good idea to make reservations at least a week ahead if possible. The Grand also offers trap and skeet shooting. Cost is $52 to play half of the course, $85 to play the entire course, gun and ammunition included. If you bring your own gun, it's $25 for half the course and $40 for the entire course.

Racquetball

Competitive players have known for years that Memphis not only produces some of the sport's best athletes but also hosts racquetball's U.S. Open, the premier championship tournament in America—and maybe the whole world! (See Annual Events chapter November listing.)

As far as public courts go, choices are limited to the Fogelman Downtown YMCA (901-527-9622) and Collierville's Schilling Farms YMCA (901-850-9622). One for-profit athletic club that has six courts for members is Wimbleton Sportsplex, which offers a whole range of membership options (901-388-6580).

Skating

For ice-skating in sweltering Memphis, you'd better head to Ice Chalet (901-362-8877) inside The Mall of Memphis at American Way and Perkins. Open all week,

special rates can be had for groups, including birthday parties. It's located on the ground floor of the west end, below the food court.

Roller-skating is still rolling at Skateland Summer (901-683-6991) on Old Summer Road, next to the movie theater. Open every day except Tuesday, rates are between $4.00 and $6.00, and the rolling goes on until 10:00 or 11:00 P.M., depending on the night. Another hip place to speed around in a circle is called Cordova Skating Center (901-755-0221). In the heart of the suburbs off Germantown Parkway, this facility includes an in-line shop, accommodations for birthday parties, and a roller-hockey league. From I-40 go south on Germantown Parkway past Dexter Road and turn right on Club Center Road; you can't miss it.

Strap on all your pads and helmet to go skateboarding at Kullison (sometimes

> **Insiders' Tip**
> Leaderboard Golf is a great place to buy grips, shafts, clubheads, or many other golf components. Located on National Avenue, they no longer have a brick-and-mortar retail shop, but you can go to www.leaderboardgolf.com for a look at their truly gigantic selection of replacement and upgrade items for your golf clubs at wholesale prices. Or you can call (901) 458-6112; they may answer the phone with their former name, Memphis Golf.

pronounced "collision"), formerly Darkside Ramp Park (901-323-3888). It's situated off Broad Avenue at 116 Cumberland Street between the railroad tracks. This set of verts, ramps, jumps, and boxes welcomes roller blades and bikes, too. For $25 you can buy a membership that includes a $3.00 discount off their standard $8.00 fee. If you're under 18 years old, you must wear a helmet, and adults as well are strongly encouraged to protect their heads. The best place to get the goods on local skating is Cheapskates (1576 Getwell Road, 901-744-1312). A visit or call to Memphis's oldest skateboard store is a good way to stay on top of the latest local news or just hang out with the "crusties."

Swimming

City Pools

The City of Memphis operates 16 outdoor swimming pools during the summer, as well as Bickford, the city's only indoor swimming pool, which is open year-round. Admission to the pools is free, as are swimming lessons. Hours and days of operation vary.

Bickford, 321 Henry Street, (901) 578–3732

Charlie Morris, 1235 Brown, (901) 272–0327

Douglass, 1616 Ash Street, (901) 323–3542

Fox Meadows, 3064 Clarke Road, (901) 365–0527

Frayser, 2907 North Watkins, (901) 353–0627

Gaisman, 4223 Macon, (901) 763–2920

Gooch, 1974 Hunter Street, (901) 276–9685

L.E. Brown, 617 South Orleans Street, (901) 527–3620

Lester, Tillman at Mimosa Streets, (901) 323–2261

Orange Mound, 2430 Carnes, (901) 458–9035

Pine Hill, 973 Alice, (901) 947–2978

Raleigh, 3678 Powers, (901) 372–1930

Riverview, 1981 Kansas, (901) 948–7609

Tom Lee (Carnes Pool), 328 Peach Street, (901) 527–3748

Westwood, 810 Western Park, (901) 789–6275

Willow, 4777 Willow Road, (901) 763–2917

Team Sports

Soccer

The Mike Rose Soccer Complex is a testament to the growing popularity of the sport here and to the dedication of Mr. Rose and others who share a dream for the youth of this community. Located in Collierville and visible from the Nonconnah Parkway, this state-of-the-art facility features 16 lighted, regulation-sized fields of the latest hybrid Sports Bermuda grass. These fields are supported by the best drainage and irrigation technology there is, and the plan is that the 2,500-seat stadium will be home to tournaments, special events, exhibitions, and clinics for years to come. Facilities for participants include showers and a food court, and in addition to the fields at this 136-acre site, you'll find

Insiders' Tip

In summer have plenty of water with you whatever outdoor recreation you're enjoying. Temperatures frequently push 100 degrees, and the oppressive humidity can be a serious health issue if you don't stay hydrated. Be sure to bring your own water, even though many golf courses place water coolers at strategic locations during summer, and other recreation sites have concessions or drink machines.

a picnic and recreation area and a three-acre lake. The Complex (www.mikerosesoccercomplex.com) is owned by the Shelby County Government and run by OS Memphis in a public/private partnership. To get here take I-240 to Nonconnah Parkway (385). Follow the parkway 7 miles east to the Forest Hill-Irene Road exit; then turn right onto Forest Hill-Irene Road. Take your first right into the Complex on Cindy Parlow Drive.

Soccer clubs in the area include, for adults, the Greater Memphis Soccer Association (901-321-3330); for youth, Collierville Soccer Association (901-854-8724), Germantown Soccer Club (901-755-6688), and Memphis Futbol Club (901-327-9444).

Other Team Sports

The parks and recreation divisions of Memphis (901-454-5220 for adult athletics, 901-454-5203 for youth athletics), Germantown (901-757-7375), and Bartlett (901-385-5590) offer adult and youth team sports like softball, basketball, and touch football. But how do you locate a team to play on? Start by contacting the Park Service in your area; they might be able to hook you up with a team. If you're affiliated with a church or other large organization, chances are there is already an existing team looking for fresh players. Another good possibility is playing on the team for the company you work for. Some of the larger businesses in Memphis field numerous teams, both single-sex and coed, or, if you can round up enough players on your own, start your own team. Again, call the city to find out about fees and other regulations.

These sports aren't big enough to warrant a local league, but they are part of larger national leagues:

Memphis Blues Rugby Football Club
(901) 522-9871
www.memphisblues.isonfire.com
This club was founded in 1998 with the combining of the University of Memphis RFC and Memphis Old #7, at one time sponsored by the Jack Daniels Distillery,

hence the name "Old #7" (talk about great parties!). Scrums are held at the University of Memphis or Toby Field at Central Avenue and Hollywood.

Memphis Ultimate Frisbee Team
(901) 278-3756
These zany but dedicated athletes have been going at it since 1988, when the "Prairie Squids" first formed. Regional tournaments begin early in the year, so practice continues year-round on the big field at Overton Park. During the short days of winter, they meet on Sundays and some Saturdays at two o'clock. The rest of the time practices are Tuesday and Thursday after work and Sunday afternoons.

Tennis

Bellevue Tennis Center
1310 South Bellevue Boulevard
(901) 774-7199
These south Memphis courts are group-friendly and allow you to arrange playing times according to your group's schedule. The tennis center, which has two indoor and four outdoor courts, is open seven days a week.

Frayser Tennis Complex
2907 North Watkins Street
(901) 357-5417
The price is right at these eight outdoor courts in Frayser. The courts are free until dusk, and even after that the rates are very low. Groups and children are welcome here. The tennis complex is open Monday through Friday.

Leftwich Tennis Center
4145 Southern Avenue
(901) 685-7905
This tennis center, situated at the south end of Audubon Park, has both indoor and outdoor courts, although the indoor courts are much pricier. Leftwich welcomes groups, and lessons also are available. It's open every day except holidays and for special events.

Whitehaven Tennis Complex
1500 Finley Road
(901) 332–0546
This facility has both indoor and outdoor courts, available at a wide range of rates depending on which court you play and when. Groups and children are welcome here. It's open seven days a week.

Wolbrecht Tennis Complex
1645 Ridgeway Road
(901) 767–2889
With two indoor courts and six outdoor courts, Wolbrecht offers both group rates and children's rates.

YMCAs

Memphis has a number of YMCAs with a variety of services, programs, and equipment available. All of them have before-school and after-school programs for kids. Keep in mind that if you're from out of town, you can use the Y (including the pool!) up to 10 times a year for $8.00 per visit without becoming a member. You must show an out-of-town ID to qualify for this deal.

The Abe Scharff YMCA
254 South Lauderdale
(901) 521–9622
This urban location serves the surrounding communities with child-care service, youth sports, adult leagues, and youth and teen programs. As for the facilities this Y has an indoor pool, a cardiovascular center with treadmills and other machines, circuit weight equipment, and free weights.

East Memphis YMCA
5885 Quince Road
(901) 682–8025
Situated next to the Lichterman Nature Center, this Y features a quarter-acre wooded walking/jogging trail and an outdoor pool. There are also workout rooms with treadmills and other equipment, a circuit weight system, and free weights. Children ages 5 through 14 can participate in organized sports activities including soccer, coed flag football, cheerleading, and basketball.

Fogelman Downtown YMCA
245 Madison Avenue
(901) 527–9622
Known around town as the Downtown Y, this is the one of the best YMCA facilities, situated near AutoZone Park and within easy reach of both downtown office workers and families in downtown and midtown. There's a full floor of exercise equipment, including cardiovascular and weight-training equipment, a gym, and a track that circles the workout floor. Three racquetball/handball courts, an indoor pool, basketball court, aerobic studio, and sundeck are also available. Members also have access to a variety of classes ranging from water exercise to pararyu karate. Sports leagues also take place here. There are spacious locker rooms, with sauna and whirlpool spa facilities. Parents can leave their children ages six months to eight years in the care of the Y's free babysitting service while they work out. An added plus is that during baseball season, you can watch the action at AutoZone Park from the window while you work out.

Mason YMCA
3548 Walker Avenue
(901) 458–9622
Situated near University of Memphis off busy Highland Avenue, this facility has an indoor pool, where water-exercise classes and swimming lessons are available. There's also cardiovascular equipment, machine weight equipment, free weights, aerobics classes, and a summer-camp program for kids. You can also take advantage of the weight-management programs, active-older-adults programs, and international dance classes. The Mason Y also has overnight accommodations for men, usually favored by seniors.

Medical Center YMCA
777 Washington Avenue, Suite 405
(901) 572–5622
Situated in the city's medical center area in the LeBonneur Physicians Office Building, this state-of-the-art fitness facility—new in 2001—includes an array of exercise equipment, including Nordic Tracks, Precor treadmills, and a boxing bag. There's also a

free-weight area, an aerobic studio with regular classes, a whirlpool spa, and full-service locker rooms. This YMCA also features three rehabilitation programs, LeBonneur's pediatric-cardiac and orthopedic rehab programs and a pediatric-asthma/obesity-control program. Membership includes aerobic classes, fitness evaluations, and strength-training classes.

Millington Family YMCA
7725 Navy Circle, Millington
(901) 873-1434
This suburban branch is one of the area's newest, built in 2001. It has an indoor pool, cardiovascular and other workout equipment, and a host of other offerings ranging from summer-day-camp and playground programs to massage therapy and Spanish lessons. Classes and programs include martial arts, weight management, kickboxing, and special weekday programs that welcome homeschoolers.

Sweeney YMCA
5959 Park Avenue
(901) 765-3105
Situated on the second floor of Saint Francis Hospital, this Y features a level-three cardiovascular rehab facility as well as full-service health and fitness facilities. Equipment includes a variety of treadmills, aerobic riders, and rowing machines, and the exercise floor is staffed at all times. Programs are available in weight management, stress management, and step aerobics as well. An important focus is fitness for seniors, who can take advantage of fitness testing, coaching, and free exercise classes including one especially for people with arthritis.

Thomas B. Davis Family YMCA
4727 Elvis Presley Boulevard
(901) 398-2366
This south Memphis facility has an indoor pool, where swimming lessons are available. There's a strong group-exercise program, with classes in yoga, toning, water therapy, and senior strength training.

YMCA at Schilling Farms
1185 Schilling Boulevard, Collierville
(901) 850-9622
This swank Collierville Y has every kind of equipment or program you could want, including both an indoor and an outdoor pool (complete with patio), a vertical climbing wall, racquetball and handball courts, a fitness-testing lab, an aerobic studio, and a full-equipped gym. Swimming lessons are available, as well as aerobic and Jazzercise classes, cardio-kickboxing, tumbling, nutritional education, and martial arts. The location just off Poplar Avenue makes this Y convenient both to employees at nearby FedEx and to those who live in this suburban community.

Spectator Sports

Baseball
Basketball
Boxing
Football
Hockey
Racing
Wrestling

Lately, Memphis has found a happy ending to its saga of attracting professional sports, with pro basketball and Triple A baseball coming to town within two years of each other. Until those welcome developments the professional sports scene in Memphis had been a real heartbreak hotel, as the city tried without success to attract a real, major-league sports team.

The city's luck first began to change in 2000, when the Memphis Redbirds, a Triple A Pacific Coast League baseball team, began its first season in a swank new downtown stadium. The year 2001 brought more good news, this time from the National Basketball Association: The Grizzlies, a basketball franchise, relocated here from Vancouver. The Grizzlies are now the perfect complement to the Redbirds, and with L. A. Lakers legend Jerry West now president of basketball operations, hopes are running high.

The Redbirds, a farm club of the St. Louis Cardinals, set attendance records in their first two years in AutoZone Park, one of the nation's finest minor-league baseball parks. In its first year in the park, the team won the league championship and went on to the Minor League World Series, where it fell to Indianapolis in seven games. The second year the team drew nearly 900,000 fans, second in the league.

Despite the city's success with these two teams, Memphians find it hard to forget the earlier frustrations of trying to win a professional sports team. Over the years Memphis has had teams in the USFL, the American Basketball Association, the Canadian Football League, the World Football League, and the North American Soccer League—all of which folded or left town. The city's XFL team, the Memphis Maniax, may have appeared on national television in 2001, but it, too, perished along with its much-hyped league.

The biggest heartbreak, though, was delivered by the National Football League in the late 1990s. It all started when NFL officials suggested that if the city expanded Liberty Bowl Memorial Stadium to its current capacity of 60,000, an NFL team would follow. What followed were innuendos and more to encourage the city's hopes, but despite all-out efforts by city leaders, Memphis was passed over when the league expanded in the late 1990s.

Humiliation was piled on top of humiliation when the Houston Oilers, in a deal to flee that Texas city for Nashville (Memphis's archrival), agreed to play in Memphis for at least two years until their new stadium could be built. Memphians, enraged by the NFL's moves, stayed away in droves. When TV cameras panned the empty stands during a nationally televised game in the 1997–1998 season, the dearth of Memphis football fans became a running joke. When the team bolted and went to Nashville early, few tears were shed in Memphis.

In the end the team became the Tennessee Titans, the first Tennessee NFL team, and went on to play in the Super Bowl. Despite the team's success Memphians find it difficult to forget the past. It may be a while before "how 'bout those Titans" is a well-received conversation starter in Memphis.

Although the Redbirds and Grizzlies rule in terms of professional sports, the University of Memphis football and basketball teams are the focal point of local college sports. Memphians, many of whom attended the school, are huge Tigers fans, especially when it comes to basketball.

In the past the Tigers basketball team has included such talents as Penny Hardaway and Eliot Perry. Today, though, hopes for the team are riding high after the arrival in 2000 of Coach John Calipari, the coach credited with taking the University of Massachusetts to five straight NCAA appearances. The Tigers tip off in the Pyramid Arena against Conference USA opponents such as Louisville, Cincinnati, and St. Louis. The Pyramid also has hosted several conference tournaments and has been the site of early-round NCAA games. The Tigers delivered in 2002 by winning the National Invitation Tournament (NIT), the team's first national title.

If you don't believe that hope springs eternal, talk with U of M football fans. They loyally follow the Tigers despite the team's mostly dismal showing season after season. The team delivers on occasion, however, as in its surprise defeat of University of Tennessee in 1996.

Memphis is also home to many fans of surrounding Southeastern Conference teams including University of Tennessee, University of Mississippi (Ole Miss), Mississippi State University, and University of Arkansas. You'll see them much in evidence during the football and basketball seasons.

The city also boasts a calendar of annual sports events, starting in February with the Kroger St. Jude International Indoor Tennis Championship. The event features top men's tennis stars in a weeklong tournament that's steeped in tradition. In summer professional golfers of national prominence play here in a PGA stop, the FedEx St. Jude Golf Classic, which has taken its place as one of the most competitive on the tour. There's also the Germantown Charity Horse Show in June, which draws top riders.

The annual matchup between two top area historically black universities, Tennessee State University and Jackson State University, fills the Liberty Bowl for the Southern Heritage Classic in September. In December the Liberty Bowl hosts the AXA Liberty Bowl Football Classic, an annual college football game pitting the champions of Conference USA and Big West. One of the oldest bowls in existence, the Liberty brings national exposure to the city.

(See the Annual Events chapter for details on the Kroger St. Jude International Indoor Tennis Classic, the FedEx St. Jude Golf Classic, the Germantown Charity Horse Show, the Southern Heritage Classic, and the AXA Liberty Bowl.)

As for other spectator sports, the Memphis RiverKings play in the new DeSoto County Center, just south of the city, as does a developmental Arena Football League team. Boxing matches take place monthly on Beale Street at the New Daisy Theater, and there's also wrestling from time to time at the Mid-South Coliseum, a venue with a rich tradition of professional wrestling, where Sputnik Monroe and Jerry "The King" Lawler built their careers. (For more information see the Close-up in this chapter.) Across the river in West Memphis, Arkansas, "The Sport of Kings," greyhound racing, is a nightly attraction at Southland Greyhound Park. North of the city in Millington, auto racing makes itself heard at the Memphis Motorsports Park.

Amateur sports thrive in the city under the auspices of the Memphis Park Commission, which operates baseball, softball, soccer, and basketball leagues for all ages, and of the city and county schools. (Check out the Parks and Recreation chapter for more information about these leagues.)

Baseball

Memphis Redbirds
AutoZone Park
8 South Third Street
(901) 721–6050 (for tickets)
www.memphisredbirds.com

The hottest summer sports ticket in town gets you into AutoZone Park, the crown jewel of downtown Memphis, where you can watch the Memphis Redbirds take on their Pacific Coast League (Triple A) rivals. The local nine plays 72 home games between April and Labor Day. The Redbirds are the St. Louis Cardinals farm team, so a number of players have seen action with their major-league parent team. The park itself is a prince among minor-league baseball parks, with a design that looks and feels like Baltimore's Camden Yards.

The Redbirds have built on a strong baseball tradition in Memphis, which dates back to the old Memphis Chicks of the Southern Association. That Double A team were champions, who captured the Dixie Series in the 1950s. Major-league rosters

The Redbirds' José Rodriguez springs into action at Autozone Park in downtown Memphis.

PHOTO: LARRY T. INMAN / MEMPHIS REDBIRDS BASEBALL FOUNDATION

Rocky the Rockin' Redbird adds to the fun at a Redbirds home game.
PHOTO: LARRY T. INMAN / MEMPHIS REDBIRDS BASEBALL FOUNDATION

were dotted with former Chicks such as Luis Aparicio, Jim Landis, and Sammy Esposito. Later, a Double A successor to the old Memphis Chicks, also called the Chicks, played at Tim McCarver Stadium here, as did another Triple A team, the Memphis Blues.

AutoZone Park opened on April 1, 2000, to a sellout crowd of 15,000 as the team hosted its major-league parent, the St. Louis Cardinals. Sellout crowds that first year were the rule rather than the exception as fans flocked to the new park. Sellouts were no fewer in 2001 as 900,000 flocked to the park to watch the beloved Birds and fan-favorites Stubby Clapp and Lou Lucca.

The Redbirds should retain their status as the hottest ticket in town for many, many more exciting years—because after all, it's baseball.

Ticket prices range from $5.00 to $15.00, and various ballpark facilities are available to accommodate groups of up to 2,500.

Basketball

Memphis Grizzlies
The Pyramid Arena (through 2003–2004 season)
One Auction Avenue
(901) 888–HOOP, (800) 4NBA–TIX
www.grizzlies.com

The Grizzlies first season (2001-2002) created great excitement in Memphis, with highlights that included the team's at-home win over the L.A. Lakers. Much of the excitement came from the performances of top players like Pau Gasol, named conference rookie of the month several times during the season; Shane Battier, the Duke University star forward, and Jason Williams. True, the team didn't excel in its NBA division, the Midwest division of the Western Conference, but coaches attribute that performance to the fact that the first season was more about developing a team.

The team's prospects, morale, and visibility got a big boost in 2002 when former L. A. Lakers executive Jerry West signed on

Insiders' Tip

For a sampling of the basketball talent for which Memphis has long been known, check out the annual Jerry Dover Memorial Classic, a three-on-three basketball tournament held each summer at Southwest Community College gym. Here, the big college players who hail from Memphis come home to play each in this annual charity event. You can watch old high-school rivalries being rekindled, as well as some great basketball action.

University of Memphis Tigers Basketball
The Pyramid Arena
One Auction Avenue
(901) 678–2332, (888) 867–8636
www.gotigersgo.com

Even though the Redbirds rule the sports roost in Memphis, the University of Memphis still boasts a strong, local following in roundball, and that should grow as Coach John Calipari builds the team's hoops fortunes after several dismal seasons under a myriad of coaches. Already Calipari helped the Tigers to their first national title, with an NLT win in 2002.

Fans have to go all the way back to the 1980s to remember when the Tigers, under the auspices of Coach Dana Kirk, were consistent winners. Before that, in 1973, another legendary Tiger coach, Gene Bartow, led the school to its first Final Four appearance in history. In St. Louis the Tigers faced off against the record-breaking national champions, UCLA. A dozen years later, Kirk would once again lead the team back to the Final Four, where it lost to Villanova in a semi-final game.

The team's long history had its beginnings in 1957, when the Tigers played Bradley for the NIT championship in New York, the program's first appearance in the national spotlight. The coach was Bob Vanetta, and the game put the Tigers on the basketball map.

Today's Tigers tip off in the Pyramid Arena against Conference USA opponents such as Louisville, Cincinnati, and St. Louis University. Memphis also has hosted several conference tournaments and served as hosts of early round NCAA games.

In 2000-2001, the team's first season under Calipari, the Tigers advanced to the NIT semi-finals before being knocked out. A big reason was high school All-American Dajuan Wagner, son of Tiger assistant Milt Wagner, who joined the team in 2001. Among other distinctions, Wagner was named Conference USA's Freshman of the Year. The team has regrouped since Wagner left to pursue his NBA career. In the past U of M squads have included other All-American players such as Penny Hardaway, Keith Lee, William Bedford, and Eliot Perry.

Hopes have been running high since the arrival of Calipari, so sellout crowds

as the team's president of basketball operations. One of the 50 greatest players in NBA history, West as an executive led the Lakers to eight NBA Championships.

The team, which had been the Vancouver Grizzlies, landed in Memphis during the 2001 off-season, bringing in professional basketball with a bang, not a whimper. Before the first game was played, the team scored points with Memphians by drafting Battier and by choosing hometown favorite St. Jude Children's Research Hospital as one of its featured charities.

The Grizzlies will continue to play at the Pyramid until the 2004–2005 season, when construction is complete on a $250-million state-of-the-art arena in downtown Memphis. Currently, Grizzlies fans can take advantage of the lowest ticket prices in the NBA.

For Pyramid games, tickets, available through Ticketmaster (901-525-1515) are $9.00 to $125 for individual tickets and $405 to $5,625 for season tickets.

should greet the Tigers for every game when they take the floor at home.

Individual game tickets are $18 and $13, while season tickets are $205 and $280.

Boxing

Boxing on Beale
New Daisy Theater
(901) 525-8979, (901) 525-8981

Boxing on Beale, a longtime tradition, takes place the first Tuesday of every month at the New Daisy. Memphis boxing fans from all walks of life gather to watch the action. There are usually four to six fights—some good, some bad—but the best entertainment may be watching the family and friends of the local boxers vociferously weighing in for their fighter.

On boxing night you'll see a main event and some underclass events, in weight classes that can include heavyweight, middleweight, junior-middleweight, and welterweight divisions. It's quite a scene, complete with "ring babes" in bikinis, beer, cigars, popcorn, and, of course, great boxing.

Ringside seats are $15, and general admission seats are $12.

Football

University of Memphis Tigers
Liberty Bowl Memorial Stadium
335 South Hollywood Street
(901) 678-2332, (888) 867-8636 (tickets)
www.gotigersgo.com

For the city's diehard, often frustrated gridiron fans, the biggest sports moment of their lives may have been in 1996 during a matchup with nationally ranked University of Tennessee Volunteers. With only seconds left on the Liberty Bowl Stadium clock, and the sun setting in more ways than one, a 3-yard touchdown pass from Tigers quarterback Qadry Anderson to tight end Chris Powers gave the Memphis team a 21-17 win over the Vols. It was the Tigers' first win in 16 meetings with this SEC powerhouse. In 2001 the Tigers, still trying to build on that upset, have called on coach Tommy West to lead the Memphis fortunes.

Things haven't been so rosy for the Tigers before or since, as they have suffered through losing season after losing season under coach after coach. Playing in Conference USA, the team is eligible for an automatic spot in the St. Jude Liberty Bowl Football Classic in December if they are champions of their league. The conference also has tie-ins with lesser bowls for second- and third-place finishers.

Despite yearly disappointments Memphis schedules two or three SEC teams each season. It has played both Ole Miss (University of Mississippi) and Mississippi State University since the 1950s and can show wins over those schools plus Auburn University, Vanderbilt University, University of Alabama, and, yes, Tennessee. Present schedules also show games with such noted institutions as Army and TCU.

Individual tickets are $10 to $30; season tickets run from $60 to $135.

Hockey

Memphis RiverKings
4560 Venture Drive, Southaven, Miss.
(662) 342-1755
www.riverkings.com

The RiverKings, the longest running professional indoor team in Memphis sports

Insiders' Tip

One of the most pleasant ways to take in a Redbirds baseball game—especially if you have young children—is to buy lawn seats for just $5.00 each. You can spread out a blanket and relax on the sloping, grassy bank behind left field to watch the game. Your ticket will also admit you into the ballpark to buy concessions, T-shirts, or just wander around.

history, play 35 home games each season beginning in October. The Central Hockey League team, which moved to the new DeSoto County (Mississippi) Civic Center in 2000, had played for many years in the Mid-South Coliseum in Memphis.

The current RiverKings team is not the original professional hockey team in Memphis. In the 1960s the Memphis Wings and their successor team, the Memphis South Stars, were members of the Central Hockey League, which at the time was a developmental league for the NHL. Presently the Central Hockey League is unaffiliated, and its teams are stocked mostly with free agents and players just out of college looking for a way into the NHL. Also, the league owns the teams, sells the franchise to locals, and has local personnel to take care of the day-to-day tasks.

Tickets are $9.00 to $20. Game times are 7:15 P.M. and, on Sundays, 2:35 P.M.

Racing

**Memphis MotorSports Park
5500 Taylor Forge Drive, Millington
(901) 358–7223, (866) 407–7333
www.memphismotorsportspark.com**
The area's racing fans can listen to the roar of

the engines, smell the gas fumes, and, more important, see the races at the Memphis Motorsports Park, located 7 miles north of the city in Millington. Some of the featured races are the NASCAR Craftsman Truck Series Memphis 200 in June, the NHRA AutoZone Nationals in September, and the Sam's Town 250 Busch Series, a NASCAR event, in October. (See the Annual Events chapter for more information on the Sam's Town event.) In addition, Memphis Motorsports Park hosts the Winston Drag Racing Series, weekly racing, and special events throughout the season.

From April to September the Mid-South's top racers gather for Friday Night Thunder at the quarter-mile, high-banked dirt track. This weekly series features four classes of cars including mini stocks, hobby stocks, open-wheel modifieds, and winged-sprint cars. These racers lay it all on the line, as they try to follow in the footsteps of other legendary racers such as Hooker Hood, Sammy Swindell, Jeff Swindell, and Greg Hodnett.

Each Thursday the park's quarter-mile drag strip becomes a drag-racing haven for its popular Test-N-Tune event. This gives the serious drag racer a final chance to tune his car before weekend's competition and gives the novice a chance to come out and put his personal car to the test.

The races always draw a crowd at Memphis MotorSports Park in Millington.
PHOTO: MEMPHIS CONVENTION AND VISITORS BUREAU

Saturday night at the park features the finest drag racing in the area as the E.T. Bracket Racing Series takes center stage. Drivers from all over the Mid-South converge on Memphis to compete in four different classes—Super Pro, Pro, Junior Dragster and a Trophy Class—as the racers vie for weekly titles.

The Thursday, Friday, and Saturday events continue into fall.

Gates open about two hours before race time. Ticket prices vary, depending on the event.

Southland Greyhound Park
1550 North Ingram, West Memphis, Ark.
(800) 467–6182
www.southlandgreyhound.com

Long before the casinos began opening up in Tunica, Memphians have been crossing the bridge over into Arkansas to watch the greyhounds race and to indulge in pari-mutuel wagering on the outcome. Southland has live races every day except Sunday and simulcasting of greyhound races from other tracks daily.

You can watch the action trackside or on TV monitors in a clubhouse environment. Southland also has a family-seating area and arcade to accommodate families with kids. The park has an adoption program for its past-prime racers, so don't be surprised if you occasionally see the sleek greyhounds on leashes around the city.

There's free admission to the park and $1.00 admission to the clubhouse level.

Wrestling

Mid-South Coliseum
(901) 274–3982 (tickets)

The days are gone when Monday Night Wrestling was a fixture at the Mid-South Coliseum, but you can still catch some live wrestling there when the World Wrestling Federation comes to town a few times a year. Memphis has a rich tradition of wrestling, producing stars from Sputnik Monroe to Jerry "The King" Lawler. (See Close-up below for details about pro wrestling in Memphis.)

CLOSE-UP

Wrestling: A Memphis Thing

For years and years grunts and groans have been emitting from the Mid-South Coliseum on Monday nights, as a pair of broad, burly, hairy-chested men (or women) clash in yet another wrestling match. This is one of the longest-running shows in Memphis and can still be seen on a local TV station on Saturday morning, just as it has in years past.

Although some people may argue that it's more show than sport, professional wrestling is one sport in which Memphis has played a huge role for more than 40 years, developing such talents as Sputnik Monroe, Hulk Hogan, and Randy Savage.

Over the years Memphians—and wrestling fans everywhere—have come to know Sputnik Monroe (good guy), Jack Dundee (semigood guy), Jerry "The King" Lawler (good guy), and Sid Vicious (baaaaad guy). This is where in the 1980s the late comedian Andy Kaufman, after years of wrestling women, came to take on the local wrestling establishment, only to leave it with his head pile-driven into the floor by Lawler. More recently, World Wrestling Federation stars The Rock and Kurt Angle wrestled in Memphis on their way to WWF fame.

Now that Monday Night Wrestling is no longer a fixture at Memphis's Mid-South Coliseum, you can still see live wrestling when the WWF comes here a few times each year. WMC-TV 5, the station that broadcasts wrestling on Saturday mornings, also sponsors some live matches. Both capture the theatrics that wrestling audiences of all ages love.

Make no mistake: Wrestling is definitely a Memphis thing, along with barbecue, Elvis Presley, soul music, and walks along the Mississippi.

Annual Events

From a celebration of Elvis Presley's birthday and Dr. Martin Luther King, Jr.'s, birthday in January to the giant New Year's Eve party on Beale Street, Memphis has a respectable calendar of annual events. There's truly something for everyone, and some events also include elements of the bizarre. After all it's not everywhere you find female, Japanese, and dwarf Elvis impersonators (Elvis Week), or a stage full of people competing for who can best squeal like a pig (World Championship Barbecue Cooking Contest). Although many events are organized around sports and the arts, it's not surprising that the main events are organized around the things Memphis is best known for: Elvis, music, and barbecue.

Certainly the most international event is Elvis Tribute week, the August anniversary of Presley's death in Memphis in 1977. Each year, despite the sweltering temperatures, fans from all over the world roll into town for a three-ring circus of official and unofficial events, culminating with the candlelight vigil in front of Graceland Mansion on August 15, the eve of the anniversary of his death. A more modest celebration in January commemorates Elvis's birthday.

In terms of live music, the big event is the Beale Street Music Festival, which takes place in early May. It attracts national acts as well as local talent for a three-day, four-stage party next to the Mississippi River. Also notable are the annual W.C. Handy Awards, which later that month honors blues musicians and attracts a who's who of that universe to the Orpheum Theater (and to Beale Street clubs later). Other favorites include the Beale Street Zydeco Festival in February and the Memphis Music and Heritage Festival over Labor Day weekend. Just about any other weekend, though, you'll find plenty of music on Beale Street and elsewhere. Check out local papers or just ask around.

A highlight on the events calendar is Memphis in May, a monthlong celebration that gives locals a chance to shake off the winter doldrums and attracts many out-of-towners. It includes about 100 events, big and small, as the city honors a different country each year and puts on three main events. The music festival takes place during the first weekend, then the World Championship Barbecue Cooking Contest two weeks later. To wrap things up, Sunset Symphony takes place during the final weekend. It's an outdoor performance by the Memphis Symphony Orchestra along Old Man River, coupled with a Southern Food festival that features prepared foods from various restaurants.

As for professional sports events, the Kroger St. Jude International Indoor Tennis Championship takes place in February, attracting a who's who of tennis stars, whereas in June the FedEx St. Jude Golf Classic is a stop on the PGA Tour, which attracts top players to Memphis. College-football fans flock to the city each year for the Southern Heritage Classic in September, an annual matchup between Tennessee State University and Jackson State University, and for the AXA Liberty Bowl in December, when the Conference USA champion takes on the top team of the Mountain West Conference.

Another focal point for annual events is black history, as the National Civil Rights Museum commemorates both the birthday of Dr. Martin Luther King, Jr., and the anniversary of his assassination in Memphis in 1968. In October there are two arts-and-crafts fairs, featuring local artists and artisans as well as their counterparts from all over the country.

In this chapter we list Memphis's top annual events, but you can find great stuff to do on just about any given weekend. Beale Street has a number of other music festivals each year, including the Labor Day Music Festival and its St. Patrick's Day celebration, and it offers great music even on ordinary weekends. Plus, there are neighborhood festivals, 10K races, and other fund-raising events, parades, independent film festivals, and outdoor concerts. For more information, check *The Memphis Flyer*, the city's free alternative weekly, or the Playbook section of the city's daily newspaper, *The Commercial Appeal*, which comes out on Fridays.

January

Elvis Presley Birthday Celebration
Graceland Mansion
3734 Elvis Presley Boulevard
(901) 332–3322, (800) 238–2000
www.elvis.com
For Elvis fans who can't celebrate their idol enough, every year Graceland Mansion sponsors a weekend-long series of events to commemorate Elvis Presley's January 8 birthday. The events vary but always include a traditional proclamation of Elvis Presley Day ceremony on the front lawn of Graceland. In prior years the events have included a dance party, free birthday cake to Graceland visitors, and a special musical event, Elvis—The Concert. It's a miniversion of the big event, Elvis Week, which takes place in August to commemorate The King's death.

Dr. Martin Luther King, Jr.'s Birthday
National Civil Rights Museum
450 Mulberry Street
(901) 521–9699
www.civilrightsmuseum.org
Every year on the federal holiday designated as Dr. King's birthday, the National Civil Rights Museum sponsors programs aimed at educating children about the life and work of Dr. King. A highlight is always a birthday celebration that takes place at the museum on that Monday. In April on the anniversary of his death, there's also a candlelight vigil or other event to commemorate his untimely death in Memphis in 1968.

February

Beale Street Zydeco Festival
Beale Street
(901) 526–0110
www.bealestreet.com
The street gets a dash of Louisiana spice at this popular festival, which features small family bands as well as zydeco stars such as Wayne Touts and Chubby Carrier. An

annual event since 1989, the festival also brings you Cajun cooking, a crawfish-eating contest, and (only for the truly brave) a crawfish-bobbing contest. Some years, Mardi Gras falls on the same weekend, which means a big parade and other festivities. It's a wristband event, so $15 gets you into most of the clubs on Beale, where the bands put on their shows.

Kroger St. Jude International Indoor Tennis Championship
The Racquet Club of Memphis
5111 Sanderlin Avenue
(901) 765–4400
This annual men's tennis event, which takes place in mid- to late February, brings in some of the biggest names in tennis as they compete on state-of-the-art indoor courts at The Raquet Club in East Memphis. This all-indoor tour event, one of only seven championship-level tennis tournaments in North America, is also the nation's oldest indoor-tennis tournament, attracting 48 singles players and 24 doubles teams to compete for $800,000 in prizes. The tournament organizers point out that of the 10 men who have ranked Number One in the world since 1976, eight of them have played and won the Memphis tournament. Past winners have included Michael Chang, who made this his first pro tournament in 1988, Pete Sampras, and Andre Agassi. Singles and doubles matches are

Insiders' Tip

The Memphis Convention and Visitors Bureau publishes a detailed calendar of events four times a year, which is available free. Call (901) 543-5333 to have one mailed to you.

Insiders' Tip

Volunteering can be a great way to enjoy some of these annual events, while meeting some new people and helping organizers put on a successful show. Even if there's no money involved, there's usually a free T-shirt and free admission. Call organizers of the individual events for more information.

played Monday through Sunday, with finals on Sunday afternoon. Daily tickets range from $9.00 to $40, weeklong tickets are $175 and $260, and weekend tickets are $125 and $160.

April

Africa in April Cultural Awareness Festival
Robert Church Park
Beale and Fourth Streets
(901) 947–2133
www.africainapril.com

This four-day festival is a point of pride for the city's African Americans, who gather here to reconnect with their African roots. The festival, which honors a different country in Africa each year, includes children's activities, performances by colorfully costumed African dancers and musicians from the honored country and elsewhere, as well as storytelling, both onstage and in booths. Visitors of any heritage enjoy browsing the marketplace—with vendors selling jewelry, artifacts, and colorful African-made shawls and other clothing—and taking in performances that might include Jamaican reggae or African American gospel. An annual event for more than 15 years, Africa in April

takes place in and around Robert Church Park, having outgrown the smaller W. C. Handy Park farther down Beale Street. Admission is free.

May

Beale Street Music Festival
Tom Lee Park
Riverside Drive at Beale
(901) 525–4611
www.memphisinmay.org

For music-minded Memphians and a growing number of visitors, attending the annual Beale Street Music Festival is a rite of spring not to be missed. Held the first weekend in May along the Mississippi River at the foot of Beale Street, the festival celebrates Memphis music and the musical sounds it has produced or influenced, including blues, rock, gospel, R&B, alternative, and soul. The event, which outgrew Beale Street years ago, is now a three-day, four-stage extravaganza with performances by some 60 bands. The lineup generally includes a remarkable range of performers, from headliners such as Bob Dylan, Van Morrison, Sheryl Crow, or the latest chart-topping alternative band to homegrown gospel and blues groups. The 2001 festival, for example, featured Dylan, Koko Taylor, bluesman R.L. Burnside, George Clinton & Parliament Funkadelic, and Willie Nelson, as well as hometown-bands-made-good North Mississippi Allstars and Three 6 Mafia. In addition to the music, there's a great view of the Mississippi River (particularly at sunset), plenty of people-watching, cold beer, and vendors selling barbecue, pronto pups, grilled corn, and other festival food. Do bring cash and an ID (if you're drinking), but don't bring your own food and drink, cameras, or lawn chairs.

The festival, part of the monthlong Memphis in May International celebration, attracts more than 140,000 people over the three days. Recently, tickets began to sell out in advance, so it's a good idea to buy them early. Tickets are $17 per day if purchased in advance or $40 for a three-day pass. If any tickets are left the day of the show, they sell for $22 each.

The Beale Street Music Festival, one of the most popular Memphis in May events, takes place along the banks of the Mississippi River. PHOTO: MEMPHIS CONVENTION AND VISITORS BUREAU

Memphis Kemet Jubilee
Various locations
(901) 774–1118

Formerly known as the Cotton Makers Jubilee, this annual event has a rich history dating back to when the city's African American community, excluded from Memphis Cotton Carnival across town, created a celebration of its own. The highlight is the Jubilee parade, the city's largest, which takes place the first Saturday in May. The parade, which goes along Second Street from Exchange Street to Beale Street before turning east, features more than 100 marching bands from Tennessee and surrounding states as well as floats carrying Jubilee participants, including its king and queen. It's mainly a family event and features a youth leadership program as well.

World Championship Barbecue Cooking Contest
Tom Lee Park
Riverside at Beale
(901) 525–4611
www.memphisinmay.org

This is Memphis's biggest, craziest, most eccentric party of the year. Here, some 250 barbecue teams, with names like Pork Me Tender and Squealer Dealer, gather in mid-May to compete for cash prizes at this, the largest pork-barbecue cooking contest in the world. While team members tend to the serious business of cooking prize-winning ribs and other pork delicacies in preparation for the judges' visits on Saturday morning, there's plenty of time for fun. Its organizers describe it as "the Super Bowl, Mardi Gras, and one bodacious party rolled into one," but one might just as easily describe it as bizarre. There's a hog-calling contest, the Ms. Piggy contest (contestants tend to be hairy and male despite the makeup and dresses), and other eccentricities such as the Viva Las Porkas chapel for renewing wedding vows.

The atmosphere is reminiscent of an oversized fraternity cookout, producing clouds of barbecue aroma that permeate downtown Memphis as well as your clothes. One of the oddities of the festival is that unless you are invited by a team, you won't get to taste the barbecue you smell

The fine art of cooking ribs and other meats is at the core of the yearly World Championship Barbecue Cooking Contest. PHOTO: MEMPHIS IN MAY

cooking. Organizers have remedied that situation by setting up vendors, including contest winners, to sell barbecue. Other festival food and cold beer are available as well.

It goes without saying that if anyone invites you to visit his or her barbecue team, say "Yes!" immediately and get passes if possible. Although it's fun to people-watch, see the entertainment, and check out the sometimes outrageously decorated team sites, it's a better party if you hang out with a team.

Admission is $6.00 per day for adults, $3.00 per day for children 7–12, and free for children age 6 and under. On Thursday and Friday admission is free during lunchtime (10:00 A.M. to 2:00 P.M.). The party atmosphere gets rowdy later at night, so plan an early visit if you're bringing the kids.

W.C. Handy Blues Awards
Orpheum Theatre
203 South Main Street
(901) 527– 2583
www.handyawards.com

This annual awards presentation, where the blues' highest honor is bestowed at the foot of Beale Street, attracts some of the best-known names in the blues. In 2001, for example, there were appearances by Ruth Brown, Little Milton, and Levon Helm; Dr. John was host, and both Taj Mahal and Clarence "Gatemouth" Brown performed. Named after the Father of the Blues (who lived in Memphis), the awards show takes place at the ornate Orpheum Theatre the Thursday before Memorial Day weekend. The Handy Awards presentation, which has been struggling since its 1980 beginning, is now a weekend-long event that includes a blues symposium with workshops and panel discussions. It's also a great time for blues fans to go club-hopping on Beale Street, as many of these stars find their way to the birthplace of the blues after the ceremony.

June

Memphis Carnival
Various locations
(901) 278–0243

Established in 1931 as Memphis Cotton Carnival to draw attention to the cotton industry and to promote business, this yearly event mimics New Orleans Mardi Gras festivities by featuring a royal court with king and queen as well as krewes, the participating clubs. Each year Carnival honors an industry that has had a major impact on the local economy, and participants come from all over the Mid-South. It continues largely as a society event, although at one time it was much more visible, with public festivities such as a parade and fireworks. At present most of its parties and events are invitation only, taking place in early June.

Germantown Charity Horse Show
Germantown Charity Horse Show Arena
7745 Poplar Pike, Germantown
(901) 755–1200
www.gchs.org

This five-day event, held over the first weekend in June, is one of the largest all-breed horse shows in the country, with more than 300 classes. As a Mid-America States Cup (MASCUP) event, it draws the top national riders and features Tennessee walking horses, saddle horses and hunter jumpers as well as amateur events such as horse-drawn carriages. A major highlight is the awarding of the $25,000 Lincoln Grand Prix of Germantown. For spectators there's plenty of picnicking room in the grassy natural bowl in which the arena is built, as well as cotton candy, barbecue, snow cones, and other goodies for sale. The events take place in an arena built in 1954 especially for the horse show, where 35,000 to 40,000 people gather over the five days to watch the horses, and to see and be seen.

Ducks Unlimited Great Outdoors Sporting and Wildlife Festival
Agricenter International
7777 Walnut Grove Road
(901) 758–3825
www.ducks.org

This three-day festival, which takes place in early June, is geared toward hunters and other outdoors enthusiasts, with interactive exhibitions and demonstrations of the latest in sporting equipment. You can check out canoes, camping equipment, bows and arrows, fishing gear, and other equipment. There are even special tracks for testing

Insiders' Tip

Interested in becoming a judge for the World Championship Barbecue Cooking Contest? Each year the organizers of the contest have BBQ school, a seminar on the fine points of barbecue, which a requirement for all judges. To learn more check out www.mem phisinmay.org or call (901) 525-4611.

ATVs, bikes, and climbing equipment. The sponsor is Ducks Unlimited, a wetlands conservation group whose members are mostly waterfowl hunters. Its headquarters is in Memphis, just a stone's throw from the festival location..

Tickets are $10 for adults and $5.00 for children (6–12) in advance; at the gate, tickets are $12 for adults and $5.00 for children. Kids under 6 and dogs on leashes are free (rabies tag and cleaning up after dogs are required), as is parking.

FedEx St. Jude Golf Classic
Tournament Players Club at Southwind
3325 Club at Southwind, Germantown
(901) 748–0534

This annual stop on the PGA tour brings top players to Memphis every summer, along with television cameras. An estimated 150,000 spectators watch as the players compete for a $3.5-million purse. The FedEx St. Jude Classic is played at Tournament Players Club at Southwind in the suburb of Germantown, a 71-par course with eight lakes and three streams that affect play on 11 holes. The tournament takes place in early June, a switch from the early days when it was in August, which in Memphis means 90-plus temperatures and high humidity. The tournament was started in

1958 as the Memphis Open and later changed names as TV actor Danny Thomas, then St. Jude Children's Hospital, and finally FedEx sponsored the event. The event has raised more than $11.5 million for St. Jude Children's Research Hospital since 1970. One of the tournament's highlights occurred in 1977, when golfer Al Geiberger shot a 59, a PGA tour one-round record. Memphis fans have a soft spot for home-town players, including John Daly, Loren Roberts, and David Gossett.

One-day tickets are $24 in advance and $18 at the gate for adults. Season tickets, which are good all week, are $60 in advance and $80 at the gate for adults, and for youth (5–16) $13 in advance and $17 at the gate.

July

July 4th Fireworks
Various locations
(901) 543–3333
In Memphis instead of one main event, you'll find a number of fireworks exhibitions, usually coupled with a concert or other festivities, all over the Memphis metropolitan area. Some take place on July 4th proper, whereas others take place the night before. Check local newspapers for the exact locations, dates, and times. The two major fireworks displays are held downtown and in Shelby Farms. Among the most popular is the annual WMC Star-Spangled Celebration, which after years downtown has moved to Shelby Farms near Germantown. Taking its place downtown is the Red, White & Blues celebration at Tom Lee Park. Both events also feature musical entertainment and are free to the public. In east Memphis the Memphis Botanic Garden hosts a pops concert that features fireworks; lawn seats are $15. Other free fireworks exhibits take place in Millington, Bartlett, Germantown, and Collierville. Don't forget about Tunica, Mississippi, where Sam's Town casino puts on a splashy fireworks show in fine Las Vegas style.

August

Elvis Week
Graceland Mansion
3734 Elvis Presley Boulevard
(901) 332–3322, (800) 238–2000
www.elvis.com
At a time when Memphians are hitting back-to-school sales or looking to escape the heat, thousands of Elvis Presley fans are pouring into Memphis from all over the world to commemorate the anniversary of The King's death. It has been at least 25 years since Elvis left the building, but the flame still burns bright in the hearts of his fans, some of whom have been making the pilgrimage each year for 20 years. Usually about 30,000 to 35,000 come through Graceland that week, and a special year, such as the 25th anniversary in 2002, that number may double. The highlight is the candlelight vigil in front of Graceland Mansion the evening of August 15. The street is closed off that night, as mourners line up in front for their turn to walk up the driveway of Graceland, candles in hand, to pay their respects at his grave in the Meditation Garden. Everyone should see this ritual once, but remember, it's as serious as church for many, so if you go to observe, be respectful to the true faithful who've saved all year to be here for this moment.

Dozens of other events take place during the week, many of them sponsored by Graceland, such as Elvis—The Concert. This virtual-reality show at the Mid-South Coliseum features vintage footage of Elvis singing, along with former band members who perform the music live. "Tribute artists" from all over the world compete in what most of us would call an Elvis-impersonator contest, which runs for several days.

All over Memphis locals get into the act as well. The Orpheum summer film series features the 1970 classic concert film, *Elvis, That's the Way It Is,* this week, while the Pink Palace's Sharpe Planetarium puts on its annual Elvis: Legacy in Lights laser show. Various forums are held around town to allow fans to hear about their hero from professional and personal associates of the late King. There's no charge to visit the grounds of Graceland Mansion on vigil night, and charges vary for other events. You'll find a calendar of Elvis Week events and ticket information in local newspapers.

September

Memphis Music & Heritage Festival
Downtown Memphis
(901) 525–3655
www.southernfolklore.com
If you are interested in hearing the music that originated in Memphis and the surrounding Delta area, don't miss this Labor Day weekend festival held each year by the Center for Southern Folklore. The organizers bring together a remarkable collection of musicians, ranging from local gospel quartets and homegrown bluesmen to the original Sun Records rockabilly hit-makers and Memphis soul royalty such as Carla Thomas. With modest stages set up in and around the Center for Southern Folklore, the event is on a much smaller, more human scale than the Beale Street Music Festival in May. You may not hear the latest, slickest chart-toppers, but you won't miss them, not with performers such as blues performers Blind Mississippi Morris and Roscoe Gordon, Mississippi-bred folksinger Kate Campbell, rockabilly legends Eddie Bond and Billy Lee Riley, and the Last Chance Jug Band. Best of all, the performances are all free.

Southern Heritage Classic
Liberty Bowl Memorial Stadium
(901) 398–6655
www.classicmemphis.com
This mid-September football contest between archrivals Tennessee State University and Jackson State University fills the Liberty Bowl and spills over into one of the biggest party weekends of the year. Alumni of these historically black colleges and other football fans pour into the city for the Saturday-night game and other activities, ranging from concerts and tailgate parties to the Ed "Too Tall" Jones Golf Classic and the Classic Fashions & Brunch

event. The weekend is also an opportunity for informal reunions of the schools' alumni, many of whom live in the region. Many of the events are fund-raisers that funnel tens of thousands of dollars to the two schools and to charities, so very few of them are free. A highlight is the Dr. Pepper High School Battle of the Bands, which features top high-school show bands and their dance routines. During the game's halftime show, the contest moves from football to music as the JSU Aristocrat of Bands and TSU Sonic Boom of the South strut their stuff. Tickets for the game range from $10 to $30 for box seats.

The Mid-South Fair
Mid-South Fairgrounds
(901) 274–8800
www.midsouthfair.com
The Mid-South Fair, a Memphis tradition since 1856, attracts about half a million people each fall, as Memphians and country-come-to-town visitors alike pour in to check out carnival rides, pronto pups, and other junk-food classics, exhibitions, concerts, and rodeo events. The fair starts in late September and runs for 11 days, usually coinciding with the welcome arrival of cooler weather.

There's truly something for everyone at the fair, which has more than 60 rides, 150 food vendors, 200 exhibitors, youth programs that include 4H competitions and the largest amateur youth talent contest in the world, the Championship Rodeo, and concerts by name performers who have included Gladys Knight, Kansas, and the Marshall Tucker Band. Many go for the rides and the dazzling array of carnival favorites such as candied apples and funnel cakes, whereas others are there to compete in livestock shows, homemade-ice-cream contests, and other events. Agriculture continues to be the backbone of the fair, so you'll find livestock exhibits, sheep-dog trials, farm-and-garden-produce exhibits, and horticulture educational programs. The fair takes place at the 176-acre fairgrounds, bound by Central Avenue, East Parkway, Southern Avenue and Hollywood. Parking is free and can be accessed from all sides except from Eastern Parkway.

Insiders' Tip

If you're inclined to shop early for Christmas gifts, do what many locals do and shop at the two October arts-and-crafts fairs, Arts in the Park and Pink Palace Museum Crafts Fair. You'll find unique jewelry, pottery, paintings, handmade children's toys, and other items that make great gifts.

Admission is $7.00 for adults (48 inches and taller), $3.00 for children (under 48 inches), and free for children 3 and under. Ask about Wristband Days, when in addition to the admission you can also pay $14 for a wristband that admits you to unlimited rides.

October

Pink Palace Museum Crafts Fair
Audubon Park
(901) 320–6320
www.artsandcraftsfestival.org

To the casual observer, this festival and Arts in the Park, which follows two weeks later, seem pretty similar: two big arts-and-crafts fairs in East Memphis with fair food and some music. But Memphians see them as very diverse, given their different beginnings. This fair was the original event, a big, yearly fund-raiser for the Pink Palace Museum System, with its focus on crafts, whereas Arts in the Park, which started in Midtown's Overton Park, is oriented more toward fine art and performances.

This four-day fair, a favorite since 1973, draws at least 30,000 people each year. Held the first weekend in October and organized by the Friends of the Pink

Palace, it features craftspersons from all over the country selling one-of-a-kind jewelry, fused and blown glass, pottery, and other handmade goods. You can watch artisans making baskets, spinning and weaving, turning wood, and demonstrating other crafts. If you have a sweet tooth, don't miss the Friends' Donut Tent, featuring fresh, homemade donuts.

Advance tickets are $5.00 for adults, $3.00 for seniors, and $2.00 for children. Admission at the door is $6.00 for adults, $4.00 for seniors, and $3.00 for children. Two-day adult passes are available for $8.00 in advance, $10.00 at the door. Parking is $2.00.

Arts in the Park
Memphis Botanic Garden
(901) 761–1278
www.memphisartsfestival.org

The three-day festival is held the second weekend in October. Arts in the Park started out as a small event in Overton Park but quickly outgrew the location, necessitating a move out east (to the chagrin of many midtowners).

Its organizer, Memphis Arts Festival, differentiates the event as the only fine-arts festival celebrating the visual and performing arts, with a focus on fine arts. You'll find booths for around 150 artists, including talented locals, and more than 80 performances by the Memphis Ballet and others. Local restaurants set up booths to sell their specialties in the Taste of This Town section, and participatory activities range from T-shirt decorating for children to ballroom-dance lessons.

Admission is free on Friday, and tickets at the door costs $10 for adults and $4.00 for children. Advance tickets are $7.00 for adults and $3.00 for children, students, and seniors on Saturday and Sunday. Two-day passes are available in advance (but not at the door) at $9.00 for adults and $4.00 for children, students, and seniors.

November

Hilton U.S. Open Racquetball Championships
The Racquet Club of Memphis

Every November The Racquet Club of Memphis provides space on center court for a glass racquetball court to be erected, and the faithful fill the stands to watch the biggest tournament of its kind anywhere, with more than 200 pros and 400 to 600 amateurs doing battle. Tickets are $10 to $20 for each session, or there are packages that cover the whole shebang. The United States Racquetball Association is in charge of the event, so for ticket info and other questions, call them in Colorado at (719) 635-5396.

December

AXA Liberty Bowl Football Classic
Liberty Bowl Stadium
(901) 795-7700
This annual matchup between the winners of the Conference USA and the Mountain West Conference draws thousands of college-football fans to Memphis in late December to cheer on their team. Okay, it's not the Sugar Bowl or one of the more prestigious football contests that take place around the New Year, and it rarely fills Liberty Bowl Stadium, but it's a great party for fans of the two teams. The Liberty Bowl originated in Philadelphia, which explains the name, and was moved to Memphis in 1965, when its founder decided the Northeast was too cold. This bowl game made history in 1982, when legendary University of Alabama head coach Paul "Bear" Bryant ended his career with a game against University of Illinois. *Note:* If the University of Memphis Tigers, a Conference USA Team, ever make it to the Liberty Bowl, expect the party of the century.

Beale Street New Year's Eve Celebration
Beale Street
(901) 526-0110
www.bealestreet.com
On New Year's Eve Beale Street is to Memphis what Times Square is to New York

Beale Street is the place to be on New Year's Eve, as hundreds gather to ring in another year.
PHOTO: PERFORMA ENTERTAINMENT REAL ESTATE, INC.

City, namely, the place where crowds gather to bring in the New Year. It's a huge, rowdy outdoor party, whether there's an organized event or not, and revelers also can buy wristbands that will admit them to most of the clubs on Beale Street. A wristband is often a smart investment, given the cool temperatures at that time of year. During some years sponsors have set up a stage, on which an official Countdown on Beale program takes place.

Casinos

In less than a decade, Tunica County, Mississippi, has grown into the third-largest gaming destination in the United States, second only to Las Vegas and Atlantic City. Ten casinos operate in this rural county 30 miles south of Memphis, including Grand Casino, Harrah's, and Sam's Town. They offer 24-hour-a day Las Vegas–style gaming with no limits, 40 different restaurants, their own luxury hotels, and amenities that include nightly live entertainment, PGA golf courses, and health spas.

Locals still rub their eyes when they behold the mini-Las Vegas in their midst, with its high-rise hotels and neon lights. After all, until the casinos started flocking to Robinsonville in the early and mid-1990s, Tunica County was an expanse of cotton and soybean fields, with a handful of restaurants and a rich blues history but little else to recommend it to visitors.

The situation changed, however, when authorities voted to allow riverboat gambling, and Splash Casino opened in October 1992, a few miles south of the present-day cluster of casinos. When locals and Memphians flocked here—standing in line and paying a cover to come in and lay their money down—it got the attention of the major casino operators, who quickly moved in. To date the casinos have invested more than $3 billion in their Tunica County operations.

The present clientele is a combination of locals, Memphians, and out-of-towners, both people who drive from their hometowns and those on group tours. The crowd is pretty consistent from casino to casino, and during the week it consists mostly of retirees. On the weekends there's usually a good crowd, with a steady stream of traffic pouring in from Memphis. Some come in for the evening or the day; others spend the night in one of the 6,000 hotel rooms in Tunica County.

The differences among the casinos lie in their decor, comp policies, size, and number of slot machines and tables; otherwise, they're pretty similar, with the same games—blackjack, craps, and roulette—and the same types of slot machines. Some cater to the lower end of the market with $2.00 and $3.00 blackjack and penny slot machines. The electronic din of hundreds of slot machines all jangling at the same time is standard as well.

Players are always attracted to casinos by the chance they'll win big, but the chances of that are, in fact, slim. The odds are in the casinos' favor, both at the table games and the slot machines, and the longer you play, the greater your chance of losing. The best approach is to decide before you go how much you can realistically afford to lose, then to walk away once you spend that amount. Some advise stricter rules: Leave your credit cards behind to avoid the temptation to continue beyond your budgeted amount or to stop playing when you're ahead.

Each casino issues comp cards, which it uses to calculate how much time and money you've spent there. Free meals, hotel rooms, and other comps are based on those amounts, although drinks are free to anyone who's playing. Points can also be used in gift shops, or some casinos will cash out the points. You can ask the casino's hostess about their policies (for example, how much do you have to play to get a free meal).

Another draw is live entertainment. The casinos bring in a variety of musicians, comedians, and other entertainers, from Mr. Las Vegas himself, Wayne Newton, to Beale Street headliner Ruby Wilson. Although much of the entertainment consists of acts on the casino circuit, others are touring performers who in years past would have gone to Memphis instead of Tunica. The casinos advertise lavishly in Memphis newspapers, so it's not hard to find out who's playing down in the Delta and how to get tickets.

Each casino also has at least three restaurants, including a buffet and an upscale eatery, and gives away meals to players under certain circumstances. Reservations are generally recommended for fine-dining restaurants only.

The hotels at the casinos are fairly new and are a favorite among Memphians for a quick weekend or overnight getaway. They generally fill up on the weekends, including Thursday, so booking ahead is a must. If you're venturing out from Memphis to see the Mississippi Delta, you might want to make Tunica an overnight stop. Tunica County is in the heart of the Mississippi Delta, which produced the blues and many of its legends including Muddy Waters and Robert Johnson. It's just half an hour away from Clarksdale, where you'll find the Delta Blues Museum and Madidi, a restaurant owned by Mississippi-born actor Morgan Freeman. Other Mississippi day-trip destinations are nearby, notably, Oxford, Holly Springs, and Tupelo. (See the Day Trips and Weekend Getaways chapter for more information.)

Remember, if you spend a lot of time in the casinos, you won't see much of the Delta, as the gaming halls have no windows, no clocks, or anything else to distract you from the gaming tables and slot machines. Often gaming patrons never even see the Mississippi River, which is less than a mile from the casinos. The recent addition of Tunica River Front Park next to Fitzgeralds, with a visitor center and aquarium, makes it easier for visitors to appreciate the river.

To get here take U.S. Highway 61 from Memphis. You can get here by taking I-240 to I-55 North, then turning onto the Highway 61 South exit, or take Third Street from downtown Memphis going south (it will eventually turn into Highway 61). The casino exits are well marked. Once here, you can take a shuttle between casinos for $1.00 per ride.

For more information about Tunica and its casinos, call the Tunica Convention and Visitors Bureau at (888) 4TUNICA or check out www.tunicamiss.org.

Here's a description of what the Tunica casinos have to offer in terms of gaming, dining, lodging, and amenities.

The blackjack tables are popular spots at the Tunica casinos, just south of Memphis.
PHOTO: TUNICA CONVENTION AND VISITORS BUREAU

Bally's Casino Tunica
1450 Bally's Boulevard (off Casino Center Boulevard), Robinsonville, Miss.
(800) 382-2559
www.ballysms.com

One of the first casinos built in Tunica, Bally's has more than 1,200 slots and 40 tables as well as free live performances in an entertainment center that's built into an authentic grain silo. It also houses Bonkerz, the only comedy club in Tunica. Bally's has a country feel: The decor is down-home barn on the outside, with a rustic Delta theme inside, complete with exposed wooden beams and 1800s-style wallpaper. Gaming options include $2.00 and $3.00 blackjack tables. In terms of amenities Bally's has three restaurants, which include a buffet restaurant and a snack bar, and 230 hotel rooms, each with a whirlpool tub and minirefrigerator, and a swimming pool for guests.

Fitzgeralds Casino/Hotel
711 Lucky Lane, Robinsonville, Miss.
(800) 766-5825
www.fitzgeraldstunica.com

This is one casino where you can get a good look at the Mississippi River. Fitzgeralds, the only one overlooking the river, touts the luck of the Irish to draw visitors. It's a favorite among retirees, who flock to play the penny and nickel slots and $2.00 and $3.00 blackjack. The casino is built to resemble an Irish castle, with a whimsical ceiling painting of clouds, castles, and leprechauns in the gaming hall. The 500-room hotel is a modern style, with an indoor swimming pool and exercise room. It has four restaurants, including a sports pub and steakhouse, and indoor parking, a welcome amenity during the summer hot-car season.

Gold Strike Casino Resort
1010 Casino Center Boulevard, Robinsonville, Miss.
(888) 245-7829
www.goldstrikemississippi.com

With its marble floors, brass, and elaborate decor, Gold Strike draws the usual crowd as well as the high rollers. Its 31-story luxury hotel tower, with 1,200 rooms and suites, wins raves from visitors, who consider it to be one of the best. Players enjoy

the 1,400 slot machines and the 40-plus game tables. Its 800-seat, state-of-the-art Millenium Theater attracts national acts such as magician Brett Daniels and Tony Bennett. Restaurant choices range from a food court with McDonald's and Little Caesar's to its Chicago Steakhouse.

Grand Casino
13615 Old Highway 61 North, Robinsonville, Miss.
(800) 946-4946
www.grandtunica.com

Grand has the distinction of being both the largest casino in Tunica County and the closest one to Memphis. Four gaming areas—each with a different theme—feature 3,100 slot machines and 110 game tables for players. The amenities are more extensive here than at any other place in the area: Eight restaurants (plus two poolside cabanas in summer) include two steakhouses and an Italian cafe, three hotels offer more than 1,300 luxurious rooms, and an RV park provides 200 spaces for guests who bring their homes with them. Its 18-hole Cottonwoods Golf Course, designed by Hale Irwin, offers tee times as well as a golf school. Its Willows Trap, Skeet & Sporting Clays allows sportsmen to shoot a variety of targets in a controlled environment, one of the few places like it in the region. Live entertainment at its event center includes such acts as Patti LaBelle and Alabama. The Grand also has its own convention center and a child-care facility.

Harrah's Casino & Hotel
1100 Casino Strip Boulevard, Robinsonville, Miss.
(800) 427-7247
www.harrahs.com

Harrah's, a big name in casinos, offers 50,000 square feet of slot machines and game tables at its Tunica property, as well as 200 hotel rooms and four restaurants, including Harrah's Steakhouse & Grill. Its 1,400 slot machines offer nickel, quarter, or $1.00 slots. There are 20 game tables as well. Harrah's, in partnership with Hollywood and Sam's Town, also offers River Bend Links golf course, a links-style course designed by Clyde Johnson.

Horseshoe casino, one of the 10 world-class casinos in nearby Tunica, is a great favorite among Memphians. PHOTO: TUNICA CONVENTION AND VISITORS BUREAU

Hollywood Casino Tunica
1150 Casino Strip Boulevard, Robinsonville, Miss.
(800) 871-0711
www.hollywoodcasinotunica.com

This casino has plenty of star quality, with 54,000 square feet of gaming (1500-plus slots, 50 game tables) that includes $2.00 and $3.00 blackjack. You'll even find great movie memorabilia, including the DeLorean car from *Back to the Future.* Three restaurants include the ornate Fairbanks Steakhouse, and the Safari Bar features live entertainment, with acts as diverse as David Allan Coe and the Dick Jergens Orchestra. For accommodations Hollywood has a hotel with 500-plus rooms and an RV park with 123 spaces, and there's an indoor pool for guests to enjoy. Golf aficionados will enjoy the River Bend Links golf course, a challenging links-style course designed by Clyde Johnson, which Hollywood operates in partnership with Harrah's and Sam's Town.

Horseshoe Casino & Hotel
1020 Casino Center Drive, Robinsonville, Miss.
(800) 303-7463
www.horseshoecasinos.com

Horseshoe is a big favorite among Memphians, who rave about the friendly ambiance, the generous comp policies, and its steakhouse. Expanded and refurbished to the tune of $40 million in 2001, Horseshoe now has more than 2,000 slots and 70 tables as well as a new Asian restaurant, Yasmin's. The casino caters to high rollers as well as the more general player. Of all the casinos this is the one that pays tribute to the blues heritage of its Mississippi Delta location, with a tiny blues museum featuring memorabilia. Its Bluesville entertainment complex is a big draw, featuring rock and blues acts that have included Art Garfunkel and Kenny Chesney. Horseshoe's 24-story hotel tower has 500 suites for guests.

Isle of Capri Casino and Entertainment Resort
1600 Isle of Capri Boulevard,
Robinsonville, Miss.
(800) 843-4753
www.isleofcapri.com

This casino has a Caribbean flavor, with indoor waterfalls, a palm tree, and bright colors. More intimate than most of the other casinos, Isle of Capri has about 900 slots and

15 game tables, including penny slots as well as $3.00 blackjack. A recent $14-million expansion in 2000 added 227 hotel rooms, many of them deluxe suites, as well as its Paradise Entertainment Center. There you'll find two theaters that feature flashy, Las Vegas–style musical-production shows.

Sam's Town Tunica
1477 Casino Strip Boulevard, Robinsonville, Miss.
(800) 456-0711
www.samstowntunica.com

Expect to see some cowboy boots here. Although Sam's Town retains the exterior look of an old West town, its interior was updated to the tune of $21 million in 2000, replacing the rustic look with a more polished ambiance. The gaming area consists of two floors with 1,500 slots and 60 tables. Sam's Town is known for its country flair, both in the music and general ambiance. A

favorite among its restaurants is Corky's BBQ, where you can get your Memphis barbecue fix. The hotel has 850 rooms and suites, and a new RV park has 60 spaces and plenty of amenities. Sam's Town gets some of the hottest acts around, including James Brown and Merle Haggard, at its 1,600-seat arena. It also operates River Bend Links golf course in partnership with two other casinos, an amenity that's popular with golf-playing visitors.

Sheraton Casino & Hotel
1107 Casino Center Drive, Robinsonville, Miss.
(800) 391–3777

This casino resembles a Tudor mansion on the outside, with 31,000 square feet of gaming on the inside that includes 1,300 slots and 50 game tables. The Sheraton prides itself on its full-service spa and luxurious accommodations, with a whirlpool bath in every room.

Day Trips and Weekend Getaways

We include this chapter not because there isn't enough to do in Memphis. We believe the city has enough attractions, nightlife, and good food to keep any visitor entertained and happy, but if you're in the mood for a road trip, there are plenty of excursions you can take to experience rural and small-town life in the Deep South.

You can venture down to the Mississippi Delta, to see firsthand where the blues were born, and across the river to Helena, Arkansas, home of the "King Biscuit Time" radio show and annual blues festival. Elvis fans may want to visit Tupelo for a look at The King's birthplace, with a stop in Holly Springs to visit the shrine assembled by the world's most committed Elvis fan. Oxford, Mississippi, where writer William Faulkner lived and worked, is the quintessential small Mississippi town, a favorite day trip among Memphians (and especially Ole Miss fans, as Oxford is home to the University of Mississippi). West Tennessee has plenty to offer, including Civil War battlefields and the birthplace of *Roots* author Alex Haley.

If you like gambling, you can check out 10 world-class casinos in Tunica County, Mississippi, all within about a 45-minute drive from Memphis. (See the Casinos chapter for details.)

These destinations are within two hours' drive of the city. If you wish to venture farther for the weekend, Hot Springs, Arkansas, is a favorite getaway for Memphians. At this historic resort, you can bathe in the natural hot-spring water at bathhouse spas, enjoy live horse racing in season, and tour lavish restored bathhouses dating from the 1920s.

Hikers, fishermen, and others who like the great outdoors can learn more about state parks and other getaway options in the Parks and Recreation chapter.

Birthplace of the Blues

Head south from Memphis on the legendary Highway 61 (now four lanes all the way through Clarksdale), and you'll be in the heart of the Mississippi Delta, the land where the blues were born. From downtown Memphis take Third Street to the south, which eventually turns into U.S. 61; otherwise, take I–40 to Interstate 55 North, and take the exit to Highway 61 South. Once you leave the city, you'll drive past cotton fields (you'll actually see the white stuff on the plants in late summer and fall), plantation houses, sharecropper shacks, and simple African American churches. (The casinos at Tunica are a recent development.) These were the fields where workers' hollers gradually evolved into the blues as we know them, and many of the greatest

bluesmen in the world once lived and worked in the fields you're seeing. (See Memphis Music chapter for a full account.) If you're looking for the legendary crossroads, where blues-great Robert Johnson made his mythical deal with the devil to get a guitar, you'll find many intersections claiming to be The One. A likely candidate is where Highway 61 crosses Highway 49, the road that takes you across the Mississippi River into Helena, Arkansas. It's about 75 miles from Memphis to Clarksdale and about 65 miles to Helena, home to the "King Biscuit Time" blues show.

Blues fans may want to time their visit to coincide with one of the Delta's annual blues festivals, including King Biscuit Blues Festival (870–338–8798, www.kingbiscuit fest.org), one of the world's largest blues festival, which takes place in October in

231

Helena. There's also the August Sunflower River and Gospel Festival in Clarksdale (662-627-6820, www.sunflowerfest.org), or the Mississippi Delta Blues and Heritage Festival in Greenville (888-812-5837, www.deltablues.org). Book accommodations as early as possible in the local area or expect to drive back to Memphis after the festival.

Clarksdale, Mississippi

If you're looking to experience the raw feel of the Mississippi Delta, this town of 20,000 is the place. As you approach Clarksdale, take the right hand turn to stay on U.S. 61 (also called State Street) as it meanders through town. Look for signs to the **Delta Blues Museum,** 1 Delta Blues Alley (662-627-6820, www.deltabluesmuseum.com), a good first stop in your tour. The museum, established by the Carnegie Library after members of ZZ Top and other musicians raised the necessary money, is housed in the Clarksdale railroad depot (a separate building houses the archives, which also are open to the public). You enter the museum proper through double screen doors, which every Delta country store once had, and into a rustic exhibit space. The museum re-creates the plantation lifestyle that produced the blues, with old photos, guitars, and harmonicas that belonged to blues greats including John Lee Hooker and Sonny Boy Williamson II. You'll also find the original headstone from the grave of Mississippi Fred McDowell, the sign from the Three Forks juke joint where Robert Johnson played and was poisoned, and the shack where Muddy Waters lived (with a life-size statue of the man inside). From the displays you learn exactly where W.C. Handy heard the blues for the first time and the name of the Delta plantation where locals say the blues originated. The museum is open Monday through Saturday. Admission is $6.50 for adults and $3.00 for children ages 6–12 (this may seem steep for a small museum, but think of it as your contribution to keeping the blues alive). The museum director or other staff can tell you about live music, both at the museum and in area clubs, taking place

during your visit. Just west of the blues museum (to the left as you leave the building) is a former grocery store/cotton seed company that has been converted into **Ground Zero Blues Club,** 0 Delta Blues Alley (662-621-9009, www.groundzerobluesclub.com). Co-owned by actor Morgan Freeman and named for Clarksdale's position as "ground zero for the blues," the lofty, old-fashioned club serves home-cooked plate meals, as well as burgers and such for lunch during the week and for dinner on Saturday nights. The big draw, though, is live music, which cranks up about 10:00 P.M. on weekends.

Another claim to fame is that playwright Tennessee Williams lived in Clarksdale as a child with his grandfather, the Reverend Walter Dakin. You can see the brick church, St. George's Episcopal Church (106 Sharkey Avenue), where Reverend Dakin was rector for many years, and may recognize some of the names you see in the area from Williams's plays.

Clarksdale food options include Abe's Bar B Q, U.S. 61 at U.S. 49 (662-624-0047), one of the Delta's oldest barbecue joints where you can get also get hot tamales. Farther south on U.S. 61 is Chamoun's Rest Haven restaurant, a diner that features Southern home cooking, Lebanese specialties, and great homemade meringue pie. For fine dining that seems far too elegant for a place like Clarksdale, have dinner at Madidi, 164 Delta at Second Street (662-627-7770), a swank restaurant that serves dishes such as herbed rack of lamb and pecan-coated fried oysters. Like Ground Zero, it's partly owned by actor Morgan Freeman, who frequently stops in when he's not filming or making appearances out of town.

As for accommodations Clarksdale has some chain hotels on U.S. 61 such as Hampton Inn (662-627-9292) and Days Inn (662-624-4591). The most unusual accommodations are found at Hopson Plantation's **Shack Up Inn** (662-624-8329, www.shackupinn.com), where you can stay in a sharecropper shack, complete with the corrugated tin roof as well as modern amenities such as indoor plumbing, which the sharecroppers never had. The shacks are near the former plantation commissary, now a blues club with a bar, occasional live blues music, and errant hours. It's worth checking out for the cool old signs, cash register, and other antique stuff, but it's sometimes reserved for private parties.

For more information about Clarksdale, call (800) 626-3764 or check out www.clarksdale.com.

Note to steak lovers: You can't be this close and not check out the legendary grocery-store-turned-steak-joint in Greenville, Mississippi, **Doe's Eat Place,** 502 Nelson (662-334-3315). Greenville is about 85 miles as you continue north on U.S. 61; then go west on U.S. 82. You may be eating in the kitchen, but it will be the steak of your dreams. Be sure to try the hot tamales, too. Reservations are recommended. If you spend the night, the Greenville Suites and Inn (662-332-6900) next to the levee is a good bet or try the Hampton Inn or Holiday Inn Express on U.S. 82. Literary buffs will want to visit McCormick Book Inn (825 South Main, 662-332-5068) to learn about the many writers from this river town, including historian Shelby Foote and novelist Walker Percy. For more information about Greenville, check out www.thedelta.org.

Helena, Arkansas

Incorporated in 1833, this small, historic river town caught the eye of Mark Twain for its picturesque perch above the river. To get here take U.S. 61 from Memphis, then go west on U.S. 49, going about 10 miles past the Isle of Capri casino and across the Mississippi River bridge into Arkansas. Although you may want to first take a detour to the Visitors Information Center, to get to historic Helena, turn right at the end of the bridge. Once in town, check out **The Delta Cultural Center,** 141 Cherry Street (870-338-4350, www.deltacultural-center.com), where staff can answer your questions about the area (admission is free). The center is actually two buildings, one of which is housed in a former railroad depot. In that regard it's like Clarksdale, but it differs in that the exhibits are new and modern looking, not rustic in a Delta sort of way. The depot's exhibits give the history of the area, including photos and descriptions of life on the river. The second building, a storefront on Cherry Street, is a visitor center with temporary art exhibitions as well as a permanent exhibit highlighting blues musicians who came from or passed through the Arkansas Delta. One of its eccentricities is that the center omits bluesmen without Arkansas connections, so you won't find much about Muddy Waters or Howlin' Wolf. The main attraction, though, is the "King Biscuit Time" radio show, broadcast from the visitor center every day at 12:15 P.M. by Sonny Payne. The blues show, broadcast from local station from KFFA since the 1940s, launched the careers of Sonny Boy Williamson and Robert Jr. Lockwood and brought blues music to many Deltans, including B.B. King and others who went on to become blues greats. Although there's occasionally live music, as in the program's early days, today Payne usually spins CDs and spins yarns during the half-hour show. You can hear the program at www.kingbiscuit.com. Now in his 70s, Payne likes mingling with visitors, and he might even invite you to be on the radio show. King Biscuit also lends its name to the annual blues festival, which has grown into the third-largest blues festival around with a who's-who of performers. The 2001 lineup included Robert Jr. Lockwood, Sam Carr, Alvin "Youngblood" Hart, Pinetop Perkins, and Marcia Ball. Best of all, it's free. You can see footage of the most recent festival at the center.

Elsewhere downtown are antiques and gifts shops to browse, as well as Bubba's Blues Corner, 105 Cherry (870-338-3501), a shop inside a shop that buys and sells blues records and CDs.

One of the more celebrated options for food is Pasquale's Tamales, a company that makes and ships its homemade tamales all over the country. You can sample the tamales as well as muffalettas, spaghetti and meatballs, and other items at its restaurant, situated next to the Delta Cultural Center depot building (870-338-6722). A few blocks up the main drag is Cherry Street Deli, a deli-pizzeria (420 Cherry Street, 870-817-7706) that's decorated with vintage toys. For barbecue try Armstrong's Pit Barbecue (303 Valley Drive, 870-338-7746). Turn west onto Perry Street, and you'll see it across from Kroger between Helena and West Helena.

When it comes to accommodations, Helena has an embarrassment of riches in the form of antiques-filled, historic bed-and-breakfast inns, all with large verandas, private baths in the rooms, and full breakfasts. The Edwardian Inn, 317 Biscoe (870-338-9155 or 800-598-4749, www.bbonline.com/ar/edwardian) is a 1904 Colonial Revival mansion that features quartersawn oak woodwork on the interior. Magnolia Hill, 608 Perry Street (870-338-6874, www.bbonline.com/ar/magnoliahill), is a Queen Anne Victorian home with original fireplaces that at one time served as a club for World War II soldiers. Foxglove, 229 Beech (870-338-9391, www.bbonline.com/ar/foxglove), is a 1900 home with beautiful interior woodwork that overlooks the city of Helena from Crowley's Ridge (children not allowed). Stone Ridge Inn, 1202 Perry Street (870-338-9390), is actually two turn-of-the-century homes with lavishly furnished rooms, some with private sitting rooms and kitchens. These are just a few of more than 30 Helena homes found on the National Register of Historic Places. You can also get a free tour of some homes, including the Pillow-Thompson House, 718 Perry Street (870-338-8535, www.pccua.cc.ar.us/pillowthompson).

If bed-and-breakfast inns aren't your thing, try the Palm Terrace or Coral Reef hotels at Isle of Capri casino (888-782-9582), across the river in Lula, Mississippi, or the Best Western Inn on U.S. 49 (870-572-2592) in neighboring West Helena.

For more information about Helena, get in touch with the Helena Tourism Commission at (877) 899-3263.

Elvis's Birthplace and Mississippi Towns

If you drive southeast from Memphis out U.S. 78, the four-lane highway to Holly Springs and Tupelo, you'll discover the hilly terrain of Mississippi's piney-woods area. It's a marked contrast to the flat farmland of the Mississippi Delta, and Mississippians will tell you that people from the hills are a different breed from the party-loving Delta folk. Holly Springs is the closest of the towns we list here, about a 35- to 45-minute drive from Memphis, whereas Tupelo is about 100 miles from Memphis. Oxford is about a 30-minute drive east of Holly Springs. It would make for a long day to try to see all three towns in one day, but it can be done if you plan carefully. The towns form a triangle, so once you get to Holly Springs, you can continue east on U.S. 78 to Tupelo, from Tupelo west on U.S. 6 to Oxford, then from Oxford back to Holly Springs via U.S. 7 and U.S. 78 back to Memphis. Alternatively, from Oxford you can go east on U.S. 6 to I-55, then north to Memphis. Of course, you can choose to concentrate on one or two of these towns or make it an overnight trip, particularly if you want to stay in one of the bed-and-breakfast inns in the area.

Tupelo

Probably every person in the world knows that Tupelo is the birthplace of Elvis Presley, who lived there until moving with his parents to Memphis at age 13. Tupelo, a vibrant town of 35,000, also has other things going for it, including a furniture-making industry that's one of the largest in the world and a convention arena (BancorpSouth Center) that seats 10,000 people. To go straight to the Presley house from U.S. 78, you pass a number of Tupelo exits and take the Veterans Boulevard exit and follow the signs to the **Elvis Presley birthplace and museum,** 306 Elvis Presley Drive (662-841-1245). The house is a tiny two-room shotgun shack that Elvis's father, Vernon Presley, built himself for $180, which he borrowed for materials. Elvis was born there on January 8, 1935. You'll see a wood-burning stove, an icebox, and furnishings of the era, although none is original to the house. Behind the house is a museum with a collection of memorabilia from the collection of Janelle McComb, a family friend of the Presleys. You find notes written by Elvis and childhood photos as well as photos, outfits, and mementos from his rise to fame through his Las Vegas days. There's also a large gift shop there. Just over from the museum is a modern chapel, built with funds from Elvis fans and dedicated two years after his death. Admission to the home is $2.00 for adults and $1.00 for children 7–12; admission to the museum is $5.00 for adults and $2.50 for children. If you're hungry and don't want to venture far, check out Johnnie's Drive-In Bar-B-Q, a 1950s-style place that serves barbecue sandwiches and other fare. When you leave the birthplace, turn left onto Veterans Boulevard, and look for the drive-in at the corner of Main Street. For a map with other Elvis points of interest, including his schools and the hardware where his mom bought him a toy guitar, go to the Tupelo Convention and Visitors Bureau at 399 East Main Street at Franklin Street (662–841–6521, 800–533–0611). Main Street is also U.S. 6, the highway that links Tupelo to Oxford.

As for other attractions, you can continue west on Main Street/U.S. 6 to check out the **Oren F. Dunn Museum** (662–841–6438), a modest but interesting town museum with a mishmash of displays and artifacts. You'll find a 1949 bookmobile, a space suit worn on the *Apollo 15* mission, and other items related to the U.S. space program, Civil War artifacts, and a dogtrot house built in 1870. Admission is $1.00 for visitors 5 years and older. There's talk of moving the museum, currently housed at James L. Ballard Park off Highway 6 West, to a new location near the Elvis birthplace, so call before heading over.

The city's newest attraction is the Tupelo Automobile Museum, 399 East Main Street, set to open in late 2002 with 100 restored classic and antique cars from a local collector. Few specifics were available as this book went to press, so contact the Convention and Visitors Bureau, which has its offices near the museum site.

Tupelo is home to one of Mississippi's top bed-and-breakfast inns, **The Mockingbird Inn,** 305 North Gloster Street (662–841–0286, www.bbonline.com/ms/mockingbird). Situated in the heart of the city within walking distance of several restaurants and across the street from Milam

School, where Elvis attended the sixth and seventh grades, The Mockingbird Inn features seven rooms, each with a geographic theme. The Africa room has rattan furniture, mosquito netting, and faux zebra skins; the Venice room has a tapestry of Venetian gondolas and European styling—you get the idea. A hot breakfast is served, and nonalcoholic beverages are available throughout the day. No children under 12.

Other accommodation options include chains such as Ramada Inn and Hampton Inn.

The best restaurants are on or near Gloster Street. There are two fine-dining establishments within walking distance of the Mockingbird Inn, the best of which is Park Heights at 825 West Jefferson (662–842–5665). Around the corner is Gloster 205, at 205 North Gloster (662–842–7205). Both are open for dinner.

Other dining options in Tupelo include Vanelli's, 1302 North Gloster Street (662–844–4410), a large family-owned restaurant/pizzeria that serves lunch and dinner. It's kid-friendly, with a huge menu that has something for everyone. For lunch try Harvey's, a bustling downtown eatery at 424 South Gloster (662–842–6763).

While in Tupelo you can also check out the historic **Natchez Trace Parkway,** which goes from Nashville to Natchez, Mississippi. This famed highway was originally an Indian trail, which two centuries ago, became a key route for early pioneers, travelers, and post riders carrying mail between the two cities. Unfortunately for those early travelers, it was popular among robbers, too. The parkway fell into disuse with the advent of steamboat travel, but now it is part of the National Park system. For more information contact the Natchez Trace Parkway Headquarters and Visitors Center at Tupelo (662–680–4025, 800–305–7417).

Oxford

This college town, with its charming square and stately homes, has become one of the South's most celebrated small towns, and not just among University of Mississippi fans. In 2001 it was named by

The sidewalks around the main square of Oxford, Mississippi, are favorite places to relax and shop.
PHOTO: OXFORD TOURISM COUNCIL

Money magazine as the best place in the South to retire. It was also home to William Faulkner, the novelist who won the Nobel Prize in literature in 1950. Many of his novels were set in Yoknapatawpha County, a fictional stand-in for Lafayette County, where Oxford is the county seat. You'll probably want to see Faulkner's home, Rowan Oak, but also spend plenty of time at Courthouse Square, where you'll find great restaurants, shops, and Square Books, an outstanding independent bookstore. Unless you want to share your experience of Oxford with hundreds of rowdy Ole Miss fans, you should avoid football weekends in the fall.

To get to the square, take the downtown/South Lamar exit off Highway 6 and stay on Lamar, which runs right into the handsome, white Lafayette County Courthouse, with its statue of a Confederate soldier facing south. On the east side of the square is the Oxford Tourism Council (111 Courthouse Square, 662-234-4680, 800-758-9177), where you can pick up a map and brochures and ask about tours. If you're interested in Faulkner, ask for the *Faulkner Country* brochure.

On the south side of the square, you'll find **Square Books,** with its extensive selection of Southern literature and other fiction and nonfiction. Go up the stairs, lined with photos of writers who have done book signings here, and you'll find a quiet cafe, where you can linger over coffee, espresso, dessert, or a light meal. Its upstairs porch is nice during good weather. There are plenty of other shops to browse on the square as well.

Take South Lamar and then go right onto Old Taylor Road to visit **Rowan Oak,** the antebellum home Faulkner purchased in 1930 and occupied until his death in 1962. He wrote some of his most acclaimed novels here, and you can still see the outline for his novel *A Fable* scrawled on his study wall. The home is open Tuesday through Sunday; call ahead for hours (662-234-3284).

To see the **Ole Miss campus,** take South Lamar from the square, turn onto University Avenue, and you'll drive through the main part of campus. Ole Miss, incidentally, has one of the world's most extensive collections of blues recordings and related materials at Farley Hall,

but tourists only have access to a bit of memorabilia.

As for dining in Oxford, **Courthouse Square** offers many of the best options, particularly City Grocery (152 Courthouse Square, 662-232-8080), an urbane restaurant with a good wine list and a changing menu that includes imaginatively prepared fresh fish, quail, and its famous shrimp and grits. This is a hands-down favorite among local gourmands. (Upstairs at City Grocery is a casual bar, a good hangout for happy hour or later.) Another uptown option is Downtown Grill (upstairs at 110 Courthouse Square, 662-234-2559), which features a piano bar overlooking the square. On the more casual side is Old Venice Pizza Company (1112 Van Buren, 662-236-6872), which serves gourmet handmade pizzas; Proud Larry's (211 South Lamar, 662-236-0050), a bar just south of the square serves good sandwiches; and Bottletree Bakery (923 Van Buren, 662-236-5000), an excellent bakery, also serves breakfast, lunch, and specialty coffees. Steak lovers might want to seek out Doe's Eat Place (1536 University, 662-236-9003), a satellite of the original Doe's in Greenville, Mississippi. Its steaks are legendary. A short drive to the country brings you to the Yocona River Inn (842 Highway 334, 662-234-2464), a former general store that's now a fine-dining restaurant.

As for accommodations there are a number of quaint bed-and-breakfast inns. The most popular are two restored antebellum mansions: The Oliver-Britt House (512 Van Buren Avenue, 662-236-2816), which is 2 blocks from Ole Miss campus, has five rooms with private baths; Puddin' Place (1008 University Avenue, 662-234-1250) has suites with private baths. Both are within walking distance of the square. The Tree House (53 County Road 321, 662-513-6354, 887-849-8738) is a modern log cabin with fireplace and nice rooms, situated about 4 miles from the square.

Other lodging options include The Downtown Inn (400 North Lamar, 662-234-3031), a modest motel within walking distance of the square, and several chain hotels on the outskirts of town, including Holiday Inn Express and Comfort Inn.

Holly Springs

Situated about 45 minutes' drive from Memphis, this quaint town boasts 64 antebellum homes, mainly because General Ulysses S. Grant decided to spare Holly Springs from the usual torching. The town may be familiar to moviegoers as the backdrop for the Robert Altman film, *Cookie's Fortune*, and it's home to Rust College, Mississippi's oldest historically black college. The best time to see the homes—and the only time for many of them—is during the Holly Springs Pilgrimage, which takes place the last weekend in April each year. These gracious homes open their doors to show off their period furnishings, with guides in period costumes giving history and other information. Some other properties, including several historic churches, open for the Holiday Tour of Homes the first weekend in December.

Otherwise, stop by the Holly Springs Tourism and Recreational Bureau (104 East Gholson, 662-252-2515, www.visit hollysprings.org), which makes its home in an 1832 house known as the Yellow Fever House. The staff can supply you with a map for a driving tour of the homes. You may want to call ahead to arrange to see some of the homes.

You'll see the exteriors only of most of these antebellum structures, although a few are open to visitors by appointment, including Montrose, an 1858 home maintained by a local garden club. Contact the tourism office to see Montrose, the Yellow Fever Martyrs Church on East College Avenue, or other homes. Ask, too, about Strawberry Plains (662-252-4143), an antebellum home that serves as headquarters for the Mississippi Audubon Society. Not only is the home magnificent, there are also wildlife educational programs for children.

The **Holly Springs town square** also is very well preserved, with a courthouse that hasn't changed since before the Civil War and streets built double wide in order to accommodate large cotton bales. You might want to check out Booker Hardware (119 South Market Street, 662-252-2331), an old-fashioned general hardware store, or Tyson Drug Company (145 East Van Dorn, 662-252-2321), a vintage drugstore with a soda fountain.

By far the most bizarre attraction in Holly Springs is **Graceland Too** (200 Gholson, 662-252-1918), which might be described as the world's most intense personal shrine to Elvis Presley. Paul MacLeod, the generously sideburned, self-proclaimed number-one fan of Elvis, has converted his 1853 home into a museum of Elvis minutiae, including The King's report card, all his albums, and stacks of *TV Guide* magazines with every mention of Elvis marked with colored paper clips. He and his son, Elvis Aaron Presley MacLeod, monitor TVs to make note of all references to The King. The senior MacLeod will not only show you around, with rapid-fire commentary (just try to interrupt this man), he'll also take your picture (to join the 200,000-plus others he has collected) and entertain you by singing along with Elvis records. Your enjoyment of Graceland Too depends on the strength of your interest in Elvis and tolerance of personal eccentricity. Graceland Too is open 24 hours a day every day, as the MacLeods sleep near the door to be ready for guests. As you come into Holly Springs after turning off Highway 78, go through the first stoplight and then take a right onto Gholson.

The most famous place to eat in Holly Springs is **Phillips Grocery** (541 East Van Dorn, 662-252-4621), known for its hamburgers. It's housed in a rustic grocery store decorated with early 1900s memorabilia. Ask for directions, as it can be hard to find. Other dining options are on or near the square, including City Café (135 East Van Dorn, 662-252-9895), a plate-lunch restaurant, and Annie's (198 North Memphis, 662-252-4222), which serves a good lunch buffet.

The premier choice for accommodations is Fort-Daniel Hall (184 South Memphis Street, 662-252-6807), a bed-and-breakfast inn housed in an 1850 mansion in the style of George Washington's home, Mt. Vernon. The staff will cook other meals as well upon request for a group of at least four. On the same street attractive accommodations can be found at Somerset Cottage and Rutledge Carriage House (both at 662-252-4513).

There's also a Hampton Inn on the outskirts of town.

West Tennessee Travels

As you venture into West Tennessee from Memphis, you pass some great little towns and plenty of cotton fields and other agrarian sights. We recommend two loops, one of which will take you to Shiloh National Military Park, the site of one of the bloodiest battles in the Civil War. It's a little more than 100 miles from Memphis, going east on U.S. 57, and on the way you'll pass some interesting old towns, a state park, and an off-beat museum devoted to hunting dogs. Shiloh is only a short drive from Pickwick Lake, one of the largest lakes in the area. (See the Parks and Recreation chapter for details about the lake.) Although you can retrace your steps back on U.S. 57 to Memphis, a faster, but not particularly picturesque, option is to swing south to Corinth, where another important battle took place, then back to Memphis via U.S. 72. Either way your best

route in and out of Memphis is to take Nonconnah Parkway, getting on or off at the Collierville exit. If you plan to stay overnight in the Shiloh area, bear in mind that there are very few accommodations.

A second West Tennessee loop takes you north from Memphis on U.S. 51, where you'll pass the picturesque town of Covington on the way to Henning, the boyhood home of Alex Haley. From Henning go west on Route 87 to Fort Pillow State Park. On the way back, via Covington, take 59 South to Mason to Gus's for some of the best fried chicken on the planet. Even though they are probably not worth a detour, other points of interest include Nutbush, the birthplace of Tina Turner, and Benton County, where singer Patsy Cline died in a plane crash.

The Road to Shiloh National Military Park

Once you pass the Memphis suburbs, the first point of interest is the historic town of

Shiloh National Military Park is the site of one of the bloodiest battles of the Civil War.
PHOTO: MEMPHIS CONVENTION AND VISITORS BUREAU

LaGrange, worth a short jog off the highway, given its old storefront and antebellum homes. Just a few miles down U.S. 72 you'll come to Grand Junction, home of the **National Bird Dog Museum** (901-764-2058, www.fielddog.com). Believe it or not, west Tennessee is recognized as the birthplace of America's pointing-dog field trials and is home to the National Field Trial Championship. The museum pays homage to the canine worker that finds birds, rousts them from their hiding places, and retrieves them for the hunter. It features art, photography, and memorabilia highlighting the accomplishments of more than forty breeds of bird dogs, including pointing, flushing, and retrieving breeds. A highlight is a lighted glass case that contains the taxidermied Count Noble, a setter, imported into the United States in 1880 from South Wales, who sired the accomplished American-Llewellin setter dynasty. Field trials take place at nearby Ames Plantation in February.

Continue traveling east on Highway 57, and you'll see signs directing you to **Shiloh National Military Park,** Shiloh (901-689-5275, www.nps.gov/shil). The Battle of Shiloh was fought here on April 6-7, 1862, between 45,000 Confederate soldiers and 66,000 Union soldiers. It was the bloodiest battle in American history, resulting in more than 23,000 casualties, more than all casualties in previous American wars put together.

History buffs will recall that Confederate General A. S. Johnston began concentrating men at Corinth, with the intention of moving against General U.S. Grant's Union Army of the Tennessee. The plan was to attack the Union army before it could reinforced by General D. C. Buell's Army of the Ohio. When Johnston's army attacked the Union camps around Shiloh Church on the morning of April 6, it was a complete surprise, and the South advanced throughout the morning. Then the Union finally held a line, which was dubbed the "hornets nest" because the fighting there was so ferocious. It resisted many Confederate attacks but later fell under fire from 62 cannons, at that time the largest artillery concentration ever seen on a North American battlefield. The fighting ended for the day, and during the night, unbeknownst to the Confederates, Buell's army arrived so that by the following day, the Union force far outnumbered the Confederates. The next day things went well for the Confederates initially, but the army withdrew once its leaders realized the strength of the Union numbers. The Rebels fell back to Corinth.

Start your visit by stopping at the visitor center for a self-tour map of the park as well as a look at Civil War soldiers gear and a 25-minute film about the battle. Nearby is a bookstore with souvenirs as well as books and videos about the war for Civil War buffs. The map will guide you to key locations, including Pittsburg Landing (where Buell's troops arrived), the Hornets Nest, and the peach orchard, where witnesses say bullets cut down peach blossoms that fell like snow over the battlers. The entrance fee is $4.00 for a single-family car or $2.00 for an individual, both good for seven days. Every year near the anniversary of the Battle of Shiloh, the park has a special program that includes re-enactors portraying parts of the battle and others demonstrating such skills as rifle-musket firings.

If you plan to spend the night, try the Hampton Inn or accommodations at Pickwick Landing State Park (see Parks chapter for details), but reserve ahead, as this is a popular spot in the summer. You can also try Savannah, where you'll find a Days Inn and Comfort Inn, or continue about 20 miles to Corinth, where you'll find Hampton Inn, Holiday Inn Express, and other chains along U.S. 72.

Fort Pillow, Alex Haley's Boyhood Home, Gus's Fried Chicken World Famous

Take U.S. 51 North through Millington, home of the USA Olympic Baseball Team stadium, journeying north through the suburbs until you reach Covington, a picturesque town about 40 miles from the city. This charming town features a well-preserved town square complete with two vintage movie theaters, antiques shops, a few restaurants, and other businesses.

Roots *author Alex Haley grew up in this Henning, Tennessee, bungalow, where he heard many family stories that inspired his books.* PHOTO: MEMPHIS CONVENTION AND VISITORS BUREAU

Another 7 miles brings you to Henning, where you can follow the signs to the **Alex Haley House Museum,** 200 South Church Street (901-738-2240). This ten-room bungalow was built by Will East Palmer, Haley's grandfather and manager of a local lumber mill. Haley lived with his grandparents as a child, hearing accounts of family history from his grandmother and aunts that later inspired him to write *Roots.* Tours are given by Fred Montgomery, the town's mayor and a boyhood friend of Haley. Admission is $2.50 for adults, $1.00 for students.

From Henning take Highway 87 west toward the Mississippi River about 20 miles to **Fort Pillow State Historic Park,** 3122 Park Road (901-738-5581, www.state.tn.us/environment/parks). Fort Pillow was set on a bluff high above the Mississippi River, although the river has since shifted away from the bluff. The South held the fort during the Civil War until 1962, when the Confederates evacuated and the Union took it over for the next two years. Fort Pillow is best known, however, for the raid by Confederate General Nathan Bedford For-

rest, who in 1864 with 1,500 soldiers attacked the fort, where some 550 federal troops—almost half of them African American—were stationed. Because of the high casualties, particularly among the black soldiers, controversy continues to surround the raid. At the time some considered it acceptable wartime action, whereas others considered it a massacre, enough so that Congressional hearings were held to investigate Forrest's actions. The visitor center has a modest exhibit that includes artifacts and information about the fort, blacks in the Union army, and how soldiers lived. A short hike from the visitor center takes you to the site of the battle (ask for directions because the signs and maps are confusing). You can see the breastworks and some restored fortifications. The park also has a fishing lake, hiking trails, a camping area, and an overlook with a great view of the river.

If all this sightseeing has worked up an appetite, you're in luck. Take U.S. 51 back to Covington, then Highway 59 to Mason, home of **Gus's Fried Chicken World Famous,** 520 U.S. 70 (901-294-2028).

This small shotgun shack has three big skillets working overtime to turn out perfect mahogany chicken that makes Mason a favorite road trip for hungry Memphians. In 2001 GQ magazine named Gus's as one of the 10 restaurants in the world worth flying to for a memorable meal. Unfortunately, Gus's was damaged by a fire in early 2002 but should have reopened by the time you read this write-up. Open every day for lunch and all afternoon. No credit cards. If Gus's is full, try Bozo's Hot Pit Bar-B-Q down the road, which serves up great barbecue sandwiches and other menu items in a diner atmosphere that's like a trip back in time.

Taking the Waters in Hot Springs, Arkansas

Hot Springs, Arkansas, is a favorite weekend getaway for Memphians, who flock here for live horse racing at Oaklawn Park in winter, the spas that feature local hot-springs water and massages, and the charms of the vintage Arlington Hotel. To get to Hot Springs, take I-40 West to Little Rock, then take I-30 South, following the signs to Hot Springs via Highway 270.

One of the first areas to be preserved by the United States government as a national park, Hot Springs was a popular resort, particularly in the early part of the 20th century. Although we focus on the historic downtown area of Hot Springs National Park, there are many other reasons to visit this part of Arkansas, including five beautiful lakes, each dotted with resorts, cabins, and rental homes, and attractions for families that range from the Arkansas Alligator Farm & Petting Zoo to the Magic Springs and Crystal Falls Theme Park. You can get more information from the informative Hot Springs National Park Web site at www.hotsprings.org.

If the horses are running at **Oaklawn Park** (2705 Central Avenue, 501-623-441, 800-OAKLAWN, www.oaklawn.com), you should definitely spend a day watching the thoroughbred races and betting on your favorites. You can do it uptown style by

going up to the boxes, or you can mix with the regular folks on the grandstand level. Wherever you are at Oaklawn, don't miss the legendary corned-beef sandwiches and jumbo shrimp. Admission to the track is a few dollars, and minimum bets are usually $2.00. Boxes and club memberships are generally available for the season only, but sometimes boxes become available the day of the race, if you're in the mood for a splurge. The season lasts generally from early January through March, and at other times of the year you can enjoy simulcast racing at Oaklawn.

You should also spend some time exploring the historic area of **Central Avenue,** where you'll find shops, restaurants, and eight huge, exquisite bathhouses, built at the turn of the century and carefully restored. The entire area is part of Hot Springs National Park.

You can tour **Fordyce Bathhouse Museum** (501-623-1433) to get an idea of what the bathhouses were like during their heyday and to learn about the lifestyles of those who frequented them back when hot springs were considered the best available treatment for arthritis and other ailments. This is also the park's visitors information center, where you can inquire about other attractions and amenities including hiking trails.

Buckstaff Bath House (509 Central, 501-623-2308, wwwbuckstaffbaths.com) is the only remaining continuously operating bathing facility on Bathhouse Row, and you can still get baths, massages, or other treatments here. They don't take reservations, however.

Also check out the park areas, where you can see the steaming springs water bubbling forth, as well as other attractions, which include the Josephine Tussaud Wax Museum (250 Central, 501-623-5836), where, of course, you can see a wax likeness of Hot Springs native-son Bill Clinton, and the Mountain Valley Spring Water Co. (150 Central, 501-623-6671), where you can get a free sample.

The park also includes an extensive network of hiking trails, where you can experience anything from an easy walk to a challenging mountain hike.

By far the most popular place to stay is **The Arlington Resort Hotel & Spa** (239 Central Avenue, 501-623-7771, www. arlingtonhotel.com), which feels like a step back in time with its opulent lobby bar, vintage elevators, and uniformed valets. The Arlington has its own bathhouse and spa, supplied with local thermal mineral water, and you take a private elevator from the hall of your room to this old-fashioned spa when it's time for your appointment. A hot-bath-and-massage combination is the most popular, although other services are available, and it's best to reserve ahead, especially during weekends. Definitely spend some time in the lobby, where there's a great bar, great people-watching, and later in the evening, big-band music and dancing. Restaurants, shops, and the bathhouses are a short walk away.

If you are a fan of bed-and-breakfast inns, you will find a number of elegant choices. A number of them are in historic homes, including the Stitt House (824 Park Avenue, 501-623-2704), built in 1875; the 1890 Williams House (420 Quapaw Avenue, 501-624-4275), and Wildwood 1884 (808 Park Avenue, 501-624-4267). Contact the local tourism office at (888) 772-2489 or check out www.hotsprings. org for more ideas.

Other accommodations include The Majestic (101 Park Avenue, 501-623-5511, www.themajestichotel.com), another historic resort hotel with its own springs-fed spa. Hot Springs also has its share of chain hotels, including Comfort Inn (501-623-1700) and a Best Western that's close to Oaklawn Park (501-624-2531).

For fine dining Belle Arti Ristorante (719 Central, 501-624-7474) is a warm, elegant family-run restaurant that features a large menu of Italian specialties and live piano music. Hamilton House (130 Van Lyell Terrace, 501-525-2727) is a romantic restaurant on nearby Lake Hamilton with continental cuisine. In the historic downtown area, The Faded Rose (210 Central, 501-624-3200) serves a casual menu for lunch and dinner that includes sandwiches, New Orleans specials, and their famous soaked salad, which is bathed in homemade Italian dressing before arriving at your table. Just a few doors down is The Pancake Shop (501-624-9465), a bustling breakfast diner that serves great pancakes, omelets, and other favorites.

Neighborhoods and Real Estate

Memphis is a city of neighborhoods with all kinds of houses. You can find historic mansions, roomy new homes, charming bungalows, ranch houses, and cottages, not to mention apartments, townhouses, and, in the outlying areas, farms. Plus, there's a pleasant surprise in store for people who move here from high-cost areas such as the East Coast or West Coast: You can get a lot of house for your money in Memphis.

Memphis is one of the most affordable housing markets in the country for a city of its size. A 1999 survey of 20 cities by Chicago Title Insurance Co., entitled "Who's Buying Homes in America," found that Memphis had the lowest median price of homes purchased, $110,000. It's not unusual to be able to find a good home for $75,000 or even a good bit less, and of course you can pay more than $1 million. More recent figures show that the average sale price for a home inside the city was $113,438 in 2001, according to the Memphis Area Association of Realtors Multiple Listing Service. For the Shelby County suburbs outside the city, that figure is higher, ranging from $160,423 in Bartlett to $295,351 in Germantown.

In addition to having no state income taxes and affordable home prices, Memphis also has a low cost of living that's well below the national average—about 89 percent of the national average in 2001, according to the American Chamber of Commerce Researchers Association. The bottom line is that you can live well in Memphis for much less than in many other cities. You also won't have to commute as far. The average commute in Memphis is 21.4 minutes, compared with a 39-minute commute in New York and a 33-minute average commute in Chicago, according to a U.S. Census Bureau study published in 2001. As the city grows, so does traffic, although building of new roads such as Nonconnah Parkway and widening existing roads help to offset the impact of the extra cars. It's not surprising that a lot of new development is taking place along these arteries.

The city of Memphis includes downtown Memphis, midtown, and East Memphis, as well as neighborhoods in north Memphis, including Raleigh, and south-Memphis neighborhoods that include Hickory Hill and Whitehaven. The city is ringed by bedroom communities, including Millington, Bartlett, Cordova, Germantown, Collierville, and the DeSoto County, Mississippi, suburbs of Southaven and Olive Branch. Outside this ring of suburbs, you'll find additional housing options in Tipton County, Arlington and elsewhere in northeast Shelby County, and Fayette County.

Although City of Memphis schools serve residents inside the city limits, children who live in the county but outside the city limits attend Shelby County schools. (See Education chapter for more details.) Tipton, Fayette, and DeSoto Counties have their own school systems.

Property taxes in Shelby County are $3.79 for every $100 of assessed value, plus city tax (unless you live outside a municipality). Property tax in the city of Memphis is $3.23 per $100 of assessed value, whereas in other municipalities, that amount ranges from $1.00 to $1.45 per $100 of assessed value.

Property taxes in Fayette County, Tipton County, and DeSoto County are generally lower than in Shelby County. In Tennessee there's no state income tax, and although Mississippi does have a state income tax, that's somewhat offset for homeowners by the state's homestead exemption program. (See the section on DeSoto County, Mississippi, in this chapter.)

The Memphis metro area experienced 13 percent growth in population during the 1990s to 1,135,614, according to the U.S. Census Bureau. The growth was particularly dramatic in the suburbs, particularly in DeSoto and Tipton Counties, Collierville, and Lakeland. This growth is seen as continuing, and new construction is expected to keep pace in the coming years.

Neighborhoods

City of Memphis

Downtown

Residential development has been an important part of the revival of downtown Memphis in the last 15 years or so, and as a result, you can find beautiful homes ranging from lofty condominiums in renovated historic warehouses to spacious new houses with views of the river. A standout is Harbor Town, widely considered one of the most successful traditional neighborhood developments in the country. Situated on Mud Island just across the Auction Street Bridge, this neighborhood is easily accessible to downtown and its attractions but is self-contained, with its own grocery store and parks. The homes, some of which have river views, are beautifully designed and are frequently featured in the pages of *Southern Living* and other magazines. They feature updates of traditional Southern elements such as porches and columns, and the smaller ones are designed like a shotgun house—so called because a shot from the front door can go through the back door without piercing any walls. Home prices here range from the low $200,000s to $500,000 or more, and the homes feature all the modern amenities. You can also find plenty of apartments and condominiums on Mud Island at a variety of prices. Whereas Harbor Town flourishes on the north end of downtown, neighborhoods on the south end, such as South Bluffs and Founder's Pointe, provide homes on the bluffs of the Mississippi River. Actress Cybill Shepherd has a home in this area, and more homes are under construction.

An alternative to these neighborhood houses with yards is downtown proper, where apartments have been developed in some of the historic buildings. They range from huge luxury penthouses to the moderate-income apartments in the Exchange Building. Downtowners love the easy access to restaurants, bars, and other attractions, as well as proximity of the river and parks alongside it. It's one of the few areas where you can get along without a car except for long commutes or trips to the grocery.

Midtown

If you like unique older homes with high ceilings and lots of charm, midtown is where you'll find them. Here, the options range from historic mansions in Central Gardens to modest bungalows built in the 1920s, and everything in between. The real-estate community places midtown starting at I-240 West (next to the medical-center area) and going east to Eastern Parkway at the edge of Overton Park, although Memphians tend to think of midtown as stretching farther east than that. Midtown has the feeling of being a small town within a city and is more culturally and economically diverse. It's not unusual to see a $500,000 house on the same block as a $100,000 house. Memphians think of midtowners as being more avant-garde than their counterparts in the suburbs. That's probably overstating the case a bit. Although you'll find some punked-out artists and musicians living here, it's mostly families with kids who prefer the charms and quirks of midtown to the anonymity of the suburbs. Among the swanker neighborhoods in this area are Central Gardens and Hein Park, and you'll find more modestly priced homes all over. The most typical architectural styles in this part of town are bungalows, with exaggerated porches and eaves, and foursquares, with four square rooms on the ground floor. In addition to the older homes, which are constantly being renovated by owners and investors, you'll also find new "infill" homes, so called because they are built to "fill in" areas of older neighborhoods. A

The quiet neighborhood of Harbor Town on Mud Island is just over a bridge from downtown Memphis.
PHOTO: TROY GLASGOW

notable collection of these homes were built near Overton Park in a portion of the city that years ago had been cleared for an interstate that never materialized. You'll find both Memphis City schools as well as some parochial schools in midtown. Although homes can cost $1 million or more in midtown, it's also possible to find homes in comfortable neighborhoods for around $75,000, depending on the condition and if they have been recently renovated.

East Memphis

East Memphis is the area that stretches between midtown Memphis and the I–240 loop. While there's a difference of opinion as to where East Memphis begins, the real-estate community considers that midtown ends and East Memphis begins at East Parkway, just on the eastern edge of Overton Park, and continues east to Germantown. Given the fact, however, that the center of the city has shifted to the east over the years, Highland Street and the area around University of Memphis are generally thought to be more midtown than East Memphis.

East Memphis is the nearest suburb to central-business-district downtown and is convenient to shopping at Oak Court Mall, Laurelwood shopping center, and elsewhere as well as to excellent public and private schools. Public schools include White Station High School and Grahamwood Elementary, and private schools include St. Mary's Episcopal School and Memphis University School. The homes are older, dating back to the 1940s, 1950s, and 1960s, although some are brand-new "infill" homes. Families or developers buy lots and replace the existing home with brand-new structures, or they make a separate lot out of a large yard.

You'll find homes in all sizes and price ranges, with "starter" homes in the sought-after High Point Terrace neighborhood as well as near University of Memphis, where there's a concentration of 1940s homes built under the GI bill. In the middle range are ranch homes in neighborhoods along Mendenhall, White Station, and Yates. The average sales price in 2001 for this part of East Memphis, between Perkins and I-240, was $152,406, according to the Memphis Area Association of Realtors Multiple Listing Service.

The larger East Memphis homes are found in enclaves near Galloway Golf Course and elsewhere, along Walnut Grove, and in new areas such as Valley Brook, an area where huge new homes are being built.

Between I-240 and Germantown you'll find larger, newer homes. In 2001 homes in this area had an average sale price of $248,949, according to the Memphis Area Association of Realtors Multiple Listing Service.

Whatever the location or price range, the homes in East Memphis tend to appreciate in value, because the neighborhoods are so established. Plus, you'll find plenty of large trees and good-sized yards.

North Memphis

This area of Memphis, north of downtown Memphis and tucked between the river and Bartlett, includes the working-class neighborhoods of Frayser and Raleigh. Frayser features many different styles of homes, such as bungalows and ranch homes, and enjoys easy access to the city. It's one of the hillier areas of the Memphis area, with plenty of stately trees, and homes are very affordable, with prices in the $50,000 range.

Raleigh dates back to the early 20th century, when it was home to a popular mineral spring that attracted visitors from the city. It, too, with its rolling hills, is a refreshing break from the relatively flat terrain of Memphis. Raleigh, as home to Raleigh Springs Mall and numerous shopping centers, has plenty of shopping options.

Home prices are in the $90,000 range in Raleigh.

South Memphis/Hickory Hill

This part of Memphis consists of several neighborhoods, including Whitehaven, the South Parkway area, Oakhaven, and Hickory Hill, many of which have very affordable home prices. Whitehaven, best known as home to Graceland, is close to Memphis International Airport and I-55. Here, you'll find subdivisions with homes built in the 1950s and 1960s, with the average price around $75,000, as well as apartment complexes. Along South Parkway are beautiful old homes with grand trees and roomy yards. Oakhaven, tucked between the airport and Mall of Memphis, features moderately priced homes and subdivisions, although homes near Holmes Road are wooded and spacious. Home prices are in the low $60,000s. Hickory Hill, situated in southeast Memphis, has homes in all price ranges, although the average sales price for a home in 2001 was $88,386, according to the Memphis Area Association of Realtors Multiple Listing Service. The area has lots of shopping, with Hickory Ridge Mall and centers that feature national chains as well as local retailers.

Suburbs

Germantown

Germantown is considered the posh suburb of Memphis, and although it has traditionally been thought of as a horsey, elite town, it has become more diverse in recent years. It began as a separate town in the 1820s but, over the years, has grown into a suburb of Memphis with a population of 37,348, according to 2000 census figures. Homes can be spectacular and fairly expensive for the Memphis market. The average sales price for a home in this area in 2001 was $295,351, according to the Memphis Area Association of Realtors Multiple Listing Service, although more modestly priced homes can be found as well. Germantown is proud of its parks, its state-of-the-art performing-arts center, its annual charity horse show, and its shopping, including the Shops of Saddle Creek. The city of Germantown has exacting planning standards, so here expect businesses to have discreet signs rather than flashing neon. The area is well known for its horses, and both polo and fox hunting are still popular sports. Germantown schools are part of the Shelby County school system, which includes four elementary schools, two middle schools, and two high schools. There are also several private schools. The city's property tax is $1.30 for every $100 of assessed value, in addition to the county property tax of $3.79 per $100 of assessed value.

Cordova

This fast-growing suburb, tucked between Germantown and Bartlett, is where many young families with children choose to make their homes. The atmosphere is comfortingly familiar if you're at home in a modern American suburb; if not, it may seem overly homogeneous. The subdivisions of Cordova are convenient to shopping and restaurants, and you'll find many familiar chains represented both in the many strip shopping centers and the mall, Wolfchase Galleria. Part of the suburb is in the Shelby County school district, although a 2002 annexation of part of Cordova by the city may change that for some schools. Cordova favors the first-time buyer, with homes that are more affordable than in neighboring Germantown, generally considered the swank suburban address. Cordova homes start at $110,000, going up to $250,000 and sometimes beyond. The median sales price for a home in Cordova in 2001 was $166,453, according to the Memphis Area Association of Realtors Multiple Listing Service. Most of the homes here were built fairly recently, and more are under construction, so they have oversized bathrooms and kitchens and other up-to-date amenities.

Cordova offers many affordable homes like this one.
PHOTO: CRYE-LEIKE REALTORS

Cordova is also adjacent to Shelby Farms, a large urban park with recreational activities available. Cordova residents pay only county property taxes of $3.79 per $100 of assessed value, although those in annexed areas pay Memphis city taxes as well.

Collierville

Collierville, situated about 10 miles east of the Memphis city limits and 25 miles from downtown, has become a popular bedroom community, particularly for families with children. During the 1990s it nearly doubled in population to 31,872, according to the U.S. Census Bureau, and an annexation is in the works that will add about 20 more square miles to this historic town. Residents love its picturesque town square with shops and restaurants, as well as its family-friendly attitude, and there are plenty of shopping centers and other commercial businesses along West Poplar Avenue (Highway 72), the main thoroughfare. A few years back the area economy got a boost when FedEx opened its World Technology Center in Collierville, but many residents commute to Memphis for work. The completion of Nonconnah Parkway a few years ago has made the commute between Memphis and Collierville much shorter, thus making this historic town more convenient to the city. As for homes, there is a lot of building going on in the area, as well as more established homes that change hands. Homes start around $90,000 and go all the way up to $2 million, but the average sales price for a home in Collierville in 2001 was $247,167, according to the Memphis Area Association of Realtors Multiple Listing Service. Property taxes here are $1.47 per $100 of assessed value, in addition to Shelby County property taxes.

Bartlett

This family-oriented suburb, with a population of 40,543, according to the 2000 census, is situated in the center of Shelby County and about 11 miles from downtown Memphis. It started off as a stagecoach stop in the 1820s and has grown dramatically, especially in the last 30 years, from a sleepy town into a thriving suburb that manages to keep its small-town feel.

You'll find most homes in the $100,000 to $250,000 range, which makes it an affordable option for first-time buyers. The average sale price of a Bartlett home in 2001 was $160,423, according to the Memphis Area Association of Realtors Multiple Listing Service. The older section of Bartlett is to the west, where you'll find the town proper, and to the east are newer subdivisions as well as a plethora of shopping centers and stores. There's continuing construction of new homes, which start at about $140,000-$150,000. City property taxes are $1.23 per $100 of assessed value, in addition to Shelby County property tax. Bartlett is part of the Shelby County school system, and has six elementary schools, three middle schools, and two high schools. The town also boasts a new Bartlett Performing Arts Center, as well as lots of new retailers, including national chains.

Arlington/Lakeland

This quiet municipality in the northeast corner of Shelby County is seen as an up-and-coming area that will soon be the next Cordova or Collierville in terms of development. Already census figures show that Arlington's population grew nearly 70 percent between 1990 and 2000, as subdivisions have been built with more on the way. Situated beyond the town of Lakeland off I-40, Arlington had few shopping centers or other commercial development, but that's expected to change as the number of rooftops grows. Most of the homes are in the $200,000 range, although the median sales price for a home in Arlington in 2001 was $173,156, according to the Memphis Area Association of Realtors Multiple Listing Service. Property taxes here are $1.00 per $100 of assessed value, in addition to Shelby County property tax. Arlington is served by Shelby County Schools, with two elementary schools, two middle schools, and nearby Bolton High School. Lakeland is closer to Memphis, and actually just 2 miles from Wolfchase Galleria Mall. It has been around for many years, but during the 1990s its population grew by 400 percent. As a result, you'll find more established neighborhoods as well as lots of new subdivisions to accommodate all the new residents. Lakeland also offers the advantage of having no city property tax, only Shelby County property taxes.

Millington

This community of 10,400 people, just 10 miles north of downtown Memphis, has traditionally been a navy town. Now it is home to the Bureau of Naval Personnel, although until the 1990s Millington's naval operation was a much larger air station engaged in training. People choose to live in Millington for its small-town ambiance and easy highway access, both to the city and to I-40. It's popular among retirees, many of them former navy officers who like having access to the base and its facilities and in some cases were once stationed in Millington. A number of subdivisions have been built in recent years, or are still under construction, ranging from neighborhoods with modest homes for first-time buyers to those with 3,500-square-foot homes that command prices near $200,000. In 2001 the average home sale price was $109,911, according to the Memphis Area Association of Realtors Multiple Listing Service.

Millington is in the Shelby County school system and has five elementary schools, a middle school, and a high school; there are also several private schools. Meeman-Shelby Forest State Park is nearby.

Taxes in Millington are lower than those in some municipalities, with a city property tax rate of $1.23 for $100 of assessed value plus the county property tax rate of $3.79 per $100 of assessed value.

Fayette County, Tennessee

Fayette County, which is just east of Shelby County, has grown into a bedroom community in recent years for persons who like rural or small-town living but want to be close to the city. Another plus is that property taxes are lower here than in Shelby County. Fayette County property owners, as of 2002, paid $1.845 per $1,000, or about half of what Shelby County property owners paid in taxes.

Most of the county's residential development has followed Highway 64, and in the more densely populated west part of

Fayette County, you'll find Hickory, Withe, and Oakland, towns where a lot of new homes and subdivisions have been built. Prices range from $100,000 for a starter home to $350,000 and more. There's very little commercial development here, although supermarkets and other retail stores are being built in the Oakland area. This area is about a 20-minute drive away from Wolfchase Galleria Mall and the surrounding shopping area and an additional 15 minutes or more from Memphis proper.

As you go farther east, Fayette County becomes more rural, appealing to homeowners who want more seclusion and more elbow room, whereas tiny Somerville is attractive to those who like small towns. This area is not growing as quickly as the western part of the state, but this trend could change.

Tipton County, Tennessee

Situated 18 miles north of Shelby County, this fast-growing county saw its population increase 36 percent during the 1990s to 51,271 people, according to the U.S. Census Bureau. For those persons who want to get away from the city, Tipton County fills the bill, so you'll find that many residents work in Memphis but live here, attracted in part by lower property taxes. There's plenty of new development, particularly along Highway 51, with new homes and subdivisions being built in the tiny towns of Munford, Atoka, and Brighton. Shopping centers and other commercial development has been slow but is beginning to pick up in the area. Farther out is Covington, a small town with a charming, vibrant downtown that includes vintage movie theaters as well as stores housed in turn-of-the-century buildings.

Property taxes in Tipton County, at $2.92 per $100 of assessed value, are lower than those in Shelby County. The Tipton County school system has four elementary schools, three middle schools, and three high schools, located in Brighton, Covington, and Munford.

DeSoto County, Mississippi

Drawn by low housing prices and other factors, many people are opting to make their homes just south of Shelby County and across the Tennessee state line into Mississippi. As a result, DeSoto County was one of the fastest-growing counties in the country during the 1990s, with a 58 percent increase in population to 107,000 people in 2000, according to the U.S. Census Bureau. Most of the residential development is in the towns of Southaven, Olive Branch, Horn Lake, and Hernando, where you'll find numerous subdivisions with homes of all sizes and in all price ranges. There are also homes in the rural pockets in between these municipalities. A big draw is the state's homestead tax exemption, which can save a homeowner some $240 in taxes each year. The exemption is much more generous for homeowners who are 65 or older or disabled. Otherwise, property taxes are $3.64 per $100 of assessed value, somewhat lower than the rate in Shelby County, plus municipal taxes where applicable. Residents say they like the small-town feeling of the Mississippi neighborhoods while still being close enough to the city of Memphis to enjoy its offerings. Another draw is the DeSoto County school district. It's the second-largest system in the state of Mississippi, and one of the state's best, with more gifted education students than in any other district in Mississippi. DeSoto County has well-developed amenities, including plenty of shopping centers with familiar chain retailers as well as locally owned stores and other commercial businesses—and there are more under construction. The average sale price of a home in DeSoto County in 2001 was $127,035, according to the Northwest Mississippi Association of Realtors Multiple Listing Service.

Real Estate

Existing homes are constantly changing hands, and new homes are always being built in the Memphis area, both in the heart of the city and in the surrounding suburbs. Of course, as in any other market, Memphis real estate is buoyed when times are good and quiets down a bit when the economy slows down. By and large, though, the local real-estate market has been very strong, thanks in part to low interest rates, a phenomenon that has allowed many people to buy their first home or to trade up to a larger home. Interest rates were below 8 percent from about 1995 to at least 2002, and at times below 7 percent.

Real-Estate Agencies

To help you find your way through the local real-estate market, there are hundreds of real-estate agents in all areas of the city and its surrounding suburbs who can help, whether you are buying or selling a home. Here, we list the largest and best-known residential real-estate brokerage firms. Bear in mind, though, that Memphis has dozens of other reputable and knowledgeable agents and firms, so this is by no means a complete listing. For more information about other companies, contact the Memphis Area Association of Realtors at (901) 685-2100 or visit its Web site at www.maar.com.

The Sunday edition of the city's daily newspaper, *The Commercial Appeal*, is an excellent source of information about homes for sale or rent and also has news about the local housing market, real-estate agents, and lenders. The weekly *Memphis Flyer* also features homes and apartments in its classified-advertising section.

Century 21 River Oaks, Inc.
1926 Exeter Road, Germantown
(901) 756-1622
Opened in 1985, and part of the Century 21 organization since 1997, this real estate firm works mainly in Germantown, Collierville, and Cordova as well as East Memphis. Century 21 River Oaks specializes in relocation, as an affiliate of the large transferee network, Cendant Mobility. In addition, because it represents a large homebuilder, the company shows a lot of new homes. Its main office is in Germantown, but it also maintains an office in Bartlett. River Oaks is known locally for buying and selling properties in Germantown. With 51 agents the firm has about $142 million in annual gross sales.

Coldwell Banker/Hoffman-Burke, Inc., Realtors
1709 Kirby Parkway
(901) 759-1651
This real-estate company, with 42 agents and two offices, prides itself on its work with upper-tier homes in Memphis, Germantown, and Collierville. The firm also provides relocation services, as well as new construction and commercial real estate, and does about $78 million in gross annual sales.

Coleman-Etter, Fontaine Realtors
651 Oakleaf Office Lane
(901) 767-4100
www.cef-realtors.com
This full-service residential real-estate company, which has been in operation since 1951, prides itself on its personal service to customers. One of the city's premier realty companies, it's best known for high-end properties in the downtown, midtown, and East Memphis areas but also works with first-time buyers and sellers of middle-income properties. The company is also knowledgeable about all aspects of Memphis and will help newcomers with recommendations for lenders, movers, day-care providers, or whatever else that customer needs. Coleman-Etter, Fontaine realtors has more than 30 full-time realtors and does about $129 million in gross sales each year. The president and owner is Fontaine Taylor.

Crye-Leike, Inc.
6525 Quail Hollow
(901) 756-8900
www.crye-leike.com
Started in 1977 by two Memphians, Crye-Leike has become the largest real-estate company in Memphis as well as the largest in Tennessee, with 2,200 agents in five states. You can count on finding a Crye-Leike office with knowledgeable agents in every neighborhood. That's because with 1,100 agents and 22 offices in the greater Memphis area, Crye-Leike covers every part of Memphis as well as much of the Mid-South region outside the metropolitan area. In addition to handling home

sales and purchases, Crye-Leike also offers an array of services, including relocation (it's part of the RELO network) and home improvement. It also publishes its own home-buyer's guide with listings of properties for sale in Memphis and the surrounding suburbs. The company does about $1.5 billion in annual gross sales.

John Green & Co., Realtors
108 Mulberry Street, Collierville
(901) 853–0763, (800) 772–2052
www.johngreen.com

Based in Collierville, this realty company handles new and existing homes in Collierville, Germantown, Cordova, East Memphis, and other suburban areas. John Green is the owner and has 50 real-estate agents on his staff as well as a relocation specialist to take care of those types of client needs. The company works with properties in all price ranges, but most are $150,000 or more, given the home prices in the Collierville area.

Although primarily a residential real-estate firm, the company also does some commercial and land transactions. John Green & Co. does about $79.7 million in annual gross sales.

The Hobson Co., Realtors
5100 Poplar Avenue
(901) 761-1622
www.hobsonrealtors.com

This family-owned residential real-estate company is best known for buying and selling midtown and East Memphis properties at the upper price range but actually handles homes in other areas of the metropolitan area as well as more moderately priced homes.

The company does about $121 million in yearly gross sales, and prides itself on its 24 agents, each of whom averages $5 million in sales and has an average of 15 years of experience in residential real estate. The company is owned and managed by Joel Hobson III, the son of the couple who founded it in 1972.

Lawrence Johnson Realtors
4222 Millbranch Road
(901) 345–1600, (800) 760–4661
www.lawrencejohnson.com

Started in 1976 by Lawrence Johnson, this company has 110 agents, making it one of the largest agencies in Memphis. The focus is on properties in all neighborhoods in Memphis and northwest Mississippi, with plenty of homes below $100,000 as well as more expensive properties. The firm, which also offers relocation services and some commercial listings, does about $55.6 million in annual gross sales.

Mallard Creek Realty, Inc.
7556 Highway 70, Bartlett
(901) 372–9933
www.mallard-creek.com

Mallard Creek Realty got its start in 1994 selling newly constructed homes. These days the firm continues to sell lots of new homes, particularly in the Collierville, Bartlett, Cordova, and Millington areas. Existing homes are equally important to them, however, and account for almost half of the agency's business. Those listings tend to be in the same area, although agents handle listings all over town. Mallard Creek has 50 agents and maintains offices in both Bartlett and Cordova. It does some $57.7 million in annual gross sales. The owner and founder is Stan Holmes.

Marx & Bensdorf Real Estate & Investment Co.
959 Ridgeway Loop
(901) 682-1868
www.marx-bensdorf.com

This is the city's oldest real-estate agency, founded in 1868, and continues to operate under the same name. With 36 agents Marx & Bensdorf covers all of Memphis and Shelby County, as well as Tipton and Fayette Counties, and sells homes in all different price ranges. Although the company retains the original name, the present principals are David Okeon and Jimmy Reed. As part of the RELO referral network, the firm reaches customers who are moving to Memphis, and it provides relocation services. The company does about $137.2 million in annual gross sales.

The Neilson Group LLC GMAC
1296 Peabody Avenue
(901) 474–6600
www.greatmemphishomes.com

Owned by Don Neilson and staffed with 24 agents, this real-estate company does about half of its residential business in downtown Memphis and midtown, where the company started. The remainder of the residential business, which accounts for 90 percent of the business, is properties in all areas of the city. The firm handles homes in all price ranges and does about $34.5 million in annual gross sales.

Prudential Collins Maury, Inc., Realtors
1352 Cordova Cove, Cordova
(901) 753-0700
www.collins-mauryrealtors.com

This locally owned and operated franchise of Prudential, with offices in Cordova, Collierville, and East Memphis, handles residential properties at all prices. Collins Maury is most active in Germantown, Cordova, Collierville, and Bartlett but works with properties in all parts of the metropolitan area. Prudential owns several relocation companies, so it's not surprising that this agency does a good bit of relocation work. The owners are Doug Collins and Bill Maury. Annual gross sales are $140 million.

RE/MAX Elite of Memphis
6363 Poplar Avenue
(901) 685–6000
www.memphismidsouthhomes.com

RE/MAX Elite of Memphis has three offices, including locations in Collierville and Germantown, and has 125 agents who specialize in all parts of the Memphis metropolitan area. The agency is independently owned and operated by Richard Sharpe and does quite a bit of relocation work as part of the RE/MAX referral network. The agency works mainly in residential real estate, buying and selling properties at

every price. Annual gross sales are about $223.8 million.

RE/MAX On-Track
2075 Exeter Road, Germantown
(901) 758–1200
www.memphismidsouthhomes.com

Started in 1990, this residential realty company has 55 agents who cover all areas of the metro area, including Germantown, Cordova, Collierville, Memphis, and Mississippi. The office is independently owned, but as part of the RE/MAX system, it does lots of relocation work, both for companies and individuals. The principal broker and owner is Peter Ritten. The company has annual gross sales of about $146 million.

RE/MAX Preferred Realtors
7555 Highway 64, Bartlett
(901) 372–1777
www.memphis-homes.com

This real-estate agency is located in Bartlett near Cordova, but its 30 agents buy and sell properties all over Memphis as well as its suburbs and Fayette and Tipton Counties. Many of them have their own Web sites, too. RE/MAX Preferred Realtors, independently owned and operated, is also active in relocation work through RE/MAX Relocation and handles properties in all price ranges. Annual gross sales are $59.5 million.

Sowell and Co. Realtors
54 South Cooper Street
(901) 278–4380, (888) 799–4235
www.sowellandco.com

This company, which has been helping customers buy and sell homes since the mid-1970s, specializes in homes located in neighborhoods within the I–240 loop. This includes midtown, downtown, and East Memphis, with a specific interest in historic homes such as those found in the Central Gardens neighborhood of midtown. The homes range from starter homes in the hip Copper Young area to historic mansions in Central Gardens and other upscale midtown enclaves. The company also handles properties in suburban areas such as Germantown or Collierville. Founded by Linda Sowell, the firm has 29 agents and annual gross sales estimates at around $51 million.

Apartments and Rental Housing

Many residents opt to rent apartments or homes rather than buying, and there's something to satisfy every taste. You'll find large modern apartment complexes with every possible amenity, both in the suburbs and downtown Memphis, as well as charming older apartment buildings in midtown and downtown. You can also choose from duplexes, garage apartments, and carriage houses, most of which are peculiar to midtown, and loft apartments in downtown historic warehouses and other buildings. Whatever part of town you're interested in, you'll likely find plenty of freestanding houses available for rent as well in all price ranges.

Memphis's local newspapers, the daily *The Commercial Appeal* and the weekly *Memphis Flyer*, have listings of rental properties currently available, which is where many Memphians turn when they're looking for new digs.

Also look for the *Greater Memphis Area Apartment Guide*, a free publication with plenty of information about the larger apartment complexes around town, found in racks at supermarkets, library branches, and other

locations. There's also a growing number of apartment Web sites, where you can check out different properties on-line. They include Memphis Apartments (www.apartments-memphis.com) and ePartment Finder: Memphis (www.epartmentfinder.com/memphis).

Chambers of Commerce in the Memphis Area:

Bartlett Area Chamber of Commerce, (901) 372–9457, www.bartlettchamber.org

Collierville Chamber of Commerce, (901) 853–1949, www.colliervillechamber.com

Fayette County Chamber of Commerce, (901) 465–8690, www.fayettecountychamber.com

Germantown Chamber of Commerce, (901) 755–1200, www.germantownchamber.com

Memphis Regional Chamber, (901) 543–3500, www.memphischamber.com

Millington Chamber of Commerce, (901) 872–1486, www.millingtonchamber.com

Olive Branch (Mississippi) Chamber of Commerce, (662) 895–2600, www.olive branchms.com

Southaven (Mississippi) Chamber of Commerce, (662) 342–6114, www.southaven chamber.com

South Tipton County Chamber of Commerce, (901) 837–4600, www.southtipton.com

West Memphis (Arkansas) Chamber of Commerce, (870) 735–1134, www.wmcoc.com

Health Care and Wellness

Memphis is one of the largest medical centers in the South, providing health care to a five-state region. It has changed dramatically with the times and is fast becoming one of the nation's premier centers for medical research.

Here, the practice of medicine is dominated by two large health-care systems, and benefits from the presence of the state medical school, University of Tennessee Health Science Center. The city also is home to world-renowned St. Jude Children's Research Hospital, which boasts a Nobel Prize for medical research and treats children from all over the world. (See Close-up in this chapter.)

The primary competitors in Memphis health care are Baptist Memorial Health Care Corp. and Methodist Healthcare, Inc. The two large systems operate hospitals, surgery centers, and health plans throughout the Mid-South. Whatever the name is on your insurance card, if you could peel the label back and peek, it would probably say Baptist or Methodist.

Baptist and Methodist each claim to be unique, but they both offer most of the same services, and compete on quality and price. This competition has proven to be very beneficial to the community because it has meant a wide range of services and access throughout the city. By virtue of the dominance of the Baptist and Methodist systems, the other hospitals in Memphis work on the fringes, filling their own niches.

Saint Francis Hospital, an additional provider on most health plans, controls about 15 percent of the market. Saint Francis is building a new hospital in the suburb of Bartlett. Delta Medical Center specializes in behavioral health and is attractive to physicians who prefer a smaller, cozier atmosphere.

Baptist and Methodist have set aside their competitiveness when the community's needs have been great. Both systems have agreed not to pursue vital services provided at the Regional Medical Center at Memphis (The Med), like its trauma center equipped to treat the sickest and most seriously injured patients or its world-class burn center. Competing in these areas would undermine The Med, which would be bad for everyone. The two systems also cooperate in a helicopter air ambulance, and they co-own a surgery center. Both work with the Church Health Center, which provides health care to the city's working poor (see Close-up in this chapter).

Le Bonheur Children's Medical Center (no need to dust off your high-school French, because it's pronounced luh-BON-ner) is the region's primary provider of pediatric care. Courted by both health systems for several years, Le Bonheur merged with Methodist in 1995. Since then, Baptist has developed its own pediatric services so that now only about 3 percent of Baptist's pediatric patients are treated through Le Bonheur.

University of Tennessee Health Science Center keeps health care in the city both friendly and first rate. The med school operates in Memphis, even though the main university campus is in Knoxville, and also includes UT Bowld hospital here.

Many of the region's physicians, nurses, and other medical professionals are graduates of UT, and more than 800 Memphis physicians donate their time to teaching students about the real world of medicine beyond the school's walls. Most of the faculty of UT also practices medicine in the community. Some 375 faculty members are part of UT Medical Group, Inc. and, as such, staff area hospitals, clinics, and surgery centers. The result is a dynamic, professionally charged environment where there is no barrier between academics and private practice.

University of Tennessee is also linked to St. Jude, which was started by 1960s TV star Danny Thomas. Here, no child is turned away, regardless of the seriousness of the illness or ability to pay. St. Jude is also unique in that almost all the scientists there have medical degrees as well as PhDs. Most of St. Jude's scientists have dual appointments at UT, creating even more cross-pollination of medical creativity.

Like their counterparts elsewhere, the city's health-care providers have been pressed by rising health-care costs, resulting in the establishment of outpatient surgery centers. By far the biggest pressure has been from TennCare, enacted by the state in 1994 to put Medicaid under the discipline of managed care. What followed was financial chaos for several years and the effective disappearance of mental health care for the poor. At present hospitals and doctors complain that TennCare covers only half of the actual cost of providing care to those patients. Efforts are ongoing to improve the program.

History

Memphis health care dates back to 1855, the year that the first of a series of yellow-fever epidemics began. The disease killed off much of the population and earned Memphis a reputation as one of the three deadliest cities in the world, alongside Prague and the Chilean port of Valparaiso.

To the rescue came Catholic priests and nuns from three different orders, many of whom died while caring for the stricken during the epidemics of 1873 and 1878. In 1889 a priest and two nuns from Lafayette, Indiana, started the city's first civilian hospital. Fund-raising for the hospital was directed by Rabbi Max Samfield of Temple Israel. Thus, the religious tradition of health care in Memphis was established at the very beginning, and it's still evident in the names of the primary health-care institutions: Baptist, Methodist, Saint Francis, St. Jude.

Baptist and Methodist started early in the 20th century, as much of the city's health care shifted to institutions. Previously, it was customary for all but the very poor to be treated at home by family physicians.

Since that time health care has grown dramatically, and as the city has grown, health care has followed the population growth. That movement led to the addition of suburban and regional hospitals, and the 2000 closing of what was once the world's largest private general hospital: Baptist Medical Center, near downtown Memphis.

As a sign of the times, the property is shifting over from patient care to research. In partnership with Baptist and the Mem-phis Biotech Foundation, UT Health Science Center is building the UT–Baptist Research Park, a new campus integrating research, teaching, and biomedical development. It includes a biotech business incubator, where scientists from UT can develop and commercialize their medical research.

Health Department

Memphis and Shelby County Health Department
814 Jefferson
(901) 544-7600
The health department provides a wide range of services, including primary care in poor neighborhoods and oversight of a wide range of public health matters. It also has a role in the two county nursing homes, Shelby County Health Care Center and Oakville Health Care Center.

Hospitals

Baptist Memorial Health Care Corp.
899 Madison
(901) 227-2727
www.bmhcc.org
Baptist, as locals call the local health-care system, has evolved into one of the world's largest and most comprehensive health systems since leaders from Tennessee, Arkansas, and Mississippi first opened their hospital here in 1912. At present, with about 8,000 employees in metro Memphis alone, Baptist operates 17 hospitals in three states. In Tennessee those hospitals are in Memphis, Collierville, Germantown, Cov-

Baptist Memorial Hospital/Memphis, one of the city's largest medical centers, was recently expanded.
PHOTO: GREG CAMPBELL/ BAPTIST MEMORIAL HEALTH CARE

ington, Ripley, Huntingdon, and Union City. In Mississippi they are in the Memphis suburbs of Southaven, Booneville, Columbus, New Albany, and Oxford. Arkansas hospitals are in Blytheville, Forrest City, and Osceola. In just the metro Memphis hospitals, Baptist treated 54,500 patients in fiscal 2000.

This expansion at the regional level reflects the desire among consumers to be treated closer to home. At one time, however, regional hospitals provided basic care to local patients but referred their most complex cases to Memphis, either to the facility traditionally known as Baptist Memorial Hospital/East or, until it closed in 2000, Baptist Medical Center near downtown Memphis.

At its peak the medical center was the nation's largest private general hospital, with a capacity of 1,800 patients, and until the mid-80s usually ran a full house. This was where Elvis Presley was pronounced dead after his untimely collapse and, during happier times, where his daughter Lisa Marie was born. The center opened some 90 years ago as a nine-story, 150-bed hospital on land donated by Physicians and

Surgeons College. Baptist Hospital ran into financial problems, and just two years after opening, a group of Methodists declined to buy the place for $1.00. They were already planning to build the new Methodist Hospital up the street. Today, Baptist and Methodist are the Coke and Pepsi of Memphis-area health care.

One reason for the medical center's demise is that during the 1990s, much of the system's health-care activity shifted to Baptist East, now the system's main hospital and renamed Baptist Memorial Hospital/Memphis.

In east Memphis, besides the main hospital, Baptist also operates a busy emergency department and recently expanded to bring its total capacity to 766 beds, including the 20-bed Hardin Pediatric Center.

In 2001 Baptist opened the 140-bed Baptist Women's Hospital, which has an adjacent physician's office building and its own secure parking. As one of only 15 women's hospitals in the United States, the facility has 36 birthing rooms, capable of delivering 8,000 babies a year. There are also six operating rooms, a 40-bed neonatal intensive care unit, and a laboratory.

Nearby, Baptist recently opened a $86-million heart institute, which combines medical and surgical heart care, with one floor dedicated to cardiac research. The system also owns and operates Baptist-Trinity Home Care and Hospice.

Baptist Hospitals in the Memphis Metropolitan Area:

Baptist Heart Institute, 6019 Walnut Grove Road, (901) 226–2328

Baptist Memorial Hospital/Collierville, 1500 West Poplar, Collierville, Tennessee, (901) 861–9000

Baptist Memorial Hospital/DeSoto, 87601 Southcrest Parkway, Southaven, Mississippi, (662) 349–4000

Baptist Memorial Hospital for Women, 6225 Humphreys Boulevard, (901) 227–9000, 861–9000

Baptist Memorial Hospital/Memphis, 6019 Walnut Grove Road, (901) 227–2727

Crittenden Memorial Hospital, 220 Tyler, West Memphis, Ark., (870) 735–1500 www.crittendenmemorial.org

Crittenden Memorial Hospital is a 152-bed facility about 7 miles from downtown Memphis. It's a full-service hospital with referral relationships across the river with Tennessee hospitals, and many of Crittenden's physicians also practice in Memphis.

The newest addition at Crittenden is a cardiac-imaging center, providing a service that formerly was routinely referred to Memphis. The hospital is the new home for the University of Tennessee School of Dentistry pediatric-residency program, as well as a medical education center that includes a 75-seat auditorium. The hospital also has a new women's and children's health center.

Delta Medical Center
3000 Getwell Road
(901) 369–8100
www.deltamedcenter.com

Delta Medical Center is a 134-bed hospital that has changed hands frequently over the years. It started 30 years ago as Doctor's Hospital, when a group of physicians sought to separate their professional fate from the two big systems, and it later oper-

ated as Eastwood Medical Center, a name that has stuck despite its most recent name change. Entrepreneurs Craig Watson and Neil McLean, who bought the hospital in 1999 (renaming it), have committed themselves to making the place a success. Under their control the hospital has expanded its behavioral-health areas, which grew 20 percent in 2000, and they've recruited more physicians to take up shop in the neighboring office building and to practice at the hospital. The emergency department, which has come under new management in the past year, does a steady business.

Le Bonheur Children's Medical Center
50 North Dunlap
(901) 572–3000
www.lebonheur.org

Children are not just little adults, and that's the point behind Le Bonheur Children's Medical Center. At the 1952 dedication a key attached to a balloon was sent skyward, symbolizing that the hospital would always been open to sick and injured infants, children, and adolescents.

Presently Le Bonheur, with 225 beds and more than 1,600 employees, enjoys an international reputation for clinical care, research, and benevolence. It became part of the Methodist system in 1995 and treats more than 100,000 children each year. It also distributes about 38,000 popsicles and 13,000 crayons to patients each year.

A long list of accomplishments includes the city's first pediatric open-heart surgery in 1959, the region's first intensive-care unit. At its main hospital Le Bonheur operates the only emergency and trauma unit in the Mid-South that's fully staffed and designed specifically for children.

Because it's home to the University of Tennessee Health Science Center's department of pediatrics, UT doctors staff the hospital and provide much of the high-intensity care. Between the university and the community, some 650 doctors practice at Le Bonheur in 42 different medical specialties. The hospital is also home to pediatric organ transplants, providing liver, kidney, heart, and lung transplants.

Other additions to Le Bonheur's services include the Sam Walton children's pediatric imaging center (opened in 1990) and a neurosciences center for children and adolescents (opened in 1995). The latter specializes in brain tumors, epilepsy, spinal-cord injuries, sleep disorders, and attention and behavioral problems.

Although all the heavy-duty surgery takes place at the main hospital, Le Bonheur also operates the Le Bonheur East Surgery Center at 786 Estate Place in East Memphis (901-681-4100). That's where many of the city's children have surrendered their tonsils or had other minor surgery.

Methodist Healthcare, Inc.
1265 Union Avenue
(901) 726-8274
www.methodisthealth.org

This major health-care system includes a network of fourteen Tennessee hospitals and surgery centers, the hub of which is Methodist University Hospital, a 917-bed medical center near downtown Memphis, newly affiliated with the University of Tennessee. It's the same location where 125-bed Methodist Hospital was first built in 1924, after John H. Sherard convinced fellow Methodists in the region to start a hospital.

Methodist operates, in addition to its central medical center, three other Memphis area medical centers as well as hospitals and surgery centers in Brownsville, Dyersburg, Somerville, Jackson, Lexington, McKenzie, Martin, and Selmer.

Methodist has aggressively expanded its other hospitals in Shelby County into freestanding medical centers. They provide most of the care people need, from advanced cardiac care to birthing centers, but close to home. That frees much of Methodist University Hospital to concentrate on the most complex cases, from heart transplants to brain surgery.

Methodist University Hospital has four Centers of Excellence, providing research, training, and treatment in cardiology, oncology, women's services, and neuroscience.

A neonatal intensive care unit, equipped to care for the sickest of babies, is staffed by board-certified neonatalogists and nurses certified for advanced cardiac life support.

Methodist University Hospital is also home to the Memphis Gamma Knife Center, which provides a specialized type of radiation for tumors too deep in the brain to be reached through surgery.

Methodist University Hospital, a major provider of health care, operates in the medical center area near downtown Memphis. PHOTO: METHODIST HEALTHCARE

Emergency and Information Numbers

Emergencies: fire, police, ambulance, 911
Al-Anon, (901) 278–5953
Alcoholics Anonymous, DeSoto County, (901) 280–3435
Alcoholics Anonymous, Memphis, (901) 458–7845
American Cancer Society, (901) 278–2000
American Diabetes Association, (901) 682–8232
American Heart Association, (901) 526–4616
American Lung Association, (901) 276–1731
Civil Defense, (901) 528–2780
Crisis Center, (901) 274–7477
Gamblers Anonymous, (901) 371–4083
LifeBlood: Regional Blood Center, (901) 522–8585
Memphis Light Gas & Water emergencies, (901) 528–4465
Memphis & Shelby County Health Department, (901) 544–7600
Narcotics Anonymous, (800) 677–1462
Overeaters Anonymous, (901) 458–5261
Red Cross, (901) 726–1690
Social Security Administration, (800) 772–1213
Southern Poison Center, (901) 274–7477

Physician Referral Services
Baptist Physician Referral, (901) 362–8677
Delta Medical Physician Referral, (901) 369–8293
Methodist Med Search Physician Referral, (901) 726–8686
Saint Francis Physician Referral, (901) 765–1811
UT Medical Group Physician Referral, (901) 448–6610

Its emergency department treats more than 48,000 patients each year.

Since merging with Le Bonheur Children's Medical Center, Methodist has expanded the reach of the pediatric hospital into many Methodist facilities. For example, the children's hospital staff has helped the system's regional hospitals upgrade and equip their emergency rooms for pediatric care.

Methodist Hospitals in the Memphis Metropolitan Area:

Methodist–Le Bonheur Healthcare/
Germantown Hospital, 7691 Poplar Avenue, Germantown, (901) 754–6418

Methodist Healthcare/North Hospital,
3960 New Covington Pike, (901) 384–5200

Methodist Healthcare/South Hospital,
1264 Wesley Drive, (901) 346–3700

Regional Medical Center at Memphis
877 Jefferson Avenue, (901) 545–7100
www.the-med.org

The Med, as everybody calls this medical center, started in the 1980s as a partnership between the Shelby County government and the University of Tennessee. They wanted to organize a new kind of medical center, an academic and research hospital that would provide the most acute care possible for patients within a 150-mile radius.

The Med, with 321 beds, is part of the training ground for UT and serves as the county's safety-net hospital to the poor. It's also home to five Centers of

Excellence, including its Level III trauma center, where the most seriously injured accident victims from a 150-mile radius are airlifted for emergency care.

The best known of the five is the Elvis Presley Memorial Trauma Center, where saving lives is a daily miracle. It was established in 1983 by surgeon Timothy Fabian, who remains medical director to this day. The center is staffed around the clock with on-site trauma surgeons, nurses, anesthesiologists, and other service personnel, all of them specially trained in severe trauma care.

The newborn center at The Med is one of the oldest and largest newborn intensive-care units in the United States. More than 1,300 premature or critically ill newborns are treated here each year. It is one of only 14 member institutions of the National Research Network, which is supported by the national Institute of Health's Child Development Program. Since its founding in 1968, this facility has successfully treated more than 39,000 premature babies, some weighing as little as one pound.

In general, the Med delivers more than 3,600 babies each year. More than a quarter of those mothers are considered high risk before birth and are therefore treated at the hospital's high-risk obstetrics center. This includes the 1,500-plus referrals of women with complicated pregnancies that The Med gets each year.

The 14-bed burn center treats adults and children with severe burns and cares for more than 300 patients a year. It also operates a skin bank used for transplants. The Med's wound-care center is an outpatient facility that treats slow-healing injuries, such as diabetic foot ulcers, and provides hyperbaric oxygen therapy. The center also has treatment vans that provide wound care to patients in area nursing homes.

Saint Francis Hospital
5959 Park Avenue
(901) 765–1000
www.saintfrancishosp.com

This 609-bed hospital, on Park near the Germantown line, anchors a campus near the geographic center of the metropolis, which also has an on-site nursing home and two physician's office buildings. Saint Francis operates a trauma center, a chest pain center, and an emergency stroke center. It is also home to the Saint Francis/UT Family Practice Residency Center, staffed by University of Tennessee Health Science Center faculty and residents.

In 1994 the chain that is now Tenet Healthcare Corp. bought out the hospital for $100 million, a sum used to fund the Assisi Foundation of Memphis. Since then the foundation has awarded tens of millions of dollars in health-care and education grants.

Reflecting a growing population, Saint Francis is building a 90-bed full-service community hospital in Bartlett, which will offer an emergency room, intensive care, labor and delivery, and surgery. Those beds will be transferred from the main hospital, which is evolving into a place for more intensive care.

St. Jude Children's Research Hospital
332 North Lauderdale
(901) 495–3300
www.stjude.org

This unique hospital focuses on childhood catastrophic diseases, such as leukemia,

Actress Marlo Thomas continues to support St. Jude Children's Research Hospital in Memphis, founded by her father, Danny Thomas.

PHOTO: ST. JUDE CHILDREN'S RESEARCH HOSPITAL

St. Jude Children's Research Hospital

In the winter of 1940, an out-of-work comedian, with just $7.00 in his pocket and a pregnant wife at home, was in a Detroit church when he fell to his knees in desperation before a statue of St. Jude Thaddeus, the patron saint of hopeless cases. The entertainer, Danny Thomas, prayed, "Help me find my place in life and I will build you a shrine, where the helpless may come for aid."

Thomas remembered his vow, and as his career advanced, he used his position and fame to launch St. Jude Children's Research Hospital, which opened in 1962. True to its namesake, St. Jude has always concentrated on research that leads to survival of childhood catastrophic diseases that were at one time considered hopeless. The prospect of survival today for most of these diseases is dramatically better, thanks to St. Jude research.

St. Jude now operates 56 inpatient beds but provides nearly 50,000 outpatient treatments each year. It has more than 2,200 employees, including clinicians, scientists, social workers, and administrative staff. Thousands of children from more than 60 countries have been treated at St. Jude, and no child has ever been denied care for lack of money. Food, lodging, and transportation are provided free of charge to the family while in Memphis for treatment, with the help of the Ronald McDonald House and Target House in town.

The hospital is in the midst of an ambitious $1-billion expansion, which is adding laboratory space and other facilities to attract the best scientific minds in the world. St. Jude is at the forefront of the newest forms of gene therapy. The work is expected to be complete in 2005, but further expansion is planned beyond that. The hospital is one of the most international places in town, with scientists from all over the world.

Research at St. Jude has opened up new windows in understanding things such as AIDS and sickle-cell disease. St. Jude continues these types of research for the clues they can provide in treating childhood diseases.

One of the most exciting events in St. Jude history came in 1996 when Peter Doherty, chairman of the Immunology Department, was awarded the Nobel Prize in medicine. He was recognized for key discoveries he made about the workings of the immune system.

The focus at St. Jude is still pediatric leukemia, solid-tumor cancer, and biomedical research, but it has grown into basic and clinical research in bone marrow transplantation, chemotherapy, the biochemistry of normal and cancerous cells, radiation treatment, blood diseases, viruses resistant to therapy, hereditary diseases, and influenza.

St. Jude is also reaching out into the world. Under an innovative relationship with a children's hospital in Brazil, doctors there bring their most difficult cases to a teleconferencing center to be examined by Memphis doctors over a closed-circuit TV system.

St. Jude Children's Research Hospital is dedicated to finding treatments and cures for catastrophic childhood diseases and also provides care to children who have those diseases.

PHOTO: ST. JUDE CHILDREN'S RESEARCH HOSPITAL

The system also allows Memphis doctors to guide their South American counterparts step by step through complex surgeries.

St. Jude is also creating an Internet-based training system by which surgeons from around the world can access the latest data and take advanced coursework, without leaving home.

The impact of St. Jude's research and treatment can be seen in improved survival rates for many childhood diseases. For example, the survival rate for leukemia was 80 percent in 2001, compared with 4 percent in 1962, and Hodgkin disease had a 90 percent survival rate in 2001 compared with 50 percent in 1962.

that were formerly considered hopeless, and it is at the forefront of medical research in many areas. More than 17,000 children from 60 countries have been treated at St. Jude, and no child has ever been denied care for lack of money. (See Close-up in this chapter for more information.)

UT Bowld Hospital
951 Court
(901) 448–4000
www.utmem.edu

Tucked into a corner of the University of Tennessee Health Science Center campus is UT Bowld Hospital, a 100-bed facility with 500 employees, which specializes in transplant surgery and in the development of new surgical techniques.

Kidney, liver, and pancreas transplants are almost routine, and much of the basic research into cryosurgery was developed here. Cryosurgery is used on organs that cannot be cut and sewn; instead, a cyst or tumor on the liver is frozen with liquid nitrogen and simply trimmed away.

Bowld also saw much of the development of laparoscopic surgery. Rather than cutting a large incision in the abdomen, three small punctures are made. One puncture is for a TV camera, and the other two are for surgical instruments, while the surgeon watches his work on a TV monitor. It's often called Nintendo surgery, and instead of weeks to recover from an incision, patients who get the Nintendo version are usually up and about the same day.

Veterans Affairs Medical Center
1030 Jefferson
(901) 523–8990

The city's VA hospital, with 322 beds and 1,500 employees, includes one of the best facilities for treating spinal-cord injuries in the entire VA system. Before moving to the medical district in the 1960s, local VA medical facilities were concentrated at Kennedy VA Hospital on Shotwell Road. Some people thought the street's name unfortunate and thus moved to have it renamed Getwell Road, which it is still called today.

VA Memphis treats more than 35,000 patients each year, almost entirely on an outpatient basis. The hospital offers a full range of services to military veterans, many of whom have no place else to turn. The hospital is staffed primarily by University of Tennessee physicians, and many of the clinics there are operated by advanced practice nurses who are also on faculty at the UT College of Nursing.

For a variety of reasons, veterans account for a disproportionate number of homeless persons and those with alcohol and drug addictions. VA Memphis has several programs specifically designed to find and treat these veterans.

Walk-in Clinics

Many Memphians turn to walk-in clinics when a sudden illness or injury comes up, but they can't get into their doctor's office and don't want to risk a long wait at a hospital ER, where ambulances have priority. Fast, convenient, and reasonably priced, these centers also are choices for getting treatment for colds, flu, bug bites, sprains, and cuts. As with most everything else in Memphis health care, the minor meds are

Methodist Healthcare Inc.

The system operates two minor medical centers and two with Le Bonheur Urgent Care facilities devoted to treating children.

Cordova Minor Medical Center, 8045 Club Parkway, Cordova, (901) 758–6035 open seven days a week 9:00 A.M. to 10:00 P.M. including holidays

Winchester Minor Medical Center/Le Bonheur Urgent Care, 8071 Winchester, (901) 756–6056, (901) 756–9634 (Le Bonheur) Center hours: seven days a week 9:00 A.M. to 10:00 P.M. including holidays; Le Bonheur hours: Monday through Friday 4:00 P.M. to 11:00 P.M. and Saturday and Sunday 8:00 A.M. to 11:00 P.M.

Le Bonheur Urgent Care, 1335 Germantown Parkway, (901) 758–6000 open Monday through Friday 4:00 P.M. to 11:00 P.M. and Saturday and Sunday 8:00 A.M. to 11:00 P.M., including holidays

Independent Walk-in Clinic

There is one independent clinic in the area.

Med-Emergency Clinic, 5270 Knight Arnold, (901) 362–2811 open Monday through Friday 7:00 A.M. to 5:00 P.M. and Saturday 9:00 A.M. to noon

Insiders' Tip

Although physicians can administer childhood immunizations, the Memphis & Shelby County Health Department operates five childhood immunization clinics throughout the metro area where the costs are less than $10 per visit.

dominated by Baptist and Methodist health-care systems. You may want to check your health insurance before your visit to make sure you are covered, as there may be some restrictions.

Baptist Minor Med, Occupational Health and Urgent Care Centers

All eight centers are open Monday–Saturday, 8:00 A.M. to 8:00 P.M.; three are also open the same hours on Sundays (see below). All are closed Thanksgiving Day and Christmas Day.

Locations

5366 South Mendenhall Square Mall, (901) 795–0385

2087 Union Avenue, (901) 274–3336

5096 Stage Road, Raleigh, (901) 382–5537

6570 Stage Road, Bartlett, (901) 683–7937 (open on Sundays)

5030 Poplar Avenue, (901) 683–7937 (open on Sundays)

584 North Germantown Parkway, Cordova, (901) 753–7686 (open on Sundays)

1164 West Poplar, Collierville, (901) 854–5167

8990 Germantown Extension, Olive Branch, Miss. (901) 525–1160 or (662) 893–1160

Alternative Medicine

Not all health care in Memphis is of the cut, sew, and medicate variety. As a large city with a particular focus on health care, Memphis offers alternative therapies, ranging from Christian Science healing and acupuncture to midwives who will deliver babies at home.

In addition, UT Bowld Hospital has developed techniques for most surgeries that can be performed without donated blood. The Church of Scientology operates the Mission of Memphis, which includes classes on physical and mental health. Its

Church Health Center

Scott Morris is a doctor who preaches and a preacher who heals, and the Church Health Center is both the result of his vision and the template of similar clinics across the United States.

The idea for the center started when the Atlanta native, after attending both medical school and seminary, became associate pastor at St. John's Methodist Church in midtown Memphis. He set out to organize a clinic for the 150,000-plus people in the Memphis area who work yet lack adequate insurance. These people often fall through the cracks in terms of health care, as they earn too much to qualify for Medicaid but cannot afford to buy into their employer sponsored health plan.

The Church Health Center opened its doors in 1987 in a boardinghouse purchased by St. John's, and on its first day Morris and his nurse treated 12 patients. At present Church Health Center has more than 30,000 patient files and employs five on-site physicians, a full-time dentist, six nurses, and two pastoral counselors. There's also a network of more than 600 volunteer physicians, nurses, dentists, optometrists, and other health professionals. They volunteer their time in the clinic—even nights and weekends—or treat the center's patients in their own offices.

Keeping with the spirit of its name, the Church Health Center is funded not by the government but by more than 200 Memphis congregations, including churches of all denominations as well as synagogues. Donations from these groups, individuals, businesses, and other entities provide almost all of the budget.

Hospitals set aside their competitive ambitions when it comes to the Church Health Center. They make their MRI units, CT scanners, and even operating rooms available for the center's patients, who pay based on their income.

Morris's continued innovation has led to two successful outgrowths of the Church Health Center: the Memphis Plan and the Hope and Healing Center.

The Memphis Plan provides a way for people who make $7.50 an hour or less to prepay for their health care and gain access to primary and specialty care, hospitalization, and other medical services. The plan works, thanks to the hundreds of physicians, hospitals, labs, and other facilities who donate their services. Many small businesses that employ minimum-wage workers sponsor these employees by paying the monthly $20 fee.

The Hope and Healing Center provides a place where patients can go for wellness care, such as exercising, aerobics classes, cooking lessons, prayer time, and whatever else a person needs to live a healthy, balanced life. It addresses the reality that more than two-thirds of illnesses can be prevented. It opened in 2000 in a building donated by Baptist Memorial Health Care Corp. and renovated to the tune of more than $6 million.

The Church Health Center is located at 1210 Peabody Avenue (901–272–7170). The Hope and Healing Center is at 1111 Union Avenue (901–259–4673, www.church healthcenter.org).

focus is on health maintenance and preventative care, rather than treatment.

Memphis has more than 40 trained acupuncture specialists, many of them registered nurses who use acupuncture within a physician's practice. Most acupuncturists are also well versed in the uses of herbs, vitamins, and other nutritional interventions. The Healing Arts Center (see below) combines acupuncture, internal medicine, massage therapy, and Eastern medicine.

For more information, or if you're seeking a specific type of treatment, you can do as many Memphians do and head for Wild Oats Market, the local health-food store. Get some gourmet coffee, scan the bulletin board, and ask around. Chances are somebody will be able to help you. Wild Oats is at 5022 Poplar, (901) 685-2293.

Acupuncture and Acupressure Center, 5733 Nanjack Circle, (901) 795-3900

Healing Arts Center, 6005 Park, (901) 763-0909

Chinese Acupuncture Center, 515 North Highland, (901) 323-1202

William L. Faulkner, MD (acupuncture), 969 Peabody Avenue, (901) 527-1153

Mid-South Center for Natural Medicine, 4515 Poplar Avenue, (901) 766-9355

Church of Scientology Mission of Memphis, 1440 Central Avenue, (901) 276-5686

Insiders' Tip

Hospital emergency departments are usually busy and crowded, especially at the larger hospitals, where ambulances go first. But for nontrauma care the emergency department at the much smaller Delta Medical Center, at 3000 Getwell Road, is usually a quicker trip.

Education

Memphis offers a highly diverse assortment of educational choices, from preschool to continuing education. Of the 14 institutions of higher education, the city is home to two major universities, including Tennessee's leading medical school. Colleges in Memphis are also at the forefront of the emerging world of on-line education, and it's possible to earn an entire degree in Memphis in front of a computer terminal.

For elementary and secondary education, there are two public-school systems: Shelby County Schools and Memphis City Schools. Although Shelby County schools are generally seen as better than those in the city, the Memphis system boasts a number of schools so outstanding that parents from outside the city pay tuition for their children to attend them. Parents can also choose from a roster of private schools for children of all ages, many with longstanding traditions of academic excellence.

Memphis has been shaped over the years by its schools and by the public's perception of their quality. Sometimes entire neighborhoods have been disrupted by a change in schools, often based on unfair and unreasonable fears. For example, after more than a decade of legal wrangling, the City of Memphis in 2000 finally annexed the Hickory Hill area of southeast Shelby County, bringing a number of county schools under the authority of Memphis City Schools. Within a year the entire area was dotted with FOR SALE signs in front yards, with the shift in school systems a major reason.

In both the city and the county, many families base their home-buying decisions on the neighborhood's schools. Word of mouth among parents is often the best source of information about the schools, particularly city public schools, which vary significantly due to parental involvement and other factors.

Some families are drawn to Southaven, Olive Branch, and other parts of DeSoto County, the fast-growing Mississippi county just south of Memphis. The DeSoto County School District, which had 24 schools and two more under construction as of 2001, is the second-largest school district in Mississippi and gets high marks from the state education department for its academic achievement.

Public Schools

Shelby County, which operates 46 schools with almost 50,000 students, includes the lion's share of middle- and upper-income areas, with virtually no poverty. Memphis City Schools is the largest school system in Tennessee and the 20th-largest school district in the nation, operating 165 schools with an enrollment of nearly 120,000.

Memphis City Schools are a mixed bag, so each school must be considered on its own merits. For example, White Station High School in East Memphis is considered one of the best college-prep schools in the United States and routinely has more National Merit semi-finalists of any public school in Tennessee. Yet in 2001, after the Tennessee Department of Education toughened some of its criteria, some 64 city schools were identified by the department as low performing and in danger of being placed on probation.

Many of these troubled schools face significant challenges, including locations in impoverished, crime-ridden sections of the metropolitan area, and parents who in many cases don't get involved with their children's education or schools. The same schools usually have a high percentage of students qualifying for free or subsidized school lunches.

Insiders' Tip

Memphis City Schools encourage parents to take an ownership role in their neighborhood school and allow parents to develop programs based on local need. One example is a 501(c)3 nonprofit corporation formed by parents at Richland Elementary, which raised enough money to hire two extra reading assistants to help the slower readers catch up.

conduct, and attendance records, plus they must pass rigorous audition standards to be admitted to the program. About 600 of Overton High's 1,400 students are enrolled in the creative- and performance-arts program at the school, which also offers honors, advanced placement, and standard courses in English, mathematics, and other subjects as well as business education and vocational courses.

The operating budget for Memphis City Schools was $645 million for the 2001–2002 school year, and the system has also made extensive capital expenditures. A few years ago the city school system completed its six-year, $1-billion project to install air-conditioning in every school, which makes sense for a city where temperatures in August and September are often in the 90s. Schools that could be retrofitted were, but many older schools were replaced with modern facilities. Recognizing that each school is a long-term investment in neighborhood stability, Memphis City Schools officials designed each school to fit its particular neighborhood.

Capital improvements continue, with a number of new schools being added and existing schools being renovated or expanded.

In contrast new Shelby County schools have been less expensive to build, but they tend to look very much alike. The system includes all areas of the county outside the Memphis city limits, including the incorporated towns of Arlington, Bartlett, Collierville, Germantown, Lakeland, and Millington. It's the fourth-largest school system in the state.

The Shelby County government has spent about $1.5 billion on public education in the past decade: $1.1 billion in operations and $400 million in capital improvements. Because every property owner in the city of Memphis pays taxes to the city and the county, a major portion of tax collections from the county find their way back to city schools.

In order to comply with laws requiring county government to equally fund students in both systems, 70 percent of county tax collections for education go to the city. That means that half of every dol-

The system is working to improve the low-performing schools. In addition, more than 600 business and community partners give time and money to students at all the schools through the Adopt-a-School program. The school system also encourages parents to get involved with their child's school, and as a result many parents volunteer their time and help to raise money for improvements ranging from new playground equipment to extra teaching assistants.

The city school system also offers an optional program at 30 schools, with enrichment areas ranging from fine arts to engineering, from international business to aviation technology. Optional programs are available at no extra charge to residents of the district, but others clamor and compete for a limited number of slots. Noncity residents pay $600 per year, Tennessee residents outside Shelby County pay $2,600, and out-of-state residents pay $5,300 to attend Memphis City Schools.

For example, Overton High School offers the area's only creative- and performing-arts optional high-school program. Students must have good grades,

lar collected in property taxes and 100 percent of the local sales taxes support public education.

For more information about Memphis City Schools, contact the student enrollment office at (901) 325-5830. You can also check out the city schools' Web site at www.memphis-schools.k12.tn.us, or call (901) 325-5628 for a free brochure. For more information on Shelby County schools, contact the pupil services offices at (901) 321-2560 or check out the system's Web site at www.scs.k12.tn.us.

Private and Parochial Schools

The Memphis area has more than 100 private elementary, middle, and secondary schools. Most are affiliated with a church or denomination, but some are purely academic. Tuition and fees can range from $1,500 a year to more than $10,000 a year.

A number of private schools also offer special education for children with various learning disabilities. By law, city and county schools are obliged to provide these services to residents at no additional charge. The reality is that the public-school systems do their best but are overwhelmed by the demand. Those who have grown weary of the struggles and the waiting have found refuge in private schools.

The Catholic Diocese of Memphis operates the single largest private-school system in Memphis, with 7,500 students at 24 schools. In 1999 the diocese launched an ambitious plan, the Jubilee Project, to reopen six inner-city schools beginning with kindergarten and first grade in each and adding one grade each year. The response from the neighborhoods has been overwhelming. Most Jubilee schools are 80 to 100 percent black and about 90 percent non-Catholic. The percentage of children qualifying for free or subsidized lunches is in the same range.

Another major private-school system in Memphis is Harding Academy. Affiliated with the Church of Christ, Harding operates eight schools with a total enrollment of about 2,000.

Private Elementary/ Middle Schools

Holy Rosary Elementary School
4841 Park Avenue
(901) 685–1231
www.cdom.org

Holy Rosary is a Catholic school under the auspices of the Catholic Diocese of Memphis. It's a coed school founded in 1954, along with the founding of Holy Rosary Parish, and offers classes in kindergarten through the eighth grade.

The school has a reputation as being academically rigorous—and very Catholic. That's reflected in daily Bible studies, weekly Mass, and a faculty that is 85 percent Roman Catholic. It is one of the largest parochial grade schools in the diocese.

The East Memphis campus includes 29 classrooms, a library, a media center, a computer lab, a science lab, a music room, a gym, and athletic fields. The teacher-pupil ratio is 1:22, and virtually all graduating eighth graders are accepted into the high school of their choice.

St. Ann-Bartlett Elementary School
6529 Stage Road, Bartlett
(901) 386–3328
www.cdom.org

St. Ann has been part of the Bartlett Community since 1960, when the parish school opened with 150 students. Presently St.

Insiders' Tip

Some of the city's best private education can be found at one of the more than 20 Catholic schools in the area. For more information call the Catholic Diocese of Memphis at (901) 373-1219 or check out www.cdom.org.

Ann has an enrollment of nearly 700, and 95 percent are Catholic. It has classes for kindergarten through the eighth grade.

The school has a staff of 40 certified teachers, plus a full-time counselor and administrators. There are 30 classrooms, plus a library, a computer lab, a science lab, a music room, a band room, a full-service cafeteria, and a gym.

In addition to Catholic religious instruction, St. Ann puts a high value on enrichment activities. Those include academic competitions, community-service projects, sports, and music. The school also offers child care before and after school, as well as summer programs.

Private Elementary/ Secondary Schools

Briarcrest Christian Schools
6000 Briarcrest
(901) 765-4600
www.briarcrest.com

Briarcrest was founded in 1972 as a ministry of Briarcrest Baptist Church, and since then has evolved into a large, coed, nondenominational Christian school with an enrollment of nearly 1,600 students and a strong sports program.

The main campus is on 20 acres near Poplar and I-240 in East Memphis, with an elementary school (K–5), a middle school (6–8), and a high school (9–12). Briarcrest also operates an elementary school at Ridgeway Baptist Church, at Ridgeway near Nonconnah Parkway in southeast Memphis.

Briarcrest offers a wide range of sports, including soccer, football, and tennis. The school's sports complex is on 90 acres near Walnut Grove and Raleigh–LaGrange Road in east Shelby County.

Christian Brothers High School
5900 Walnut Grove Road
(901) 682-7801
www.cbhs.org

CBHS is an all-boys Catholic high school in East Memphis operated by the same LaSalle order that operates Christian Brothers University in midtown Memphis. The school, on a 32-acre campus on Walnut Grove near I-240, has a reputa-

tion for solid academics and college prep. It's one of the few schools in Memphis that still teaches Latin, and it prides itself on its commitment to technology, with a computer-learning center and computers also woven into other classroom areas. The curriculum is heavy on math, science, computers, fine arts, and even business, another rarity for a high school.

Christian Brothers has an enrollment of about 875, and a very intimate teacher-pupil ratio of 1:14. The students are required to perform 44 hours of community service in addition to satisfying academic requirements. The student body consists of grades 9 through 12.

Evangelical Christian School of Memphis
7600 Macon Road, Cordova
(901) 754-7217
www.ecseagles.com

Tucked away in a wooded area of Cordova, ECS is an independent, nondenominational, coed school with an enrollment of about 1,400. As its name implies, the school comes from the evangelical tradition, which means a strong emphasis on moral character, clean living, and service to others.

ECS teaches children from kindergarten through 12th grade. It's known for its rigorous science programs, especially in high school, where chemistry and biology get special attention.

The school prides itself on the fact that 70 percent of the 2001 graduating class were offered academic, athletic, or achievement scholarships.

Harding Academy
1100 Cherry Road
(901) 767-4494
www.hardingacademymemphis.org

Harding Academy, affiliated with the Church of Christ, operates eight schools across Shelby County with a total enrollment of about 2,000, including a high school at 1100 Cherry Street in East Memphis. Its system covers all ages, from prekindergarten through 12th grade.

The school, which was founded in 1952, has expanded by going into growing neighborhoods and adding schools to church campuses there. The newest addition is a 54,000-square-foot school in fast-growing Cordova, located on 6.1 acres next to the current building on Macon Road. The additional space provides 18 classrooms to serve 432 elementary students in grades 1 through 6.

Harding is unabashed about its Christian foundation and also seeks to instill a sense of pride in being an American and the responsibility that citizenship entails.

Hutchison School
1740 Ridgeway Road
(901) 761–2220
www.hutchisonschool.org

Hutchison is one of the premier, all-girls schools in the Mid-South, with a college-prep program. The school was founded in 1902 and is known for its high-quality, academically rich instruction. Enrollment is about 820, covering kindergarten through 12th grade.

The school has been expanding and adding new services recently, including a new athletic center and a learning and technology complex complete with a NASA satellite feed, interactive media, wireless technology, and an e-classroom. Hutchison completed a new early-childhood center in 2001.

Foreign-language classes begin as early as age three, and hands-on science classes begin in the 1st grade. One popular area of study has been robotics.

Hutchison also provides instruction in fine arts and offers a summer program that's also academically rich. About 25 percent of the school's students each year are recognized as National Merit Scholars.

Lausanne Collegiate School
1381 West Massey Street
(901) 683–5233
www.lausannekth.com

Part of the 28-acre campus of Lausanne is the Blue Herron Lake, where students often gather to read poetry, paint, or discuss studies. And that reflects the Lausanne philosophy of incorporating learning into all of life's activities.

Lausanne is a coed, college-prep school with about 600 students and 100 faculty and staff. It offers classes in kindergarten through 12th grade.

The school has embraced technology in almost every way, from teachers who post assignments on the Internet so that parents can stay involved to word processing in English. Kindergartners use calculators in math instruction, and science labs are equipped with the latest devices. The school also provides a variety of athletic options, so all children can find something they enjoy. In addition to the usual soccer, basketball, and track, sports programs also include dance, karate, weight training, fencing, and lacrosse. Outdoor leadership features rock climbing, canoeing, rafting, and more.

Memphis University School
6191 Park Avenue
(901) 260–1300
www.musowls.org

Since 1893 MUS has existed with three goals: preparing boys for competitive colleges, providing them with a well-rounded liberal arts education, and helping them to develop into cultured gentlemen.

On 94 rolling acres in East Memphis, MUS teaches boys in the 7th through 12th grades. The student-faculty ratio is 12 to 1. The school still has the same general goals, and the numbers tell the story.

The class of 2001, for example, had 91 graduates accepted into 42 different colleges and universities; 53 percent received merit, leadership, athletic, or military scholarships. The class had 10 National Merit Finalists and another 21 Letters of Commendation.

Traditionally, connections made at MUS have continued into adult life, with about 70 percent of the school's alumni remaining in the Memphis area. Many of the city's movers and shakers, including AutoZone founder Pitt Hyde and many others, are MUS graduates.

St. Agnes Academy–St. Dominic School
4830 Walnut Grove Road
(901) 767–1356
www.saa-sds.org

St. Agnes Academy–St. Dominic School is a Catholic independent school with a history—at least in the case of St. Agnes—that predates the Civil War. St. Agnes, founded in 1851, is a college-prep school for girls.

Insiders' Tip

The leading private schools in town take pride in having a student body that is diverse, both ethnically and socially, so if there's a school you really like, don't write it off because the tuition might be $7,000 or more. Most schools offer scholarships and grants based on need, and most will trade for services. That top school might be within reach with a combination of partial tuition, financial aid, and maybe painting the gym.

St. Dominic was founded in 1956 as a school for boys. The two were joined in 1978 but still retain some of their single-sex character.

The school provides coed education in early childhood and kindergarten, single-sex classes in grades 1 through 6, and coordinated classes in 7th and 8th grades. High school is for girls only. Total enrollment is about 830, with upper-school enrollment of 335.

As a college-prep high school, St. Agnes provides a well-rounded academic education and offers a number of advanced-placement courses. It is known to shine in liberal arts and language, and is one of only two high schools in the state at which the University of Tennessee will grant college credit for foreign language instruction, in both French and Spanish.

St. Agnes teaches from a philosophy of service and requires all upper-school students to perform community service as part of their education.

Of the 62 members of the class of 2000, 58 percent won academic, athletic, and achievement scholarships.

St. Benedict at Auburndale (K–12)
2100 Germantown Parkway, Cordova
(901) 388–7321
www.stbenedictatauburndale.org

St. Benedict started as a private school in 1966, founded by Stanley and Alice Smith, and was known as the Auburndale School System. They sold the 22-acre campus in 1988 to the Catholic Diocese of Memphis, which gave it the current name. It serves students in kindergarten through 12th grade.

St. Benedict is college-prep school with a total enrollment of about 1,025, including 400 in the high school. The school emphasizes honors and advanced-placement coursework, along with foreign language, music, art, and computer instruction. Virtually all of St. Benedict's graduates are accepted to college.

St. Benedict plans to merge with the school across the street, St. Francis of Assisi Parish, effective in 2004.

St. Mary's Episcopal School
60 Perkins Road Extension
(901) 537–1405
www.stmarysschool.org

St. Mary's is a girls-only college-preparatory school in East Memphis that is academically rigorous and carefully sequenced from prekindergarten through 12th grade. Founded in 1847, St. Mary's now has a total enrollment of about 840, with a student to faculty ratio of 10 to 1.

St. Mary's graduates have a reputation for being able to analyze and act and are highly sought for the critical thinking skills they possess. The school emphasizes a classic, rigorous liberal arts curriculum that is designed to allow each girl to reach her individual potential.

The rigorous program has paid off for St. Mary's students. In the class of 2002, for example, 27 of the 47 students were recognized by the National Merit Scholarship program, including 10 National Merit semifinalists. The school's class of 2001 ranked eighth in the nation for its ACT composite score.

The school shares a 20-acre campus with Church of the Holy Communion, an Episcopal church in East Memphis.

Southern Baptist Educational Center
7400 Getwell Road, Southaven, Miss.
(901) 349-3096
www.sbecschool.org
SBEC was founded in 1973 as a ministry of Broadway Baptist Church, with the goal of providing Bible-based, academic education. The school is situated on 61 acres in northern DeSoto County. It provides classes from kindergarten through 12th grade.

The school has an enrollment of about 1,100, with a faculty-to-student ratio of 1:15.

SBEC offers 11 honors courses in high school and four advanced-placement courses; 98 percent of its graduates pursue college.

Home Schooling

Nearly 2,000 children in the Memphis area go to school at the kitchen table, in one of the most dynamic home-school communities in the United States. This is partly as an outgrowth of the city's position in the Bible Belt, as many parents choose to home-school for religious reasons.

Home school is almost a misnomer, because, through the Memphis Area Home Education Association, students can still participate in competitive sports, including basketball and cheerleading. They have field trips, dances, graduation ceremonies, even their own scholarship fund. Parents share teaching duties so that numerous home-school families can combine talents, resources, and materials. For more information about all aspects of home schooling in the Memphis area, call the Memphis Area Home Education Association at (901) 788-6432 or check out its Web site at www.memphishomeed.org.

In this state the Tennessee Department of Education has certain requirements for enrolling home-school students. For more information contact the agency at (865) 579-3749 or visit its Web site at www. state.tn.us/education/aahomsch.

Child Care

Memphis is a very family-oriented city, and you'll find many providers of quality day care. There are nearly 400 licensed child-care centers in the Memphis area and probably twice as many unlicensed places that also provide care to children. The licensed centers include large national chains such as La Petite Academy and Kinder Care. But, in a city like Memphis, where churches play a central role in the lives of so many families, it's not surprising that church child care dominates the scene.

In finding care for your child, your best resources may be friends, neighbors, and coworkers with young children. You'll probably want to visit a number of child-care centers and take time to ask questions as well as observe how the care providers interact with the children.

Also, many churches, including Calvary Episcopal Church in downtown Memphis and Christ the King Lutheran in East Memphis, operate excellent day-care centers that welcome children from outside their own flocks. Of course, if you choose to join a church, it may well offer day care, allowing you to leave the little ones with people you know. Also check out private schools; many of them have waiting lists, and by starting with their child-care center, it may be easier to get a slot a few years later when it's time for school to start.

Memphis Association for the Education for Young Children
815 North McLean Boulevard
(901) 274-9440
http://taeyc.oofamily.com/maeyc.html
This group is primarily a provider of training opportunities to the child-care community that's also involved in policy issues related to early-childhood licensing standards and programs. The group is up to speed, however, on what's happening in the local child-care community and can be a good source of information.

Tennessee Department of Human Services
400 Deaderick Street, Nashville
(800) 462–8261
www.state.tn.us/humanserv

The Tennessee Department of Human Services is in charge of overseeing child care in the state. Under state law any child-care provider caring for more than four children must have a license from this agency. The department provides a free child-care resource and referral service, offering customized child-care listings, literature, and counseling.

Check out the Web site, which maintains a list of licensed and registered child-care centers, organized by zip codes within Shelby County and other nearby counties. It also has information on licensing and updates on proposed child-care rules and legislation.

Higher Education

A 2000 study compiled by the city's 14 academic higher-education institutions indicates that education is almost as big an industry in Memphis as motor freight, in employment and payroll, with an economic impact of $1.4 billion. These schools, ranging from Southwest Tennessee Community College to the University of Memphis, boast 2,500 faculty members and another 8,500 staff employees. Among the public colleges and universities, the primary issue is state funding. By some measures Tennessee ranks 47th in the nation in support of higher education. State budgetary problems have resulted in tuition increases for most state schools. Worse, the financial strain has caused a steady drain of faculty, especially from the University of Memphis and the University of Tennessee Health Science Center. Instructors are being lured away not just with better salaries but with offers of better research facilities and support.

Generating more funding for the schools is a constant debate. In place of wholesale tax reform, which seems unlikely, one idea that won't go away is the creation of a state lottery, with all proceeds going to higher education. To do that would require amending the state constitution, which prohibits all forms of gambling.

Students can find an active campus life at University of Memphis, Rhodes College, or another of the city's institutions of higher learning. PHOTO: BILLY HOWARD/ RHODES COLLEGE

Memphis also has a wide range of smaller trade and technical schools.

Baptist Memorial College of Health Sciences
1003 Monroe Avenue
(901) 227-4330
www.bmhcc.org

Part of Baptist Memorial Health Care Corp., the College of Health Sciences represents the consolidation of several schools, primarily Baptist College of Nursing. At present the school awards degrees in nursing and other health related fields.

Christian Brothers University
650 East Parkway
(901) 321-3200
www.cbu.edu

CBU is a Catholic school in the tradition of the Christian Brothers of the LaSalle Order, and it's a common sight to see the brothers on campus and teaching classes. The college has a strong program of evening classes to accommodate working students as well as traditional daytime classes for full-time students.

U.S. News and World Report, in its Year 2000 Annual Guide of America's Best Colleges, ranked CBU number 23 in the top regional Southern colleges and as one of the top-50 schools in the nation offering bachelor's and master's degrees in engineering. CBU also offers degree programs in management and education, as well as an MBA and executive MBA programs. Enrollment is about 2,000. CBU is not to be confused with Christian Brothers High School, which maintains its campus on Walnut Grove Road in East Memphis, although the LaSalle Order oversees both.

Crichton College
255 North Highland
(901) 367-9800
www.crichton.edu

Crichton (pronounced CRY-ton) is a non-denominational Christian college, known for intimate classroom experiences and fostering an attitude of service. It recently moved to a new campus on Highland Avenue. Enrollment is about 925.

LeMoyne-Owen College
807 Walker Avenue
(901) 774-9090
www.lemoyne-owen.edu

LeMoyne-Owen is a traditionally black, private liberal arts college that was one of the original schools that formed the United Negro College Fund. Enrollment is about 1,000.

The school awards bachelor's degrees in arts, sciences, and business administration. It is affiliated with the United Church of Christ and The Tennessee Baptist Missionary and Education Convention. The college is committed to providing a holistic education for the traditional and non-traditional student and to providing leadership and service to the Memphis and Mid-South community and beyond.

Memphis College of Art
1930 Poplar Avenue
(901) 272-5100
www.mca.edu

Nestled in the heart of Overton Park in midtown, the College of Art, as it's known locally, is one of the nation's leading art schools. It teaches traditional forms in sculpture and painting as well as computer graphic design, and it recently added a photography program. With an enrollment of about 250, the school awards the bachelor's and master's degree of fine arts. The school prides itself on its 11-to-1 student-teacher ratio.

MCA is a hip place, so there's great people-watching in the area around the main building.

Students have showings throughout the year, including an annual holiday show and sale. The college's lobby is also the scene for some of the city's more inspired art shows, including an annual show of original black-velvet art by local artists.

Rhodes College
2000 North Parkway
(901) 843-3000
www.rhodes.edu

Rhodes is a private liberal arts college, with a reputation for academic excellence. With an enrollment of about 1,500, Rhodes awards bachelor's degrees in sciences and

Rhodes College in midtown Memphis features a beautiful campus in the English tradition.
PHOTO: TREY CLARK/ RHODES COLLEGE

arts and master's degrees in accounting. Affiliated with the Presbyterian Church (USA), Rhodes is also known for teaching from a perspective of humility. In addition to classroom work and extracurricular activities, students are required to perform public service in the community.

Rhodes (formerly known as Southwestern at Memphis) has one of the most beautiful campuses in the South, with soaring stone buildings in the English tradition, and lots of trees in a residential area of midtown Memphis. About 75 percent of its students live on campus, which makes for a lively atmosphere.

The school has a 12-to-1 student-faculty ratio, which encourages students to get to know their teachers. About 60 percent of students participate in Rhodes's internship program, working at local businesses that include Federal Express, the Orpheum Theatre, and the Memphis office of Ernst & Young.

Through the Meeman Center for Lifelong Learning, Rhodes faculty members also teach adult enrichment courses in a wide variety of disciplines. The school also maintains a link to the off-campus world through music, theater, and lecture presentations that are open to the public.

Southern College of Optometry
1245 Madison Avenue
(901) 722-3216
www.sco.edu

SCO is a private college of optometry, awarding doctor of optometry degrees. It is one of the more competitive optometry schools in the United States, with an enrollment of about 480 in its four-year graduate program. The school estimates that it has trained 14 percent of all optometrists in the United States.

The school also operates the largest optometry clinic in the city and is just completing construction of a 46,000-square-foot, state-of-the-art eye and vision center on its campus to accommodate demand for eye care.

Southwest Tennessee Community College
737 Union Avenue
(901) 333-4368
www.stcc.cc.tn.us

Southwest Tennessee Community College was formed in 2000 with the merger of two community colleges, and people still refer to the midtown campus as Shelby State and the East Memphis campus as State Tech. Plans are to build a third campus, but in light of state fiscal problems, the plans may not get off the drawing board for some time.

Still STCC is the largest two-year college in the state higher-education system. For now Southwest Tennessee has been energetically seeking places to offer classes and has satellite locations as far away as Fayette County. Currently it has seven off-campus sites in addition to the two main campuses.

STCC is a progressive community college known for providing a nurturing, safe environment for students, many of whom are the first in their families to attend college. Local industry often turns to Southwest to develop specialized training for new processes for its employees. Enrollment is about 12,000.

Union University/Germantown
2745 Hacks Cross Road, Germantown
(901) 759–0029
www.uu.edu/gtown/

Union University is a private, Christian liberal arts college based in Jackson, Tennessee, that in 2000 opened a permanent Memphis campus in Germantown. Previously, it had offered classes in various places in Memphis, mostly for nurses seeking a bachelor of science in nursing. The school has a local enrollment of 380 and awards degrees in nursing and education.

University of Memphis
Central Avenue at Patterson
(901) 678–2000
www.memphis.edu

The University of Memphis is the second-largest university in Tennessee (after University of Tennessee in Knoxville), with enrollment of more than 20,000 students. The school's main campus covers more than a dozen city blocks near East Memphis. Classes are also available at other locations in Shelby County and West Tennessee. Most people call it "U of M," but

don't be surprised to hear it called by its former name, Memphis State.

U of M is an urban commuter university, with only a fraction of students living on campus in a traditional college arrangement. Demand for student housing was so low that at one point the university ended up selling two high-rise dorms to Wesley Housing Corp. to be used as senior housing.

The university has nine colleges and schools that award bachelors, masters, and doctoral degrees in multiple disciplines. It's also home to the Cecil C. Humphreys School of Law and the Fogelman College of Business and Economics.

The University of Memphis Tigers—both the basketball and football teams—help raise the school's visibility around town, and many alumni turn out to watch the teams play. (See the Spectator Sports chapter for more details.)

> ## Insiders' Tip
> These days you don't have to go to a campus to work on your college degree. Southwest Tennessee Community College and the University of Memphis are part of the new Regents Online Degree Program, a state program that allows students to earn an entire college degree on-line. To enroll call University of Memphis at (901) 678-2000 or Southwest Tennessee at (901) 333-4000 or, for more information, check out www.tn.regents degrees.org.

U of M has a particularly deep involvement within the city of Memphis. It's not uncommon for logistics companies to tap expertise in the college of business, for example. Memphis businesses also play a significant role at the university: Kemmons Wilson, the man who created Holiday Inns, is funding a new college of hospitality at the university, and the city's biggest employer is the title sponsor of the FedEx Emerging Technology Center.

In addition the U of M Department of Criminal Science works on projects with the Memphis Police Department and the FBI. The Urban Institute was formed in 2000, to coordinate the community projects of five departments. Examples of its work include a project that documents changes in social patterns in the area north of downtown, where a massive housing project is being torn down and replaced with a blend of subsidized and market-rate housing. The Urban Institute is tracking changes as part of a national project that aims to break the circle of welfare and cultural dependency.

University of Tennessee Health Science Center
800 Madison Avenue
(901) 448–5500
www.utmem.edu

Known as UT-Memphis, this school is the state's main medical school and training center, with an international reputation for its emphasis on hands-on training. Enrollment is about 2,000.

The goal of the College of Medicine is to get every student into a clinical environment in their first semester. Rotations also take med students through the pediatrics hospital, the trauma center, suburban and rural hospitals, and doctors' offices. Its philosophy, which is promulgated in every class, is that students must always understand that there's a patient who's affected by their education.

An innovative program to address the shortage of doctors in rural areas recruits young people from the underserved areas. Their communities support their education with the understanding that they will return and hang a shingle in their hometowns.

The College of Medicine also is aggressively expanding its research efforts, working with a local hospital to build the UT–Baptist Research Park, a biotech business incubator near the Memphis campus. In 2000 the college received $60 million in research grants and hopes to increase that number.

The school also has a strong link to area health care, with more than 800 Memphis physicians teaching its students and with many of its faculty members practicing medicine. (See Health Care and Wellness chapter for more information.)

The College of Nursing is equally responsive to the communities it serves. The school awards only graduate degrees, and so is designed for mid-career nurses who are already in practice. UT-Memphis also has programs in dentistry, pharmacy, allied health, and other health-related subjects.

Other Higher Education

The Memphis area also is home to a number of schools that offer specific technical or vocational training or a limited number of courses, primarily intended for adults seeking to advance their careers. Others offer degrees and instruction in religious studies. In addition, there are some other community colleges located just outside the city in Mississippi and Arkansas.

Belhaven College, 5100 Poplar Avenue, (901) 888–3343, www.belhaven.edu

Concorde Career Institute, 5100 Poplar Avenue, (901) 761–9494, www.concordecareercollege.com

Embry-Riddle Aeronautical University, 2990 Airways Boulevard, (901) 332–4300, www.embryriddle.edu

Harding University Graduate School of Religion, 1000 Cherry Street, (901) 761–1352, www.hugsr.edu

ITT Technical Institute, 1255 Lynnfield Road, (901) 762–0556, www.itt-tech.edu

Memphis Theological Seminary, 168 East Parkway, (901) 458–8232, www.mtscampus.edu

Methodist Hospital School of Nursing, 251 South Claybrook Street, (901) 726–8516, www.methodisthealth.org

Mid-America Baptist Theological Seminary, 2216 Germantown Road South, Germantown, (901) 751–8453, www.mabts.edu

Mid-South Community College, 2000 Broadway, West Memphis, Arkansas, (870) 733–6722, www.mscc.cc.ar.us

Northwest Mississippi Community College, 5197 W.E. Ross Parkway, Southaven, Mississippi, (662) 342–1570, www.nwcc.cc.ms.us

Southeast College of Technology, 2731 Nonconnah Parkway, (901) 345–1000, www.educationamerica.com

University of Mississippi/DeSoto Center, 5197 W.E. Ross Parkway, Southaven, Mississippi, (901) 342–4765, www.olemiss.edu

Vatterott College, 6152 Macon Road, (901) 761–5730, www.vatterott-college.edu

William R. Moore College of Technology, 1200 Poplar Avenue, (901) 726–1977, www.williamrmoore.org

Retirement

Retired Memphians—rather than retired New Yorkers, Michiganers, or other transplants—make up the majority of senior citizens in the city. As a result it's not surprising that the retirement amenities available in Memphis tend to focus on the people who live here already and are simply reaching the age at which they have different needs in terms of housing, recreation, assistance, and care. This situation is a contrast to that in Florida, the Ozarks, and other places in the Sunbelt, which attract retirees from other parts of the country.

Memphis is a place where people have strong ties to their neighborhoods, so one welcome trend is toward retirement communities geared toward local neighborhoods. Thus retirees who decide they need a little more assistance can still be close to familiar amenities and the neighbors they care about by choosing one of these communities. Many offer meals, transportation, activities, assisted-living services, and other amenities.

This approach differs from that in senior housing seen in the late 1980s, when a construction boom of retirement communities took place in Memphis and in many major cities in anticipation of a surge in demand that never materialized. These were centers with maintenance-free living, social activities, and personal assistance available on an a la carte basis. Many of them fell flat when it turned out retirees didn't flock to these types of residences immediately upon retirement.

Since then the retirement industry has retrenched. The great consolidator of retirement living in the region has turned out to be Wesley Senior Ministries, an affiliate of the United Methodist Church, which stepped in to take over distressed retirement centers. Presently Wesley serves more than 2,400 residents in three nursing homes, four assisted-living communities, and 22 senior-housing communities across three states. In addition, several large operators of assisted-living facilities have entered the Memphis market, including Atria and Brighton Gardens by Marriott.

Of course, retirees need more than just a place to live. Resources are plentiful in this area, and it's easy to find meals, recreation centers, volunteer opportunities, and a variety of activities. Local government agencies are important players, as are churches, as they often have programs, activities, and outreach for that segment of the population.

City life isn't for everybody, though, and those who prefer small-town life will find dozens of options within a short drive of Memphis. Many retirees and urban professionals are buying property in these small towns, the most celebrated of which is Oxford, Mississippi. *Money* magazine in 2001 named this college town as the best place to retire in the South. Home to University of Mississippi, Oxford has a picturesque town square and a population of 11,800 (see Day Trips chapter for more information).

Ballroom dancing is among the many activities available for seniors at Lewis Senior Center, one of many operated by the City of Memphis Division of Park Services. PHOTO: CITY OF MEMPHIS DIVISION OF PARK SERVICES

Senior Services

These local agencies serve as clearinghouses, with information on all types of services available to senior citizens. In some cases they operate their own facilities and programs.

Aging Commission of the Mid-South
2670 Union Avenue, Extended
(901) 324–6333

The mission of the aging commission is to serve as the focal point for aging services and as a liaison between senior citizens and the agencies and programs that serve them. It coordinates and funds community services that promote independence and choice for retirees age 60 and older.

In partnership with other groups, the commission funds programs that provide housekeeping assistance, legal advice, and Alzheimer's day-care services as well as a retired senior volunteer program.

County Mayor's Office on Aging
2670 Union Avenue, Extended
(901) 525–2273

The mayor's office on aging was set up in 1979 to help solve the problems of senior citizens in more than 60 areas. These include dealing with Medicare/Medicaid and social security, taking care of dental needs, and counseling. It publishes the *Senior Citizens Handbook*, which is updated twice a year. This valuable tool has a wealth of information on everything from a complete listing of available services to the warning signs of serious illnesses and advice on protecting one's self from fraud. It's available by calling the office.

Memphis Inter-Faith Association (MIFA)
910 Vance
(901)527–0208, (901) 521–0536 for MIFA Meals
www.mifa.org

MIFA is a major provider of meals to seniors, serving 3,000 hot lunches every day both at central locations and through its home-delivered meals program. Through its Long-Term Care Ombudsman advocacy program, MIFA works to improve the quality of life and care in nursing homes and other long-term care facilities. Through other programs active, low-income seniors work as companions to frail seniors, and volunteers provide handyman services. MIFA also operates two senior centers.

Senior Services
4700 Poplar Avenue
(901) 766–0600, (800) 487–5207
www.memphisseniors.com

Although it's reaching out to other age groups these days as well, Senior Services can put you in touch with providers of an array of services, including stay-at-home assisted living, career assistance and transportation. The organization also operates two senior activities centers and a free information and referral service, available to the public and to professionals.

Volunteer Opportunities

Memphis Inter-Faith Association (MIFA)
910 Vance
(901) 527–0208
www.mifa.org

MIFA has an ongoing need for volunteers to staff its meals operation, Long-Term Care ombudsman advocacy, and other programs.

RSVP
910 Vance
(901) 527–0208, Ext. 229

RSVP (Retiree & Senior Volunteer Program) matches interested seniors with community needs. Under this local branch of the Corporation for National and Community Service program, more than 700 retired Memphians over age 55 volunteer their time to help out in the community.

Volunteer Memphis
326 Ellsworth Street
(901) 458–3288
www.volunteermemphis.org

This group recruits volunteers and refers more than 4,000 of them each year to area nonprofit organizations in Memphis and Shelby County. The volunteer assignments range from helping children as part of the Volunteers in Schools program to being a

Insiders' Tip

The City of Memphis division of park services operates six senior-citizens centers in various locations around the city. Each one offers activities, low-cost meals, and other programs. For more information call (901) 454-5200.

docent at a Wonders exhibit. Although Volunteer Memphis isn't specifically a retiree program, many of its participants are senior citizens.

Retirement Communities

When it comes to choosing a retirement home, you'll find numerous options in Memphis. There are more than 100 retirement centers and other residences for seniors in the city, ranging from independent-living residences to nursing homes.

Where to live during the golden years is a very personal decision, and one that requires careful research and thought. People have different ideas of what they're looking for in terms of amenities, food, and social activity. For example, a very sociable environment with loads of organized activities might be heaven to one retiree and hell to another. The chances of finding a fit are good, because the services of each center can be closely tailored to the individual needs of the resident. "Continual care" is a buzzword you'll hear a lot, and it means that when a resident needs more care or services, they're available.

Once you narrow down your choices to a few favorite candidates, go and spend time at each facility. Try the food, stroll the grounds, talk to the residents, and ask lots of questions. This way, you can be confident about your decision.

Remember that there are four categories of housing for senior citizens: senior housing (often called independent living), assisted living, homes for the aged, and nursing homes. In Tennessee assisted-living facilities, homes for the aged, and nursing homes are all licensed by the state Department of Health.

Senior housing is designed for independent living, sometimes with personal services. As the term can mean just about anything—including simply an apartment complex that doesn't allow families with children—it's always a good idea to ask what amenities are available. Assisted living is for those who are able to maintain their independence, thanks to help with such things as meals, housekeeping, monitoring of medicines, bathing, and dressing. Homes for the aged are a variation on assisted living, small with as few as four licensed beds. Nursing homes are for residents who need 24-hour licensed nursing supervision and assistance with most activities of daily living.

We list some of the city's best facilities for independent living and assisted living, but you may want to obtain a more complete listing of what's available, especially since new facilities are always in the works. Contact Aging Commission of the Mid-South's information and assistance hotline at (901) 324-3399 or try *The Best Times* at (901) 523-1561 for the annual listing of retirement living communities that appears in its November issue.

Belmont Village
6605 Quail Hollow Road
(901) 624-8820

A village atmosphere, complete with neighborhoods and town hall, restaurant-style dining, and plentiful activities, made this 120-unit assisted-living facility popular among seniors. Belmont has one-bedroom and studio units with kitchenettes if you want to cook, three meals served daily in its bistro if you don't. Activities include lots of outings to plays, art exhibits, restaurants, and attractions; services include transportation, help with daily-living chores such as dressing and bathing, and 24-hour-a-day emergency response. Other amenities include wellness and learning centers, exercise classes, library, and beauty salon. Belmont also has a 24-unit Alzheimer's facility.

Brighton Gardens of Memphis
1645 West Massey Road
(901) 763-3232
Brighton Gardens, part of the Marriott Corp. chain, is known for its young, lively staff and its full schedule of daily activities. The 115-unit assisted-living community offers a choice of one-bedroom or studio apartments and four levels of care. Residents can get assistance with the everyday tasks of living and eat three meals a day, ordering from the menu in the restaurant-style dining room. Activities and entertainment range from bridge and bingo to theme parties and outings to museums. Twenty-five of the units are in a special facility devoted to caring for residents with Alzheimer's or other related memory disorders.

Colonial Estates
2600 Colonial Tower Drive
(901) 382-8852
This retirement community, located at the Colonial Country Club golf course, has a swimming pool, tennis courts, an activities program, a library, and a beauty shop. The 83 one-bedroom and two-bedroom apartments have satellite TV, and laundry and housekeeping services are available. Home health services also are available.

Kirby Pines
3535 Kirby Road
(901) 365-3665
Its complete roster of services, good cooking, and well-planned activities program make Kirby Pines a standout for independent living. The retirement community, which offers continuing care, has 471 units, ranging from studio apartments to three-bedroom apartments or garden homes. Three meals a day and an array of services are available; special amenities include walking trails and a greenhouse. Kirby Pines requires a significant initial entrance fee, which starts at $53,800, but residents get a money-back guarantee and decorating allowance.

The Parkview Retirement Community
1914 Poplar Avenue
(901) 725-4606
Situated on the western edge of Overton Park, the Parkview was built originally as a hotel in the 1920s and still has the lobby frescoes and the high ceilings of the era. This independent-living facility, a favorite among retired midtowners, has 130 apartments, ranging in size from efficiencies to three-bedroom units. There's an "anytime" dining policy, so residents can have their three meals a day as they wish, ordering from the menu. Daily activities are available, and services include transportation, weekly housekeeping, 24-hour nursing support, and an emergency response system. The Parkview offers only limited assisted-living services, but residents are free to hire personal sitters as needed. The property is gated, with 24-hour security.

Plough Towers
6580 Poplar Avenue
(901) 767-1910
There's a definite international flair at Plough Towers, an independent living facility where about 40 percent of the residents are Russian-speaking. The 11-story, high-rise facility has 150 one-bedroom and two-bedroom apartments and serves a noon meal five days a week. On the premises you'll find a computer center, library,

> ## Insiders' Tip
> If reading the newspaper has become a chore for your eyes, tune into WYPL-FM 89.3, the Memphis and Shelby County Public Library station. Here volunteers read from *The Commercial Appeal, Memphis Business Journal,* and other local publications.

Insiders' Tip

Senior discounts are available for everything from Main Street Trolley fare to concert tickets and admission to museums. So always ask when buying tickets or placing orders.

convenience store, and beauty shop. A full calendar of activities is available. There's also a full-time social worker on staff, and a nurse, podiatrist, and psychologist visit each week. Limited transportation services also are available, and because it's a government rent-assisted building, the monthly fee is determined by income. Plough Towers is overseen by the Memphis Jewish Housing Development Corp.

Trezevant Manor Lifecare Retirement Community
177 North Highland
(901) 325-4000
Trezevant Manor, which began as independent-living apartments in the mid-1970s, today has 166 independent living apartments as well as 12 cottages, 25 assisted-living units, and a 104-bed nursing home. The residents may live in a cottage or apartment at first, then move to one of the other units if they require more care. This gated community, known for its elegant, traditional decor and excellent service, offers restaurant-style dining, transportation, housekeeping services, and daily activities that include parties, exercise classes, and on-the-premises concerts as well as excursions to plays or out to dinner. Amenities include library, fitness center, chapel, grocery store, and bank. The apartments range from studios to three-bedroom units, and the cottages have either three or four bedrooms.

Wesley Highland Towers
400 South Highland
(901) 325-7810
Formerly University of Memphis women's dormitories, the two 10-story towers presently operate as an independent-living facility with 396 efficiencies and one-bedroom apartments. Wesley Highland Towers offers three meals a day in its cafeteria, a wellness program, transportation services, a beauty shop, and a sundry store. There are some activities and social functions, too. Rental assistance is available for qualified residents through HUD. Residents of the tower who need assisted-living or nursing-home care are given priority at Wesley's other facilities, where those services are available. Wesley is convenient to University of Memphis, a plus for residents interested in taking classes on campus.

Worship

Given its location well within the nation's Bible Belt, it's not surprising that Memphis is richly endowed with churches and other places of worship. By one estimate there are at least 5,000 identifiable houses of worship in Memphis, and there may be many more than that. These range from the mammoth Bellevue Baptist Church, which claims 27,000 members, to tiny community churches that might consist of the preacher and a handful of followers.

If you drive around Memphis, you'll see churches everywhere. There are historic downtown churches that date back to the 1800s, clustered in the area north of Jefferson Street, including Calvary Episcopal Church, well known for its "street ministries" to aid the homeless. Also downtown is Clayborn Temple AME Church, a meeting place during the 1960s for civil rights activists, and Beale Street Baptist Church, the first brick-constructed, multi-story church in the United States built for African Americans (presently it's the First Baptist Church Beale). You'll find the Cathedral of the Immaculate Conception in midtown, not to mention numerous other churches.

Every neighborhood of the city has its own houses of worship, so in addition to churches, synagogues, temples, and other religious venues can be found all over. Although Protestant Christian churches dominate the scene, with the Baptist church particularly visible, Memphis also has a number of Catholic churches, Jewish synagogues that include the largest Orthodox congregation in the country, as well as Hindu, Muslim, and Sikh temples. You'll also find Quakers, Korean Baptists, and Scientologists.

Memphis has some famous churches, among them, the Full Gospel Tabernacle, where singer Al Green is pastor. After his successes of the 1960s and early 1970s, this Grammy-winning performer was called to start his own church, and he is known for his charismatic preaching. Memphis also is the seat of the Church of God in Christ, whose historic Mason Temple is the site of Dr. Martin Luther King, Jr.'s, "I've Been to the Mountaintop" speech in April 1968.

A notable characteristic of the Memphis worship community is that leaders from different religions tend to pull together during times of crisis. For example, the Memphis InterFaith Agency, a charitable organization, started out as a banding together of churches in 1968, when the assassination of Martin Luther King, Jr., in Memphis and the ensuing riots threatened to tear the city apart spiritually. More recently, an ecumenical group of local religious leaders have united in the wake of the events of September 11, 2001, praying together and raising money to send aid to Afghanistan refugees. On King's birthday in 2002, a group of churches and congregations committed themselves to fight against racism.

In Memphis you'll find that many families build their lives around their chosen house of worship, and it's not unusual for large churches to offer not only worship services, musical programs, and religious education, but also social events, sports leagues, workout facilities, and many other activities that reach beyond simply worship.

Probably the best and most inclusive source for information on local houses of worship is, believe it or not, the Yellow Pages. Look under Churches, Synagogues, Mosques, or Temples, depending on the type of worship you are seeking. The Churches listing is particularly extensive, organized both by geographical area and by denomination.

As for other sources of information, the Saturday edition of *The Commercial Appeal* has religious news and some listings of churches with information about services, and a regular column by journalist David Waters on faith appears several times a week. The Web site www.memphisareachurches.com features a limited listing of area churches.

Just about every Protestant denomination you can think of is represented in Memphis, including the Baptist, Southern Baptist, Missionary Baptist, Methodist, Episcopal, Lutheran, Unitarian, and Seventh Day Adventist churches. There are also many independent and community churches that aren't affiliated with a particular denomination. The Catholic Church is represented by the Cathedral of the Immaculate Conception and some 27 other churches in the Memphis area.

The religious right also has a presence here. Adrian Rogers, pastor of Bellevue Baptist Church, is a leader in the Southern Baptist Convention, generally credited with bringing the organization back to its conservative roots. Memphis is home to the ultra-conservative Religious Roundtable, founded by Ed McAteer with the aim of bringing biblical principles into public policy.

Memphis also has a growing number of community churches, a type of church favored by those who want more control and the ability to write their own theology. These churches aren't affiliated with an organized religion per se; instead, a pastor is answerable only to his congregation, and not a church hierarchy. These tend to be churchgoers who find the policies of established churches too liberal for their tastes.

Among the most important African American churches in Memphis is Mason Temple, the seat of the Church of God in Christ, founded by C. H. Mason. It holds its annual convocation in Memphis, a gathering that brings thousands to the city each year (it's actually the city's biggest annual convention). Mississippi Boulevard Christian Church is the largest Disciples of Christ congregation in the country. The Christian Methodist Episcopal Church also has its headquarters in Memphis.

One trend that's being seen in Memphis is a move by some congregations to large, new suburban churches with all kinds of amenities. A key reason is that so many members of churches are moving farther out into the suburbs as Memphis continues its development, and the churches are looking to keep pace. In some cases the new locations are big campuses, offering a range of amenities in addition to worship opportunities.

The Reform, Conservative, and Orthodox movements of the Jewish faith are well represented in Memphis, with six synagogues. About half of the Jews who attend services go to Temple Israel, a Reform congregation with some 1,800 families. It's also the city's largest and oldest congregation, founded in 1853. Baron Hirsch Synagogue of Memphis has the largest Orthodox congregation of any synagogue in the United States. There are other synagogues, one that includes a Hasidic gathering, Eruv of Memphis. In general, the city's Jewish community is a mixture of native Memphians from old families and newcomers to the city.

The city also has at least four mosques as well as a Hindu temple, which operates in nearby Eads. There is a Sikh community that's active in Memphis, and there are other faiths as well, a reflection of the city's growing international population.

Media

Memphis media are much like those of other major urban centers, given their lineup of publications and stations. These days Memphis is a one daily-newspaper town, with *The Commercial Appeal* publishing seven days a week. Filling the role that otherwise would be played by a second major daily are two weekly newspapers, *The Memphis Flyer* and *Memphis Business Journal*. In addition, a number of suburban and small-town newspapers in the area focus on local politics, high-school sports, and other news of interest to their respective readerships.

The city's most visible magazine is *Memphis* magazine, which has been published since 1976. This glossy monthly has an urbane and sometimes offbeat take on the city and its cultural scene, personalities, and restaurants. You'll also find numerous free publications around town (look for racks in the foyers of local supermarkets or libraries), including *Downtowner* magazine (a monthly with news and features about downtown Memphis) and *RSVP* (a monthly with society news and photos).

Memphis has the country's ninth-largest African American population, which is served by *Tri-State Defender,* a weekly newspaper that focuses on civil rights and other issues of interest to that audience. The city's growing Hispanic population is served by two free Spanish-language weeklies, *La Prensa Latina* and *El Horizonte*.

The current editions of most local newspapers are available on newsstands as well as from individual vending machines. In addition, many have Web sites with some or all of the newspapers' content as well as breaking news or other extra features.

Radio is the Memphis medium with the most colorful history, given its ties over the years to the music produced here. For example, WDIA was the first station in the United States to have an all-black format, with Nat D. Williams as its first black DJ. The station also helped to launch the careers of B.B. King, Rufus Thomas, and others. (See the Memphis Music chapter for more information.) Memphis DJs also were the first to play Elvis Presley's music, back when he was an unknown, and some, including Rick Dees, have become nationally known radio personalities. Currently the airwaves here offer a broad range of stations, and in 2001 Memphis ranked 45th among U.S. radio markets, according to Arbitron.

Memphis has seven television stations, including affiliates of the major networks and a religious broadcast station. The top stations compete for viewers by touting their local news coverage and the quality of their weather-tracking equipment (a good thing, given the thunderstorms and the occasional tornadoes that come through this area). Memphis had the 40th-largest TV market, with 642,000 TV homes as of Jan. 1, 2001, according to Nielsen Media Research.

As with media in other markets, many Memphis television stations also make their news coverage and other offerings available on the Internet, so you can watch the news at your own convenience.

Many Memphians opt for cable television or direct satellite dish for a bigger selection of channels. Time Warner Communications has consolidated most of the local cable TV systems, and now serves more than 230,000 customers in 53 communities in West Tennessee, North Mississippi, and East Arkansas. The lone cable holdout is Millington CATV, which serves customers in and around Millington. Direct TV and other companies are making inroads to this market, as is evidenced by the discreet dish receivers found on many Memphis rooftops.

Print Publications

Dailies

The Commercial Appeal
495 Union Avenue
(901) 529–2211
www.gomemphis.com

The Commercial Appeal, or the *CA* as locals call it, is a morning daily newspaper with a circulation of about 200,000, published by the E. W. Scripps Co. chain. Editorially, it has a definite liberal slant, and from a business standpoint, it's believed to be one of the most profitable papers in the Scripps chain. *The Commercial Appeal* serves 71 counties in Tennessee, Mississippi, and Arkansas and promotes itself as the largest circulation newspaper in the Mid-South (which simply means it's bigger than the newspapers in Little Rock, Arkansas, and Jackson, Mississippi). It maintains a network of bureaus in the region, including state capitals in the three states, to stay on top of regional news.

The paper dates back to 1841, when Memphis was a rowdy 20-year-old river town, and has been the city's only daily newspaper since 1979, when the evening paper, the *Memphis Press-Scimitar,* ceased publication. If you're used to a meaty, in-depth urban newspaper, you may find this one a bit thin. The quality is consistent with that of most Scripps-Howard newspapers, and in 1994 the *CA* won a Pulitzer Prize for editorial cartoons by Michael Raminez. Like most daily papers the newspaper carries a mix of local, national, and world news, as well as feature sections. Each Friday's edition of the *CA* includes "Playbook," a pull-out section with details about entertainment and events scheduled for the weekend as well as listings of what's available at area museums, galleries, theaters, casinos, and other venues. The *CA* also provides thorough coverage of the Memphis music scene.

Much of the newspaper's content, as well as breaking news, is available on its Web site. You can also search the newspaper's archives, and although you can read the headline and first paragraphs for free, there's a charge for viewing or downloading the entire article.

The newsstand price for the daily edition (Monday through Saturday) is 50 cents, and $2.00 for the Sunday edition. A one-year subscription is $224.25 for both the Sunday and daily paper ($17.25 per four-week billing period), and $140.40 for Monday through Friday only.

The Daily News
193 Jefferson Avenue
(901) 523–1561
www.memphisdailynews.com

The Daily News publishes Monday–Friday with a circulation of about 2,000, with most readers being attorneys, real-estate agents, and others who track lawsuits, public notices and property transfers. Although its strength is this information, which it culls from local government sources, it also runs business news stories. From its Web site you can look up all kinds of information without stepping into a courthouse or dealing with bureaucracy. The paper also publishes the monthly *WWWdot,* with technology news and information, and *The Best Times,* a monthly newspaper for senior citizens (see the Retirement chapter for more information). *The Daily News* is 50 cents a copy on the newsstands and $80 for a one-year subscription. *WWWDot* and *The Best Times* are free, although you can get home delivery of *The Best Times* for $15 a year.

DeSoto Times Today
8625 Highway 51, Southaven, Miss.
(662) 393–6397

DeSoto Times Today is the daily paper, published Tuesday–Saturday, for fast-growing DeSoto County, Mississippi. Its circulation is about 8,500 (around 27,000 for the weekend edition, which is also delivered to nonsubscribers). Under the guidance of Editor Tom Pittman, the paper has taken an energetic approach to covering local government, politics, economic development, and lifestyle issues. And of course, there's local high-school sports. The cost is 50 cents on the newsstand and $108 for a year's subscription.

The Evening Times
111 East Bond, West Memphis, Ark.
(870) 735–1010

The Evening Times is an afternoon newspaper that publishes Monday through Friday. It covers Crittenden County and eastern Arkansas, with a circulation of around 9,000. The paper's niche is the collection of small towns in Crittenden County, such as West Memphis, Marion, Crawfordsville, and Earle. The paper also extends its coverage to Hughes, in neighboring Street Francis County. The newspaper is 50 cents a copy on the newsstand and $75 for a year's subscription.

Weeklies

Bartlett Express
6187 Stage Road, Bartlett
(901) 388–1500

The *Bartlett Express* covers news and local sports in the bedroom suburb of Bartlett, located northeast of Memphis. The weekly paper, which comes out every Thursday, has a circulation of about 6,500. Cost is 50 cents a copy on the newsstand and $22 for a year's subscription.

Collierville Herald
148 North Main Street, Collierville
(901) 853–2241

The *Herald*, one of Tennessee's oldest newspapers, is distributed weekly with a circulation of about 7,200. Because the suburb of Collierville has a second weekly newspaper, local wags say it enjoys a more competitive newspaper scene than Memphis proper. The *Herald* also carries local sports and community news. Cost is 50 cents an issue, $18 for a year's subscription to an address inside the Collierville zip-code area, and $22 a year to an address outside the area.

Cordova Beacon
6187 Stage Road, Bartlett
(901) 388–1500

This suburban weekly, with a circulation of 3,000, covers news of interest to residents of the bedroom community of Cordova. The newspaper is 50 cents a copy on the newsstand and $18 for a year's subscription.

Covington Leader
2001 Highway 51 South, Covington
(901) 476–7116

The *Covington Leader* is a weekly newspaper with a circulation of about 9,000. Its focus is local news, sports, and features in the city of Covington and surrounding Tipton County, north of Memphis. The cost is 75 cents on the newsstand and $23 for a year's subscription to an address within the county.

DeSoto County Tribune
8885 Goodman Road, Olive Branch, Miss.
(662) 895–6220

The *Tribune* is a weekly paper with a circulation of about 10,000 and covers local news, government, and sports for DeSoto County. Its greatest strength is in covering the eastern part of the county, especially in the boomtown of Olive Branch. The cost is 50 cents a copy on the newsstand and $23.50 for a year's subscription.

Fayette County Review
14750 Highway 64, Somerville
(901) 465–4042

A weekly newspaper with a circulation of about 3,200, the *Fayette County Review* could be the next newspaper to suddenly expand. It covers the county just east of Memphis, which is seeing some of the most aggressive home building in the region. As the county becomes a major bedroom community for the metro area, the paper's coverage of local government, economic development, and sports will likely expand. The newspaper costs 35 cents a copy on the newsstand, $10 for a year's subscription to a local address, and $24 for a year's subscription to an out-of-town address.

Germantown News
7545 North Street, Germantown
(901) 754–0337

The *Germantown News* is a weekly paper published Wednesdays with a weekly circulation of about 6,700. The paper, published by Crittenden Publishing Co. in West Memphis, concentrates on news and features in the city of Germantown. The cost is 50 cents a copy on the newsstand and $25 for a year's subscription.

The Independent
151 North Main Street, Collierville
(901) 853–7060

The Independent is Collierville's other weekly paper and has a circulation of about 12,000, mostly distributed free. It competes with the *Collierville Herald* on local news. The newspaper, although free to the town's homeowners, is 50 cents a copy or $15 for a year's subscription.

Memphis Business Journal
88 Union Avenue
(901) 523–1000
www.bcentral.com.memphis

Memphis Business Journal is a weekly newspaper with paid circulation of about 12,000 and readership of about 60,000, published every Friday. A must-read for the business community, this well-respected weekly is often first with many important stories. The paper's primary focus is covering local business: real estate, economic development, health care, education, tourism, and other segments of the economy.

MBJ was started in 1970 by journalists Deborah and Barney Dubois plus a group of local executives, and it immediately established its reputation as an aggressive newspaper that breaks a surprising number of local news stories. At present *MBJ* is one of about 40 city business newspapers owned and operated by American City Business Journals, headquartered in Charlotte, North Carolina.

In addition to its news coverage, *MBJ* also features weekly special sections that zero in on a particular industry plus exhaustive listings of tax liens, judgments, commercial property transfers, and other news of record. *MBJ's* annual *Book of Lists*, published the last week of the year, is a valuable resource, and its Web site provides daily breaking news in addition to articles from the print edition of the newspaper. The cost is $1.50 a copy on the newsstand and $69 for a year's subscription.

The Memphis Flyer
460 Tennessee Street
(901) 521–9000
www.memphisflyer.com

Every week Memphians flock to nearby news racks or to one of the distinctive green dispensers around town for the latest issue of *The Memphis Flyer*. The attraction: both lively coverage of what's happening around town as well as stories that often are the most talked-about in town.

The Flyer is a weekly free paper that tries to fill a number of niches, from liberal alternative news source to exhaustive listings of restaurants, nightlife, and live music. It is part of Contemporary Media, Inc., which also publishes Memphis magazine.

The Flyer does some investigative reporting but specializes more in long, detailed explanatory articles for the cover and lots of short tidbits throughout the paper. Notable for his political coverage is the work of

Insiders' Tip

One of the most valuable tools available for newcomers and old-timers alike is the *Memphis Business Journal's Book of Lists.* Published around the first of the year, it lists the top companies, schools, and other entities in 70 different categories, including banks, private companies, shopping centers and private schools. To order a copy, call (901) 523-1000 or check out www.bcentral.com.memphis. The cost is $29 for the book, although it's free with a subscription.

reporter Jackson Baker, whereas music-editor Chris Herrington is responsible for the newspaper's thorough coverage of the local music scene.

Because its advertising rates are favorable to small retailers, many people find the assortment of ads for small local business at least as valuable as the writing itself. *The Flyer* also does a brisk business in classified and personal ads; though most of the ads are middle of the road, some of them are the most risqué in Memphis.

Depending on your neighborhood the new issue is available on Wednesday or Thursday. *The Flyer* has a circulation of about 120,000.

The Millington Star
5107 Easley Street, Millington
(901) 872–2286
www.millingtonstar.com

The Millington Star, with a weekly circulation of about 3,200, focuses its coverage on this northern suburb and, to a lesser degree, on the smaller towns of Munford and Atoka. The paper has adapted to the changing life of Millington; 10 years ago it was a U.S. Navy–base town, but it has now become a middle-class suburb, since the base has been replaced with a Bureau of Naval Personnel office and commuting Memphians have discovered the area. *Millington Star* reflects this transition and has become more of a community and lifestyle paper. The cost is 50 cents a copy on the newsstand, $20 for a year's subscription to a local address, and $26 for a year's subscription to an out-of-town address.

North Shelby Times
3518 North Watkins Road
(901) 358–8034
www.northshelbytimes.com

The *North Shelby Times* is a weekly paper that covers news and sports in the northern third of Shelby County. Ten thousand copies are circulated each week, by delivery and racks. It's free, both for single copies and for a subscription.

Shelby Sun Times
7508 Capital Street, Germantown
(901) 755–7386

The *Shelby Sun Times* covers local news and events for a broad swath of East Shelby County but mostly covers Cordova and Germantown. It distributes 33,000 copies a week, mostly thrown into residential driveways. The newspaper is free if you pick it up, but you can subscribe for $20 a year.

Tri-State Defender
124 Patterson Avenue
(901) 523–1818

The *Tri-State Defender,* a weekly newspaper with a circulation of about 38,000, was formerly a part of the crusading Sengstacke newspaper chain, based in Chicago.

The *Defender* was known as a fearless force at the peak of the black civil rights era and served, along with black churches in Memphis, as one of the rallying points for the civil rights struggle. Those days are mostly in the past, but the *Defender* still takes a powerful, civil rights–oriented voice in other issues, from local schools to welfare reform. The paper in recent years has expanded its offerings of society and lifestyle news and information as it seeks to become both an urban community paper while maintaining its political edge.

The newspaper is 75 cents a copy on the newsstands or $28 for a year's subscription.

Magazines

Memphis
460 Tennessee Street
(901) 521–9000
www.memphismagazine.com

This glossy monthly was started in the mid-1970s with an eye toward celebrating the popular culture, the important issues, and the culinary landscape of Memphis. It continues this mission, providing a witty and informed take on what's happening around the city. *Memphis* magazine also has probably the most complete listing of restaurants in the city, as well as reviews of both new eateries and perennial favorites. Newcomers to Memphis should check out the magazine's *City Guide,* published in August. Its *Restaurant Guide,* published in January, has a listing of the restaurants chosen as favorites by the magazine's annual readers' poll, as well as features about what's hot on the culinary scene. Both are for sale on the newsstands all year. The magazine, published by Contemporary Media, is a sister publication to *The Memphis Flyer*. The magazine is $5.00 an issue on the newsstand or $15 for a year's subscription.

Specialized Publications

Memphis sports are the subject of a wide array of specialized publications, often with a very narrow focus. *The Contract Bridge Bulletin* is a monthly magazine for bridge players, published by the American Contract Bridge League, with a circulation over 140,000.

Ducks Unlimited, a wetlands conservation group, publishes its bimonthly magazine, *Ducks Unlimited*, in Memphis, with a circulation of 615,000. Other publications include two quarterly magazines, *Puddler* with 65,000 copies, and *DULeader* with a circulation of more than 90,000.

Memphis Automotive Report is a monthly newspaper just for the local auto-repair and body-shop industry. Perhaps it's a comment on Memphis drivers that the paper has a circulation of 66,000.

Spanish-Language Publications

El Horizonte
P.O. Box 751482
(901) 566–9958
horizontes@bellsouth.net

This free weekly newspaper, which covers both the Memphis and Jackson, Mississippi, markets, consists mainly of articles about current events and sports in the Caribbean, Mexico, and other areas of Latin America. It also features advertising and classified advertising targeted at the Hispanic market.

La Prensa Latina
376 Perkins Road Extension
(901) 751–2100
www.laprensalatina.com

The city's other free Hispanic weekly considers itself bilingual, publishing some arti-

cles in both Spanish and English. *La Prensa Latina* features local, national, and Latin American news; some of its articles are from *The Commercial Appeal* translated into Spanish. It, too, runs ad for goods and services targeted at the city's Hispanic population. The publisher is Memphis-based Mendelson & Associates. Circulation is 40,000 (includes markets beyond Memphis).

Television

In the Memphis market you'll find all the major networks represented through local affiliates, which also deliver local news, weather, and some local programming.

The stations' news departments compete on the big local stories, often hyping them on the air to attract viewers. All the major network affiliates feature local newscasts between 5:00 and 6:30 P.M. and again at 9:00 or 10:00 P.M. Most of them also do a local early-morning show, which leads into network morning shows. Although the stations brag a lot about their weather-forecasting and tracking equipment, the truth is that they all have pretty similar resources.

WMC-TV 5, with Action News 5, is generally considered the news leader in this market, with the most professional anchors and reporters. The station's top anchors in news, sports, and weather have held their positions for more than 10 years, earning them a loyal viewership over the years and building a reputation for dependability for the station.

WREG-TV 3, which calls itself News Channel 3 On Your Side, also has a solid reputation, positioning itself as an advocate for the people of Memphis and making weather coverage its top priority. Viewers enjoy the station's "Does It Work?" feature, in which a reporter tries out a gadget and reports on the experience. This station is a bit more promotional than its colleagues, and more likely to hold contests in which viewers can win money or prizes. It's the CBS affiliate in town.

Both these stations cater both news and programming to viewers in the 50-plus age group.

In contrast Fox 13 and ABC 24 WPTY target a young audience, the 18–49-year-old age group. These two stations created some confusion in the marketplace in 1995, when they swapped network affiliations. One outcome of the swap is that ABC 24, under the terms of the deal, had to start a news department from scratch, whereas its seasoned news team became the Fox 13 news team. (ABC 24 shares its newsroom and reporters with UPN 30 WLMT, so the two stations have the youngest news operation in town.) WPTY and UPN 30 also are young in terms of the ages of their reporters and anchors.

The Fox 13 news team has in Claudia Barr and weatherman Jim Jaggers two of the city's most experienced anchors. The news team was affiliated with ABC before the deal between the two stations.

UPN 30 WLMT, one of the top-rated UPN stations in the country, gears its coverage toward the region's African American viewers. You'll find more news stories about the city's African American community and leaders and a programming lineup with lots of reruns of sitcoms featuring African Americans. It's also where you can watch University of Memphis basketball, a great favorite among Memphis viewers.

WKNO-TV Channel 10 is the PBS affiliate, which features not only PBS standards such as *Masterpiece Theatre* and *Charlie Rose*, but also has some strong local programming. It broadcasts the annual W. C. Handy Awards, the Memphis ceremony recognizing excellence in the blues, and Redbirds baseball games; it has also offered documentaries on such topics as the Memphis radio station WDIA and Kallen Esperian, the noted soprano who calls Memphis home. More than 70 percent of the station's operating budget comes from local supporters and viewers.

WPXX-TV Channel 50 is part of the PAX-TV network, committed to what it calls "family-friendly television." It features off-network runs of popular shows such as CBS's *Touched by an Angel* as well as its own programming, such as its prequel to the *Bonanza* television series. In 2001 it scored a major coup, getting the contract to air some Memphis Grizzlies basketball games.

Television Stations

WHBQ-TV Channel 13 (Fox)
www.fox13whbq.com

WKNO-TV Channel 10 (PBS)
www.wkno.org

WLMT-TV Channel 30 (UPN)
www.upn30memphis.com

WMC-TV Channel 5 (NBC)
www.wmcstations.com

WPTY-TV Channel 24 (ABC)
www.abc24.com

WPXX-TV Channel 50 (Pax)
www.paxtv.com

WREG-TV Channel 3 (CBS)
www.wreg.com

Radio

A quick spin of your Memphis radio dial will turn up every kind of station, from National Public Radio to hip-hop, talk radio to Christian to album-oriented rock. This is the 45th-largest radio market in the United States, according to the industry's 2001 Arbitron rankings, and in addition to entertaining and informing listeners, it has produced some well-known and influential disc jockeys. The most recent is Isaac Hayes, the legendary Memphis musician who has his own syndicated radio show featuring "hot-buttered love songs." Memphis radio launched the careers of Elvis crony George Klein and radio personality Rick Dees, who created the hit "Disco Duck" while a Memphis DJ in the mid-1970s. In the 1950s WHBQ disc jockey Dewey Philips was instrumental in getting Elvis and other musicians onto the airwaves. In 1948 WDIA was the first radio station in the country to adopt an all-black format, and it continues to be one of the top urban adult-contemporary stations in Memphis.

In recent years Memphis radio has seen a lot of consolidation among radio and television stations, as have other U.S. media markets. As a result most of the top stations are owned by one of four large companies. Of the public companies Clear Channel Communications owns seven Memphis radio stations plus two TV stations, whereas Infinity and Entercom own three stations apiece. Among private companies Flinn Broadcasting owns six stations, and Boston-based Barnstable Broadcasting owns four.

Urban oldies and adult contemporary are currently the hottest format in Memphis. WRBO-FM 103.5, which specializes in rhythm-and-blues oldies that include a hefty dose of Memphis legends such as Otis Redding, was the number-one ranked station, according to 2001 Arbitron surveys.

Note: Don't be surprised if you tune into a station listed as country and hear adult-contemporary Top 40 instead. As in other markets new radio stations are constantly appearing as old ones fade away, and stations often change formats, rushing to cash in on the latest hottest trend.

Radio Stations

Adult Contemporary
WEVL-FM 89.9 (community radio)
WMC-FM 99.7
WMBZ-FM 94.1
WRVR-FM 104.5

Christian and Gospel
KKLV-FM 94.7
KSUD-AM 730
KWAM-AM 990
WAVN-AM 1240
WBBP-AM 1480
WCRV-AM 640
WKRA-AM 1110
WKVF-FM 94.9
WLOK-AM 1340
WOOM-AM 1380
WPLX-AM 1170

Classical
WKNO-FM 91.1 (NPR)

Country
WGKX-FM 105.9

Insiders' Tip

Beloved among Memphis radio listeners is Weevil (aka WEVL-FM). Its disc jockeys are volunteers who bring their own records and CDs to the studio for their one-hour shows. The programming includes probably the city's best blues listening, Cap'n Pete's Blues Cruise, and other shows ranging from gospel to World Music Dance Party. Tune in to 89.9 or visit www.wevl.org for a schedule and other information.

Information
WQOX-FM 88.5
WYPL-FM 89.3 (Memphis and Shelby County Public Library)

Jazz
WJZN-FM 98.9
WUMR-FM 91.7

News/Talk
KBTM-AM 1230
WMC-AM 79
WREC-AM 600

Oldies
WJCE-AM 680 (easy listening)
WOTO-FM 95.7
WRBO-FM 103.5 (rhythm and blues)
WSRR-FM 98.1

Rock

WEGR-FM 102.7 (classic rock)
WMFS-FM 92.9 (album-oriented rock)
WMPS-FM 107.5 (album-oriented rock)
WOWW-AM 1430 (Disney)

Sports

WHBQ-AM 560
WTCK-AM 1210

Urban

KJMS-FM 101.1
KXHT-FM 107.1 (hip-hop)
WDIA-AM 1070 (rhythm and blues)
WHRK-FM 97.1

Spanish

AM 1030

Index

About the Author

PHOTO: DAWN B. HAYES

Nicky Robertshaw is a freelance writer who's also the food writer for *Memphis* magazine. She has been in and out of Memphis all of her life, starting as a child and teenager growing up in the Mississippi Delta. She and her family were constantly driving to Memphis to shop, take in a concert, catch an airplane to another city, or attend to healthcare matters. So she found that after living for a while on the East Coast (she lived in New York, then worked as Washington correspondent for *Women's Wear Daily, Crain's New York Business,* and other business publications), Memphis seemed like a pretty good place to live. She arrived in 1993 and got acquainted with the city through her work as a reporter for the *Memphis Business Journal,* a respected local business weekly. During that time she covered everything from restaurants and retail to aviation and trucking. On her own time she discovered a lively arts scene, lots of friendly people who quickly became friends, a surprising diversity of restaurants, and some peculiarly Memphis pleasures such as great blues and funk, gnawing on barbecue pork ribs, and contemplating the meaning of life while gazing at the Mississippi. In her years here Memphis has only gotten better and better. Although travel is a hobby and a passion, she says it's always good to get home to Memphis. Nicky Robertshaw currently lives in a midtown bungalow with her husband, daughter, and various pets.